INTRODUCTION

Our forefathers never dreamed of it. Honest men, making an honest living, working until their fingers bled and their calluses grew, never fathomed building a knife empire, just knives. The men who carried lunch pails to work at the Imperial Knife Co., to Case Brothers or Western Cutlery, to the Keen Kutter plant or the Cattaraugus factory rarely thought past payday or a Saturday shopping trip downtown for food and supplies. Pride? Yes, and then some. The tools they built were sharp, dependable and necessary. Just consider what it took to get through a day back then. The meals they put on the table were the result of a hard day's work. The smoke they inhaled was from the fires they stoked, the steel they forged, the blades they cut, the burrs they burnished.

It made sense in those days. There was a product at the end of the day, something that worked and would work. Folks who continue to build things with their hands today know the feeling, but most of them have high-tech tools to lighten the load. Technology has mapped out paths toward jobs well done. The smoke is clearing, literally, with laser- and water-jet cutters. Heck, the CAD program on the computer can design the knife with a little help. The parts can be bought, the labor cut in half, or thirds, or sixths. The CNC machines can be programmed; the heat-treat oven set; the furnaces fired; the temper lines practically brazened on; the locks set, tested, molested and adjusted; the springs bounced, stretched and squeezed into the tiniest crevices; the tolerances held to within tens of thousandths of an inch; the blades precut; the edges ground with one fell swoop of the double-bevel grinder. Pride? Yes, and then some.

Dedicated factory owners, entrepreneurs, designers and engineers have built a knife industry on top of yesterday's knife industry and brought it into a realm of marvelous magnitude. Folding knives are so slick that they no longer click. Fixed blades feel good and travel well, too. Factory blades not only come polished but lubed, oiled and filtered with little tags that warn the consumer about the dangers of running fingers across blades or pointing them in the wrong direction. Some carry pamphlets describing steels, grinds, blade coatings and locks. Others come with wrenches for adjusting pivot tension. Still others have built-in wrenches for adjusting the wheels of roller blades or the brakes of mountain bikes. Forget the old nail nicks: These things have thumb studs, pocket clips and breakaway bead chains for around-the-neck carry.

Not satisfied? With carbon-fiber handles, anodized-titanium bolsters and blued blades, they're fabulous fashion statements worn clipped to a vest or shirt pocket. Most are relegated to cleaning fingernails and slicing threads off girlfriends' blouses, but others are actually ridden hard. People still employ knives to hunt, camp, fish and serve their country. They need sharp tools built to last, and most modern factory knives won't rust if left in a bucket of salt water. Knives fresh from high-tech production facilities are clean, cost-efficient cutters with the finest steels imaginable and practically indestructible handles and frames.

The newest concern isn't whether they'll cut, or how lon~ +h~,'ll ~,,+ h,,+ whether a knife sharpener will even hone the strato-steels. credit is due. Innovators haven't gone out of style; they're ju fedoras. Their fingers still bleed, their temples ache and the the knife industry has come a long way. It is better. The blad consumer is happier. The hunters are more efficient. The sounder. Workers wake for another day at the shop, but in about Saturday downtown shopping, they look forward to summer vacations and a substantial slice of the proverbial pie.

Sporting Knives 2002
CONTENTS

FEATURES

REPORTS FROM THE FIELD

About our covers

Front cover:

Kershaw has moved itself from a reliable builder of basic hunting and everyday knives to a cutting-edge company whose designs do much more than cut.

Kershaw, founded in 1974, has retained some of its traditional designs such as easy-to-grip black, co-polymer handles and fixed-blade sporting knives, some with gut hooks or time-tested drop-point and skinning blades.

Then along came custom knifemaker and designer Ken Onion, moving Kershaw into the new millennium with some flashy handles, streamlined shapes and the revolutionary Speed-Safe torsion bar design for assisted blade opening at warp speed.

Once even a grizzled old-timer gives the Speed-Safe mechanism a try, he will discover — with a satisfying click as the blade snaps into place — that this new design is reliable, and just plain fun.

The Speed-Safe mechanism is found on seven models: the Boa (offered with flashy blue, purple and black, or plain black, aircraft aluminum handles), Whirlwind, the Polyamide-handled Scallion, the Elk (which benefits the Rocky Mountain Elk Foundation), the small, stainless steel-handled Chive, and the Avalanche and Black Out (both with black ti-nitride-coated blades).

Aluminum handles with non-slip, co-polymer inserts combine with AUS6A stainless steel blades (in drop or tanto points) and liner locks in the Liner Action series. D.W.O.s (named for Delley Wade Officer, a man killed in a hunting accident) are traditional folders with co-polymer handles in black, blue, orange and yellow. Rugged, working folders also include the Black Horse, featuring a finger-contoured co-polymer handle and 440A stainless blade. A combination Black Horse and Mini-Mag flashlight is offered, which includes a nylon sheath to stow both.

When you want a pocketknife with that extra touch of class, there are Officer Ranch models with satin-finished steel bolsters and sandalwood inlays, as

Ken Onion Boa Model 1580MC

well as Cascade Meadow models with slim, satin-finished handles also inlaid with sandalwood.

If space is at a premium, as in camping or backpacking situations, consider the Blade Traders: one knife handle that accepts many different blades with a Quik-Lock mechanism. Blade options include a saw, skinning blade with gut hook, fillet blade, carving blade, fork, spoon and even a spatula.

Kershaw also offers a variety of fillet knives — including one with an adjustable-length blade — as well as several models of shears for field dressing, fly tying and other uses.

Kershaw also has entered the multi-tool arena with a model that has locking-jaw pliers that lock at *Indian Ford Model 2155* a 45- or 90-degree angle, and can be coupled with a tool adapter for drive bits.

The company — part of the KAI Corp., one of Japan's premier blade producers

Kershaw Multi-Tool

for 90 years — uses high-grade steels, including 440A, CPM-440V and AUS6A stainless, for its blades. Partially serrated edges are an option on many models.

Deer Hunter Model 1030

Sea Hunter Model 1008

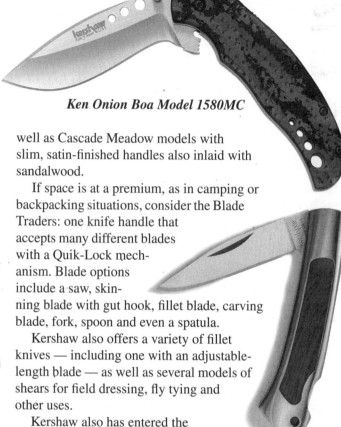

Fillet Knife Model 1257

Pictured on front cover (clockwise from lower right) are: Sea Hunter Model 1008, Deer Hunter Model 1030, Indian Ford Model 2155, Fillet Knife Model 1257, Ken Onion Boa Model 1580MC with multi-colored handle and the Kershaw Multi-Tool.

Back cover:

Whether your outdoors adventures take you to the deep Northwoods, a mountain stream or a trek through an urban jungle, Gutmann Cutlery has you covered.

Since 1947, Gutmann has been building sturdy, sharp cutlery for hunters, anglers, campers, tinkerers and anyone who feels comforted by the presence of an ever-ready blade.

Gutmann is well-known for its Junglee® line of hunting, self-defense and tactical knives.

All Junglee® models come with full-grain leather sheaths and offer a limited lifetime warranty.

Chefs and serious home cooks know about the company's Master Culinaire and Professional Series kitchen knives. Smith & Wesson multi-tools, gunsmithing tools, binoculars and other items also are produced by Gutmann. Baby Stubby® models provide small-but-strong blades as close as the keyring.

The company recently added a line of Walther® fixed-blade and folding knives that are built with the same attention to quality and detail as their famed Walther® PPK, P38 and P99 namesakes. There are shooting glasses and binoculars with the Walther® name, too.

Junglee® — and most of Gutmann's other knives — uses AUS-8 and ATS-34 steel alloys for their ability to hold an edge, without being brittle. These steels also offer great resistance to corrosion.

Pictured Junglee® models (from top) are: Tak Fukuta Skinner, Alaskan Hook Cleaver, Tak Fukuta Hunter with ebony handle, Tak Fukuta Caper and Baby Hook Cleaver.

TakFukuta Skinner

Alaskan Hook Cleaver

Tak Fukuta Hunter

Tak Fukuta Caper

Baby Hook Cleaver

Knives With A Competitive Edge

Chris Reeve runs a good race ... and builds a better knife

By Mike Haskew

CHRIS REEVE WILL never settle. As a grand prix motorcycle racer, he rode to win. Being thought of as just another knifemaker won't get it either.

The likelihood that the father of the Sebenza and the designer of the versatile one-piece range of knives could ever be thought of as an also-ran is pretty slim. Since he began making knives in 1975, Reeve's credo has been one of sustained excellence. Ideas have never been in short supply, and hard work simply goes with the territory.

"I've absolutely always wanted to be the best," explained Reeve, who was born and raised in Durban, South Africa, and came to the United States in 1989. "In the knife industry, my object is to create a company which is world renowned

The Classic 2000 Sebenza (top) is an award-winning pattern Chris Reeve first introduced in December 1987, and re-introduced into production because of continued interest in the design. Never content to rest on his laurels, Reeve and his production team debuted a new member of the Sebenza family, the Wood Inlay Sebenza (bottom), with a pocket cut into the handle and inlaid with stabilized wood.

for making the best knives, period." During an interview some time back, he stated matter-of-factly that he wants Chris Reeve Knives to be the "Rolex of knives."

With initial training and 13 years of practical experience as a tool-and-die maker, Reeve brings a practiced eye to the knifemaking business and has made the most of an opportunity to combine his love of high-performance cutlery with his trade.

"My father did a lot of wood-working," he said, "and he passed that along to me. The first custom knives I saw had handles of pink ivory, ebony and African blackwood. When I saw these knives in a magazine, I fell in love with the shapes and the beauty of the steel."

While he views knives as useful tools that are at the same time a paradox of the simple and the complex, Reeve's focus on the basics has produced spectacular results. His flag-ship design, the Sebenza, has virtually become a household word among those familiar with knives. "I wanted simplicity," he commented. "The Linerlock® was popular

"I've absolutely always wanted to be the best." — Chris Reeve

when I started taking a look at the design. I didn't like the flimsiness of the thin liner, so I came up with the Sebenza Integral Lock."

The Integral Lock was created by cutting a slot into the titanium handle slab so that gentle thumb pressure would disengage the spring section, allowing the knife to close.

A recess pin in the back of the BG-42 steel blade is made to bear on the stop pin. In the open position, the increased area of contact ultimately reduces wear that could otherwise result in a loose lock.

Each Sebenza comes with an Allen wrench so the knife can be dismantled and cleaned thoroughly. The knife is available in both large and small versions, as is the similarly designed and smaller Umfaan.

A tour of duty with the South African military persuaded Reeve to explore the possibilities of one-piece designs. The Project, Sable, Shadow, Mountaineer, Aviator and Skinner models are some of those available in the one-piece line of knives.

"I came up with the one-piece design because I didn't want anything on the knife that would crack or break, and we've been making one-piece models for the past 16 years.

Models in Chris Reeve Knives' one-piece series, the Project I and Project II with spear-point and clip-point blades, respectively, were the results of a collaboration with Sgt. Karl Lippard of the U.S. Marine Corps. The concept was to include all the features Lippard believed were vital for a knife carried by a Marine. (Gelson photo)

Each knife is made from a solid billet of A2 tool steel," he related. "The stock-removal method (of shaping blades by cutting away steel from a billet) results in two distinct advantages: the strength/weight ratio is exceptional; and there is no handle/blade juncture. This means that there is no area where the blade and handle could come apart, a weakness in the design of other hollow-handle knives."

From One Man's Hands

While he no longer makes custom knives himself, Reeve is continually involved in the design and manufacturing processes. Chris Reeve Knives currently employs 10 full-time workers in addition to Reeve and his wife, Anne. The process of developing into a manufacturer from an award-winning, one-man operation has been planned and deliberate.

"I guess I looked down the road into the future and realized that if I continued along the same path, there would be little in the way of retirement for me other than making knives continually," he reasoned. "One man's hands can only make a certain amount of knives. If you're hurt or sick, that stops. Someone has to support you to continue your life. As an insurance policy, I began to bring other people in and teach them."

Of course, insurance policies can be purchased to protect income, but those policies are expensive and, generally, knifemakers don't make much money, Reeve said. Besides, if a knifemaker puts 100 hours of work into a knife, it is difficult to successfully sell such a knife at, say, $50 an hour.

At age 46, Reeve admits that he will probably never retire completely, but he does have plans for the future, including more time with his wife and their 9-year-old son, Timothy. "One day, I probably will be semi-retired, and that is one reason why this business is in place," he explained. "Maybe when I'm in my mid-50s, I would like to work four days a week instead of five or six. I would like to watch some motorcycle racing, and I love to spend time in the mountains and outdoors. Then, I'll reclaim all those weekends that I've spent working during these years."

As long as he is on the job, Reeve will continue to push the innovation and technology envelopes. The Sebenza itself remains a work in progress. After all, what does it mean to be satisfied? "The

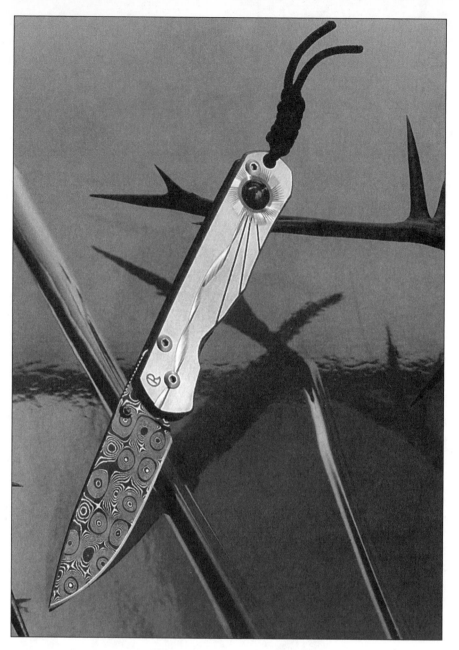

Chris Reeve fancied up his Umfaan model with a futuristic graphic design, a star-sapphire inlay, a blued-raindrop-pattern damascus blade and a titanium handle. The damascus is forged by Devin Thomas. (Weyer photo)

Sebenza has evolved over 13 years," Reeve said. "We've done little things like tightening up a gap or a toler-

"If Henry Ford had said the Model T is as good as it gets, nobody would be driving a Ford today." — Chris Reeve

ance by 2/10 of a thousandth of an inch. People think we're crazy, but that is what makes it smoother or click that much better, a radius here

or a curve there, or changing the material used in a blade or pivot bearing, or the type of screw used."

According to Reeve, a perfectionist is always nagging himself. "If Henry Ford had said that the Model T was as good as it gets and had stopped right there, nobody would be driving a Ford today, I can assure you. When I raced motorcycles, there was never a time that I thought the bike was perfect. There was always something you could do to make it go faster, and if you weren't doing that, then you would be running at the back of the field because everybody else was doing it. There is continuous evolution in every field because of competition."

In order to assure the continued success of Chris Reeve Knives, skilled employees are a prized commodity. As a taskmaster, the boss admits that he is not the easiest person to work for. There again, demanding the best is just the way it is at Chris Reeve Knives.

"Teaching someone to make a knife is a minimum of a two- or three-year process," Reeve remarked. "I wish we could speed it up, but that's where it's at, and I'm not known to be the most patient and forgiving man. I'm pretty hard on them (employees), but you've never had a coach who was a pushover win the Super Bowl, either."

"There is continuous evolution in every field because of competition."—Chris Reeve

A Rewarding Career

Maybe, there are some life lessons in Reeve's knifemaking philosophy. The value of hard work and the quality product that results are rewards in themselves. Add to that a genuine concern for his employees, and apparently Reeve offers more than just a job. The fruits of their labor and the work ethic of the man in charge were validated recently by the BLADE Magazine Manufacturing Quality Award© for 2000, awarded at the BLADE Show in Atlanta.

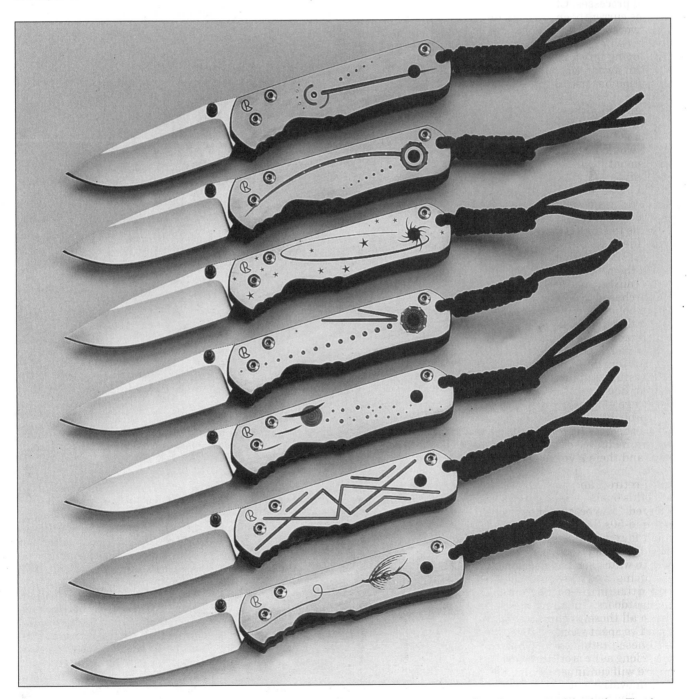

The handles of seven Sebenzas display computer-generated graphics, each with names to reflect the concept of the design. The designs began with sketches on paper, and were entered into the computer using CAD/CAM (computer-aided drawing/computer-aided machining) software. (Weyer photo)

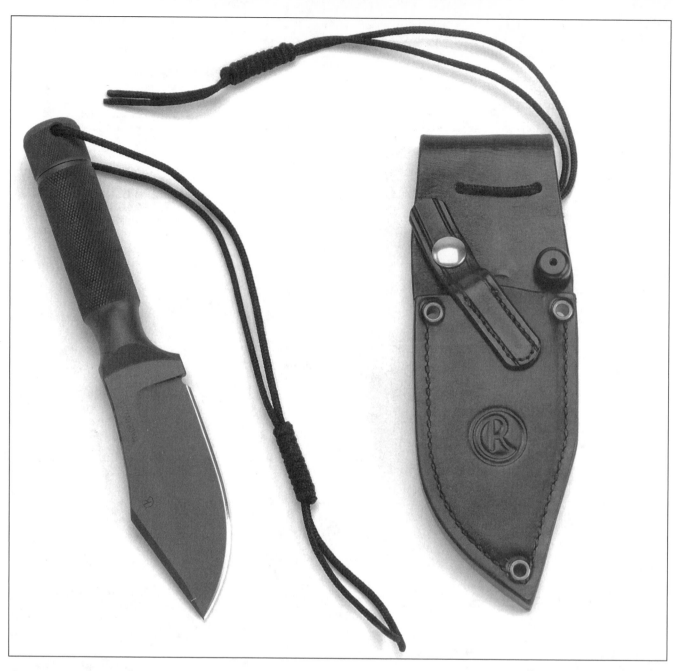

Chris Reeve says his one-piece Ubejane skinning knife is rugged enough to take punishment, but if properly sharpened, will perform the most delicate cutting tasks. Incidentally, "Ubejane" means "rhinoceros" in Zulu, the native language of the area in South Africa where Reeve was raised. (Gelson photo)

"The crew is working hard, and a day will come when they want to retire or semi-retire," Reeve said. "Until then, I think the most important thing for them is that they can go home at the end of the day with their fingers sore or their necks stiff from bending over a grinding machine, but saying that they had a part in making some of the finest knives in the world. That satisfaction is one of the most important things you can have. You can bumble through life not ever achieving anything, and that is a hollow life. Achieving something is the essence of life, and I want people here who hold that view and want to succeed."

> *"You can bumble through life not achieving anything, and that is a hollow life." — Chris Reeve*

Last year, Chris Reeve Knives produced nearly 4,300 knives, the most in its history. The possibility for expansion exists, but that expansion must be compatible with the mission of continual operational improvement, streamlining and consolidation. The number of knives produced may increase in the years ahead, but such an increase may be the byproduct of a larger selection of models. In 2001, both a new fixed blade and a folding knife have been set for introduction at the BLADE Show. Construction of a new building in the company's hometown of Boise, Idaho, is also a possibility.

Continued investment in both people and technology will mark the progress at Chris Reeve Knives.

State-of-the-art, computerized equipment and committed craftsmanship set the standard for the days to come.

For more information, contact Chris Reeve Knives, 11624 W. President Dr. B, Boise, ID 83713 (208) 375-0367.

This limited-edition Large Sebenza features a 1/10th-Krugerrand gold coin inlaid into a titanium handle and complemented by Reeve's rendition of springbok tracks machined into the handle.

Like all one-piece knives in the Chris Reeve line, the Sable IV is crafted from a single billet of A2 tool steel and stretches 10 1/2 inches overall. (Gelson photo)

Great Minds Think A Lock

Chris Reeve isn't necessarily eager to take on the title "innovator." Ask him, and he'll quickly defer to a friend and colleague.

"If you want to talk about innovation," he smiled, "then the man you must talk to is Michael Walker. He is a brilliant man, and I have incredible respect for him."

While the Integral Lock has become a Reeve signature development, he tells a story of remarkable coincidence. "Yes, I have made that lock mechanism synonymous with my name," he begins, "but Michael Walker was working on a similar lock mechanism around the same time. There were two people working on a similar idea at the same time on different sides of the world."

In fact, Reeve realized only recently that such a coincidence had occurred. He telephoned Walker to make sure that there was no misunderstanding. "I just became aware of this not long ago," he recalls, "and I thought, 'Oh no, I hope Michael doesn't think I copied his lock mechanism.' I telephoned him, and we had a long chat about the history of that mechanism — not about who did it first, but about all the things that were happening around that time."

So, Reeve tips his hat to Walker, another pioneer. Walker, you can bet, returns the compliment.

Founded on a Passion For Puukkos

From Viking swords to fencing foils, boarding axes to pole-arms, Eiler Cook has sold them all

By Edward R. Crews

Eiler Cook, owner of Historic Edged Weaponry, holds a Venetian cinquedea Renaissance dagger. Part of his knife collection is visible in the background.

"A knifeless man is a lifeless man." — Norwegian proverb

EILER COOK FOUNDED Historic Edged Weaponry, a viable and fruitful company, on a passion for Finnish puukkos. The story from there to here is as riveting as the man himself and no less involved.

When Eiler Cook was 11 years old in the 1930s, his Swedish grandparents gave him his first knives. They were Finnish puukkos, simple, strong work knives honored in Scandinavian legend and history. Even as a boy, Cook loved the knives, admiring their simple, practical designs, their heft and handiness.

During the ensuing 70 years, Cook's interest in Scandinavian knives grew deeper, leading him to collect a wide range of knives and edged weapons from Northern Europe, including cavalry sabers, a military ax and military knives.

Those first puukkos also inspired him to form Historic Edged Weaponry in 1984, and to import a variety of modern Scandinavian knives, from hunting blades to pocketknives. Thanks to Cook, an increasing number of American collectors now have access to the premier products of one of the world's oldest metalworking traditions.

Cook's passion for Scandinavian knives is as strong as it ever was. His knowledge of their history and production is encyclopedic. He still finds these items handsome and appreciates the way today's producers use traditional materials to create thoroughly modern interpretations of ancient tools that served both Vikings and Lapland villagers.

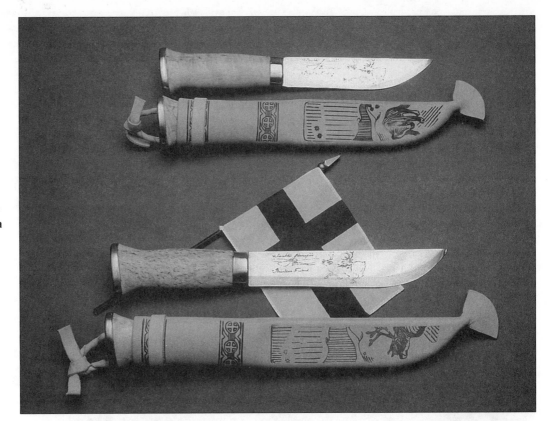

The varied offerings of Historic Edged Weaponry include Finnish Jarvenpaa Co. Lapp hunters with etched blades.

"I like the clean design that all these knives have," he said. "Modern Scandinavian knives are functional and simple. They are works of art with pleasing lines."

Cook combines a love for the workmanship with a strong emotional attachment to Scandinavia itself. While traveling on business, Cook's father, an American working for Pan American Airways, met and married the daughter of a Swedish cavalry officer. Harald Spens, the cavalry officer who became Cook's grandfather, gave him his first puukko.

A Rich Source of Knives

Although Cook's interest in knives began in boyhood, he did not start collecting in earnest until 1947, the year he became a diplomatic courier with the U.S. Department of State. He received a commission in the U.S. Marine Corps during World War II and purchased his first knives at the Paris flea market. Attracting people from around the world, the flea market offered a surprisingly rich source of edged weapons, finds that ranged from Cossack knives to an 18th-century knife from India.

During the next 33 years, the State Department sent Cook to Europe, Latin America and Asia. The

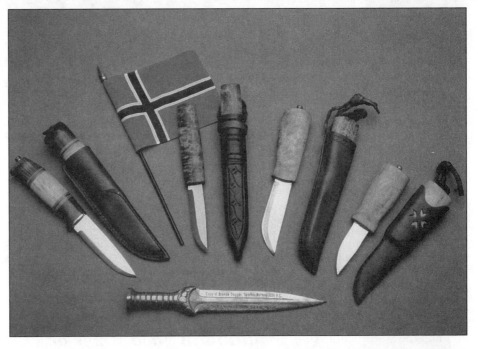

Norwegian knives imported from the Helle Co. are (from left) a Harding hunter, a Viking model, a mountaineer knife, a small camper's model, and the Trondheim Museum's Bronze-Age replica of a "Sparbu Dagger."

travel that came with a life in the diplomatic service allowed him to purchase knives from far-flung diplomatic posts. Cook soon found himself with an eclectic selection, including a Zulu fighting spear, a Hindu assassin's tiger claw, a Javanese kris, a Central American "murder" machete, and a Spanish gypsy fighting knife. He recently chronicled his collecting experiences in the book

Travels for Daggers—Adventures in Collecting.

Cook retired from the foreign service in 1980, and, although he had acquired items from across the globe, he still had a vibrant interest in Scandinavian knives. He began sharing this passion with other collectors through the launching of Historic Edged Weaponry in Hendersonville, N.C.

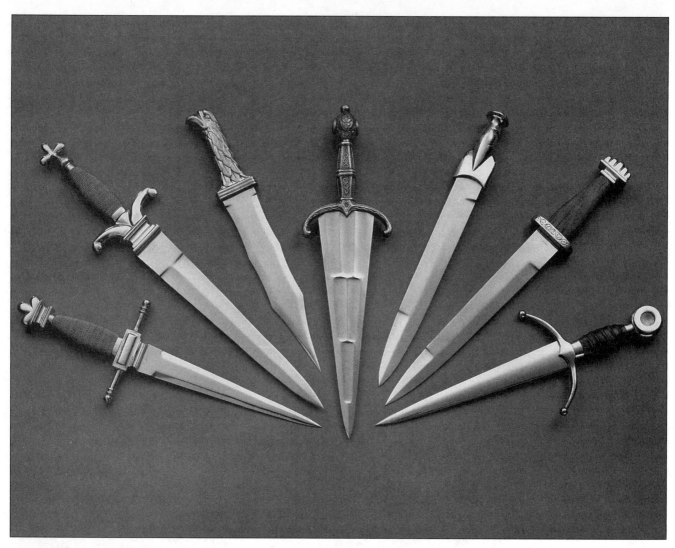

Until recently, Eiler Cook sold reproduction daggers imported from Spain where they were made by fencing expert Oscar Kolombatovich. Unfortunately, Kolombatovich has retired, and thus, the line is to be discontinued. (Weyer photo)

The company has offered two product lines for most of its 16-year history. The first features reproductions of historical weapons, while the second line features modern knives made by relatively small manufacturing companies in Scandinavia.

The traditional weapons were brought over from Spain, where Oscar Kolombatovich, former fencing master at West Point and the Metropolitan Opera, began making these reproductions in the 1970s. Impressed with the quality and appearance, Cook imported the entire product line, including Viking swords, fencing foils, boarding axes, Crusader swords, Scottish daggers, pole-arms and dozens of daggers and smaller edged weapons. He is closing out the line as Kolombatovich has retired.

Centuries-Old "Knifecraft"

Today, Historic Edged Weaponry deals mainly in a wide range of mod-

ern Scandinavian knives varying greatly in design, size and function, and sharing certain characteristics. For starters, they come from a centuries-old crafting tradition that sets a premium on fine metalworking.

Small manufacturers based in

"A puukko is a Finn's good friend. It is always at hand in good times or bad." —
Finnish saying

traditional knifemaking regions produce many of the products Cook brings to America. Today's knives are often modern interpretations of historic pieces, spare in design and incorporating native reindeer-horn or curly birch handles. Even sheaths reflect a rich heritage, often allowing knives to ride low so they won't fall out and become lost in the deep snow.

Many are embossed with Scandinavian symbols, crests and motifs.

Generally, the most popular knives Cook offers come from Finland, and among these, the puukko has the widest appeal. An all-purpose working knife, the puukko was born into use by Laplanders, a nomadic people living in the northernmost reaches of Scandinavia and herding reindeer by trade.

Modern puukkos sport blades of Swedish carbon or stainless steel, and tend to be short and comparatively wide. Though horn is used, curly birch handles have a special significance for the Finns. The native tree is a national symbol of toughness and perseverance, and has even been used as a form of money in years past.

Over the centuries, the puukko has acquired a mythic quality. It figures in the Finnish national epic poem, "Kalevala," and is part of the country's reputation for courage, ex-

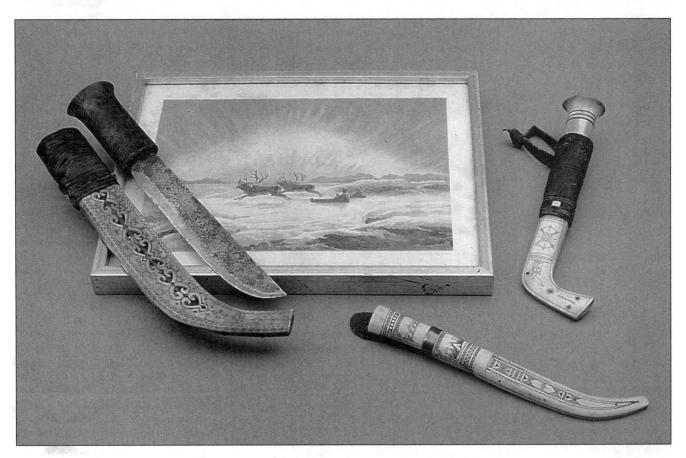

Original Lapp reindeer antler-handle knives include a large 1800s-era hunter (left) and two 1940s Swedish Lapland knives. Below, a close-up of the reverse side of the sheath of the large Lapp hunter reveals detailed scrimshaw of reindeer sleds.

pressed by the word "sisu." This fame has spread to neighboring Russia, where knowledge of the fighting qualities of Finns with puukkos was established ages ago and re-emphasized during World War II.

The Russian word "finka" describes the strike of a fighter armed with a Finnish weapon, a word Russian writers have borrowed and used as a metaphor for speed. "Love is lightning fast," wrote Mikhail Bulgakov, "and sudden as the Finnish knife."

Finnish legend attributes magical power to the puukko. Old stories claim that the blade gained supernatural strength from frog and serpent blood mixed into the water used to temper the metal. The puukko's mystical energy was believed to be so great that it could be transferred through ritual. At one time, Finnish farmers adhered to a rite that required them to thrust their knives into the soil before sowing in spring, supposedly ensuring a good harvest.

Puukkos are so deeply ingrained in Finnish culture that they have inspired sayings attesting to their utility and versatility:

"A puukko is a Finn's good friend. It is always at hand in good times or bad."

"Keep your puukko at your belt, and your wife at your side."

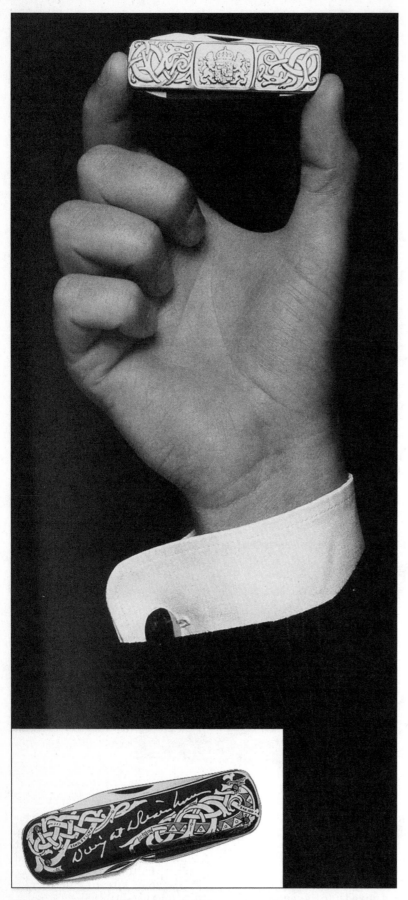

While many Scandinavian knives are rooted firmly in metalworking traditions, including materials used centuries ago, products from EKA in Eskilstuna, Sweden, are thoroughly modern. Eiler Cook imports a line of pocketknives the company makes using high-grade Swedish steel and featuring modern designs. President Dwight Eisenhower frequently had EKA pocketknives engraved with his signature and gave them as gifts.

"A man should have three puukkos — one to eat with, one to strike with and one to hold fast to."

Long Live the Lapp Knife

Cook handles two lines of puukkos — the L Series and the J Series. Both embody this rich cultural heritage.

The L Series comes from the 70-year-old Lauri firm in Rovaniemi, a town in Lapland, located in northern Finland. Lauri puukkos follow long-held knifemaking traditions. Handles are made from either reindeer antlers or great sallow and curled birch. The bottom halves of the blades are polished, while the top halves are left rough, giving them a rugged look. Lauri puukkos are handcrafted, and reindeer horn carvings are done by traditional craftsmen.

The J Series comes from Iisakki Jarvenpaa in the Ostrobothnia area of southwest Finland. This firm was founded in 1879 and was a knifemaker to the Russian czar. The J Se-

"Love is lightning fast and sudden as the Finnish knife." — Russian writer Mikhail Bulgakov

ries puukkos follow traditional customs and designs from the area. Their main characteristic is a relatively long and narrow blade, and each has a traditional birch hilt and a brass horsehead pommel. The company relies heavily on traditional production methods, including a great deal of handwork.

As they do in Finland, knives hold a special place in Norwegian history and lore. The Vikings relied on them for war and work. "A knifeless man is a lifeless man," is an old Norwegian saying that captures the importance knives play in the country's culture.

Cook imports two Norwegian companies' goods and markets them as the Nor Line and the Nor Pewter Line. Helle of Holmedal, Norway, produces the Nor Line. The company makes a variety of knives from Laplander models to traditional hunting knives and creations based on Viking knives.

Helle approaches knifemaking with the same dedication to craftsmanship found in traditional Norwegian valley knifemakers who have plied their trade for centuries. The firm also makes its knives using

Three antique Cossack "kindjal" dirks make as much of an impression in a photograph as they must have made on Eiler Cook when he bought them. The Russian icon in the background is just as visually pleasing.

a Norwegian technique of layering steel. This involves sandwiching a core piece of high-alloy steel between two layers of softer steel, creating a durable, robust knife.

The Nor Pewter Line features elegant knives from the Haugrud firm that follow traditional design and production techniques. The "Birkebeinerkniven," for example, is a presentation knife made in the spirit of 13th- and 14th-century knives produced for Birkebein warriors of Norway. Baglerknogen are knives made in the tradition of similar weapons carried by "Baglers," members of a 13th-century clerical party during the Norwegian civil war.

While many Scandinavian knives are rooted firmly in metalworking

traditions, including materials used centuries ago, products from EKA in Eskilstuna, Sweden, are thoroughly modern. Cook imports a line of pocketknives that the company makes using high-grade Swedish steel and modern designs, in some cases generated by computer.

The Presidential Seal

EKA, which also boasts a line of modern knives designed for hunting, outdoor and survival pursuits, has an interesting connection with America. President Dwight Eisenhower frequently had EKA pocketknives engraved with his signature and gave them as gifts.

Although built on a foundation of tradition, Scandinavian knifemak-

ers actively seek ways to honor their past while developing products for today's demanding customers and collectors. Accordingly, Cook sees trends developing that will affect the types of knives that Scandinavian manufacturers will produce.

Makers are now creating more commemorative knives that appeal to collectors or individuals wanting a souvenir connected to an event or historical anniversary. A recent example of this is the issuing of knives honoring the exploits of Norwegian polar explorer Roald Amundsen.

In addition, knife enthusiasts seem to like reproductions and modern interpretations of historic Scandinavian weapons from the Viking period through the Middle Ages. Ex-

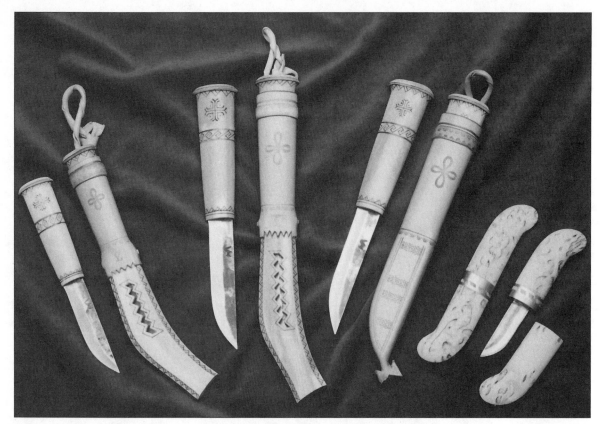

Historic Edged Weaponry makes Finnish Lapland knives by the Lauri Co. available in the United States, where they wouldn't otherwise have found homes. Two hunting knife models and a small pocket-knife puukko feature reindeer-antler handles.

A group of Finnish puukkos begins with (from left) a stubby "grandfather's knife" by Roselli, a classic 1940s Vaakuna knife, a large Lapp hunter by Marttinni, a 1930s-vintage horsehead puukko from Kauhava and large and small versions of Tapio Wirkkala-designed puukkos.

pect to see more of these items in the future.

Whatever other changes are ahead in Scandinavian knifemaking, Cook is sure some things won't change. "Scandinavian knives will always share two features," he said. "They will remain firmly anchored in national and regional traditions, and they will reflect a pride of craft that has endured for centuries."   •

For more information, contact Historic Edged Weaponry, attn: Eiler Cook, 1021 Saddlebrook Dr., Henderson, NC 28739 (828) 692-0323.

Can a Folder Replace a Fixed Blade?

The author's folder lineup for field testing includes (from left) the Chris Reeve Sebenza; the Microtech SOCOM; the Al Mar SERE; the Benchmade Axis Lock; the Spyderco Chinook; and the Spyderco Military. (Justin Ayres photo)

The author recruits a group of willing teen-agers to test folders and fixed blades

By James Ayres

Fixed for the cutting were (from left) the Benchmade Nimravus; the Kellam Ilari; the Kellam Hunter; the Fallkniven H1; the Fallkniven A1; the Chris Reeve Shadow IV; the Chris Reeve Project 1; and the Wayne Goddard Custom. (Justin Ayres photo)

ONE HIGH SIERRA morning, under a thin blue sky with stars faintly pressing through, I stopped to rest on a granite slab by the trail. As I basked in the clear spring sunlight and stretched the kinks out of city-soft legs, I heard bells tinkling in the distance. Soon four backpackers appeared.

The healthy young men were lumbering along under enormous backpacks festooned with bear bells and filled with, I guessed, 60 or 70 pounds of lightweight gear. With their heads down, sweating and staring at the trail in front of them, they would have passed by without noticing me 3 feet from the trail had

The students decided the Chris Reeve Project 1 fixed blade won the "bodacious award" for its lightweight and well-balanced properties. (Justin Ayres photo)

I spent the next half-hour explaining the many uses of a sheath knife. I demonstrated how to split kindling from a dead log and some other simple tasks. I made no converts. They remained convinced that there was no need for anything other than maybe a Swiss Army knife in the wilderness. They agreed that a lock blade was a good thing for safety, but that any lockable folder would perform all necessary tasks. In any event, none of them had a Swiss Army knife, let alone a lockable folder.

They were zealous practitioners of the "leave no trace" movement and could not imagine the need for a fire. After all, they had their stoves, tents, sleeping bags, and lightweight, folding camp chairs, and would admit no possibility of a problem that they might need a knife to solve. I don't leave much trace, either, but if I need to warm a cold, wet kid, and there is no deadwood around, then it's goodbye tree.

The author refers to the Kellam Hunter as a "sweetheart" because the fixed blade was sharp when the field testing began and sharp when it was over. (Justin Ayres photo)

"My focus would be on what the average person could accomplish, not what a highly experienced person could do."

Early this fall, while kayaking in the San Juan Mountains, one of my companions questioned my use of the same Goddard. He argued that the Spyderco folder clipped to his life vest was all the knife anyone ever needed.

This seems to be a pervasive attitude, but one that bothers me. For years I carried Henckels and Hartkopf stag-handle lockbacks. Then, when it came on the market, I bought an Al Mar Eagle with a lockable blade and an ivory-Micarta® handle. It replaced the other lockback knives as my primary folder. It traveled around the world with me for years and served me well within its limitations.

I have followed the development of new-folder technology with interest. I bought Bob Terzuola's first locking-liner folder, and I have purchased at least one example of every new type of locking folder as each has become available. I use and enjoy them all, but until now, I had

I not called out a good morning to them.

They stopped to talk and rest — any excuse will do — and conversation turned, as it often does, to gear. They commented on my tiny pack and I on their huge packs.

Then David — dark hair, muscular, and the most vocal of his group — said, "So what's with the knife?"

He pointed to the Wayne Goddard custom knife I wore in a traditional

leather sheath thrust through my belt. I handed it to him to examine, and he passed it around to his companions who talked as if they had never seen a knife before. "Wow, this thing is sharp." "Look how long it is." "What kind of wood is the handle?"

David asked, "So, what do you need this for? Looks like some kind of Rambo knife. Gonna fight the bears with it?"

never considered that they could replace fixed blades.

A Fixed-Blade Fixation?

I decided it was time to test my theory. Perhaps the new, high-tech folders could replace fixed blades. Certainly it would be better to have a folder than no knife at all. In many places today, the prejudice against knives of any kind, and large fixed blades in particular, runs deep, and many people who venture into the mountains do not take knives. This seems to be especially true of young people.

More precisely, could one of these new, advanced folders replace a sheath knife in emergency situations? Could they cut 3- or 4-inch saplings for shelter, or split logs for kindling? I decided to have a group of people use a selection of the knives in an informal woodcutting and shelter-building class.

My focus would be on what the average person could accomplish, not what a highly experienced person could do. I know plenty of people who can start a fire with a bow drill. I also know quite a few people who can knap stone knives and axes, fell trees and construct entire villages with stone tools. Those are not the people likely to become lost while snowboarding or hiking, nor do they often find the need to use emergency tools and skills to sustain them while awaiting rescue.

The experienced person carries familiar tools and rarely is lost in the first place. If an emergency does crop up, it's often just another night under the stars, perhaps uncomfortable, but not threatening.

This choice of methodology was motivated by a number of conversations like those related above, but also by a well-meaning but hapless scoutmaster who led his troop into wilderness beyond his, and their, capabilities. When my brother-in-law and I came upon them, they were wet, cold and lost. Two of the kids were clearly hypothermic. Not one of them could build a fire under the prevailing conditions. Not one of them had a hatchet or any knife beyond a scout knife, which none of them seemed to know how to use.

I teach such classes from time to time. If using a folder will make acceptance of the tool easier, and if a folder will do the job, then a folder it will be.

For this experiment, I chose to work with a small group of teenagers. They are bright, amiable kids who spend too much time on the In-

The Spyderco Chinook proved to be a well-built, quality folding knife, yet no one in the group developed a feel for how to squeeze the most performance from the folder in the context of the field test. (Justin Ayres photo)

When fatigue set in, Wayne Goddard's knife was the one everyone in the test group wanted to use. It sliced through tree limbs with little resistance. (Justin Ayres photo)

ternet, who like video games and who snowboard, kayak, and wander around the mountains of the Pacific Northwest pursuing various recreational activities.

Why this group? Because teenagers and "twenty-somethings" appear to be the largest group using the wilderness today, and because this group seems to regard the outdoors as a large playground. They see no need to prepare for the unexpected.

Hapless Handymen

Their experience ranged from considerable to none. The most experienced was a 16-year-old who can, and has, built a fire in wet conditions with only a flint sparker. He can also build shelters, split logs with stone tools and set successful traps and snares.

The least experienced of the group had no outdoor instruction at all before our day together. He had been car camping once. In my experience, teenagers are harder on gear than soldiers. Any of them, like their peers, could break a bowling ball while playing with it. If the knives could stand up to these kids, they could probably serve anyone.

which challenge folders. At least, this was my assumption. I decided to use the first task, taking down a tree, as a benchmark. We cut alder, birch and ash. We were in northern Washington at about sea level. There was no snow, but it was plenty wet, as is normal for the time of year.

The only knife that was damaged at all was the Spyderco Military. I saw the strike that did the damage. The young man was holding it off-angle and struck with a home-run hit. Still, the blade was only bent, not broken. The rest of the knives suffered no damage whatsoever.

The Results

Knives	Lock	Strikes to cut 2-to-3-inch limbs	Strikes to cut 4-to-5-inch limbs
Large Fixed Blades			
Chris Reeve Project 1	n/a	1	5-7
Fallkniven A1	n/a	1	3-4
Kellam Hunter	n/a	2-3	6-9
Wayne Goddard Custom	n/a	1	3-4
Small Fixed Blades			
Chris Reeve Shadow IV	n/a	2-3	10-18
Benchmade Nimravus	n/a	5-12	15-30
Fallkniven H1	n/a	2-3	6-15
Kellam Ilari	n/a	2-3	6-15
Folding knives			
Al Mar SERE	locking liner	2-6	8-17
Benchmade Axis 710	Axis Lock	6-19	15-40
Chris Reeve Sebenza	integral lock	1-2	4-9
Microtech SOCOM	locking liner	6-17	15-39
Spyderco Military	locking liner	4-8	7-21
Spyderco James Keating	lockback	10-27	n/a

NOTE: Obviously, the fewer strikes, the better. Time can be critical when you are wet and cold. Survival can come down to a time and motion exercise. How long does it take to get tinder, kindling, fuel and start a fire?

I sorted the knives into three categories: 1) large, 5 1/2- to 7-inch fixed blades; 2) small, 4-inch or shorter fixed blades; and 3) a selection of current, lock-blade folders.

I limited the selection of folding knives to a sampling of the current crop of high-tech pieces. They seem to be stronger, tougher tools than the old slip-joint pocketknives. I know from experience that the Victorinox Rucksack is a great all-around folder to back up a fixed blade. I also know that it would be destroyed by the work we were doing. The same is true of dozens of other perfectly good knives that were designed for tasks other than taking down trees.

To set a standard, I also brought the Wayne Goddard custom that started this discussion, and which I usually carry.

I took a small group of students into the woods to teach them some basic skills, including how to use a knife and a baton to down a tree, and how to split kindling from a log. These are two basic tasks that any large fixed blade will perform, but

When the number of strikes required to cut through a tree limb increased, the time increased

"In my experience, teenagers are harder on gear than soldiers."

exponentially. The poorer-cutting knives tended to bind as they got deeper into the cut.

Students did all the work. All the students used all the knives and cut at least one tree with each knife. The activity was observed and recorded by two helpers and myself. Then, the results were averaged. While the test did not meet scientific criteria, it accurately represents what could be done with these knives by average people in moderate conditions.

The lack of damage to the folders surprised me. There were no lock failures, but this was not a test of lock strength, and although I anticipated that some of the folders would be destroyed, it did not happen.

Now I'm a Believer

I started as a skeptic, and now I'm a believer. In some cases, for well-defined uses, a modern folder can do the work of a small fixed blade. Obviously it cannot equal a large fixed blade, but neither can a small fixed blade.

The Chris Reeve Project 1 is surely one of the strongest fixed blades made. It is well balanced and feels much lighter in the hand than expected from its appearance. The students decided it won the "bodacious" award. I had to talk them out of field dressing my Suburban with it.

The Fallkniven A1 sets a new standard for factory knives. There are many production pieces touted as "survival knives." This one will do the job. The subtle, convex curves make cutting easier and safer.

The Kellam Hunter is a sweetheart. It was sharp when we started and it was sharp when we finished. Everyone loved the wood handle and the way it felt in the hand. If it was larger, it would have performed exceedingly well for this test.

The Fallkniven H1, with a VG-10 blade and a convex grind, cut through small limbs with relative ease. (Justin Ayres photo)

Wayne Goddard's knife was the one everyone wanted to use when they tired. It sliced through everything with little resistance. One of the kids said, "Wayne's knife cuts real easy and it's kind of old-timey looking and cool."

On some cuts, the Chris Reeve Shadow IV did better than its larger brother. I think this was because of less drag once it was in the cut. I have a friend who is a well-known survival instructor. He also guides river rafters, climbers and hunters in season, and carries the Shadow IV as a neck knife.

The Fallkniven H1 has a convex grind like the A1. It also has the same VG-10 steel and similar great performance. On small limbs, the Fallkniven cut right through.

After field testing the knives and without sharpening them, the author used each piece, including the Benchmade Nimravus, in the kitchen. None of them failed to slice or dice after a hard day's work. (Justin Ayres photo)

"In a survival situation, whatever knife you have is the best knife."

Kellam's Ilari is another sweetheart. It has a comfortable wood handle and a blade that cuts like the winter wind.

Benchmade's Nimravus is made of the same tool steel as the 710 folder. It is a well-designed, well-made knife that for this use needs to be thinner.

I had a hard time keeping track of the Chris Reeve Sebenza. No one wanted to give it back. One of the

students said, "Yeah, it's twice the price but it's twice the knife."

The Al Mar SERE shows its heritage. Its predecessor, the original SERE, was the first folder ever developed specifically for Survival Escape Resistance & Evasion. The new one is smaller, stronger and a better knife in every way. It was designed for extreme use and it has strength to spare. After hours of hard work in the cold, it still feels good in the hand. Everyone wanted one.

The Benchmade 710 Axis Lock is well balanced, lighter than it looks, and quite strong. If it had different edge geometry, it would have performed much better for this use. One of the kids fell in love with the balance and general feel of it. He plans to buy one and regrind it.

Spyderco's Military benefits from a flat grind and a distal taper. It cuts quite well. Unfortunately, it is light for such extreme use. By the end of the first day, it was bent out of true.

The Fallkniven A1 sets a new standard for factory fixed blades with subtle convex curves that make cutting easier and safer. (Justin Ayres photo)

The Al Mar SERE is designed for extreme use and it has strength to spare. After hours of hard work in the cold, it still felt good in the hand. Everyone wanted one. (Justin Ayres photo)

Microtech's SOCOM is a well-built quality knife. Like the Benchmade, its geometry seems designed for other uses.

Folder or Fixed Blade?

In addition to the test, we used the knives to cut cord, sharpen and scrape arrows, and make snare triggers. Then we used them for a week or so around the kitchen to slice vegetables, cut meat and other daily chores. None of them were sharpened. They all worked fine.

I conclude that a folder can replace a fixed blade under limited circumstances for well-defined uses. In a survival situation, whatever knife you have is the best knife. This or any class of folders cannot replace the versatility, and certainly not the strength, of fixed blades.

> ### "Folders are portable, convenient and discreet. They are socially acceptable."

What they do represent is a new category of knife. They are so much stronger, so much more functional than earlier generations of folders that they will perform many of the functions that previously I would have reserved for fixed blades. In addition, they all excel in the fixed blades' weakest area. They are portable, convenient and discreet. They are socially acceptable.

Any of them can be carried in a pocket, or clipped to a waistband inconspicuously, and be available in situations where a fixed blade would be inconvenient or socially unacceptable.

It is true that in some areas it is still acceptable to openly wear a fixed blade, especially a small one. In many more places, a fixed blade will cause unwelcome attention, and in some cases, alarm. I have found that from Kuala Lampur to Lima, from Prague to Tashkent, a folder is generally seen as a tool whereas, unless you are in the bush, a fixed blade is seen as a weapon.

For my immediate concern, I have found that young people who venture unprepared into the wilderness are willing to carry a good folder even when they won't accept a fixed blade. If, with the right folder, a fire starter and an afternoon of instruction, they come back alive, then that's enough for me. •

I thought teenagers could break anything, and I was surprised that they only managed to bend this graceful folder. The bend did not stop it from working.

Spyderco's Chinook is a robust, well-made knife. I just don't know what it was designed to do. No one in the group developed a feel for how to get much performance out of it in this context. It looks to be purpose-designed and I suspect it would perform well for that which it is designed.

The Factory Damascus Dynasty

Relish these production pieces with pattern-welded steel blades

By Mike Haskew

"Companies are getting back into damascus because technology reduces the learning curve."
— Greg Cook,
Bear MGC Cutlery

Boker made the 546 Damascus, a tribute to the late Col. Rex Applegate, available in limited quantities last year. A standard issue of six Boker lock-back patterns is available on a continuing basis.

WHEN BILL MORAN re-energized damascus steel in the 1970s and worked to get the American Bladesmith Society (ABS) started, he really stirred something up. Today, almost three decades later, with its rich look and variety of patterns, damascus is an integral part of the knife industry. Collectors, custom knifemakers and manufacturers share an enthusiasm for damascus that just may be greater than ever.

Part of the phenomenon is because of the emergence of a cottage industry of damascus production after the success of the ABS. As bladesmiths branched into damascus, which in turn became more available and crept into the work of many custom makers, factories naturally took notice. A number of manufacturers began offering knives with damascus blades or fittings and met with initial success. After a relatively short period of steady sales during the mid-to-late 1980s by such companies as Bear MGC, Boker, Damascus USA, and Buck, among others, the enthusiasm for factory damascus knives began to wane. For

control both the damascus end and the finished product end. When we bought Parker-Edwards Cutlery, we knew there was a market for damascus, but it had been dumped on the market everywhere. So, we purposely scaled it back to keep prices up a little bit and help our margins."

Cook cites a realization that damascus is closer to the handmade side of the knife spectrum and simply cannot be handled on a production basis in the same manner as traditional stainless steel. "There is a whole new set of rules in dealing with damascus," he reasoned. "Some people were not ready for that and fell out because of it. Now, with laser and CNC (computer numerically controlled) capabilities for parts, some companies are getting back into damascus because technology takes away some of the learning curve."

Edwards' steel company still produces damascus for Bear, which maintains 15 to 20 damascus knives in its line. Seventy-five percent of these are in Bear's lock-backs, and 25 percent are fixed-blade hunters. Bear damascus gets higher-end handle treatment, usually stag or mother-of-pearl.

Knife-Of-The-Year Damascus

After examining one of the first to use factory damascus, let's now go to one of the latest to try it in a production capacity: William Henry Knives. Even though WHK's T-10 Pearl Damascus is Blade Magazine's 2000 Investor/Collector Knife Of The Year©, it reportedly was just coming available to consumers as BLADE was going to press—though do not expect to buy one as WHK's Matt Conable said all of the 250-300 serially numbered knives had been pre-ordered and were sold out. However, Conable said WHK would be offering more models in damascus,

a variety of reasons, including production difficulties, availability of the material, profit margins, and issues surrounding the quality of damascus produced by some sources, some factories began to shy away from damascus.

While the demand for handmade damascus knives has remained solid through the years, the ebb and flow in factory damascus has created opportunities for niche production of commemoratives and the introduction of some higher-end standard models in damascus. Factory damascus is now appearing in larger quantities and well received by the buying public.

Big Damascus Bear

The link between the factory and damascus steel is central to the lin-

"The T-10 Pearl Damascus is what might be referred to as a utility fashion accessory."

eage of Bear Cutlery, which began years ago as Parker-Edwards Cutlery, continued as Bear MGC, and most recently was acquired by Swiss Army Brands. "Fain Edwards owned a damascus foundry in the 1980s and, when he and Jim Parker got together, they built their line of knives on damascus," recalled Greg Cook, Bear's vice president of operations. "Their plan was initially to with several slated for a tentative 2001 BLADE Show debut.

The damascus WHK uses is in a ladder pattern by Daryl Meier. Why Meier? "Because he's one of the top damascus makers in the world, and for his ladder pattern specifically," Conable said. "It's a particularly beautiful choice on our gent's folders." At a retail price of $395, the T-10 Pearl Damascus is what might be referred to as a utility fashion accessory. In other words, it is not just for looks — it cuts, too. "It is an extension of what we do," Conable explained, "making beautiful things that are viable as tools."

Damascus Synonym

The name Manfred Sachse is synonymous with Boker damascus. When Boker CEO Ernst Felix met with Sachse about 20 years ago, it was the beginning of a long relationship that continues to impact the cutlery industry. "To the best of my knowledge, Manfred is now retired and has turned over his business to another forger," said Chuck Hoffman, president of Boker USA. "Manfred's damascus is a 320-layer product, and we have tried some 180-layer (damascus) out of Sweden."

Boker USA, Boker's U.S. affiliate, has been operating for 15 years, and damascus has been a part of its line the entire time. "We'll continue to offer damascus and have no plans to expand or contract the line right now," Hoffman said. "We offer a new damascus knife each year in a limited edition and always sell it out. These are numbered one through 999, and the 2000 model, a Michael Walker LinerLock™ pattern, recently sold out." The 2001 Boker Damascus will be a lock-back with a snakewood handle.

A standard issue of six Boker lock-backs is available regularly. The 546 Damascus fixed-blade fighter, a tribute to the late Col. Rex Applegate, a pioneer in combat knife design, became available in limited quantities last year. As for the resurgence in factory damascus, Hoffman simply said, "Anything would be a guess on my part, but possibly it's because of a greater interest in collecting more expensive knives because of the scare in the firearms industry. I did have a call from a guy last year with $50,000 to invest, and he wanted to put that money in damascus. His idea was that this might have a better return on his investment than a CD in a bank. Our damascus values have gone up quite a bit."

Factory Damascus Comes Of Age

Its popular Commander and CQC-7 models are also tops on the list in damascus at Emerson Knives, Inc. Company CEO Ernest Emerson sees two reasons for the renewed vigor of factory damascus knives. "The education of the knife-buying public and the quality of the factory-produced

"We offer a new damascus knife each year in a limited edition and always sell it out." — Chuck Hoffman, Boker USA

knives are both higher now," Emerson observed. "The customer who was buying a $49 knife 10 years ago is now buying a $149 knife, and that allows people like us to make a damascus-bladed version of an already expensive factory knife, and charge enough to make it worthwhile without getting into the custom knife price range."

The T-10 Pearl Damascus from William Henry Knives, Blade Magazine's 2000 Investor/Collector Knife Of The Year©, was in such demand that WHK's Matt Conable said it was sold out before the first knife could be delivered. At right is the new T-10 with a coral handle.

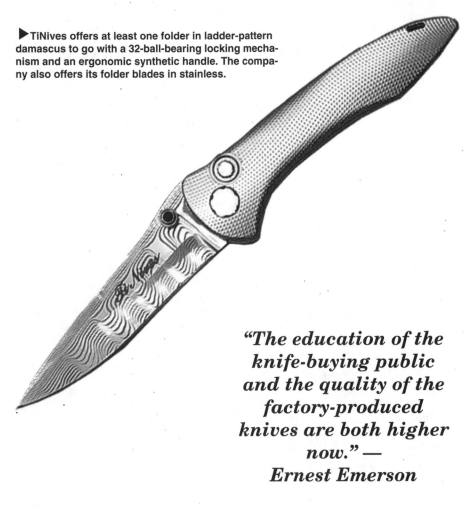

▶TiNives offers at least one folder in ladder-pattern damascus to go with a 32-ball-bearing locking mechanism and an ergonomic synthetic handle. The company also offers its folder blades in stainless.

"The education of the knife-buying public and the quality of the factory-produced knives are both higher now." —
Ernest Emerson

Emerson may charge prices $150 to $200 higher to upgrade his standard factory models to damascus, but he believes the knowledgeable knife consumer takes the difference in stride. "Some knives from factories are already expensive, but they are well made. So, people are already paying a higher price and the extra speed bump is not that much to get a damascus blade. Plus," he maintained, "we've got guys like Devin Thomas, who we buy from, that are now making damascus of superior quality in higher quantities."

Though the maintenance of damascus is something of a challenge, Emerson said the steel is more of a collectible grade. It does require cleaning and reasonable care, just as any carbon steel would. Emerson encourages those who buy damascus knives for functional purposes to consider stainless instead.

Back In The USA

Along with Bear Cutlery and Boker, Damascus USA is one of the survivors from the factory damascus movement of the mid-to-late '80s. Rob Charlton and Co. offer a wide selection of collector and user pieces

and have presented them to such luminaries as Ronald Reagan, George Bush, Chuck Yeager and others. Among the company's offerings is a holdover from the late '80s—the HOG Limited Edition set commemorating the fifth anniversary in 1988 of the Harley Owners Group. The set consists of a bowie and dagger with cocobolo handles, both mounted on a handsome wood display. Only 100 were made.

Salts Of Nitre

Chris Reeve Knives offers damascus on its large and small Sebenzas, as well as the Umfaan, all of which are folders with Reeve's Integral Lock. The blades are high carbon and nickel etched with ferric chloride for a "black-and-white" effect. Damascus blades that are bronzed or blued, with a "Salts of Nitre" finish, are available at additional cost. The Salts of Nitre finish is for decorative purposes only. According to Reeve, the finish does not react well when used to cut items

▶Delta-Z's line of Italian-made knives includes folders with Damascus blades, polished bolsters and a selection of maple, stag and synthetic handles.

with an acid content, such as apples, oranges, etc. Other damascus steels are also available on Reeve knives.

Conclusion

Of course, there are exceptions. Camillus recently dropped the damascus knives in its line, so factory damascus is not a cure-all. However, there are enough companies trying it—Round Eye Knife And Tool, Cold Steel, Delta-Z, and TiNives among them, and even Marble's reportedly is considering offering some of its traditional fixed blades in damascus— so it warrants serious consideration.

Whatever your choice, factory damascus seems to be back in large part because of the maturing of both the knifemaking community, with more sophisticated production techniques, and the knife consumer, who appreciates a steel that is both aesthetic and utilitarian. •

▶As it has since the 1980s, Fain Edwards' steel company produces damascus for Bear MGC Cutlery, and Bear maintains 15 to 20 damascus knives in its line. Some of the pieces get higher-end handle treatment, usually mother-of-pearl or stag, the latter here on the 544D gut hook.

▼ Damascus USA is one of the survivors from the factory damascus movement of the mid-to-late '80s. The HOG Limited Edition set celebrated the fifth anniversary of the Harley Owners Group in 1988. The damascus bowie and dagger feature cocobolo handles. (Weyer photo)

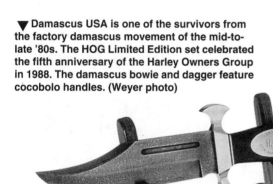

Break the Knife Code

By Richard D. White

One of the secrets of success in collecting and investing is to become familiar with the product. Whether it is stocks, bonds, antiques, toys or pocketknives, the more information available, the greater the chances of ensuring a successful venture.

It only makes sense for pocketknife companies to provide detailed pattern, model, year, brand, blade and handle information in hopes of growing the collector market. This is all good news for pocketknife collectors. Most knives made by the major cutlery companies have been well documented with outstanding bibliographies, photographs, dating systems and cutlery stamps incorporated throughout the years of production.

The documented brands include: W.R. Case, Remington, Winchester, Western States, John Primble, Schrade Cutlery, New York Knife, Pal Blade, Queen, Robeson, Cattaraugus, Camillus, IXL Wostenholm, Shapeigh Hardware, Hibbard-Spencer-Bartlett (OVB), Ka-Bar, Landers-Frary-Clark (LF&C) and Ulster Knife Co.

Many name-brand knives are listed in several different price guides, giving the collector pricing estimates that can be compared.

> ## Cutlery companies provide coded brand information to knife collectors

These documented sources are invaluable in not only purchasing pocketknives, but also for determining selling prices.

In addition, several of the major knife companies use a coding or numbering system to indicate the year the knife was produced, as well as the handle material, knife style, number of blades, and other specifications particular to a knife pattern.

The codes tell collectors whether the knife in question has the correct blades, handle material, and other inside information that reveals altered and otherwise unoriginal knives. In almost every case, the coding system or company stamp is on the portion of the blade known as the tang. The tang of a pocketknife is the flat, unsharpened area of the blade closest to the handle.

The flat area serves as the "palette," providing collectors with the

Three knives stamped "KENT" were made by Camillus Cutlery Co. for F.W. Woolworth's as early as 1934. The KENT brand popularized the use of colorful celluloid handles, including "end of day" celluloid supposedly made from sweeping up leftover celluloid pieces and molding them into knife handles.

company name, knife brand name and coding information like production dates and model numbers. An advantage of multi-blade folders is that several of the blade tangs can be used to stamp the codes.

Though several well-known companies use the tang area to detail blade configurations and handle materials (like Robeson, Winchester, Remington, LF&C, Western, Cattaraugus and Schrade), only one company uses the tang portion of the master blade to stamp production dates.

"Could that Montgomery Wards knife be a Camillus in disguise, or is it a Winchester?"

The tang stamps of W.R. Case and Sons Cutlery Co. of Bradford, Pa., are so well documented that beginning pocketknife collectors often build collections with Case knives for ease of access to individual knife production dates. Case used an extensive system of letters, symbols and dots to indicate the specific years knives were manufactured, and on the back of the master blades, a system of letters and numbers indicates each knife style, handle material and the number of knife blades.

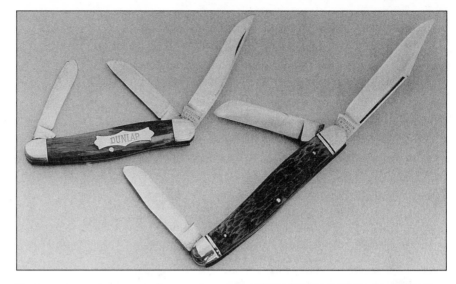

The tang stamps on two stockman patterns read "HIGH CARBON STEEL," indicating knives made by Camillus for Sears Roebuck and Co. The word "DUNLAP" on the handle shield of the knife at left refers to Thomas Dunlap, hardware buyer for Sears who created the Craftsman line of tools. The example at right is a well-constructed premium stockman pocketknife with a jigged-bone handle and a long-pull master blade.

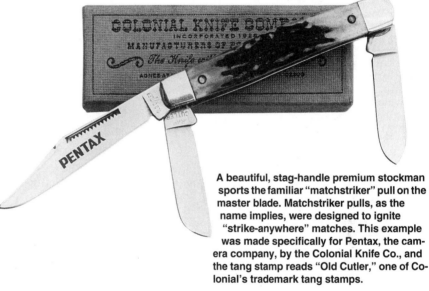

A beautiful, stag-handle premium stockman sports the familiar "matchstriker" pull on the master blade. Matchstriker pulls, as the name implies, were designed to ignite "strike-anywhere" matches. This example was made specifically for Pentax, the camera company, by the Colonial Knife Co., and the tang stamp reads "Old Cutler," one of Colonial's trademark tang stamps.

The top knife, deeply stamped "STREAMLINE" in the center of the master blade, was made by Camillus with a "Silver Sword" tang stamp. It was issued in the 1930s during the era of the streamline locomotives. At bottom is a single-blade folder with a yellow celluloid handle created by the Western Cutlery Co. of Boulder, Colo. The tang stamp of the "contract knife" for Western Cutlery touts "L. L. Bean Inc., Freeport, ME.," indicating the famous outfitter and clothing store.

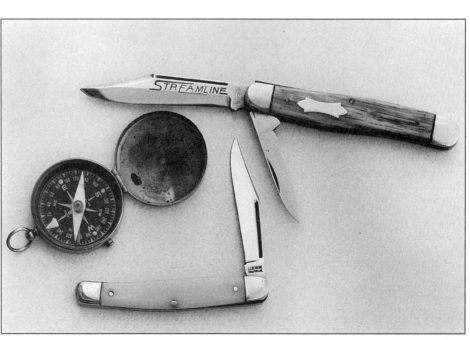

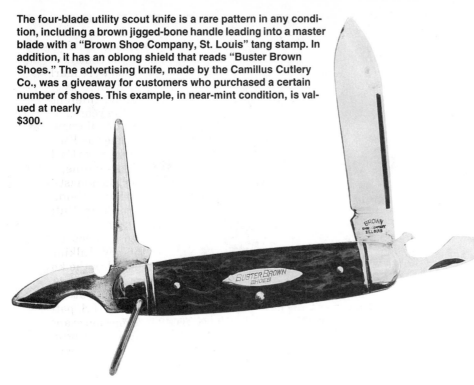

The four-blade utility scout knife is a rare pattern in any condition, including a brown jigged-bone handle leading into a master blade with a "Brown Shoe Company, St. Louis" tang stamp. In addition, it has an oblong shield that reads "Buster Brown Shoes." The advertising knife, made by the Camillus Cutlery Co., was a giveaway for customers who purchased a certain number of shoes. This example, in near-mint condition, is valued at nearly $300.

With two codes, collectors know a great deal more about specific Case knives, and collectors refer to them by their pattern numbers, not model names. The Case whittlers known as "18" and "83" patterns are

"The problem for collectors is the lack of information on little-researched knife brands."

easily identified if the code is known. Using models 6318 and 6383 Case whittlers as examples, "6" is a code telling collectors each knife has a bone handle, "3" means there are three blades, and the "8" in "80" or "18" indicates each is a whittler.

Origin Unknown

The problem for collectors arises not in identifying and pricing documented brands, but the lack of information on little-researched brands, or those not connected to a major knife company. Collectors are constantly running across knives

with unusual or unknown tang stamps.

In many cases, these knives were made by known knife manufacturers, but were not attributed to a particular company. Some non-documented stamps are the result of contractual arrangements between large companies and various hardware stores, mail-order firms and general merchandising companies.

The "contract knives," as they are called, were a source of revenue for almost all pocketknife companies. Montgomery Wards would employ a cutlery company to produce a series of knives to be sold at Wards sites throughout the United States. The handle material, size, blade configuration, production number, etc., would be agreed upon, and the contract put into effect.

In time, thousands of knives bearing the "WARDS" tang stamp would be delivered and sold at various Wards retail outlets, or offered for sale through the famous Montgomery Wards mail-order catalog.

For the collector, there is a bit of intrigue knowing the knife being examined for possible purchase, and bearing the "WARDS" stamping,

"There is a bit of intrigue in knowing a knife could have been built by a number of companies."

Two sheath knives bear the stamps "HAWTHORNE" (lower) and "WESTERN FIELD." The Western Field knife is handled in jigged bone, while the lower Hawthorne-stamped model sports a stacked-leather-washer handle with fiber and brass spacers. Both of these knives are "contract knives" and were most likely made by Western Cutlery of Boulder, Colo. A comparative analysis of the blade styles with blood grooves results in direct matches with one of Western's familiar knife patterns.

could have been built by a number of manufacturers. Could that Montgomery Wards knife be a Camillus in disguise, or is it a Winchester? Certainly, if the knife was produced by the famous and extremely collectible Winchester Cutlery Co., it has a great deal more potential value than an identical example made by Camillus.

A listing of all of the contract knives made by various companies is difficult to compile. The data is just not available. What is known, however, is nearly all merchandising companies and mail-order firms offered knives for sale. They include: Western Auto, Abercrombie and Fitch, Montgomery Wards, Sears Roebuck and Co., J.C. Higgins, Gambles Stores, F.W. Woolworth, L.L. Bean, Herter and Co., Tru-Value Hardware, Coast Hardware, and a host of others.

Some collectors use a comparative analysis method of pinpointing who made a particular knife. In this method, the knife in question is placed alongside a similar pattern by a known knife company. All of the individual characteristics (size, shape, blades, handle material, craftsmanship, etc.) are compared

> *"Some collectors use a comparative analysis method of pinpointing who made a particular knife."*

between the two, and an educated guess is made with regards to the maker of the unknown knife.

A second problem facing knife collectors is determining the manufacturers of "house brands." House brands are copyrighted stamps imprinted on various knives by knife companies but without identifying the source. Unlike the contract brands, house brands were marketed by cutlers who, in some cases, used as many as 20-30 different house brands over the years.

This list is almost endless, with such interesting names as Kwik Kut, Topper, Frontier, High Carbon Steel, Sta-Sharp, Streamline, Ranger, Old Cutler, Jackmaster, Kutmaster, Pocket Pard, Klein, Silver Sword, Western Pride, Cutco, and innumerable others.

Formal research into house brands is in its infancy. Talking to "old timers" employed in the knife industry for years is a significant source of information about stamps. Research into U.S. patent and copyright information is another valuable source, and can be used to track down the cutlery copyright application.

Three knives are stamped "WARDS" and made for the Montgomery Wards Co. Most Wards knives were made by Camillus but others were built by Winchester. The two "dogleg" jacks (top and right) are identical to a Winchester pattern, and can thereby be traced back to Winchester. The other pattern is a rather common Wards four-blade premium stockman pattern with a leather punch and sheepsfoot, spey and master blades. This knife handle is genuine jigged bone.

Contract and House Brands Revealed

KA-BAR

Kabar
UNION
Army/Navy Dept. Stores*
L.L. Bean, Freeport Maine*
OLCUT
KA-BAR-LO
IROS-KEEN
Alfred Field & Progress*
HERDER, Phil., PA*
KEENWELL
DASCO*
Ideal Cutlery Co., Reading PA.*
Supple-Biddle Hdwr.*
FOLSOM, New York*
Hoffritz, New York*
Henry Sears and Sons* (prior to 1940)
Cutco*
Union Cutlery Co.

WESTERN

Western States
Western Field (Wards)*
WEST-CUT
Coleman-Western
Westaco
Westmark
L.L. Bean, Freeport, ME.*
Coast Hardware*
Hawthorne*
Western Auto*

CAMILLUS CUTLERY CO.

Belnap Hdwr. (made also by Utica, Boker, Schrade)*
Buster Brown Shoes*
Camco
Catskill Knife Co.*
Clover Brand
Craftsman (for Sears; also by Schrade, Ulster)*
Cornwall Knife Co.*
Disston Steel (commemorative)*
Dunlap (Sears)*
Enderes*
Fairmount Cutlery Co.*
Frontier (made for Imperial)
Gambles Stores*
Hibbard, Spencer, Bartlett (Tru-Value Hardware; some also by Utica, New York Knife)*
High Carbon Steel (Sears)*
Kent, New York City (made for F.W. Woolworth's)*
Kwik Kut (Sears)*
Powercraft (Sears)*
Remington (re-issue, recent)*
Silver Sword
Sta-Sharp (Sears)*

Streamline
Syracuse Knife Co.*
Zenith (later production, earlier made by New York Knife)*
Simmons, Warden, White (turn-ring knife)*
Crosman Blades*

COLONIAL

Ambassador
Brown and Bigelow*
Old Cutler
Executive
Ranger
Forest Master
Shur-Snap
Topper (Junior Topper)
Federal Knife Co.*
Fishmaster
Master Barlow

SCHRADE CUTLERY CO.

Edgemaster
Everlastingly Sharp
J.C. Higgins (Sears)*
Master Mechanic (Tru-Value Hdwr.)*
Old Timer
Uncle Henry
Kingston
Imperial (after 1947)
Presto
Press Button
Forest King

IMPERIAL

IKCO
Hammer Brand (copyright purchased in 1938 from New York Knife)
Jackmaster
Kamp King
Made in USA (military 4-blade bone)

UTICA CUTLERY CO.

Klein*
Kutmaster
Pocket Pard
Crosman Blades (also by Camillus)*
John Primble (some also by Camillus, Schrade)*
Seneca Cutlery Co.*
Montgomery Wards (some also by Winchester)*
Western Pride*
Dura-Edge
Featherweight (Girl Scout knives)

Denotes "contract" knives made for other companies.
All others are considered "house brands," "premium brands" or "secondary brands."

Who Made It?

Putting together a list of house-brand knives and contract knives built by significant knife manufacturers is a time-consuming task that involves researching printed data, consulting historical records, interviewing former cutlery company employees, or comparing similar knives with different stamps.

Somewhat complicating the issue are retail outlet contracts with several knife companies to produce specific tang stamp requirements over a period of decades. Thus, Sears Roebuck and Co. knives were most certainly made by several different companies using numerous tang stamps. Sears had several lines of products for varying customers.

The list below represents the latest research into the stamps of the major cutlery companies, including contract knives and house brands. The list could be used as a guideline when examining a knife with an unfamiliar or unusual tang stamp. •

C.A.S. Iberia Hefts the Holy Iron of the Highlanders

Reproductions of historically accurate dirks, targes and broadswords are ripe for the picking

By Greg Bean

ALL SCOTTISH HIGHLANDERS, whether powerful clan chieftains or lowly stable cleaners, wore dirks, their "holy iron." A dirk was as significant as one's own name, parentage and clan. The most serious of oaths was sworn by the holy iron, and it was feared that supernatural forces would avenge any broken word that had thus been sworn.

Long after the end of the Highland clan's way of life, there remains a fascination with the Scots' nationalistic implements of destruction: the dirk, targe and broadsword.

Historically, a dirk was worn in the middle of the torso, dangling between the legs and protruding above the belt, as proud a display of manhood as any cock's comb. While Gaelic citizens treasured swords, only "gentlemen" could afford them. Dirks, on the other hand, were more common than shoes.

Long enough to be considered short swords, the fighting knives of northern Celts typically stretched 12-16 inches and took on various forms, depending on which century the dirks were made, their purpose, and oftentimes, the personal aesthetics of their makers.

In an era when dirks actually served in combat, they typically had long, tapered, triangle-shaped

Greg Manning poses as a Highland clansman awaiting his time in battle and displaying the C.A.S. Iberia Sterling backsword, dirk and targe.

"The most serious of oaths was sworn by the 'holy iron.'"

blades with brass disk pommels and wooden grips carved in Celtic knot work. The grips thickened at the handle/blade junctures, progressing into examples of architecture referred to as "haunches." The design served the purpose of a cross guard and kept the user's hands from sliding onto the blade.

The single-edged blade nearly always had a groove near the back edge, decorated with saw-toothed scalloping, file work or perforations called "piercings.". Blades could be fashioned from broken swords, but were most often newly forged with a preference for blades from German cities known for forging: Solingen and Passau.

Scabbards were leather with metal fittings and chapes, either suspended or thrust through the belt.

From the 18th century on, when the Highland warrior was likely in the service of the queen, the weapon became more of a distinguishing feature than a practical implement of war. As such, dirks also became more difficult to ignore. Pommels were set with stone or faceted, colored glass. Cairngorm, a smoky quartz named for a Scottish mountain range, was the favorite and set at an angle for show. The scabbard was beset with silver or

C.A.S. Iberia's Victorian-era Regimental Dirk includes a knife and fork in the scabbard suite, a holdover from use in the field. This is commonly called a piper's dirk, but was proudly worn by officers and soldiers alike throughout the years of the British Empire.

Celtic knot work. These common designations ignore the fact that basket makers in Glasgow and Stirling made both types. The leather- and wool-lined basket would keep the hand warm, and if fitted well would support the hand, making a long day a little easier.

The basket's weight also balances the weapon, allowing a faster swing of the tip. And if the conflict had become up-close and personal, the hand hardware would surely have made a great impression.

The blades were usually double-edged, though many single-edged or backsword styles have been documented. There were generally two fullers (grooves) running the length of the blade, although single fullers were common through most of the length of the blade, and double and triple fullers at the ricasso.

The targe was a round shield made of layered leather over wood. It was used to deflect an Englishman's pike or musket bayonet to allow the Scot to get inside the weapon's reach. Of course, when fighting another Scot with a broadsword, it would hold a blade sunk into it, momentarily encumbering the opponent. These shields often had spikes fixed to the front, turning the targes themselves into lethal weapons.

The "Highland charge" was the patented Scottish battle tactic, and it worked well on the Scots' own turf, which was hilly with rocky outcroppings. The charge was certainly

gold and typically housed a knife and fork.

The image of a highlander dictates a long dagger in one hand protruding from behind a spiked, round shield, a scything broadsword in the other, emerging from the covering smoke generated by primitive muzzleloaders, which roared as bagpipes screeched. This was the last sight and sound for many of the highlanders' enemies, and a favorite image of contemporary highlander "wannabes."

Let the Games Begin

Nearly all Highland games feature recreations of the Highland warrior, minus the bloodlust, and more than enough edged weaponry. Attendees first notice the broadswords, especially if banged in the knees while standing in line behind a Scotsman. One wonders how many fights have started from something as innocent as turning around and whacking someone, rather like the Three Stooges mishandling a 2-by-4. Swords seen in paintings, prints and in person are most often of the basket-hilt broadsword variety, distinguished by metal basketwork that encases the hand. The basket would protect the hand from any sword blow, and perhaps even a musket ball. The Glasgow style con-

sists of pierced plates and bars, and was usually of steel or iron.

The Stirling is a bit more of a peacock, and consists of bars that coil and twine. It typically has a look of

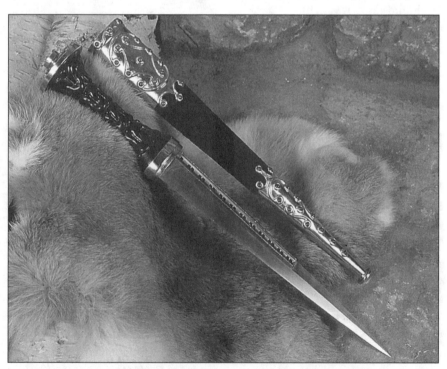

The C.A.S Iberia Civilian Dress Dirk is still in vogue, even though the handle and pommel styles date back to the Middle Ages. This particular piece is modeled after an original in the Edinburgh museum.

used in warfare between clans, but any modern Scot would prefer to remember its use in wars against the English to win or maintain independence.

The clansmen would fling themselves downhill across the broken terrain in a scattered pattern. When in musket range, they stopped to fire their weapons, dropped them and fixed in place their targe, dirk and broadsword, then resumed their frantic assault. They would emerge from the smoke of their own weapons and engage the front ranks of their enemies.

They would go low, maybe even to one knee, to allow an upward sweep with the targe to get inside of the opposing weapon's guard. They slashed or thrust with the broadsword against the opponent on the right and made a downward strike with the dirk, hopefully taking out an opponent with each hand.

"Two new C.A.S. Iberia creations capitalize on the company's close cooperation with the Royal Armouries in Leeds, England."

The Highland Furies

As one survivor of a Highland charge wrote, "The Highland furies rushed in upon us with more violence than ever did a sea driven by a tempest."

The last time the charge was seen in the British Isles was in 1746 at the battle of Culloden Moor. This was the highlanders' last grasp for independence in which they tried to put their own candidate, Charles Stuart, on the throne during the Jacobite Rebellion. The battle of Culloden, and the period of repression that followed, spelled the end of the clansmen way of life.

To a Highland descendant, Culloden Moor is as much a rallying point as the Alamo is to a Texan. What followed Culloden was a form of not-so-genteel genocide. The "pacification" was, as John Baynes wrote in the Soldiers of Scotland, "brutal subjugation, physical genocide and cultural destruction. The government's intention was to end the clan system and English Redcoats marched

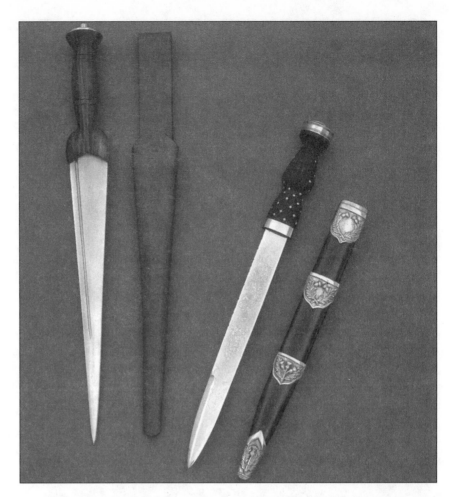

The C.A.S. Iberia Dirk (left) is patterned after an early, circa-1700 model. The blade is single-edged and wedge-shaped, and the hilt is hand-carved in Macassar ebony. To its right is the C.A.S. Piper's Dirk. Original piper's dirks were standard issue to pipers and drummers of Highland regiments of the British army from 1871 and were descendants of 18th-century Scottish dirks. This particular blade is etched in a thistle motif.

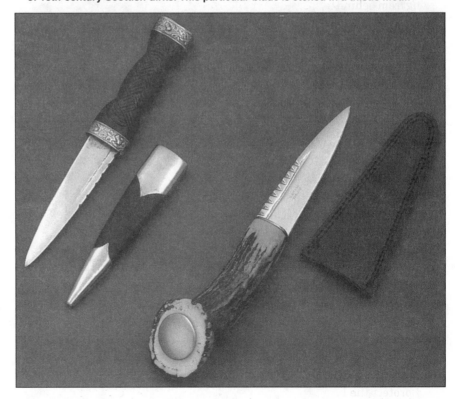

C.A.S. Iberia offers two sgian dubh dirks, one in a stag handle and silver cabochon (right), and one with a traditional military or evening dress pattern.

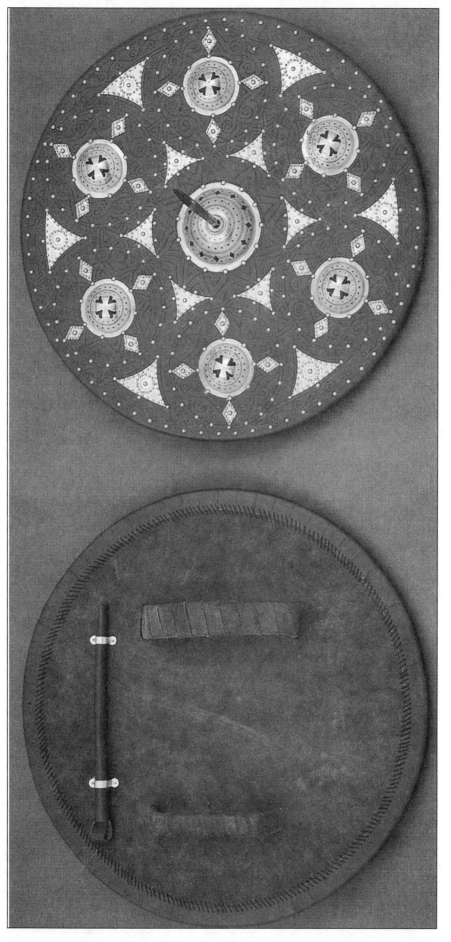

The Inverary Targe from C.A.S. Iberia is of unknown origin in a traditional pattern of tooled leather over wood with a goatskin backing. The spike screws into the central boss.

through the villages and valleys and imposed a reign of terror."

Great Britain recruited regiments of Scots in the face of any conflict. Whether the English won or lost, it was a win-win situation: winning was good, losing highlanders was good. Both were even better.

The Scots, by natural temperament, excelled as shock troops. Once equipped with military training and discipline, they proved to be the hardiest, bravest and most accomplished of Great Britain's troops. The highlanders quite mastered the retreat, but that concept was just not in their vocabulary.

The Black Watch, formed in 1725, became the best known of the British Highland regiments. These Scots, who at the time were seen as turncoats by the rebellious highlanders, became a highly respected and prestigious regiment.

By the time the sun ceased to set on the British Empire, the Highland regiments had become the greatest asset in defending the Empire.

"The highly individualistic Scots had no required style for their dirks."

As the value of Highland warriors grew, so did the esteem with which they were held. Being a highlander became all the rage, with regiments wanting kilts, bagpipes and those wonderful dirks that were to die for, literally at times. Even purely English regiments wanted to share in the glory, such that there was a Liverpool Highland Regiment.

With the cultural threat removed, the English developed a fascination with the Scots highlander, as well as all things Celtic. The British Empire hit its peak during the Victorian era, and no less a person than Queen Victoria developed a fetish for the "northern barbarians." The authors Robert Burns and Sir Walter Scott added mass media to Queen Victoria's personal stamp of approval. Scott's "Rob Roy, of the MacGregor clan," became a franchise of books and theatre pieces and (more recently) movies. Writers and royalty, through poems, prose and patronage, romanticized the highlanders.

The irony is that the Scot's national instruments, the dirk and broadsword, reached their most celebrated moment after firearms, from the Brown Bess to the Maxim gun, had taken away their military usefulness. There is still such pride in these weapons, however, that even in the modern military, the sword and the dirk are seen in parade settings and worn whenever appropriate.

For Pipers And Drummers

The highly individualistic Scots had no required style for their dirks, but once they became an ornament of the British military, they had designated patterns. There were patterns for infantry soldiers, for officers, for pipers and for drummers. Each regiment had its own pattern. There was pride expressed through the wearing of the dirks, and each regiment established its identity, at least in part, through its dirk pattern. This eventually included the "sgian dubh."

The sgian dubh, another favorite accouterment of the well-dressed Scot, is worn in the top of the stocking of the right leg and is commonly called a "sock knife." The knife part

is accurate — "sgian" means "knife" — but "dubh" means "black." A well-used blade from the era before stainless steel would have turned black, and the sgian dubh evolved from a basic utility knife.

The sgian dubh has a popular history as being from the time of British disarmament. It is thought to have

> *"If the conflict had become up-close and personal, the basket hilt would surely have made an impression."*

evolved from the "Oxter," meaning "armpit knife." The English allowed no weapons, so knives were concealed under the owners' arms. If a guest entered the home, it was a dishonor to wear a concealed weapon,

so knives were displayed in stockings.

Knives displayed in stockings gave the impression that the proprietor trusted the guest not to reveal him to the authorities and that there was no perceived threat from the guest. This honorable history of the sgian dubh partly explains why it is such a beloved artifact now.

Its realty is probably less distinguished. When battles were won with blades, it wasn't considered much of a fighting knife, and it has suffered from a bit of comical commentary. Some regiments actually forbade its wearing, as it was considered a tool for "ghilles (cattle herders) and serving rascals." The sgian dubh was the brunt of the joke in a popular Victorian song that includes in its verses, "It isn't much use for fighting, but for peeling spuds it's dandy."

Whatever the truth of its history, the sgian dubh has since earned its place as an essential piece of decoration. You seldom find a kilted gentleman not bearing his "toothpick." Where, might you ask, do you get these wonderful, antiquated, useless things?

C.A.S. Iberia offers a good selection of fine Scottish weaponry. C.A.S, a U.S.-based, historical weaponry supplier, sells dirks, sgian dubhs, targes, basket-hilt broadswords, and the two-handed claymores from earlier times, as well.

Owner Barry Ross travels around the world to museums and armories to find original Scottish weaponry. From the Tower of London to the private collections nearly anywhere, Ross spans the globe searching for edged weaponry that epitomizes an era, a people or a place. His focus then is to re-create each piece in exacting detail.

C.A.S. is appreciated for bringing history alive for the many re-creationists, collectors, enthusiasts and proud Scotsmen and descendants of Scotsmen who find that being armed is as essential and satisfying as a good meal. C.A.S. Iberia has several new additions from pre- and post-Culloden periods.

Evening Dress

C.A.S. Iberia's smallest piece is a sgian dubh with a high-carbon steel blade and a Blackwood grip carved in a basketweave pattern. Its formal purpose as decoration is made clear by its designation as an "Evening Dress" style. Yes, there is a style for daytime and casual wear, with a grip of stag horn.

Next up in size is the civilian Dress Dirk. The original of this piece, in the Edinburgh Museum, is

C.A.S. Iberia's Hanwei-made dirks are displayed with their Culloden-era targe and several camp items of a Highland soldier.

a high-quality dirk, signed and addressed by its maker, Rand Kirkwood of Thistle Street, Edinburgh. The Dress Dirk has a high-carbon steel blade with blade perforations in the fuller.

These perforations, or piercings, serve no purpose other than to attract attention. This is a wickedly sharp piece; shaving would be no problem at all. The grip is wood carved in a rope interlace. It resembles a random wrapping of cord and is typical of Celtic artwork. The flat disk pommel is a style that reaches as far back as any Scottish metalworking tradition.

The largest of the C.A.S. offerings, the Regimental Dirk, dates back to the Victorian military period. The Regimental Dirk has a high-carbon steel blade with a notched back. The scalloped teeth on the back of the blade resemble saw teeth, but were purely ornamental file work.

This type of dirk was proudly worn in many a military parade, but its origin as a field piece can be seen in the scabbard suite of fork and knife. The "stone" on the pommel of the dirk, and its suite, are canted at an angle, all the better to be seen. The wood grip is carved in a basket-weave style, another Celtic trait that goes as far back in time as the Celts do.

These historical pieces are reproduced in fine quality by the forge of Hanwei. Coming from China, as these do, may seem incongruous for a European weapon, but Hanwei has come to be recognized as a premier line of the highest quality historical weaponry. Dalian, the city of origin, now commands the same respect in knifemaking circles as Solingen, Germany.

C.A.S also sells a Hanwei-made targe from the Culloden era. It has an attractive design of embossed leather and comes with a spike for the middle, quite removable and able to be secured into its own mounted sheath.

C.A.S. also offers four flavors of the basket-hilt broadsword, with two currently in production, and two to be released early in 2001. From the Hanwei forge, the company offers a Stirling and a Glasgow-style backsword. These single-edged

Highland clansman Greg Manning displays a dirk suspended from his belt as he brandishes the Stirling backsword and targe, all from C.A.S. Iberia.

weapons have high-carbon steel blades, and are finished to a mirror-like sheen. They come with leather scabbards reinforced with a steel throat and chape.

Their two newest creations will capitalize on the close cooperation that Ross has developed with the Royal Armouries in Leeds, England. He has been given open access and enthusiastic encouragement to develop what promises to be the most accurate reproductions available.

Pre-Pacification Broadsword

The first offering is an early 17th-century broadsword, a purely Scottish creation from before the "pacification." The other is a backsword dated from 1760. The baskets of both combine bars and plates, and one will feature a gargoyle-like plaque in its protective metalwork.

The originals of both these swords have German blades, and like many German blades, have the name Andrea Ferara with the "running wolf" mark engraved on the blade. Ferara was a 16th-century Italian blade maker who achieved mythic status.

The running wolf was a mark often associated with Passau, Germany. Go figure. Many people, including the Scots, attributed magical powers to either trademark. Blade makers found it profitable to include either or both marks, even though Ferara would have been at least 300 years old to forge all the blades attributed to him.

These pieces from C.A.S will be replicated to the finest detail, including the blade maker's marks. Ross reports they are exceptionally fine weapons with such quick balance that one could fence with them, or shear tree limbs, whatever the case may be.

Most knockoffs of the Scottish basket-hilt sword are ponderous, heavy-handling things. Their weapons, though, are actually quite fleet and sprightly.

After hefting many of the actual artifacts at the Leeds Armories, Ross wished to offer dead-on replicas. While these weapons may not elevate the Scots' reputation in the areas of subtlety and finesse, the holy iron does prove itself capable of executing a skilled phrase d'arms. And that should be enough to make any Celtic connoisseur happy. •

For more information, contact:
C.A.S. Iberia
attn: Barry Ross,
650 Industrial Blvd.
Sale Creek, TN 37373
(423) 332-4700

Give Me a Factory Hunter and a Day in the Woods

Custom knives may raise the bar, but the deer don't know it, and a factory knife will do just fine, thank you

By Jack Collins

Randall knives led the way for today's custom makers, but are now considered factory knives. Whatever one considers them, they are among the best knives available.

If you believe the current knife media, you might be led to believe that only custom, or handmade, knives are suitable for hunting purposes. The perception is that factory-made knives are only suitable for use at the kitchen table, for throwing in the back of a pickup truck or for relegating to the toolbox. Well, to echo an old Johnny Mercer song, "It ain't necessarily so!"

To be fair, knife magazines find it in their readers' best interest to focus on the incredibly varied offerings of custom knifemakers, rather than the slightly more limited factory products. Additionally, many factory knives are available for first-hand inspection at local sporting

"Don't feel as though you are left behind without a custom knife on your belt."

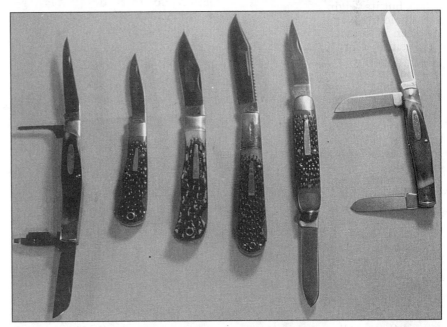

Whether reproductions or current production pieces, Remington knives come in a variety of styles and sizes. Four reproductions of the famous Bullet Knives are sandwiched on left and right by current knives. At right is a stockman pattern, and on the left is a variation of a stockman with a tool for installing or removing the choke tubes in a shotgun barrel and a punch to assist in the disassembly of Remington shotguns.

goods stores, while the more exotic custom offerings are seldom available for inspection except at knife shows.

Perhaps most importantly, the styles, shapes, materials, sheaths and finishes offered by handmade makers far outweigh the factory output, although recent manufacturing developments may skew this ratio somewhat. Finally, "new" sells, and it sells well.

Even though factories must limit the number of new offerings, I think it is safe to say that factory knives still outnumber custom knives in the field 10 to 1 (I've never been afraid to go out on a limb!). So, don't feel you are left behind or will be ostracized by your fellow hunters because you don't have a custom knife on your belt.

In my experience, there are few true custom knives. They may be handmade; they may be products of one person; they may be signed, sealed and delivered; but most are not "custom" in the true sense of the word, i.e., "made or performed according to personal order" — Webster's New Collegiate Dictionary.

Most handmade knives are merely one of the maker's knife designs, not made to order, albeit with the

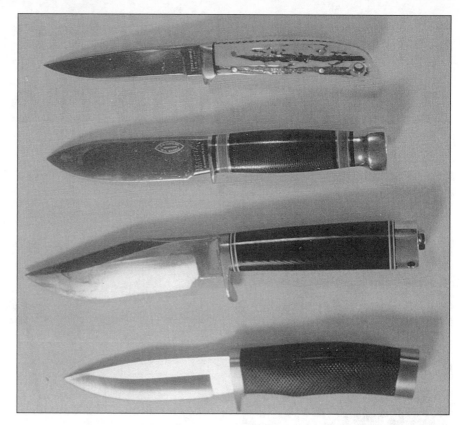

More recent styles show influence of custom makers, particularly Bob Loveless, with drop-point blades. Illustrating this feature are knives (from top) by Browning (the Model 52), Marble Arms (Sport 2000), Blackjack (Trail Guide), and Buck (Vanguard).

> ## "We as customers are better served using tried-and-true designs."

addition or substitution of one or more specifics. Makers change handle materials, vary blade lengths, finishes, or what have you. I have had one true custom knife, made to my design, and it was a miserable failure, due to the design, not the workmanship. It's not a bad thing that the knives are not "custom."

Makers prefer to design their own knives, and we as customers are better served buying and using tried-and-true designs. Few makers want to put their names on any knife of which they are not proud, and the vast majority of us, regardless of what we might think, are not good knife designers.

The Blades of Boyhood

Hunting knives were all fixed-blade knives when I was a boy. The Buck Knife Co. changed all of that in the early 1960s with the introduction of the Buck 110 Folding Hunter. Although there had been folders suitable for hunting purposes prior to that time, made by Case and others, the Buck Folding Hunter altered hunting knives for good.

It had a locking blade, and the lock worked! Good blade steel and excellent finish would have stood for little had the lock not functioned properly. The Buck 110 is still available and is a good choice for anyone who likes a folding knife.

Prior to the introduction of the Buck 110, Remington Bullet knives were also prized by many, and apparently served well. In my neck of the woods, however, I never saw a Remington folding knife until they had become collectors' items. Fortunately, they have been reissued by

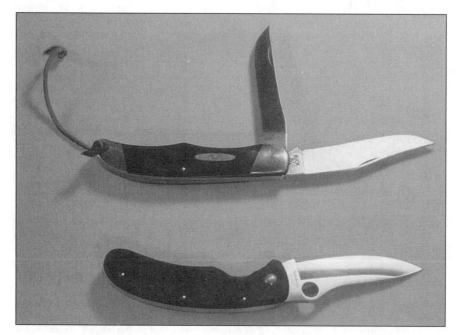

Old and new are personified respectively by the Buck Trailblazer (top) and the Spyderco Tim Wegner design. The Spyderco is considerably lighter in weight.

Remington, one model per year, beginning in the early '80s. These, too, have become collectible, but that doesn't limit their utility.

Some of the early models of the reproductions suffered from cracking of the Delrin® handle scales around the thong hole. This made them less desirable to collectors, but doesn't affect their use in the field a bit.

When compared to fixed-blade knives, folding knives have their advantages and their disadvantages. Some of their good points include their size, flexibility of carry, and safety of carry. Naturally, a knife with a blade that folds into the handle will occupy less space than one with a fixed blade.

Folded, the blade is protected and the user is protected from the blade. Many early sheath knives had their tips broken off because the soft sheaths available at the time allowed the application of unbearable stress when the user sat on the sheath or otherwise forced the tip of the sheath sideways.

On the other hand, a lock on a folding knife can fail, and according to Murphy, will do so at the most inopportune time. Used to gut, skin, butcher, or otherwise prepare game animals, hunting knives require cleaning, and folding knives have joints, crevices and other out-of-the-way spaces into which blood and tissue will intrude. Even stainless blades are not impervious to attack from blood. A fixed blade removes this concern, or at least greatly diminishes it.

The weakest point of a folding knife is its joint. This may be moot today, as the latest generation of folding knives are strong enough for anything save serious abuse. Nevertheless, a fixed-blade knife does not have that relative weakness.

One of the most popular designs for folding knives is the stockman pattern. Though a stockman will clean deer, it is better suited for squirrels, rabbits, and other small game. Popularized by hunters and trappers, the "trapper" folding knife pattern is similar to the stockman, but in most cases, it has one less blade and its blades are longer than those of the stockman. Most have slip joints and do not lock.

Recent developments in folding knife manufacture have resulted in knives with better blade steel and better heat treating. Such "super steels" as ATS-34, 154CM, CPM 440V and others were formerly the exclusive province of the custom knifemakers, and are now available from reputable knife factories.

Production sheath design has evolved, too, as evidenced by comparing the 1940 sheath (left) with the modern leather sheath to its immediate right, a style popularized by Bob Loveless. Buck offers a plastic-lined nylon sheath, and a Kydex® sheath is readily available from The Cutlery Shoppe.

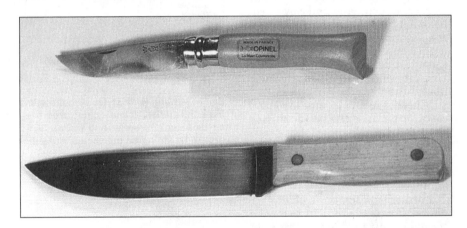

Inexpensive does not necessarily mean ineffective. The folder by Opinel (top) and fixed blade by Cold Steel were each bought for less than $20, yet are extremely useful and durable.

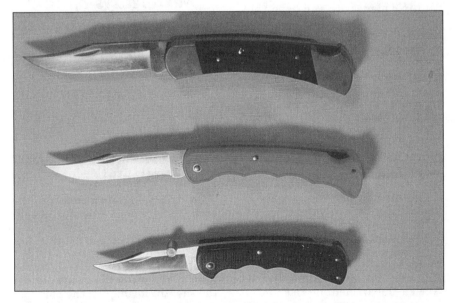

An original Buck Folding Hunter (top) and two subsequent generations of Bucklites are shown. Weight varies considerably, but cutting ability remains about the same.

Talent Scouts?

A great number of handmade knifemakers have lent their considerable design talents to factory-made knives. Also improved are handle materials. Stag is still popular, of course, but the introduction of Micarta®, G-10, and Kraton® has brought to factory knives a durability and feel heretofore unavailable.

Handle materials have changed over the years. Stag was practically standard for a time, and it is now so expensive that the antler is often saved for custom knives. There is an increasing use of high-grade steels in our current factory knives. Some companies, like Buck, have always had good reputations for supplying quality steels. When I worked in sporting goods retailing, I found that customers either loved Buck knives or hated them. I think the division fell along the lines of who could sharpen the blades, and who could not.

Companies such as Cold Steel, Gerber, Benchmade and Spyderco have led the way in the blade steel renaissance. The net result is a higher quality knife, which even though it demands a higher price point, it remains significantly lower in cost than handmade knives.

Whether in an attempt to control costs, or because the better steels are more durable, new folding knives tend to have fewer blades than those of previous generations. Indeed, a single blade is almost standard.

Formerly, when one's blade dulled, it was convenient to have a second or third blade ready to use. Just close the dull one and open the sharp one. Both could be sharpened at a more convenient time and place. Multiple blades are still handy but seldom, if ever, necessary given today's quality steels.

Most of the knives that take advantage of new manufacturing capabilities have been in the tactical genre, though this does not preclude their use for hunting. Indeed, they are tough knives and will withstand almost any field use.

Tactical folding and fixed-blade knives will also hold an edge far longer than your grandfather's pocketknife. Be careful, however, when selecting one. Many of the blade shapes are more oriented toward defense than toward hunting.

One sterling example of a hunting design in a newer "high-tech" knife is the Spyderco Tim Wegner. This knife has been endorsed by the Alaska Department of Fish and Game and has a semi-skinner-type blade shape. It is a grand knife for

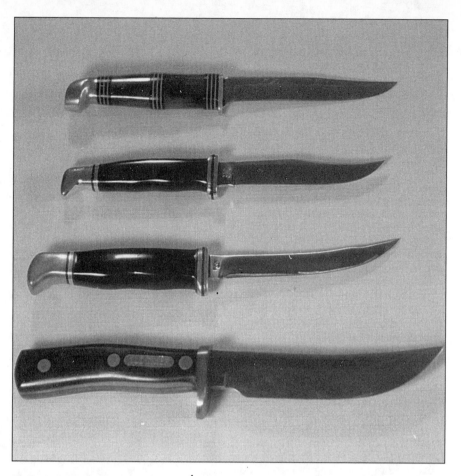

Earlier hunting knife styles demonstrate a straighter line, many having upswept or trailing-point blades. These include (from top) a circa-1940 Robeson, a Buck Woodsman, a circa-1965 Buck Personal, and a circa-1975 Schrade Old Timer. The tip of the Robeson was broken by sitting on the sheath and subsequently reground.

almost any purpose and nearly ideal for hunting.

"We may long for the yesterdays of our youth, but we are far better served with the tools of today."

Radical Changes

There have not been as many radical changes in fixed blades as there have been in folders, but there have been significant advancements in both. Factory knife designs, though made in quantity, have not remained static. Pictured in this story is a Robeson hunter circa 1940. As mentioned above, the tip of the blade was broken when the owner sat on the sheath. Reshaping the point didn't seriously reduce its utility, and may have helped it.

Notice, however, the general straightness of the blade and handle. This was characteristic of the times. Today we see the influence of custom knifemaking legend Robert Loveless in blade design, specifically in the drop-point blade style he popularized. I suggest the drop-point is most important, although not essential, in knives intended for use on big game.

Of all the factory straight knives available today, probably the most famous are those made by Randall Knives. I find it ironic that the very knives responsible for the widespread interest in custom knives are now considered factory knives, and rightly so.

Several Randall knives are pictured in this story, and despite the fact that these models are utility or combat knives, they can indeed be used for hunting, particularly in the mode of an all-around knife. The size of those shown suggests their use in hunting big game rather than rabbits or squirrels, but Randall has many smaller models.

Marble Arms has re-entered the knife scene after an absence of several years with some revived designs from their originator, Webster Marble, and some new designs. The one shown has the unmistakable look of a Robert Loveless piece, and, indeed, sports his name on the blade. The new Marbles are made of 52100 bearing steel, which is a great leap forward from the original. While not stainless, this steel will give superlative performance when properly heat treated.

One of the most significant changes to come along in the fixed-blade field is the introduction of non-leather sheaths. Kydex®, Concealex®, nylon and generic plastic are now in widespread use. Good leather sheaths are still popular, but serious inroads are being made by the newer materials. When hunting in wet weather for extended periods, these newer materials have much to recommend them.

"It had a locking blade, and the lock worked!"

SOG, Al Mar, Boker, Cold Steel, Case, Schrade, Ka-Bar and others have updated their lines with higher quality steels, handle materials, sheaths and designs as we the customers have become more discerning and demanding. In the case of these makers, the workmanship has consistently remained good, or the companies would have folded like the proverbial pocketknife years ago.

All in all, modern factory hunting knives are better than ever. We may long for the yesterdays of our youth, but we are far better served with the tools of today. ●

The Buck Folding Hunter (top) preceded more recent folders suitable for hunting such as (in descending order) the Cold Steel Voyager, the Benchmade Ascent, a Puma folding hunter, and the Gerber Gatormate.

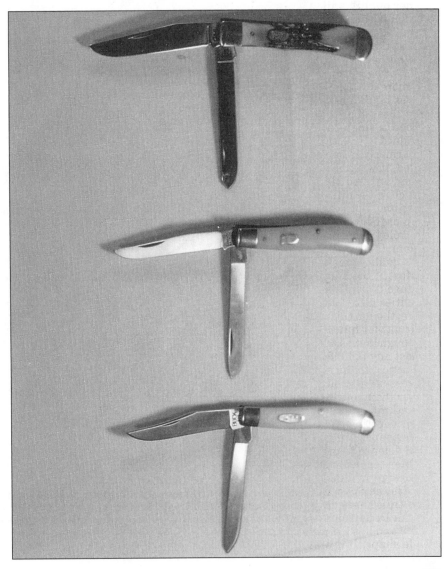

Trappers are and have been popular for hunting. Shown are models by (from top) Case, Schrade and Buck.

The Wedding of Handmade and Production Knives

Custom and factory knifemakers vow to remain faithful to each other through good times and bad

By Bob Terzuola

THROUGHOUT HISTORY, CRAFTSMEN have labored in cluttered, poorly lit home workshops to provide the world with implements from the mundane and homely to the most exquisite and complex works of art.

Giants in the crafts such as Benevenuto Cellini, Paul Revere and Faberge stand out as creators of the world's masterpieces. Such creative giants as these overshadow the countless numbers of silversmiths, blacksmiths, woodworkers, potters and the like, who made items used every day in the common household.

Not until the 19th century and the industrial revolution were items of high quality available to the average family at low cost. Factories equipped with production machinery were able to produce goods at high speed (compared to the hand craftsmen), and repeatable quality. This type of production depended on a simple principle — that of interchangeable parts.

The creator of a system of interchangeable parts was Eli Whitney, who was awarded the first contract in the United States to provide the new army with muskets, "lock, stock and barrel." Whitney realized the only way to make good on his promise was to streamline the manufacture of those muskets. Out of necessity, he devised the concept of interchangeable parts.

In the world of knives today, we reap the benefits of

The original Spyderco/Bob Terzuola C-15 was released in 1990 with an aluminum handle instead of today's G-10. "We probably made about 6,000 and the suggested retail price was $150," notes Spyderco CEO Sal Glesser. This is reportedly the only one of the original C-15s Spyderco has left.

Whitney's stroke of genius taken to a level that he could not have conceived.

At the same time, the home craftsman of the new millennium has raised the quality of handmade knives to pinnacles rarely reached before in history. The only exceptions in days past include presentation and specialty knives and swords, most often created as works of art for royalty.

The growth and advance of the modern renaissance of cutlery, led by America, has been a ballet, a "pas-de-deux," between the custom, home craftsman and the production knife factory. Like it or not, for better or worse, each has benefited from the knowledge and skills of the other.

Knives of all description have been mass-produced by factories since the early 1800s, and handmade knives have been lovingly and arduously crafted by smiths since the dawn of the age of metalworking. Only in recent years, since the 1970s, has a marriage of convenience existed between the two.

Since the early days of manufacturing, the custom knifemaker has adopted tools and machinery designed for industrial production such as the drill press, belt grinder, buffer and milling machine. No longer do most knifemakers shape their blades with files and drill holes with a crank drill. Hand-rubbed finishes remain an important part of a finely crafted custom knife, but it is now a matter of choice to do so, not necessity as of old.

Computer numerically controlled (CNC) machinery, electron discharge machining (EDM), lasers and water jet cutters are among the newest industrial blessings to the modern knifemaker. A bewildering assortment of exotic and high-tech materials, such as stainless tool steels, carbon fiber and titanium, are direct products of science and industry.

Factory Weds Workshop

It is clear that knifemakers, regardless of their level of purity as hand craftsmen, have benefited greatly from each new level of industrial advancement.

But what of the industry, the factories? How have they drawn from the humble home workshop of the custom knifemaker? Here begins the 30-year dance.

Historically, knife factories have relied on designs drawn by their own in-house craftsmen, or they have mass-produced traditional patterns tested and accepted over time. While there were many small pro-

duction shops over the decades that created exquisite examples of the cutler's art, such as Michael Price and Will & Finck around the turn of the century, their wares were generally not for the common working man. Workers rather depended on a cheap, mass-produced knife for their daily labors.

> ### *"The modern renaissance of knives has been a ballet, a 'pas-de deux,' between custom and factory knifemakers."*

Until the 1970s, most factory knives sold in the world were of well-worn but dependable patterns, especially pocketknives. True, a re-

view of some of the old catalogs will reveal a staggering compendium of different knives, but generally there was a sameness, a vague similarity to the shapes, catalog to catalog.

There was little departure from the basic materials that were common to the genre: carbon-steel blades; brass and nickel-silver frames; jigged-bone, stag or wood handles; and non-locking, slip-joint folding mechanisms virtually universal in all factory pocketknives.

The high cost of hard tooling, that is, stamping dies and power presses, required that enormous volumes of the same knife be produced to make the venture economical for the factory. The Imperial Knife Co. in the early 1950s was producing 125,000 knives per day, but the designs were limited and the materials commonplace.

A great, innovative step forward for the factory knife was the famous

Hand assembly remains a fact of life in the production of factory knives, as illustrated by a photograph taken in the Benchmade Knife Co. facility.

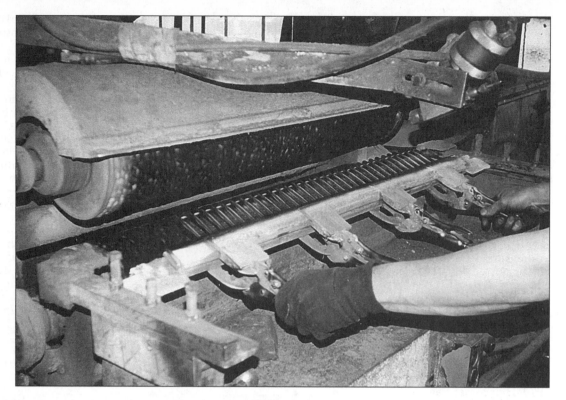

"Gang polishing" of knife blades is demonstrated at the Camillus Cutlery Co. plant.

Buck 110, a graceful design, familiar-shaped blade, and a secure, locking tang. There was no mechanical part of the knife that had not been used before, not even the materials, but it was a neat, hefty package that screamed dependability and strength. Most of all, it boasted a sexy profile that, to this day, is irresistible.

Enter the concept of innovative design into the world of factory-made knives.

Custom knifemakers, though few in number in the early 1970s, were already pioneering departures from traditional knife shapes. Bob Loveless (arguably the finest knife designer of the modern age), Blackie and Michael Collins, Lloyd Hale, Ron Lake, Rod Chappell and a few others were letting their imaginations take the humble knife to a level yet unseen.

> ## *"Enter the concept of innovative design into the world of factory knives."*

These new, innovative directions did not go unnoticed by the factories. Lo and behold, Blackie Collins was among the first custom knifemakers to collaborate with production cutlery companies in designing knives.

To this day, the Collins line of fixed blades and folders for Smith & Wesson is legendary.

The Wedding Dance

The age of collaboration between custom knifemakers and factories was born and grew stronger each year. Custom knifemakers were beginning to dance with the factories to reciprocate the benefits they had derived from advances in industrial production. They offered what the factories lacked: their unfettered imaginations and creative design spirit.

Though the trend of collaborative ventures continued sporadically throughout the 1980s, today's explosion of such ventures was touched off in large part, I am told, by a collaboration between myself and Spyderco in 1989. At that time, Sal Glesser of Spyderco was relating to me his frustrations in recruiting a custom knifemaker to design a "Clipit" knife with a hole in the blade and a pocket clip, two of Glesser's innovations in the world of pocketknives.

At that time, I had known Glesser for several years and offered to submit a design for such a knife. My only two requirements were that the blade be made of

ATS-34 (used only by custom makers at the time), and that the knives be made

Custom knifemaker Greg Lightfoot designed the Columbia River Knife & Tool "Urban Shark" to resemble (what else?) a shark. The textured-Zytel® handle is mako-shark gray and complemented by an upswept trailing-point blade.

in America. Spyderco had no production facilities in 1989, and all of their knives were being made in Japan.

Also, since the design I submitted was of a locking-liner folder, this caused a problem in finding a suitable factory since no LinerLocks® had ever been mass produced.

Glesser approached Les D'asis, who had been the entrepreneur behind Pacific Cutlery, and proposed establishing a facility that could make what would become the Spy-

"How have factories drawn from the humble home workshop? Here begins the 30-year dance."

derco C-15. D'Asis opened a small shop in Los Angeles, and later in Oregon, and set up the first production

runs of the Spyderco C-15 with anodized-aluminum handles.

Eventually, Spyderco built its own production facility in Golden, Colo., where it currently produces a variety of designs by myself, Frank Centofante, Howard Viele, Tim Wegner, Peter Herbst, Tim Zowada, James A. Keating, Bob Lum, Bram Frank, Bill Moran, J.D. Smith, D' Alton Holder, Massad Ayoob, David Boye and an impressive host of other custom knifemakers.

D'Asis took his small facility, established for the production of the

Of the incredible number of custom-designed knives offered by Spyderco, three of the company's newest are (from top) the Frank Centofante Vesuvius, the Bob Lum Chinese Folder, and the Bram Frank Gunting.

Blades roll out of a heat-treating machine en masse at Camillus Cutlery Co.

"Custom knifemakers offered what the factories lacked: their unfettered imaginations and creative design spirit."

C-15, and built it into what is now the Benchmade Knife Co., successfully riding the wave of collaborations with well-established and innovative custom knifemakers.

Part of the success of Benchmade is due to advances in modern production tooling and techniques such as laser cutting and CNC machining. These and other facilities allow the company to experiment with small-run production without the need or expense of creating permanent patterns based on stamping dies and presses.

I do not believe there is a single knife factory, large or small, that has not benefited from from the designs and creative talents of custom knifemakers. The list of collaborations is too great to include here and grows longer each day. The world of knives has changed for the better, not worse, due to collaborations between factory and handmade knifemakers.

Modern, high-speed production includes laser cutting blades, as depicted here at Benchmade Knife Co.

The custom makers have pushed the limits of what factories could or would attempt, not only in design, but in the use of new and wonderful materials. The buying public — the common, working man and woman — is the beneficiary of cooperative ventures.

The vows have been said and the wedding's a wrap, but the dance is not over. •

Growing Up Is Better With a Pocketknife

Along with the privilege of owning a knife came responsibility and respect

By Ross Bielema

I CAN'T IMAGINE life without a pocketknife. Since you are reading this book, I bet you can't, either.

That magical mechanism of steel, plastic, brass pins, locks and pure fun must sit in my pants pocket or ride on a pocket clip every day, just as I must wear a watch and shoes.

It doesn't matter much exactly which brand or blade combination. But it has to be there, a sharp comfort that can open an envelope, cut a length of twine, slice an apple or handle a dozen other tasks with ease.

This affliction struck me when I was but a lad, probably around 5 or 6 years old. My first, dim memories of my very own knife are of a stubby, extremely dull sheath knife in a tiny, beaded sheath, purchased by my kind mother at a Native American powwow my family attended.

Yes, I still have that knife, along with hundreds more of every blade

"My parents never put up a fuss when I wanted a knife. Dad just taught me how to use it."

Author's first knife was a little fixed-blade sheath knife with a compass in the handle and a beaded leather sheath — dull to be sure, but perfect for a grade-schooler's adventures.

length, brand, color and age, from a few old Keen Cutters to high-tech Spydercos and Cold Steels.

Most of us don't appreciate our parents until it's too late, but I don't remember my parents ever putting up a fuss when I wanted a knife. My dad just taught me the safe way to handle a knife. I do remember a friend's mother once scolding my mother, saying, "You always let Ross have dangerous things."

That line sticks in my mind like a bad bumper-sticker slogan.

I remember that same mother not letting her son have a pellet gun until he hit the age of 16. Then it was, "Here's your pellet gun." No safety instructions. No shooting practice with dad. Needless to say, the kid was a menace with his pellet gun, forever waving it at us, most times accidentally.

Home Schooled

My dad launched my love of "dangerous things" by teaching me to shoot a BB gun (age 3), then a 22 rifle loaded with birdshot (age 6), then a .410 bolt-action shotgun. Funny how that gun-safety stuff sticks when it's drummed into you at an early age. I couldn't imagine

Author's current carry knives include a Victorinox Swiss Army Knife with a pliers blade and a Kershaw Whirlwind.

A random selection of mostly older pocketknives from the author's collection, including an old Schrade (top) and a mother-of-pearl necklace knife (bottom). The rest were purchased at flea markets and antiques shops.

what my dad would do if I ever dared point a real gun at a person. Prison would be a safe place. Dads back then ruled with a perceived harshness that captured our attention and guided us with "loving fear." Loving fear disappears when a good swat or two on the posterior is considered politically incorrect and harmful to a kid's self-esteem.

And knives went with the guns. How would I ever learn to field dress my own rabbits — standing next to Dad and Grandpa, looking up at them demonstrating their dissecting skills as if I was watching a fireworks show — without my own two-blade Barlow? Funny how we remember the details, even when the big picture blurs. I still remember

the salty smell of that Barlow's handle, stained with rabbit blood that wouldn't wash off. Still have that knife, too.

Cub Scouts — what luck! A chance to wear a uniform with patches and pins, AND carry a knife! A special knife. Purchased at a J.C. Penney store in Clinton, Io-

wa, that blue-handled knife with several blades for opening cans and punching holes had a nifty scout emblem embedded in the handle. You bet I still have that one. The Penney store is gone.

Of course, on days when we members of Pack 342 wore our uniforms to school, the scout knife was there, too, riding in the pocket and waiting for the time when it would be needed for some high adventure on a hike to nearby Box Canyon (our sparrow-hunting woods at the edge of town) or perhaps coming to the rescue when a teacher needed a box opened.

Did any teacher ever wince at the sight of a scout knife, or any knife? I don't think so.

Author enjoys the latest innovations in blades, too, as shown by this sampling of high-tech and novelty knives.

In fact, I walked through the front door of Fulton High School, a few years later, with my .410 shotgun (cased, of course), walked into Mr. Luker's speech class and gave a decent demonstration on how to clean a shotgun.

"Is it unloaded?" Mr. Luker asked, seconds before the speech.

"Yes, it is." Then I showed them all how to remove the bolt and make sure it's unloaded and safe.

A few years ago, a school just a few miles from my high school sent a kindergarten kid home for several days because the kid came to school with a brightly colored squirt gun. Part of the "zero tolerance" effort.

I guess "zero tolerance" these days also applies to common sense at our schools.

Pocketknife Protection?

Kids are being reprimanded, suspended and worse for carrying pocketknives, fingernail clippers, maybe even Lee Press-On Nails (hey, those things are sharp). Some schools don't want kids bringing toy guns, comic books with armed heroes, or anything that brings guns to mind. Pity the poor kid whose dad is a cop or a security guard. There goes his self-esteem again.

I can understand that schools want to protect students and faculty from armed, violent students. But why go after some kid with a fingernail clippers or a pen knife? Let's then carry it further, outlawing cafeteria utensils, drafting T-squares and of course just about anything found in a high school science lab.

If you want a kid to learn responsibility, you have to give that kid some trust.

If you want a kid to rebel and crave forbidden fruit, then take away your trust and take away anything that could be considered dangerous. Make it forbidden, and he or she will want it more.

Sure, when he turns 16, you'll let him drive the family car — a 4,000-pound missile hurtling down the highway at a minimum of 55 mph — and share the road with thousands of other drivers.

Sure, you'll let him mow the lawn (maybe even when he's wearing shorts or sandals), and fill the mower's tank with one of the most explosive substances on earth: gasoline.

Just don't trust him with a pocketknife.

Maybe it's time we knife lovers call the collective bluffs of our elitist educators and shortsighted leaders.

How about a little visit to the next school board meeting, just to say, "My child is a scout, and he wants to carry his scout knife."

Better yet, maybe a few hundred Boy Scouts and Girl Scouts in uniform, with their parents, could stop by the same school board meeting.

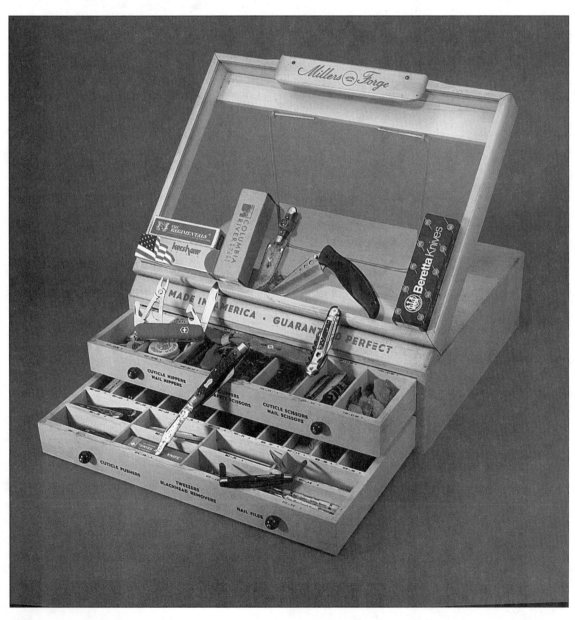

An old nail clippers hardware case provides cozy storage for some of the author's collection.

Maybe call a few TV stations and newspapers a few days before the meeting, too.

What could it hurt?

Time to Speak Up

I'm only 41, but when I look back at all the firearms laws and restrictive knife rules that have been imposed since I proudly toted my scout knife to school, I am appalled. How can Americans — the very people who claim to value freedom above all else — stand by and watch such a basic right as the right to carry a pocketknife slip away?

It's easy. It's as easy as doing nothing. It's as simple as not writing a letter to a legislator. It's as simple

"When we members of Pack 342 wore our uniforms to school, the scout knife was there."

as letting your child's school drum whatever warped sense of values it has into his or her head every day, without going to a school board meeting or talking to a teacher or principal.

Thomas Jefferson said it best: "The price of liberty is eternal vigilance."

If carrying a pocketknife ever becomes a crime in my neighborhood, I'll be a proud criminal. I have a Kershaw Whirlwind clipped to my right pocket and a Victorinox Swiss Army Knife in my left pocket as I write this.

But it doesn't matter if it's the latest tactical knife, a two-blade Barlow with rabbit-blood stains or a slightly rusty Cub Scout knife. Life is better with a pocketknife.

Growing up with a pocketknife is better, too. ●

Editor's note: The author is also project manager for "Sporting Knives 2002" and a firearms book editor for Krause Publications.

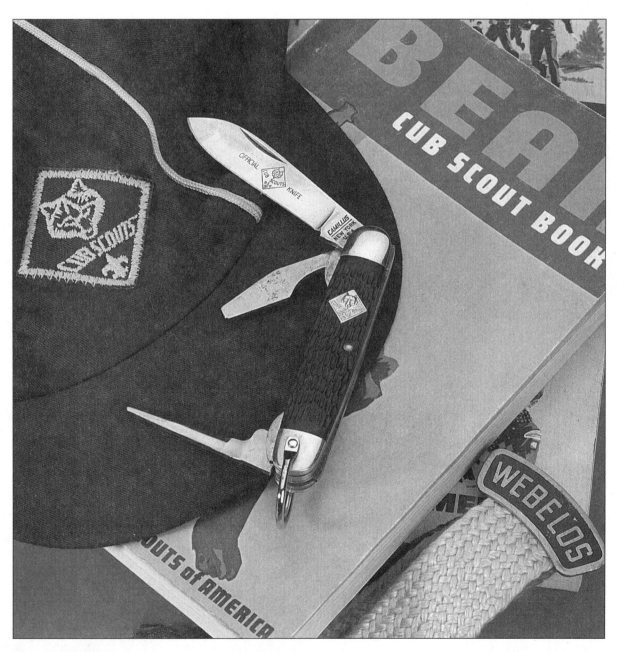

The blue-handled Cub Scout knife was the author's favorite part of his Cub Scout uniform, and he never failed to carry it to school when he and his fellow pack members were in uniform prior to den meetings. Educators today might be shocked to learn that there were no related stabbings or misdeeds from such behavior.

Mighty Columbia River Knives

Tight tolerances and dedication to quality result in knives that can hack it in the field

By Gary Kelley

LIKE ITS NAMESAKE the mighty Columbia River, Columbia River Knife & Tool rushes on in pursuit of production-knife excellence. Launched in 1994 by experienced knife industry veterans Paul Gillespie and Rod Bremer, CRKT started out with a solid philosophy: Give the customer the best materials, newest designs and highest quality production knife for the money. The company has done just that.

> *"When you're slicing meat off a 6-foot sturgeon, you need a knife that will really cut."*

From the outset, Gillespie and Bremer concentrated on producing practical working knives designed and engineered to perform on the job or in the field with user confidence. They achieved this by upping the tolerances in production to essentially make a custom-quality knife at production-knife prices.

To assure consumer interest, they signed on some of the most noted knife designers in The Knifemakers' Guild. This marriage of production-knife technology and custom-knife design have resulted

You might not think so, but Columbia River's K.I.S.S. makes a good fishing knife. Not only will it snip line, but it'll clean brook trout as well. (Kelley photo)

The K.I.S.S. is handy when clipped or tied to a fishing vest, always easy to reach and convenient to open and close. (Kelley photo)

in a line of knives that appeals to hard users and collectors alike, at a working person's prices.

CRKT has landed some proven winners in the Big Sky Hunters, Big Eddy fillet knives, the Crawford Kasper folder, the sleek S-2 titanium-handle folders, the classic K.I.S.S., Stiff K.I.S.S. and Neck P.E.C.K., and the M16 law enforcement folders with anodized T-6 aluminum or carbon fiber handles. The market has said so with consistent sales year after year.

> ## "I've used most of CRKT's outdoor knives and I can speak from experience."

This year, the company has introduced even more outstanding collaborations with custom makers to offer customers a greater variety. These include the new Wasp, a Howard Viele design; the BladeLOCK, which is the first commercial knife using Michael Walker's patented lock of the same name; Steve Ryan's Model Seven; the Tighe Tac designed by Canadian Brian Tighe; the 14K Summit series of outdoor recreation knives; and the Navajo designed by Jim Hammond, to name a few. I counted 99 different models in the new catalog.

I've used most of CRKT's outdoor knives and I can speak from experience. Two things that impressed me about the Big Eddy fillet knife are the balance and the cutting ability. I've used the Big Eddy to fillet bass and bluegills, cut cardboard boxes, completely process three deer and two elk, and steak a white sturgeon caught in the Columbia River.

Columbia River Knife & Tool's Point Guard, designed by Pat Crawford, is a consistent seller. It features substantial interframe construction with Zytel® handles, an AUS-6M stainless steel blade and ambidextrous thumb disc. Best of all, it has a LAWKS® safety lock you push forward with your thumb. (Kelley photo)

Kit Carson's M16 as produced by Columbia River Knife & Tool is a tough utility/tactical folder. A thumb stud allows one-hand opening, and also acts as a blade stop. It's a large knife with a nearly 4-inch blade. One unique feature is the "Carson Flipper" extension on the blade, which is useful for opening the knife and serves as a finger guard as well. (Kelley photo)

The Crawford Kasper folder is a heavy-duty carry knife. It has an authoritative feel with perfect balance at the deep index-finger choil, and features a black-aluminum back spacer, Zytel® scales, and a stout, modified clip-point, AUS-6M stainless steel blade. It works like a custom knife but sells for $64.99 retail. (Kelley photo)

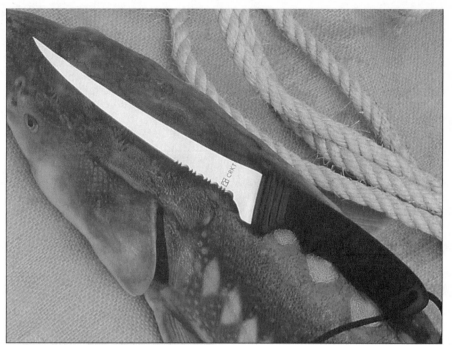

Columbia River's Big Eddy fillet knife is named after a popular fishing hole. It is unequaled when slicing and dicing fish from sturgeon (shown here) to bluegill. It's a great boning knife for processing elk as well. (Kelley photo)

The Wrangler is one of CRKT's solid old-timers. From the start, this simple and tough folder has been a seller. It has a fiberglass-reinforced nylon handle and an AUS-6M stainless steel blade with a back lock. It's a great fishing knife, too, and if you lose one, it's easy to replace at just $19.99. (Kelley photo)

When you're slicing meat off a 6-foot sturgeon, you need a knife that will really cut. The Big Eddy did. And when I had to part the tough tendons next to the notochord, the serrations sawed through without slowing the work. I was impressed.

I process game on the kitchen countertop, and it may sound sacrilegious, but I prefer the Big Eddy fillet knife for boning and cutting big game meat over any other kitchen cutter. I had to sharpen the Big Eddy occasionally, but it has the flexibility, shape and comfortable handle I look for in a meat knife.

The Big Sky Hunters series offers five blade designs — including one with a gut hook — that meet the needs of any hunting situation from skinning to general camp work. The blades are all AUS-6M stainless steel, and handles are comfortable checkered Kraton" for non-slip use under slimy or cold conditions. The 9-ounce, riveted and lock-stitched leather sheaths provide a safe carry, even in rain because of the "weep hole" in each one that allows water to drain.

K.I.S.S. Fillet?

This part may get me in trouble, but even though CRKT's K.I.S.S. folding knives are marketed as money clips, gentlemen's knives, utility folders and key-chain knives, I use my K.I.S.S. for fishing. Out of the tackle box, it's a quick one-hand-opening folder, and the short blade makes it perfect for snipping line, preparing bait, and opening those dreaded plastic wrappers. Simple, two-piece construction allows it to be sloshed in the stream for a quick cleanup. It's also handy when clipped or tied to a fishing vest, always easy to reach, and convenient to open and close.

Ed Halligan, who designed and makes the original K.I.S.S. folders, had another idea after he began his collaboration with CRKT. Why not manufacture a wharncliffe-blade model and name it the "Precision Engineered Compact Knife"—or P.E.C.K. for short? This smaller version of the K.I.S.S., officially named Delilah's P.E.CK., is handy as a keychain knife, and the perfect size for a lady's purse.

Rushing on, CRKT has introduced several new models this year. Most are folders, with the exception of the new Bear Claw. This practical utility knife shaped like its name is CRKT's production version of the knife designed by Russ Kommer, a young Alaskan knifemaker.

The Bear Claw is available in three blade styles, including a sharp tip, a fully serrated sharp tip, or serrated with a tear-drop tip for fast, safe cutting of such things as seat belts in emergency situations. Made of AUS-6M stainless steel, the Bear Claw comes with an injection-molded Zytel® sheath with lanyard holes and pocket clips, allowing it to be lashed onto a pack frame, worn on a belt, in a pocket, or around the neck.

If you've ever been to a Knifemakers' Guild Show, you may have seen custom knifemaker Howard Viele's Wasp, a very collectable high-tech locking folder. The problem with any top-drawer custom maker is the human factor: He can only make so many knives in a year no matter how many hours he works.

When CRKT approached Viele, he agreed to design a Wasp suitable for their close-tolerance production techniques. The result is a "custom" knife anyone can have today for a retail price of $114.99. The Wasp features a titanium frame, stainless-steel locking liner, custom G-10 black and blue laminate handles, machined blade pivot screws, all TORX head fasteners, and a Viele thumb stud with a soft Kraton® insert.

Michael Walker is a well-known, award-winning knife designer with more than 20 knife locking systems to his credit. Back in the 1980s, when Walker began adding thumb studs to his folders, he realized they could also be the basis for an internal locking system. He developed and patented a new BladeLOCK™, but no manufacturer had the capability of producing it until CRKT achieved its present level of close-tolerance machining.

Now, Columbia River Knives presents its first production Blade-LOCK. The entire locking system works off the thumb stud. Push it to open the blade with one hand until you hear the crisp "click" as the lock engages. Then just push the thumb stud to unlock the blade and close it into the Zytel® handle. The Blade-

is slightly smaller than Ryan's custom models, it still has the same strong deep-bellied blade for heavy cutting, the same deep finger choil for excellent grip, and dual thumb studs. For maximum safety, CRKT included the patented LAWKS®

Greg Lightfoot designed the Urban Shark as a lightweight personal security system with the design balance of a shark. It's an interframe with stainless steel liners, Zytel® handle scales, and an AUS-6M stainless steel blade. Serrations at the butt and index finger area of the handle give added purchase. (Kelley photo)

LOCK has a 3 1/2-inch AUS-6M stainless steel blade that pivots on Teflon" bearings. All this for $79.99.

This year, CRKT introduced one strong work knife designed by Steve Ryan. Though the production version

(Lake and Walker Knife Safety). This is an additional blade lock, much like a rifle safety, that guarantees the blade will not close by accident. They call this one the Ryan Model Seven, and it retails for $59.99.

The Tighe Tac fills the bill as a tough gentleman's knife. This spear-point, locking-liner folder features ambidextrous thumb studs, stainless steel liners, stainless steel bolsters and Zytel® handles. A tie-shaped cutout adorns the

Pinnacle of Achievement

One of my personal favorite CRKT offerings is the 14K Summit Series, aptly named for mountain climbers who consider the North American peaks that reach or ex-

can all be opened and closed with one hand.

With six distinct models named after such mountains as Ranier and Whitney, each piece is similar in design, differing only in size and blade styles. Razor-edged or serrated depending on the model, the Summits have a safe "reverse-tanto"-shaped tip. That's my way of describing the blunt safety clip CRKT has designed into the blade tip so it doesn't jab and cut where it isn't supposed to jab and cut.

The blades are opened with a thumb stud, and the handles have the solid heft of nickel-chrome-plated zinc alloy. To reduce weight, handles are skeletonized with five large and eight small holes. The high-carbon AUS-6M stainless-steel blades open smoothly on Teflon® bearings.

Each Summit knife is outfitted with the LAWKS blade-locking mechanism for fixed-blade strength. To close the blade, the LAWKS bar is extracted with the thumb, the locking liner is depressed, and the blade closed with the index finger. While Summit folders could be carried on an expedition, they would also be handy for hiking, everyday use, or around the office. Actually, the more comfortable you become with a knife like this, the easier it is to use in a dark environment or in adverse conditions. Each piece carries a manufacturer's suggested retail price of $44.99 to $49.99, depending on size.

"I counted 99 different models in Columbia River's new catalog."

When it comes to no-frills working folders, I have to mention CRKT's new Navajo folding knife. This one, designed by Jim Hammond, is your basic workhorse folder. The simple design includes a one-piece solid stainless steel handle with a recessed locking liner. The stainless steel blade rotates on Teflon® bearings, has thumb studs on both sides, and a thumb ramp for control when cutting.

The knife is assembled, as are all CRKT folders, with TORX-head screws. The index-finger choil is notched for added non-slip safety, and all surfaces of the knife are bead-blasted gray. The Navajo comes with a removable Teflon®-coated stainless steel clip, and retails for $64.99 to $69.99, depending on blade length.

distinctive pocket clip. Brian Tighe tests his knives by carrying one every day, and this multi-talented knifemaker has designed an artistic-yet-practical knife that retails for $69.99.

ceed 14,000 feet as particular challenges. Anyone who has reached 14K has reached the "pinnacle of achievement," so to speak. These locking folders are designed to be rugged, practical, safe, and they

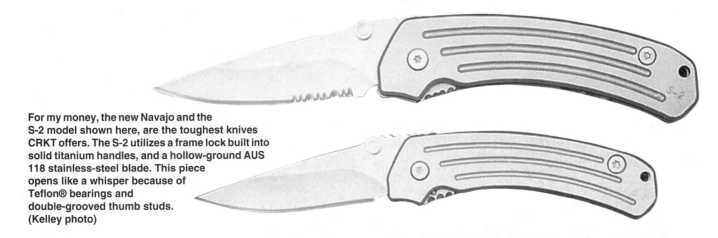

For my money, the new Navajo and the S-2 model shown here, are the toughest knives CRKT offers. The S-2 utilizes a frame lock built into solid titanium handles, and a hollow-ground AUS 118 stainless-steel blade. This piece opens like a whisper because of Teflon® bearings and double-grooved thumb studs. (Kelley photo)

There wasn't room in this article to tell about all the new models that Columbia River Knife & Tool has introduced this year. I've seen them all, and with the quality produced at the prices charged, it would be difficult to find a better deal. Before CRKT knives are packed and shipped, each one is inspected for defects in material and workmanship. The production team checks the cutting edges and actions by hand to see how they feel. If a knife needs attention, the blade tension is adjusted until it's smooth as silk and fast as the mighty Columbia River. ●

Kit Carson designed the M16-Z for Columbia River. It comes in four styles, two of which are displayed here with tough stainless steel blades, stainless interframes, and Zytel® handles. All models come with Teflon-plated belt clips. (Kelley photo)

If these don't look like bear claws, then Russ Kommer is going to be upset. He designed the Bear Claws for Columbia River Knife & Tool, and these tough but easily accessible emergency knives are meant for bush pilots, paramedics, and anyone who wants to carry a cutting tool that doesn't cut where you don't want it to cut. (Kelley photo)

The Best in Neck and Boot Knives

By Joe Kertzman

NECK AND BOOT knives are hanging in there, so to speak, and gaining popularity at every moment of the waking day. Production facilities are pumping out the newest in knife and sheath combinations to be hung, slung and strapped to the human body for quick draw or reliable release.

Neck knives might not necessarily be new to the scene, but they are a recent trend, possibly the biggest phenomenon to hit the modern knife market. It has gotten so you can't go to a knife show or visit a knife factory without custom makers and production workers alike showing off the newest in-house neck models, which most wear with the pride of new papas.

Speaking of neck models, a lightweight, sculpted, normally full-tang, plastic-handle piece looks at home around a man's neck and equally fine strapped to that of a lady. There is something about a neck knife and a pretty face that go, well, neck-in-neck.

Boot pieces have been around for a long time, and the patterns are not the most popular in the industry. If there is something to be said for longevity and endurance, however, boot knives have the staying power it takes to make it in business. They are slow-but-steady sellers that appeal to those who need a second knife, or at least one within arm's reach.

Boot and neck knives are reliable tools. There are areas of the country where police officers not only wear boot knives, but they are trained extensively in their use. Soldiers are taught the advantages of having a knife near the ankle. Pilots spend much of their time in the sitting position, where the most natural place to reach is below the knee. Aviators wear so much gear above the waist that shoulder and neck knives are buried beneath the bulk, and boot knives are a convenient alternative. Knife nuts everywhere find it hard to resist the temptation to strap on boot knives and walk a little taller.

The combination of a neck knife, a boot knife, and possibly one slung from a shoulder strap or hanging from a key chain make a sharp knife available in several natural reaching positions. The only areas left unguarded would be the hip, waist or small of the back.

Armed to the tooth? Possibly, but most folks aren't out there practicing knife fighting tactics in the street, thankfully, and most aren't as concerned with fending off attackers as they might let on to fellow passersby. The tools of the trade are bought and sold under the not-so-false pretense of being useful. They fill the need for a knife that is easily accessed in a number of awkward positions and situations.

Biking, hiking, skiing, kayaking, jogging, camping, hunting, fishing and mountain climbing are favorite pastimes of neck and boot knife enthusiasts, and in each situation, the human body is known to contort in ways that make reaching in the pocket for a knife an inconvenience. Simply put, if there wasn't a need, the sharp little pieces wouldn't be selling at the rate they are in the knife industry today. As long as people remain active, neck and boot knives will be in demand.

The demand is rising quickly with the advent of the "extreme" sportsman, the one who would rather go over the cliff on a snowboard than climb down it or avoid it altogether. Those same daredevils jump off the cliff by means of hang gliders, or parachute from heights that raise the hair on their necks and nearly dislodge the knives hung from them.

The key here is that the majority of extreme sportsmen are youngsters, those who will remain loyal to the knife industry if their needs are met. Clearly it would be advantageous to market handy knives to that burgeoning segment of the population.

Modern materials have made them so light and so unobtrusive that the wearer forgets they are there. Blade shapes and tips have come a long way. Now, rather than just a tanto, clip, drop or spear point, factories offer modified clip points, modified tantos, recurved blades, slight drop points, single- and double-bevel grinds and reinforced blade tips with choices of a dozen or more scratch-resistant blade coatings.

One major contributor to the unquestionable rise in popularity of neck and boot knives is the Kydex® sheath. Kydex® is formed and molded around blades and guards making upside-down (or blade-tip up) carry possible. The knives won't fall out of the sheaths, nor will the points puncture the skin, as is possible through traditional leather sheaths if the wearer slips and falls. With one quick tug, the knife is released from the Kydex® sheath and ready for use.

Whatever the use, however the need arises, neck and boot knives are there to answer the call of duty. It is a growing class of knives that can't be ignored, and each has that "toy factor" that makes the style playful and useful at the same time. It's fun to reach down to ensure the neck or boot knife is still in place before leaping off that cliff, jumping from that plane or biking up that mountain.

The Benchmade Model 160 TK-1 Tether knife is the brainchild of custom knife-maker Allen Elishewitz and built specif-ically for above-the-waist carry.

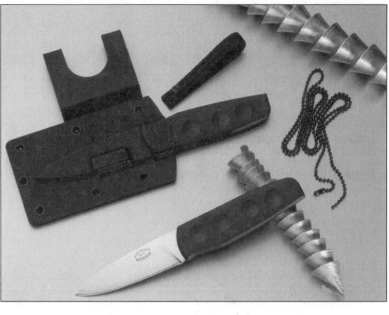

One of several Boker models available with Bud Nealy's Multi-Carry System sheath, the 580 Escort is a lightweight, drop-point, multi-purpose utility design that lends itself to neck or boot carry.

Benchmade

Benchmade boasts several collaborations with custom knifemakers, including Allen Elishewitz, who designed the Model 160 TK-1 Tether knife specifically for above-the-waist carry. A first for Benchmade, the TK-1 can be slung under the arm or around the collar for times when a waistband knife isn't practical. The one-piece GIN-1 stainless-steel, all-black fixed blade features a thermoplastic handle coating and a Kydex® sheath hung from a 64-inch beaded chain.

Boker USA

Boker USA teamed with knife-maker and entrepreneur Bud Nealy on several "back-up protection" and "personal security" knife and sheath designs. Nealy's Kydex® Multi-Carry (sheath) System allows for nine carry positions, including boot, waist, neck, hip, pocket and jacket-pocket carry. Boker offers the 580

Escort model with a fiberglass-reinforced Delrin® handle and a stainless-steel drop-point blade. Indentations in the handle provide a non-slip, firm grip. It is an ideal neck and boot knife, weighing only 2.3 ounces.

The A-F 546 Applegate Combat Boot Knife is inspired by

Boker's AF-546 Applegate Combat Boot Knife employs a Col. Rex Applegate design that is small enough for boot carry but big enough to handle any field chore.

the famous Col. Rex Applegate and built small enough to fit in a boot. Yet, the 4 3/4-inch, 440C dagger-shaped blade remains large enough to handle heavy-duty chores. It is hollow ground on one side, serially numbered and includes a Kydex® sheath.

Buck

The traditional fixed-blade and folding hunting knives company has broken into the high-tech world of locking-liner, one-hand-opening folders, multi-tools, tacky grips, colorful handles and super steels. One offering, the 3 1/4-inch Diamond-Back, is a compact fixed blade with a patterned grip that replicates that of a diamondback rattler's skin. The 420HC blade slides into a custom-made, heavy-duty black nylon sheath with belt or neck-lanyard carry capabilities.

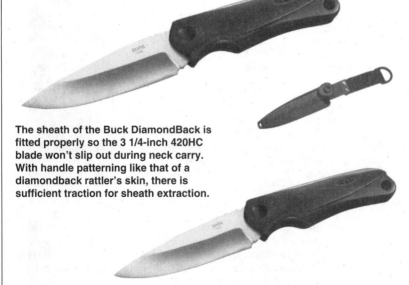

The sheath of the Buck DiamondBack is fitted properly so the 3 1/4-inch 420HC blade won't slip out during neck carry. With handle patterning like that of a diamondback rattler's skin, there is sufficient traction for sheath extraction.

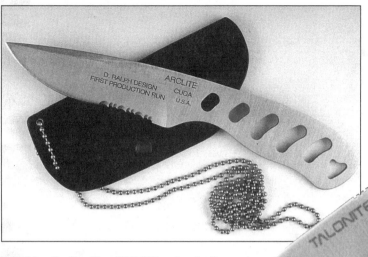

Camillus expands its neck knife offerings with a Talonite-blade model—the Mini Talon—designed by knifemaker and Talonite specialist Rob Simonich.

To lighten the Camillus ARCLITE and make it an ideal neck knife, custom knifemaker Darrel Ralph designed the piece with arc-shaped handle cutouts and a Kydex® sheath.

Camillus

Custom knifemaker Darrel Ralph designed the Camillus AR-CLITE to be the ultimate personal neck knife. Ergonomically shaped for large or small hands, the AR-CLITE features arc-shaped handle cutouts to lighten the knife and allow for a secure grip in the field. The 3 1/4-inch, flat-ground 420HC blade exhibits a slight recurve to help make short work of any cutting task. The one-piece knife comes with a molded-Kydex® necklace sheath for secure carry and fast deployment.

Camillus made the Talon model in a smaller neck-knife version

called the Mini Talon. The blade on this one is Talonite, and the knife, designed by Rob Simonich, features a contoured and grooved G-10 handle. Like the ARCLITE, the Mini Talon package is completed with a molded Kydex ® sheath.

Cold Steel

According to Cold Steel's Lynn Thompson, the company carries more neck and boot knives than any other knife manufacturer. The 2.2-ounce Cold Steel Mini Tac is designed for neck suspension as hung from a Concealex neck sheath. One tug on the checkered Kraton® handle releases the 4-inch, AUS-6A blade, in a plain or serrated edge, from its sheath.

Based on a traditional Scottish design, the Cold Steel Mini Culloden is a compact boot knife with a 3 1/2-inch AUS-8A blade and what the company refers to as a "quick-draw" Concealex sheath. The Mini Culloden is named for the location

Cold Steel's wide range of neck and boot knives includes (clockwise from right) the Mini Tac, specifically designed for neck suspension; the Mini Culloden, a compact boot knife; and the Para Edge neck knife, which weighs little more than an ounce and is housed in a Concealex neck sheath. There are other neck and boot knives in the Cold Steel line.

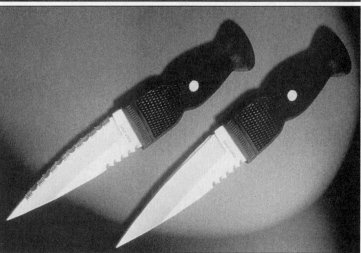

The Bear Claw from Columbia River Knife & Tool is aptly named for its claw-like appearance, but don't let the small stature fool you: It is one radical neck knife. A large finger hole allows for a secure grip on the contoured Zytel® handle.

of the last battle of the Scottish nation fought on April 16, 1746.

Cold Steel's Para Edge neck knives, with clip-point, tanto-point or double-edged dagger-style blades, weigh 1.2-to-1.4 ounces each and measure 2 3/4 inches overall.

Each is housed in a Concealex neck sheath.

Columbia River Knife & Tool

To say Columbia River Knife & Tool recognizes the value of working with the designs of custom knifemakers is an understatement. The vast majority of CRKT offerings are products of handmade knifemakers working with the company to translate their creativity and innovative designs into affordable production knives.

One such piece is the Russ Kommer-designed Bear Claw. Kommer, who hails from Alaska where conditions are rugged, thought an easy-to-grip neck knife that was hard to lose would make a big hit in the Alaskan wilderness. His original concept was a self-defense knife for women that would be lightweight and easily accessed and controlled. He found that bush pilots and commercial fishermen were equally interested.

The Bear Claw incorporates a generous finger hole that allows the knife to act like an extension of the hand in use. It is the perfect emergency cutting tool for anyone who needs to quickly cut rope, webbing or netting. The AUS 6M blade is available in three blade styles, including serrated and non-serrated, and with a blunt or pointed tip. A contoured Zytel® handle completes the piece, which weighs in at 2.9 ounces.

With a name like the "Neck P.E.C.K.," there is no doubt about where to hang the CRKT skeletonized fixed-blade offering. This one is

The AUS-6M stainless steel blade of the Columbia River Knife & Tool Neck P.E.C.K. comes razor sharp in a wharncliffe blade style that is ready to cut. Don't worry—it is held securely by a black Zytel® neck sheath.

Ed Halligan and Columbia River Knife & Tool suggest a Stiff K.I.S.S. to start your day. The fixed-blade neck knife comes with a choice of four blade styles, including a semi-serrated tanto chisel point.

A traditional Swedish sheath knife company priding itself on quality, Fällkniven debuts a VG-10 neck knife with a Thermorun handle and a Kydex® sheath.

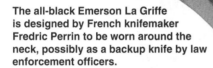

The all-black Emerson La Griffe is designed by French knifemaker Fredric Perrin to be worn around the neck, possibly as a backup knife by law enforcement officers.

designed by custom maker Ed Halligan, who adapted several of his original K.I.S.S. and P.E.C.K. designs for production. The AUS 6M neck knife employs a wharncliffe blade shape and a molded Zytel® sheath.

The Stiff K.I.S.S. is another Halligan-designed, fixed-blade neck knife, this one with four 3 1/2-inch blade choices, including tanto chisel-point, modified drop-point and plain or serrated styles. The integral piece is made from a solid bar of AUS 6M steel bead blasted to a non-reflective finish. It also comes with a black Zytel® neck sheath.

Emerson Knives, Inc.

Emerson Knives, Inc., is a growing company born of ingenuity from the mind of Ernest Emerson, custom knifemaker and modern-day knife manufacturer. Emerson knives are growing in popularity in the civilian, self-defense, military and space industries. As is common with neck knives, the handle of the Emerson La Griffe is skeletonized for lightweight carry, a style adapted by Emerson but designed by noted French knifemaker Fredric Perrin. With the addition of a gentle curve on the blade, Emerson says La Griffe is considered the ultimate backup knife by many law enforcement officers. The 154CM blade and handle are coated with a black oxide finish for a truly stealthy look, and a black Kydex® sheath holds it in place when strung around the neck.

Fällkniven

Fällkniven president Peter Hjortberger believes it is Scandinavian heritage to carry a sheath knife, and that is what the company builds, attempting to offer only the most rugged, high-quality knives. Yet, even neck knives are rugged and have sheaths, so the Fällkniven WM neck knife was born with a VG-10 blade, a Thermorun handle and a Kydex® sheath.

Gerber Legendary Blades

Rubber leg straps and secure sheaths are available for Gerber's Expedition I and II models. These high-carbon, stainless-steel fixed blades are ideal for river rafting, with Kraton rubber handles that

▶The Gerber Expedition I and II models lend themselves to nearly limitless carry options. Rubber leg straps are available for both models, and neck lanyards can be strung through holes in the molded-plastic sheaths.

▲ The Gerber River Guides are built to hold fast in the wettest of environments. Finger holes, non-slip handles and tight-fitting sheaths all combine for a sure grip. Rubber sheath-attachment straps allow for several carry options.

should hold fast in water. A lanyard is easily strung through the sheath for neck carry.

The Gerber River Guide models are whitewater and dive knives with blunt or pointed tips, molded-plastic sheaths and black or yellow handles. The two-part sheath system is available with two rubber attachment straps for a variety of carry options.

Gigand Knives

Dr. Fred Carter, an award-winning knifemaker and engraver, designed a series of smart neck knives for Gigand Knives. The Guardian and its little brother, the Mosquito, are available in spear-, tanto- and clip-point varieties of AUS 8A stainless steel blades. The handles are injection-molded, and the

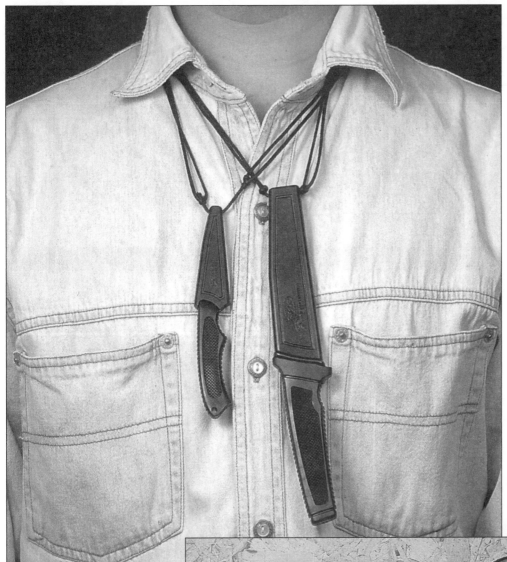

Gigand Knives teamed with custom knifemaker Fred Carter on the Guardian and Mosquito neck knives, which are fitted with special sheaths that incorporate magnets to hold the blades in place during neck carry.

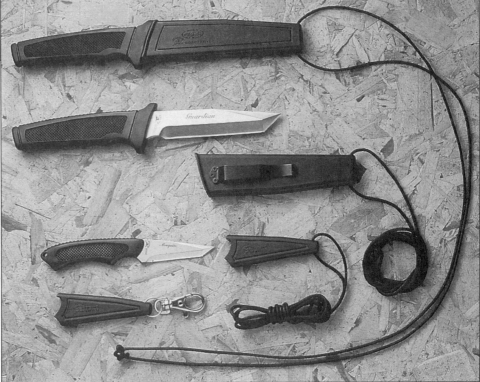

sheaths incorporate magnets that hold the blades in place, as well as neck straps for suspension.

Gutmann Cutlery

Gutmann Cutlery seems genuinely pleased to announce that the company has been awarded licensing rights for the Walther brand of knives, optics and shooting glasses for North America. Walther is a German manufacturer of pistols, air guns and knives, among other accessories. In the Walther line is the Solace, a flat, one-piece, 440A stainless-steel fixed blade that stretches 8 1/4 inches

The Walther Solace is a Gutmann Cutlery offering with a thin, one-piece profile and a paracord-wrapped handle. The 4-ounce fixed blade hangs from the neck comfortably by means of a paracord attached to a Kydex® sheath, and a belt/boot clip opens the door for other carry choices.

overall and weighs 4 ounces. The steel handle is wrapped in paracord, and the molded Kydex® sheath employs a boot/belt clip and a paracord lanyard that allows for secure neck carry.

Barging right in on the boot knife scene is Gutmann's Junglee Special Forces Knife, an all-black, tactical looking piece with an AUS 8A blade and a Kraton rubber grip. This one fits into a ballistic nylon sheath with a boot or belt clip in addition to a harness for "covert" carrying.

Joy Enterprises

Though Joy Enterprises carries a wide selection of neck and boot knives, none stand out more than the Hawg Tooth Neck or Pocket Knife line with neck lanyards. A selection of aluminum or titanium handles are anodized in a rainbow of colors, including blue, gold, purple, black, charcoal, dark purple and a multi-color rainbow effect. Black-Micarta® and black carbon-fiber handle overlays set off the underlying colors, and bead-blasted 440 stainless-steel blades complete the packages. Each is designed by Knifemakers' Guild member and handmade knifemaker Mike Franklin, with a neck lanyard that attaches to the largest of five thong holes on the butt of the handle.

Kellam Knives

Kellam Knives was established by Harriet and Juoni Kellokoski to import puukkos and other distinctly Finnish knives into the USA and to provide them for the worldwide marketplace. From there, the company took off in many directions, including a pair of boat and sailing knives with blue and silver aluminum handles and stainless steel blades with shackle slots. Each comes with a colorful lanyard for neck carry.

Kershaw

Kershaw can't be overlooked when it comes to technological advancements in the knife industry, especially considering the company's partnership with knifemaker Ken Onion and the folding knives he designed to incorporate his patented Speed-Safe assisted opening mechanism. Back to the basics, however, is the Kershaw Amphibian Model

Joy Enterprises delivers a set of Mike Franklin neck and pocketknives with anodized aluminum or titanium handles and carbon fiber or Micarta® overlays. Each can be outfitted with a neck lanyard that attaches to the largest of five thong holes on the tail end of the handle.

With a totally tactical look in a black AUS 8A blade and a black Kraton rubber grip, the Gutmann Junglee Special Forces knife is packaged with a ballistic nylon sheath for boot, belt or harness carry.

The Kershaw Amphibian has the look of a boot knife with a spear-point 420 J2 blade, a steel handle with a co-polymer handle insert and a leather boot sheath.

1006L with a spear-point 420 J2 blade and a steel handle with a co-polymer insert. This piece is not only suited for boot carry — it includes a leather boot sheath.

Masters Of Defense

A slight stray from its truly tactical knife line, the Masters Of Defense Scorpion Neck Knife is a sleek, double-edged fixed blade with a cut-out handle design and serrations on the top cutting edge. The wild blade grind, coupled with the ergonomic handle design, yields big cutting results from a small but versatile neck-knife package. The entire knife is coated black and comes with a black Kydex neck sheath.

Meyerco USA

Meyerco is another company that has reached out to custom knifemakers in an effort to better the design offerings by factories. The Buddy System was designed by knifemaker Blackie Collins to be a convenient way to carry a knife. It showcases a locking mechanism in the sheath that holds the knife in any position until released via a spring-loaded button. When replacing the knife in the sheath, the button is automatically depressed when it makes contact with the guard area of the knife. The Buddy knife includes a nylon lanyard for

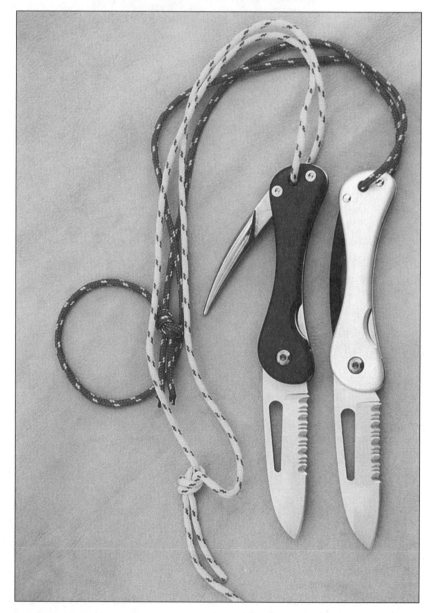

The Kellam boat and sailing knives are colorful creations, in silver and blue aluminum handles, that can be hung from the neck by equally colorful lanyards.

carrying around the neck or belt loop. Originally designed as an accessory for scuba divers, it can be carried by anyone, and the AUS 8 shouldn't rust if washed and dried after exposed to salt water.

Outdoor Edge

When one thinks of Outdoor Edge, game skinners, capers and saws come to mind. Lightweight folding knives soon follow, and neck knives are not far behind. The Wedge is one of the company's top sellers, featuring a sheath system that locks the 2 3/8-inch, wedge-shaped blade in place with the touch of a finger. The Wedge II features the same sheath system with a 3-inch blade. In addition to a cord loop for around-the-neck carry, this piece also comes with a swivel clip that attaches to belt loops and a variety of clothing and outdoor gear.

New this year is the G-Force multi-carry fixed-blade system. The stylized reverse-curve blade is extremely lightweight and balanced to cut powerfully under the most extreme conditions. Three geometric blade slots minimize weight and improve overall balance. The handle incorporates three sets of concentric pivot rings for easy rotation from a forward to a reverse grip. The sheath system includes a neck chain and clip for belt loop attachment.

SOG Specialty Knives

The acronym "SOG" stands for "Studies and Observation Group," an elite joint services military group in Vietnam practicing covert operations. Sanctioned to develop and purchase equipment, SOG created a knife for use in harsh environments. It is in this spirit that SOG Specialty Knives and Tools, Inc. was founded by Spencer and Gloria Frazer. A new addition to the SOG line is the SOG Duo, a two-blade system with a special locking frame. The Duo incorpo-

Brand new from Masters Of Defense is the Scorpion Neck Knife and sheath in all black with a double-edge blade and serrations on the top cutting edge. The cut-out handle serves two purposes: to ensure a secure grip in several holds; and to make the knife lighter, and thus more comfortable to carry.

Just when you thought there were no other options for neck-carry sheaths, Meyerco releases the Buddy System, which includes a knife with an AUS 8 blade, and a Fiberesin sheath that locks in place and is released with the push of a button.

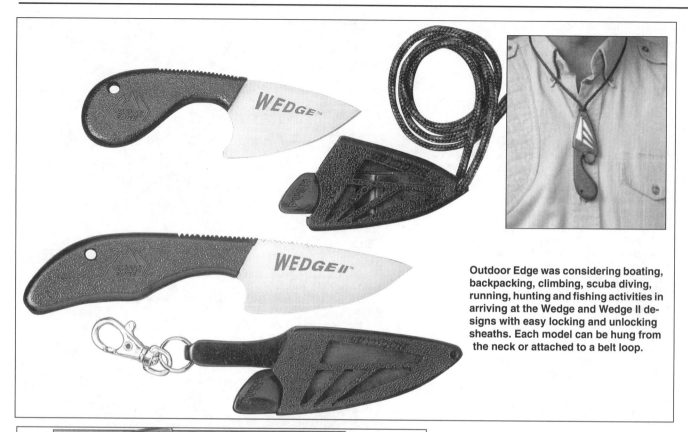

Outdoor Edge was considering boating, backpacking, climbing, scuba diving, running, hunting and fishing activities in arriving at the Wedge and Wedge II designs with easy locking and unlocking sheaths. Each model can be hung from the neck or attached to a belt loop.

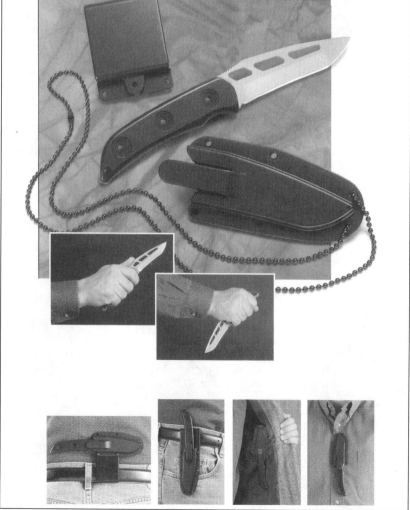

rates a serrated blade and a plain-edge blade, each of which is interchangeable by unscrewing a bolt in the handle frame and changing to the blade best suited for a specific cutting need. A removable clip and lanyard hole provide carry options to include neck carry.

SOG also offers the 1-ounce, one-piece 440A "Outline" neck knife with a 2 1/2-inch blade, a finger anchor hole in the handle and a Kydex® sheath.

Spyderco

Known for the trademark hole in the blade, pocket clips, blade serrations and knife sharpeners, Spyderco is a company dedicated to knives, tools, comfortable carry and easy accessibility. All are attributes of the Snap-It and Remote Release models. "Snap-It anywhere" says Spyderco of the C26 Snap-It, which clips to vests, bootlaces and belt loops. The snap shackle works like the clip on a dog leash and allows for quick deployment, yet keeps the

Outdoor Edge refers to the G-Force model as a revolutionary multi-carry fixed blade system. A quick-release sheath system includes a spring clip for attachment to a belt loop, and a neck chain.

Can't decide between a straight or serrated blade? Try the SOG Duo with interchangeable blades and a special locking frame. This piece includes a removable clip and lanyard hole for alternative carry modes, including neck suspension.

knife out of the way until it is needed. The Snap-It comes with a safety-style sheepsfoot blade (round-tipped) of AUS 8 blade steel, which eliminates the likelihood of puncturing skin or gear in use.

The Remote Release is designed for attachment above the waist and fast retrieval when seated or not positioned upright. The shackle on the rear of the handle is spring loaded and opens by way of a textured release pin. The knife is made to accommodate gloved hands because the hole in the blade is large, and Kra-

SOG considers the Outline neck knife "slim-line functionality," tipping the scales at 1 ounce with a hole in the handle that acts as a finger anchor.

The Spyderco C26 Snap-It has a new sheepsfoot blade shape for safety with a rounded tip that reduces the likelihood of puncturing skin or gear in use. Of course, the Snap-It shackle clips to vests, bootlaces and belt loops, and works like the clip on a dog leash.

ton handle inserts keep the knife from slipping.

The Mini Police Necklace is a pint-size version of the Spyderco Police Model folder that can be worn around the neck. The titanium handle is waterproof and stamped with the Spyderco logo bug. It features an

Spyderco's Remote Release is designed to be snapped onto clothing or gear above the waist, making use of a shackle clip with a spring-loaded, textured release pin. Spyderco's trademark hole in the blade is large in this model for opening with gloved hands.

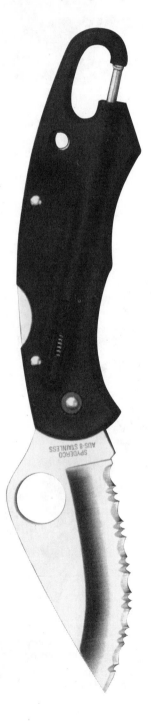

ATS 34 blade and a sterling-silver neck chain.

Taylor Cutlery

Among other sharp offerings, Taylor Cutlery is an official distributor of Smith & Wesson knives, and the Smith & Wesson line is growing considerably. Among this year's offerings are the SW990TA and SW990 Survival Neck Knives, the former with a black-Teflon-coated

tanto blade, and the latter with a bead-blasted blade. Both are 440 surgical steel offerings with neck chains, and whistles incorporated into the sheaths.

United Cutlery

United Cutlery's full range of knives includes those for hunting, camping, fishing, the military, utility, collecting, fantasy knife enthusiasts, and other specialty

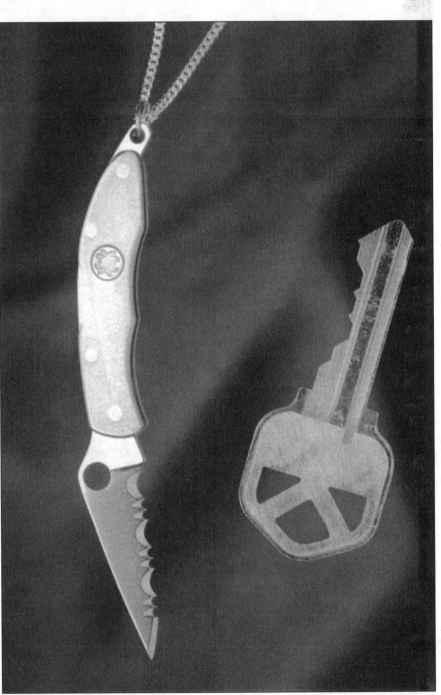

The Police Model has been one of Spyderco's more popular knife patterns, and now is available in a neck knife version with an ATS 34 blade and a waterproof titanium handle.

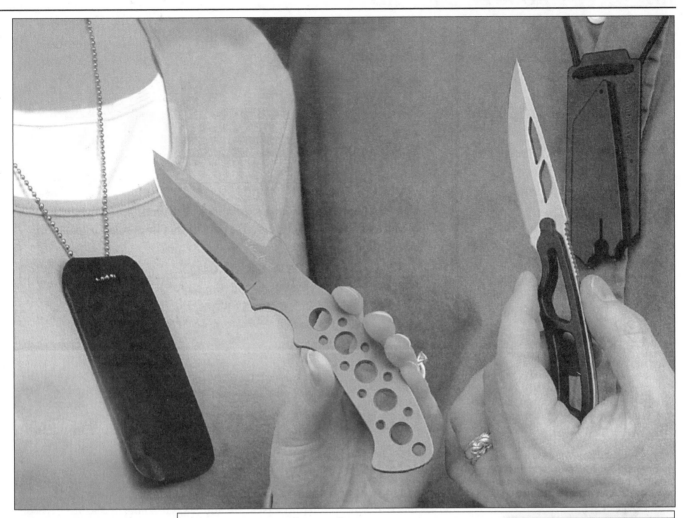

Neck knives have come into their own as useful tools. Pieces like the Pat Crawford Kasper (a handmade model at left) and the Smith & Wesson Neck Knife bring slimmed-down profiles, convenient carry systems and utilitarian designs.

knife and tool needs. Among those is a small group of little-known numbers called "T-Handle Knives." Named for their T-shaped black rubber handles, the fully functional neck knives are only 2 5/8 inches long with 420 J2 stainless steel blades. Each comes with a black fiber-reinforced nylon sheath and a nylon lanyard cord for neck carry. ●

The fully functional T-Handle neck knives from United Cutlery are only 2 5/8 inches long with 420 J2 stainless steel blades and black rubber handles.

Accessories Answered

By Joe Kertzman

YOU'VE HEARD OF computer geeks. Well, let's face it, knife enthusiasts — whether rich or poor, male or female, self-employed or slaves to the system — are gadget geeks. Gadget geeks are those unfortunate few who spend countless hours tearing apart telephones that won't ring; doorbells that won't ding, oven timers that won't ping and radios that won't sing.

New toys are torn apart for the benefit of functionality. Civilization might crumble, or worse yet, vaporize, if someone doesn't figure out how every new possession works. Folding knives are disassembled and reassembled. Fixed blades are studied for hours. Handle pommels are unscrewed if possible, and guards are regarded with constant consternation. And, when the day is done, when the mysteries of the blade world have been uncovered, there's nothing left to do but accessorize.

Knives need sheaths, sharpeners, lubricants, packs, display cases, safes and rust inhibitors. The gadget geeks, and the term is meant in the most complimentary way, get right to it. Blades are cleaned and oiled; sheaths are cleaned and oiled; pivots are cleaned and oiled; blades are sharpened, then cleaned and oiled again; pocket clips, belt loops, boot straps, shoulder harnesses and blade-totin' knife packs are opened, inventoried, tested, broken in and wrapped up again for future use.

In reality, knife nuts are not to be faulted. Sheaths, sharpeners and the like are as necessary as car wax and house paint. The more often they are applied, the longer a knife lasts and the more pleasure it brings for years to come. Accessories can be nothing but good for the burgeoning knife business.

Not long ago, there were no knife lubricants. The closest to the knife industry that lubricant companies came was to spread themselves thin enough to reach into the gun arena, coat a few Remingtons and Colts, and retreat back whence they came. Sharpeners have had a go-round with knives for a long time, but the dance has been largely reserved for kitchen cutlery.

A knife pack, harness, strap, clip, display case, or safe? Unheard of heretofore in the world of knives. Ah, with popularity comes prominence, and knives are gaining momentum in the social conscience of the people. The masses are taking notice of flashy blades, perfect handles and tight tolerances. The mood has changed toward acceptance and recognition. The kings require their presence. It's time to unsheath knives and parade them before the high courts of the bourgeoisie.

It is not all splendor. Lubricant, knife pack, sharpener and display companies are betting their bankrolls on knives and knife accesso-

The A.G. Russell Field Sharpener is a portable kit that can be set up on any flat surface for a quick blade honing job when needed. The kit includes two 4-inch diamond and two similarly sized ceramic sharpening rods and a thermoplastic base that doubles as a carrying case.

ries. These aren't Fortune 500 companies with wealth to waste and time to kill. They are moderate franchises touting quality and ingenuity in the sharp, yet small and self-propagating world of knives. Chief CEOs of accessory establishments are rolling the dice in hopes that hard work and integrity will pay off for knife manufacturers, importers and dealers, that honest people making an honest living will attract a supportive, loyal and paying clientele.

And, while the sway-backed nag sees no betting action, the odds are dropping dramatically for the knife industry, and in some ways, it seems like a profitable venture, thus the influx of accessories. Don't feel too comfortable. The chiefs of chance can retrace their steps and back out of the world of sharp as quickly as they entered the marketplace, so roll out the welcome mat and make them feel at home. It's nice to be the center of attention for once.

So far, knife manufacturers, retailers and importers have done a good job of helping finance the welcoming party for knife accessories. Innumerable companies have embraced the Blade-Tech sheath system, the Sentry Solutions Tuf-Cloth and White Lightning's line of lubricants. Others have taken a sharpening company or two under their wings and touted their wares or endorsed the products of the same.

A few sharp cutlers have packaged knives with sheaths, packs or display cases, and who could forget the first time they saw a Sack-Up knife sack? These are accessories with honest appeal, and each has a place in the knife industry. A close look at each will reveal qualities and characteristics unique in and of themselves. It truly is amazing how many such companies have sprung up over the past decade and regally stepped into the growing and endearing kingdom of knives.

A.G. Russell Knives

Established in 1964, A.G. Russell Knives is a driving force in the knife industry, not only for its high-volume sales of knives, but as a megasuccessful mail-order knife catalog company. Its catalog "Russell's For Men" is complemented nicely by "A.G. Russell Catalog of Knives" and "The Cutting Edge" catalog, widely considered one of the most comprehensive sources for antique, collectible and working knives in the world. All three do a service to knives by reaching a wider audience

than is otherwise tapped by typical knife production companies.

A mainstay in the A.G. Russell line is The Field Sharpener, a compact V-hone-type kit with two 4-inch diamond and two ceramic sharpening rods in a thermoplastic base that doubles as a carrying case.

Bianchi International

An accessories company specializing in holsters and police-duty gear, Bianchi International introduced more new products at the 2000 S.H.O.T. Show than ever before in its history, and Bianchi kept the momentum going in 2001. The AccuCase Knife

Vertical

Inverted

For those who prefer belt carry, the Bianchi International AccuCase nylon Knife Case holds most compact folding knives and attaches to the belt via a clip.

Vertical and inverted are two of five ways knife sheaths, and thus knives, can be attached to a belt with Blade-Tech's utility belt clip, the Tek-Lok. Other carry options include horizontal, cross-draw and small-of-the-back positioning.

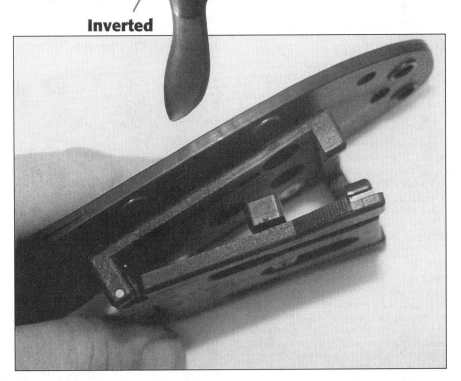

The Tek-Lok belt and knife sheath fastener from Blade Tech adjusts for different belt sizes.

Case is a simple-yet-effective nylon pouch sheath that fits most compact folding knives and attaches to a belt via a sturdy clip for convenient access. A crush-resistant tri-laminate body protects knives from damage, and a Velcro closure flap prevents accidental loss.

Blade-Tech Industries

Among the leaders in the field of thermal-molded knife sheaths is Blade-Tech Industries. Encountering thermoplastic sheaths offered with any number of production knives is often the result of a deal struck with Blade-Tech. Knife industry giants that have endorsed and struck deals with Blade-Tech to offer its sheaths and other products include Cold Steel, Ka-Bar, Camillus, Buck, Boker USA, GATCO/Timberline, Ontario, Mission Knives and Gerber Legendary Blades.

A large part of the Blade-Tech's success in the knife industry comes in the form of the Tek-Lok detachable utility belt clip designed by company president Tim Wegner and custom knifemaker Robert Terzuola. Meant to clip onto a knife sheath, and in turn, onto a belt, the Tek-Lok incorporates a system of eyelets, rivets, screws and posts for vertical, inverted, cross-draw, small-of-the-back and horizontal knife carry.

Diamond Machining Technology

"Diamond" is part of the name and the only game in town at Diamond Machining Technology, a company that has been offering diamond knife sharpening hones since 1976. Most of the stones manufactured by DMT consist of micron-sized monocrystalline diamonds bonded onto a nickel plate and electroplated to a steel base. A pattern of recessed dots on the surfaces of the diamond sharpening stones captures the fine metal particles produced in the honing process and whisks them away from the face of the sharpener.

The Diamond Mini Sharp is a Diamond Machining Technology offering that attaches to key rings for honing pocketknives. With a diamond-coated surface, the Mini Sharp is effective on the hardest stainless steel blades and features a folding handle that protects the diamond surface when not in use. It is available in extra-fine, fine, coarse and extra-coarse grits.

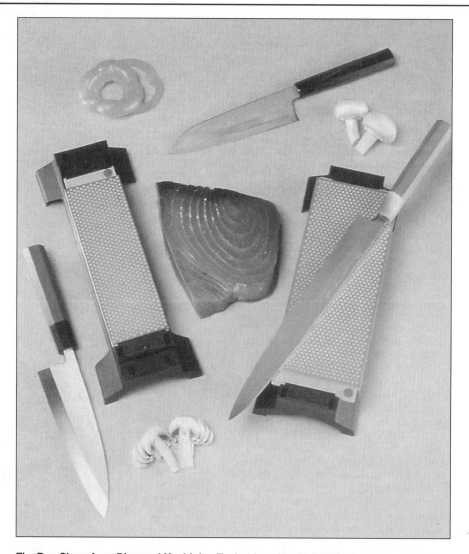

The Duo Sharp from Diamond Machining Technology is a 10-by-4-inch sharpening stone featuring an extra-large diamond surface area designed for craftsmen, professional chefs, woodworkers and large-knife enthusiasts.

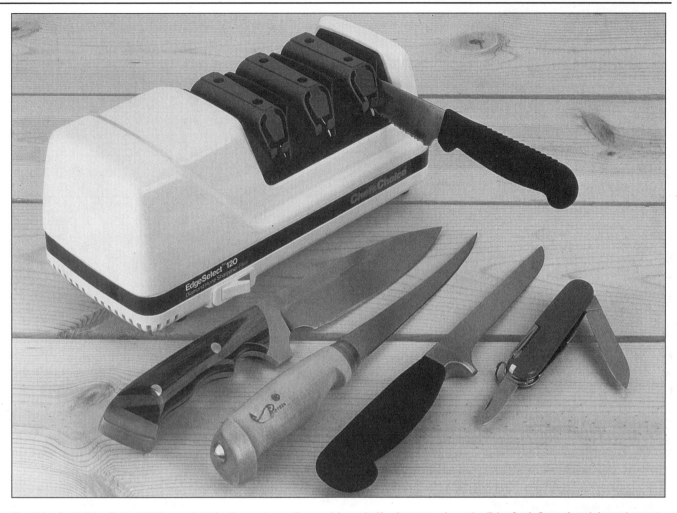

The EdgeCraft EdgeSelect 120 is an electric, three-stage, diamond-hone knife sharpener from the EdgeCraft Corp. for plain and serrated blade edges. With precision angle controls, stages one and two subject knife edges to diamond abrasives, and stage three strops and polishes blade bevels. It's ideal for gourmet, butcher, sporting and serrated knives.

EdgeCraft Corp.

Edgecraft is the home of Chef'sChoice sharpeners that come in an array of styles to hone anything from kitchen cutlery to scissors, sporting knives, fillet knives and pocketknives. Other Chef'sChoice products include knife block sets, carving sets, food slicers, waffle makers, pots and teakettles.

The Edgemaker Co.

The Edgemaker Co. builds knife sharpeners with grooved sharpening steels in cross-rod designs. The crossed rods, or steels, take the guesswork out of what angle to hone a blade bevel. By pulling a blade edge between the two crossed steels, both sides of the bevel are honed at the same time at a fixed angle. This year, the company is under new ownership, yet still premiering a

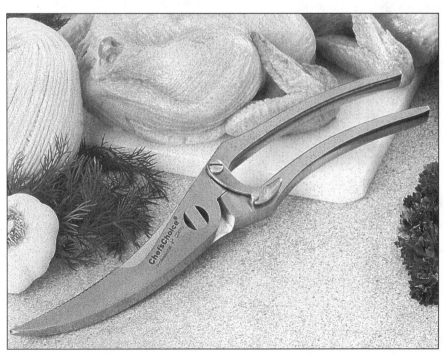

The Chef'sChoice forged poultry shears is part of the Trizor Professional 10X Cutlery set offered by Edgecraft Corp. in stainless steel blades.

Here's a hideaway knife sharpener from The Edgemaker Co. that mounts inside a drawer or workbench. The HKS Hidden Knife Sharpener features crossed sharpening steels that take the guesswork out of what angle to hone a blade bevel. By pulling a blade edge between the crossed steels, both sides of the bevel are sharpened simultaneously at a fixed angle.

product, the HKS Hidden Knife Sharpener. The design utilizes the company's existing sharpening technology of crossed steels with the added benefit of mounting inside a knife drawer or workbench. The HKS also allows for knife sharpening without requiring the user to hold the hone.

EZE-LAP Diamond Products

It is said that diamonds are the hardest substance known, and EZE-LAP takes advantage of that ultra-hard substance to hone knife blades. A heat treating process bonds industrial-grade diamond particles in a stainless steel alloy to a metal substrate. The resulting surface integrity rates approximately 72 on the Rockwell C hardness scale, a rating harder than any blade steel, and perfect for honing carbide steels, ceramic, tool steels and other hardened blade materials, including the newest stainless steels.

Flitz International Ltd.

Flitz is a metal polish, and a fiberglass and paint restorer. It cleans, polishes, deoxidizes and protects brass, copper; bronze, sterling silver, solid gold, pewter, stainless steel, aluminum, nickel, anodized aluminum, factory hot gun bluing and painted surfaces, all of which are common on knives. The metal polish contains no ammonia or abrasives that will harm knife parts.

The Model 571 EZE-Fold Diamond Sharpener from EZE-LAP employs a carrying case that unfolds into a handle and reveals a tapered diamond sharpening shaft that fits into and hones blade serrations.

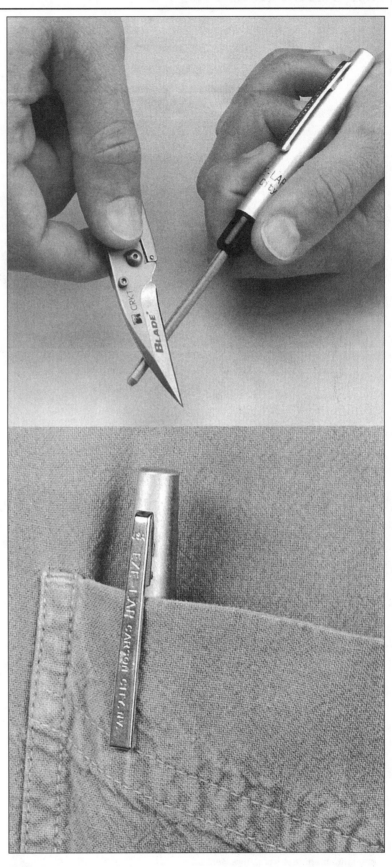

Shirt Pocket Diamond Sharpeners from EZE-LAP clip into pockets for use when duty calls, a fact that may contribute to the models being EZE-LAP's best sellers for 20 years running, according to general manager Ralph Johnson.

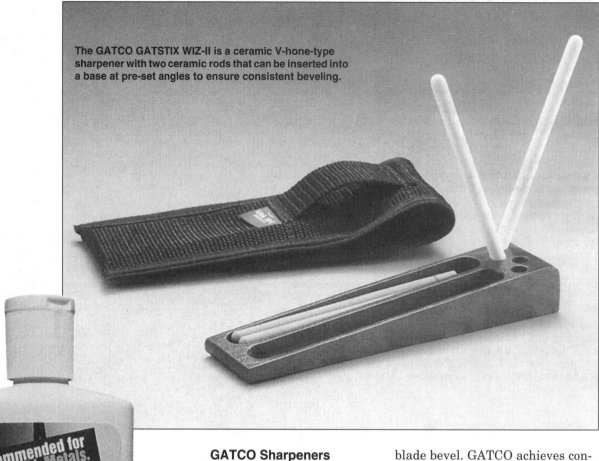

The GATCO GATSTIX WIZ-II is a ceramic V-hone-type sharpener with two ceramic rods that can be inserted into a base at pre-set angles to ensure consistent beveling.

GATCO Sharpeners

John Anthon of GATCO Sharpeners believes that holding a consistent angle in the edge-honing process is a key to achieving a sharp blade bevel. GATCO achieves consistent edge holding with the GATSTIX WIZ-II Ceramic Sharpener, a V-hone-type tool with two ceramic rods that can be inserted into a base

Flitz Metal Polish is recommended by many knife manufacturers, importers and dealers for cleaning and protecting steel blades and metal knife parts. It is safe and effective on stainless steel, gun-blued blades and anodized-aluminum bolsters and liners, among a number of other knife parts.

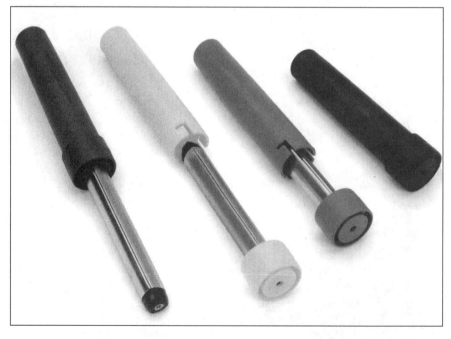

This handy Flipstik knife sharpener from Hewlett Mfg. features a handle that slides down over the diamond-coated sharpening rod when not in use for protection and ease of carrying.

at pre-set angles to ensure consistent beveling.

Hewlett Manufacturing

Known by the name "Jewelstik," Hewlett Mfg. Sharpeners are simple handle-and-rod, diamond-coated hones sold around the world. The Flipstik series is especially interesting in that the handle slides down over the diamond-coated sharpening rod when not in use and locks into a base for pocket or pack carry.

Innovative Product Design

Innovative Product Design is just what the name implies, a company offering innovative products, including the Clips-It powder-coated, stainless steel clip that attaches to knife sheaths for pocket, clothing or gear carry.

Katz Knives

Beauty is in the eye of the beholder, and Katz knives offers sharp "eye candy" for every beholder, including knives with cherry, ivory, pearl, stag and Micarta® handles. The Katz knife line is chock-full of handsome hardware, including knife sheaths.

Sheaths in the Katz line are reserved for those who favor fine leather. Some knife enthusiasts like leather because it rides on the hip comfortably and others prefer it because it is easily adjusted or repaired at home. A properly fitted leather sheath secures knives tightly and offers fast withdrawal.

Katz offers small and large cowhide hip-hugger sheaths that hold folding knives measuring 3 1/2 to 5 1/4 inches closed. Each hip-hugger features two slots for belt carry and closure flaps that snap shut.

The Clips-It is a powder-coated stainless steel clip from Innovative Product Design that attaches to knife sheaths for pocket, clothing or gear carry.

Lansky Sharpeners

Home of Crock Stick knife sharpeners and the Fold-A-Vee sharpener for field use, Lansky Sharpeners has one of those diverse product lines that holds up to the stiffest of competition.

Crock Sticks are the invention of a man named Louis Graves, who set two ceramic rods in a base at angles to each other so that when viewed straight on, they formed a "V." These V-hone-type sharpeners allowed novice knife enthusiasts to hold a knife blade straight up and down, perpendicular to the base, and sharpen one edge against the inside of one outward-angled rod, thus forming and hold-

ing a bevel angle for the inexperienced user, and then the other side of the bevel against the opposite rod. Lansky bought the patent for V-hone sharpeners, now known as Crock Sticks. Since then, Lansky has introduced dozens of new hones, including the Fold-A-Vee, another popular sharpener aimed at outdoorsmen.

REPORTS FROM THE FIELD

New for this year are the Cold Steel Sharpener, the Spyder Sharpener and the Lansky Lights. Talk about powers in the knife industry teaming up for the good of the cause, Lansky worked with Cold Steel and Spyderco, creating sharpeners built to hone each company's unusual scalloped, or serrated, edges. The handy key-ring sharpeners feature special grooves to match the mini serrations of Cold Steel knives and a range of serrated Spyderco blades. Lansky Lights are just as their name implies — new ultra-bright LED flashlights. Consider these accessories to a knife accessory line.

McGowan Manufacturing Co.

Known for its trademark Fire-Stone knife sharpening line, McGowan Manufacturing Co. offers a wide range of knife hones, including those with round, rotating stones. The freely rotating stones are made up of abrasives in a base of industrial ceramic.

Most of the company's sharpeners are built with two rotating ceramic stones butted up against each other, so with the stroke of a blade edge between the adjacent wheels, both bevels of a blade edge are simultaneously honed.

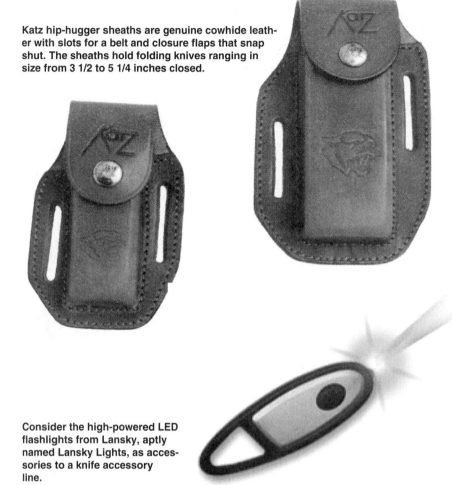

Katz hip-hugger sheaths are genuine cowhide leather with slots for a belt and closure flaps that snap shut. The sheaths hold folding knives ranging in size from 3 1/2 to 5 1/4 inches closed.

Consider the high-powered LED flashlights from Lansky, aptly named Lansky Lights, as accessories to a knife accessory line.

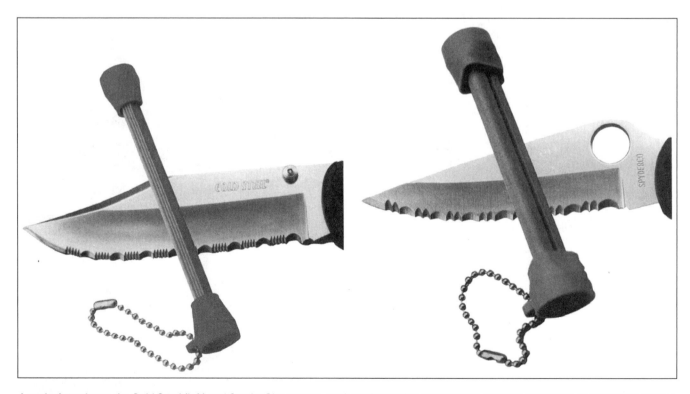

Lansky introduces the Cold Steel (left) and Spyder Sharpeners, each engineered to sharpen the unusual serrations of Cold Steel knives and Spyderco blades, respectively.

Morton Enterprises

Morton Enterprises Knife Safes are not safes at all, but rather carrying cases fashioned with Cordura® outer shells and soft, cotton poly-padded interiors to protect knife collections. A small bag holds 16 folding knives, a medium bag secures eight fixed blades and 24 folders, and a large bag holds 26 fixed blades and 38 folders. Knife Safes have double hand-loop carrying straps that wrap completely around the zipper case for a secure grip. Unzipped and open, the cases reveal rows of knife pouches padded sufficiently to prevent knives from touching adjacent pieces.

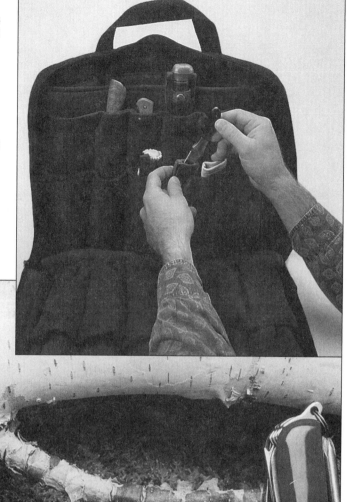

Morton Enterprises Knife Safes are not safes in the traditional sense, but they are safe ways to carry knives. Each is a carrying case with a Cordura® outer shell and a soft, cotton poly-padded interior filled with individual knife pouches.

The FireStone ShirtPocket from McGowan Manufacturing Co. is a small shirt-pocket sharpener with two round, rotating ceramic stones designed to sharpen both sides of a blade bevel simultaneously.

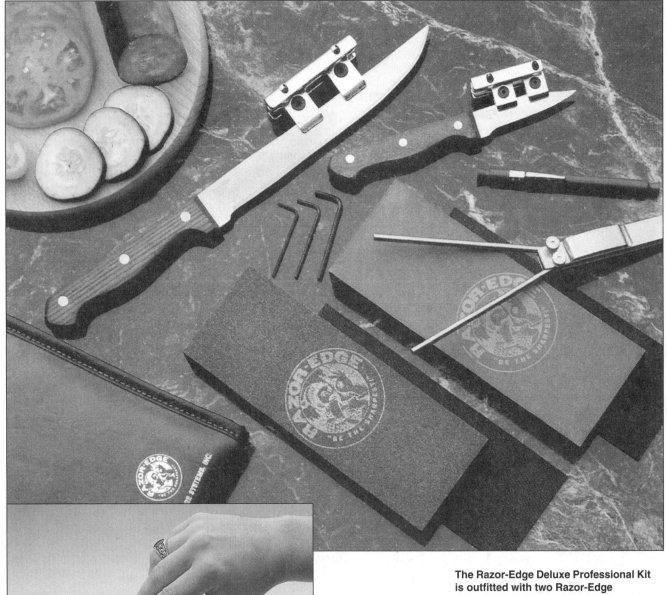

The Razor-Edge Deluxe Professional Kit is outfitted with two Razor-Edge Sharpening Guides, coarse and ultra-fine stones, a sharpening steel, edge tester, wrenches and a Naugahyde storage case. The Edge Sharpening Guides clamp to blade spines to ensure blade edges rest at desired angles on sharpening stones.

Sack-Ups protective knife pouches hold small folding knives and large fixed blades alike. Each has a cloth closure flap that extends from the back of the pouch over the top of the knife to the front, where it can be tucked inside to hold the knife in place.

Razor-Edge Systems, Inc.

John Juranitch, president of Razor-Edge Systems, Inc., is convinced that the sharpening products in his company's catalog make it possible for anyone to put a professional, razor-sharp edge on any blade or cutting bevel. Juranitch also believes a sharper blade is a safer blade, and one that gets the job done.

A product unique to Razor-Edge is the Edge Sharpening Guide, a clamp for the spine of a knife blade that, when laid on a sharpening stone with the

A foursome of products from Sentry Solutions lubricate knife blades and pivots and prevent rust and wear.

blade clamped securely, allows the beveled edge of the blade to touch the stone at a desired angle.

Sack-Ups

They look like socks, but Sack-Ups pouches and knife rolls are capable of holding anything from small folding knives to large fixed blades, and the company's knife rolls hold up to 12 or 15 knives. The single knife pouches feature a simple flap that extends from the back of the pouch over the top of the knife to the front, where it can be tucked inside to hold the knife in place. The knife rolls are secured with drawstrings.

Warren Norman of Sack-Ups claims the knife rolls can be rolled up, thrown skyward in a room with a high ceiling, allowed to drop to the floor, and the knives inside will escape without damage.

Sentry Solutions

Sentry Solutions made a name for itself in the world of knives with the Tuf-Cloth, a lint-free cloth that replaces traditional oils and silicone rags as a corrosion inhibitor and lubricant. It is a dry-film cloth that protects against rust when wiped on a knife blade.

Marine Tuf-Cloth is a similar multi-purpose dry protectant for ex-

treme conditions and salt water. Tuf-Glide is a quick-drying partner for Tuf-Cloth, and another rust inhibitor and lubricant, but it bonds to metal and won't wash or wipe off. It is ideal for the pivot area of folding knives. Smooth-Kote protects against friction and wear and elim-

inates grime: again, ideal for the pivot area of folders.

A new addition to the Sentry line is a joint effort with GATCO Sharpeners, resulting in the Knife & Tool Care Kit. The kit consists of a cloth pouch that houses the Sentry Solutions Tuf-Cloth, Tuf-Glide, a few

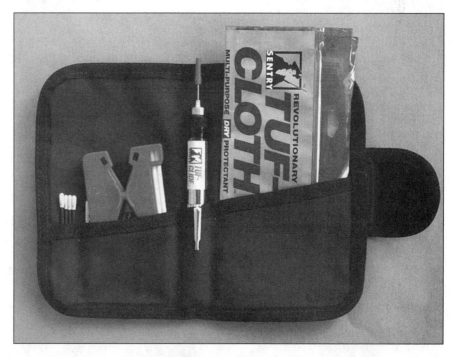

Sentry Solutions teamed with GATCO Sharpeners on the Knife & Tool Care Kit, a cloth pouch that holds Sentry's Tuf-Cloth and Tuf-Glide lubricants, rust inhibitors and protectants, cleaning tools and a GATCO Micro X Pocket Ceramic four-rod sharpener.

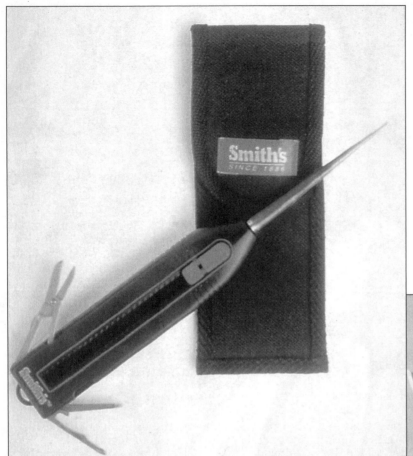

The Smith's Abrasives Diamond Retractable Plus incorporates a tapered sharpening rod for reaching into and honing blade serrations. The rod retracts with the push of a button to vary rod length, and the button is large enough to manipulate with gloved hands. The Diamond Retractable Plus also comes with a built-in scissors, screwdrivers and bottle opener.

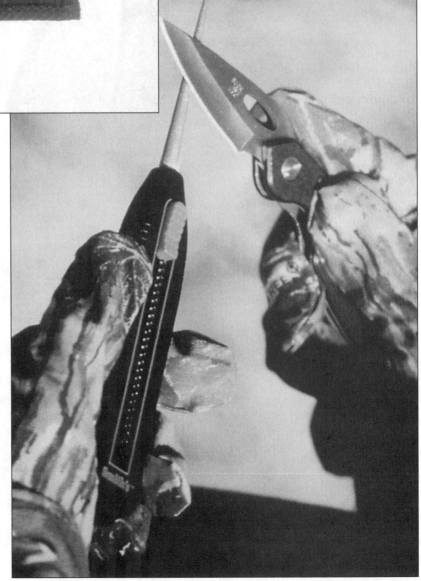

key cleaning tools and a GATCO Micro X Pocket Ceramic four-rod sharpener.

Smith's Abrasives

For more than 100 years, Richard Smith's family has been in the Arkansas sharpening stone business. Smith's is now part of the Metalrax Group, a publicly owned company in England that markets products to industrial and retail customers. Smith's, meanwhile, has expanded its line to include not only Arkansas sharpening stones, but also diamond and ceramic sharpeners, bonded abrasives and carbide sharpeners.

One such piece is the Diamond Retractable Plus, a diamond-grit sharpening rod tapered to fit into and sharpen blade serrations. The "retractable" part of the name refers to a push-button action control that varies rod length and is big enough to manipulate with gloved hands. The sharpener includes a built-in scissors, screwdrivers and bottle opener.

Spyderco Inc.

Sal Glesser of Spyderco wants his customers to know that the longer a knife goes without edge maintenance, the more difficult re-sharpening becomes. A factory knife edge, Glesser reasons, is easily maintained at home using Spyderco's Tri-Angle Sharpmaker. The Sharpmaker is known throughout the industry for its triangular-shaped ceramic rods in fine and medium grits for sharpening plain and serrated edges. A polymer base with a lid holds the rods at pre-set, 40-degree-comprehensive angles to each other for honing a 20-degree bevel on each side of the blade.

Tai Lubricants

Tai Lubricants, maker of NyOil, brings a new product to the fore-

NyOil II is a synthetic lubricant with additives for knife-blade rust protection and wear prevention.

front: NyOil II. NyOil II is a synthetic lubricant with additives for knife-blade rust protection and wear prevention.

Tru Hone Corp.

Tru Hone touts its products as "ending the Stone Age of knife sharpening." Whether that is true or not, the Crossteel is an interesting product employing two spring-tensioned, pivoting steel sharpening rods that realign themselves to knife edges. The rods are mounted on a synthetic base. The company also offers a variable-speed electric sharpener with an angle-adjust-

The Tri-Angle Sharpmaker from Spyderco is known throughout the industry for its triangular-shaped ceramic rods for sharpening plain and serrated edges.

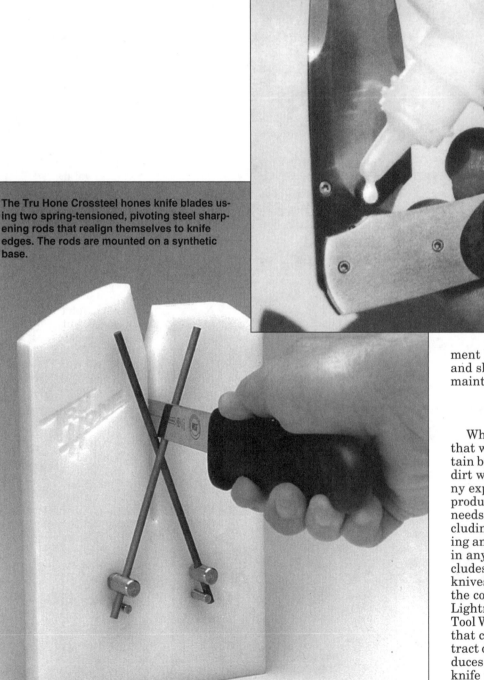

White Lightning Folding Knife & Multi-Tool Wax Lubricant is a dry-wax lube that reduces friction and wear on moving knife parts by sealing out dirt, grit and water.

The Tru Hone Crossteel hones knife blades using two spring-tensioned, pivoting steel sharpening rods that realign themselves to knife edges. The rods are mounted on a synthetic base.

ment knob to control knife angles, and sharpening wheels that help maintain a consistent angle.

White Lightning Co.

White Lightning is a lubricant that was invented for use on mountain bike chains and is said to clean dirt while it lubricates. The company expanded its scope to cover any product with a moving part that needs cleaning and lubricating, including gardening products, camping and boating products, and tools in any number of trades. That includes knives, especially folding knives with moving pivots. Thus, the company introduced White Lightning Folding Knife & Multi-Tool Wax Lubricant, a dry-wax lube that creates a film and will not attract dirt. In short, the lubricant reduces friction and wear on moving knife parts by sealing out dirt, grit and water. •

Tactical Folder Tryouts Today!

By Roger Combs

I AM NOT at all certain that every knife manufacturer agrees on what the term "tactical folder" means, but it is, if nothing else, a successful marketing term that has helped sell a tremendous amount of knives. Originally designed as a self-defense tool, somewhat larger than a typical pocketknife, the tactical folder is the definition of "tough." To be sure, most of us who carry a tactical folder have not and will not ever use it in a knife fight, but such a design has many other uses, and let's face it, nothing is more comforting than having a beefy folder at your side.

It is a cliché in the industry that a knife is not a pry bar, not a screwdriver, and certainly not a chisel. "Don't twist a knife. Don't wrench it. Don't pry with it," knifemakers admonish. Well, if there ever was a knife design that could double as a pry bar, screwdriver or chisel, it is the difficult-to-over torque tactical folder. Now for the admonishment: That doesn't mean you should use a knife for anything but cutting!

The single blade is usually at least 3 1/2 inches in length, and some will stretch 6 inches or longer, but generally 3 1/2 to 5 inches is the range. The blade always has some sort of locking system to keep it from closing up on fingers under stress.

Most tactical folders have stainless steel blades, coated or uncoated, to reduce the chance of corrosion. Such knives are built for use under adverse conditions or around water. With non-magnetic, lightweight and corrosion-resistant qualities, titanium has become the material of choice for liners, handles, and even blades on occasion. The downside is that titanium is expensive to purchase and to work, and it is extremely tough on machines such as cutters, grinders and sanders.

Handles for tactical folders, too, must be rugged enough to withstand extreme use and to provide a non-slip grip when wet or cold. That usually rules out materials such as wood, bone or antler. Most grips will incorporate checkered or textured finishes, and the shapes are often contoured, some with finger grooves. There should be no sharp edges or corners to hinder or restrict the user's hand in a tight grip during a difficult cutting task.

Tactical folding knives must have fairly thick, rugged blades, with most in the 1/8- to 3/16-inch range, and some will be thicker. All have a one-hand-opening device or mechanism. That is not to say they meet the definitions of switchblades — illegal to carry in most places and under most circumstances — but the blades must open quickly and easily, locking open as they do.

"One handers" are helped along by buttons, studs, discs, slides or holes that, with the flick of the thumb or finger, snap the blades open quickly. Each manufacturer has a favorite. One-hand operation is important to emergency medical, military or law enforcement personnel, as well as ranchers, farmers, hunters, gardeners and anyone who may have just one hand free to open a knife.

It is plain to see that there are almost as many methods for deploying a blade with one hand as there are makers. Examining each tactical knife system to determine how it works while wearing gloves is a good idea, as most are used with gloved hands at one time or another.

Tactical locking mechanisms have been undergoing changes in recent years, advancing far beyond the scope of the traditional pocketknives so many of us still carry. The ubiquitous tactical folder no longer relies on simple friction to keep the blade open or closed, but rather on locking liners, lock backs, top locks, side locks, levers, buttons or slides.

Some knives have a provision to lock the blade closed as well as open. My opinion is that as long as the lock is positive and strong, any type is satisfactory. The favorite is the one practiced with and learned inside and out, and from front to back.

Quick deployment is a requirement for tactical folders, even those worn in a belt sheath or pouch, depending on the situation at hand. It is far from unusual for military personnel in training to carry a large folder in a belt sheath, yet most tactical folders are fashioned with pocket clips. Whether stainless steel, titanium, aluminum or another relatively lightweight, durable material, today's versatile pocket clips are often made available for tip-up or tip-down carry, and made reversible for left-handers or righties. Each model has its champion and its advantages and disadvantages. You cannot know which works best for you until you try a design for some time, deploying, opening and using the knife.

Blade edges are plain, serrated or partially serrated, and the shapes of serrations are as diverse as the makers themselves. Choices made by the buyer will depend on the expected use of the knife. An emergency medical technician or paramedic will choose a different edge than, say, a construction worker or backpacker. A serrated edge will usually cut through things such as seat belts or nylon line easier than a plain edge, but a plain edge may better serve the deer hunter or angler.

Furthermore, the buyer has a choice of many different blade shapes. For some, a tanto tip will be the most practical. For others, a straight-edge wharncliffe, a drop point or curved skinning blade will serve. Keep in mind that every knife blade must at some time be sharpened, and some blade shapes and configurations are easier to sharpen than others.

Several manufacturers shy away from the term tactical folder, while others revel in it and make nothing else. In addition to the examples that follow, remember that many custom knifemakers offer their own tactical folder designs, although at considerably higher prices than the factory-made knives. As you will learn in another part of this publication, cutlery companies have learned to utilize the tactical folder designs of well-known custom knifemakers.

Benchmade Knife Co.

Here is an industry leader that features several tactical folders, some designed by company president Les de Asis, and others by well-known custom knifemakers. New for 2001 is the Model 721 Bowie AXIS Lock folder, a direct follow-up to the Mel Pardue-designed Model 720. The 721 differs in the area of a non-slip G-10 handle, which is slightly lighter than a similar handle would be in aluminum.

Blade material is 154 CM stainless steel, 3 1/4 inches long and 0.115 inch thick. Open, the knife measures 7.62 inches overall with internal liners of 410 stainless steel, and Benchmade's patented AXIS Lock developed by custom knifemakers Bill McHenry and Jason Williams. The locking mechanism is

Based on the Model 720 design, Benchmade's 721 brings a solid G-10 handle to the table for toughness, nominal weight and ease of carry. Add the ambidextrous AXIS Lock, and Benchmade feels it has a champion of a tactical folder.

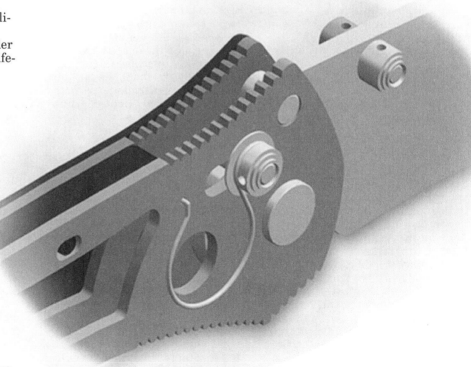

It has been one year since Benchmade introduced the AXIS Lock developed by custom knife designers and makers Bill McHenry and Jason Williams. Exclusive to Benchmade, the AXIS Lock continues to appear on more and more of Benchmade's original and new knife models.

strong, ambidextrous and smooth in operation, and the knife has a pocket clip that may be moved to either side of the knife for tip-up carry.

Beretta

New for 2001 is the Trident G-10 folder, which, as one might presume, employs G-10 for the handle over an aluminum-alloy frame. The 2 1/2-inch wharncliffe-style blade is made of VG-10 steel. Overall, the Trident is 6 3/8 inches long when open.

Boker USA

In its current catalog of knives, Boker reserves a couple pages for "tactical folders," and several other Boker knives could be defined as "tacticals."

The Model 2082 G-10 Super Liner is made in Solingen, Germany, starting with a 2 1/4-inch 440C stainless steel blade coated with black titanium nitride to give it a non-glare matte finish. The thumb stud is large for easier one-hand operation, and notched for better cutting control. Boker's Super Liner locking mechanism is best described as a side-lock. The handle material is the ever-popular and tough-as-nails G-10, finely checkered for a non-slip grip. The knife has both a pocket clip for tip-down carry and a lanyard hole to carry the knife tip-up. Clips and screws are Teflon-coated.

Browning

Browning is perhaps best known for its fine firearms, outdoor clothing and archery equipment, but the company also offers several knives, mostly for the hunter. The four Piranha Pro models fit into the tactical folder category quite well. Each has a 3 1/4-inch blade made of ATS-34 stainless steel, and each works off a titanium locking liner. The handles are of either G-10 or carbon fiber, and the buyer may select blade shapes of drop point or chisel point with plain or serrated edges.

Buck Knives

In business for nearly 100 years, Buck Knives does not fool around when it comes to making and naming new knife models. The 880 Strider is a tactical folder through and through. Designed by custom knife-

The black, stealth look is hot, judging by the Boker 2082 G-10 Super Liner with a black-coated blade and a black G-10 handle.

Browning outfits its Piranha Pro Knives with G-10 or carbon fiber handles, ATS-34 blades and full-length titanium locking liners. Fast, one-hand operation completes each package.

makers Mick Strider and Duane Dwyer, the Strider team has a reputation for top-quality knives, and each knifemaker is familiar with the requirements for a tactical folder. Buck was impressed with the twosome's insistence on rigorous field testing before the design and specs were finalized.

The Strider is rather large, reaching 9 3/4 inches in the fully open position. It is designed to be reliable in the harshest environments. Buck chose a 4-inch tanto blade of ATS-34 stainless steel for its edge-holding capabilities and toughness. The handle is a G-10 resin laminate complemented by a titanium lock and

The Buck Strider is a big, beefy stainless steel tanto with a G-10 handle and a titanium lock and liners: everything a tactical folder is supposed to be and more.

liners. A thumb stud on the blade makes one-hand opening or closing smooth, fast and easy, and the blade locks securely in place when open.

Camillus

The fast action of the Camillus CUDA makes it exciting, and I have seen no other factory-made knife that operates the same. The Camillus "Quik-Action" is just that: quick! Rather than rely on a thumb stud to open the blade, the CUDA features a sliding, checkered, flat button on the side of the handle that provides a levering action. With a little practice, a slide of the button snaps the blade open in a fraction of a second, but it does not rely on springs or gravity to operate. The blade will open even with wet or gloved hands, and it is one of the fastest one-hand openers many of us have ever tried.

The spear-point ATS-34 stainless steel blade is just under 4 inches long, bead blasted for a non-reflective look, and finished with dark titanium nitride. Handle scales are of finely checkered G-10 with dark, stainless steel liners. The CUDA is

The CUDA is a manual one-hand, locking-liner folder sporting a blade that opens via a button that slides along a channel, bringing the blade to bear smoothly.

The Chris Reeve Knives Large Sebenza model is built strong, yet weighs a slight 4 1/2 ounces because of a 6AL4V titanium handle and Reeve's own integral frame lock.

available in several blade shapes and edge configurations, some without the titanium-nitride coating.

Chris Reeve Knives

Chris Reeve, who started making knives one at a time by hand, now has a successful specialty knife company in Idaho. His rugged Sebenza folder works well, and thus the name "Sebenza," a Zulu word for "work." Zulu is the native language of the province in South Africa where Reeve was born and raised.

The Large Sebenza features a 3 1/2-inch BG-42 stainless steel blade and a 6AL4V titanium handle that makes the sharp package lightweight and strong. Reeve incorporates his own integral frame lock that moves smartly into place to lock the blade open. All spacers and pins are 303 stainless steel and the internal thrust washers are Phosphor-bronze for smooth operation. The handle is 4 1/4 inches long and the Sebenza weighs 4 1/2 ounces. A removable pocket clip is included, as is a lanyard hole.

Cold Steel

Even the name on this big folder from Cold Steel helps identify its category: Gunsite. The Gunsite Training Center, one of the leaders in firearms and defensive education, officially authorizes the model.

The larger 2001 Gunsite Folder has a 5-inch tanto-style, AUS-8A blade and a redesigned, deeply checkered Zytel® handle. The oval cross-section of the handle has been made 20 percent thicker to make it stronger and stiffer than its original design. The knife is 11 1/8-inches long overall when open and locked with a rocker-lock mechanism. The Gunsite weighs 5.3 ounces with a coated stainless steel pocket clip, a lanyard hole at the tip of the handle and a thumb stud for fast deployment.

The Gunsite Folder II is slightly smaller with a 4-inch blade, but otherwise similar, and both models feature half-serrated blade edges.

Columbia River Knife & Tool

Regular readers of BLADE Magazine® may recall the Tighe Tac folder being described as "artfully tactical." The knife is designed by Canadian custom knifemaker Brian Tighe and produced by Columbia River Knife & Tool (CRKT) in two sizes with AUS-6M blades. Each piece showcases 420-J2 stainless steel liners, a black Zytel® handle and a gray Teflon®-plated stainless steel pocket clip. The thumb disc is rectangular and protrudes from both sides of the blade for ambidextrous one-hand operation. The knife is assembled with Torx fasteners, and the blade pivots on smooth Teflon® bearings. CRKT offers a choice of a plain or half-serrated spear-point blade.

Delta Z Knives

The knife has been around for many thousands of years and it is one of man's first tools, but there is always room for another knife company. One of the newest is Delta Z, which has its knives produced in Italy and is making a mark in the cutlery industry with innovative designs and well-made knives. Delta Z's fixed blades and folding knives are distinctive and attractive.

Among the models that fit into the tactical folder category is the DZ 6114 model, available in a variety of colors and edge options. What gives the Delta Z folder distinction is the various finish colors of aluminum handles, anodized gray, black or clear. Other models are available in blue, dark green or natural materials and colors. The 6114 has a 3 1/4-inch 440A stainless steel, Teflon®-coated, matte-black blade, and a stainless locking liner, pins, spacers, screws, thumb stud and pocket clip.

Set your sights on the Cold Steel Gunsite with a half-serrated, tanto-style AUS-8A blade and a deeply checkered Zytel® handle.

Emerson Knives Inc.

Each year, the new designs introduced by Emerson Knives create a stir at trade and consumer shows. As martial artist Ernest Emerson says, "The new Mach 1 folder is at home on the trail, at the range or on duty."

The 3 1/2-inch blade is made of 154 CM stainless steel and features a conventional V-grind edge. The liners are lightweight titanium and the handle material is non-slip

Described as "artfully tactical" by BLADE Magazine®, the Columbia River Knife & Tool Tighe Tac folder is the design of Canadian custom knifemaker Brian Tighe. It is offered in two sizes with AUS-6M blades, 420-J2 stainless steel liners, a black Zytel® handle and a gray Teflon®-plated stainless steel pocket clip.

black or green G-10 epoxy-glass laminate. The Mach 1 is 8 1/4 inches overall and weighs 4.7 ounces.

Naturally, the knife includes a pocket clip and a thumb stud for fast, positive opening. It is easy on the hand with no uncomfortable sharp edges or angles, whether open or closed.

Gerber Legendary Blades

It was a decade ago that the Gerber Gator ATS-34 Drop Point received a Blade Magazine® Knife-Of-The-Year© Award, and it remains popular as ever. As the name implies, the blade is ATS-34 stainless steel and is 3 3/4 inches long in several blade configurations other than the award-winning drop-point design. The handle material is a non-slip, rubberized material made of a hard inner core of glass-filled nylon with Kraton® rubber molded around the outside. The handle is soft yet tacky when gripped and the texture looks like alligator hide. This Gator weighs 5 ounces.

Delta-Z's Teflon®-coated locking-liner folders are stainless steel wonders with anodized aluminum handles in a rainbow of colors.

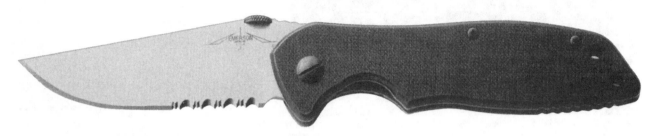

The Emerson Knives Mach 1 is a classic tactical folder with a 154CM blade, titanium liners and a non-slip, black or green G-10 handle.

Gutmann Cutlery

The Gutmann Walther P99 Tactical Knife II features a 3 1/8-inch 440C stainless steel blade with a razor tip and serrated belly. The skeletonized handle is made of bead-blasted black aluminum and utilizes a locking liner to hold the blade locked open. It comes with a right-hand thumb stud only and weighs 4.1 ounces.

KA-BAR Knives

No doubt, one of the best-recognized knives of all time is the Ka-Bar USMC Fighting Knife, still carried by many Marines on duty today. But Ka-Bar has some large tactical folders, too. Among them, the Model 2781 one-hand-opening side lock folder has a stainless steel blade that stretches 2 7/8 inches. The handle material is plastic and the pocket clip is stainless steel. A thumb stud helps get the blade open quickly.

Kershaw

The new series of Liner Action folding knives from Kershaw has proven popular for the company. The standard tanto tactical knife utilizes AUS-6A stainless steel with a blade measuring 3 5/8 inches. The handle is matte-finished aluminum with a non-slip co-polymer insert.

In a variety of blade shapes, the Gerber Gator is an ATS-34 lock-back folder with a textured Kraton® handle that looks strikingly like alligator hide.

With a skeletonized black, aluminum handle, the Walther P99 Tactical Knife II by Gutmann Cutlery has a classy look and weighs only 4.1 ounces.

The pocket clip is removable, and the knife weighs 3.3 ounces. The blade comes in plain or partially serrated edges and works off a locking liner to hold it open and release it easily. Kershaw also offers similar-sized folders with drop-point blade shapes.

Meyerco

Blackie Collins designs all the Meyerco knives. The titanium locking liners are light and corrosion resistant. Four models, all with 4-inch blades, are delivered in a choice of tactical-serrated edges, honed edges, and tanto-serrated or tanto-honed. The ATS-34 stainless steel blades are coated with titanium nitride for improved surface wear. The handles are non-slip G-10, and instead of a thumb stud, each opens via a slotted hole at the top of the blade. A stainless steel pocket clip is reversible and is fastened directly to the metal liners with stainless steel screws. The knife weighs 4.3 ounces.

Matte-finished aluminum handles with co-polymer inserts provide a sure grip in a gentlemanly look for Kershaw. The series of Liner Action folding knives also features removable pocket clips and plain or partially serrated blade edges.

Five circles in a row are machined into the plastic handle of the Ka-Bar Model 2781 one-hand-opening tactical folder with a stainless steel blade.

Tactical folders with state-of-the-art components, Meyerco's Tactical Knives rely on an all-black look with G-10 handles and titanium-nitride-coated ATS-34 blades.

For covert operations, tactical folders don't get any better than the Mission Knives & Tools All-Titanium Multi Purpose Folder 1 in black and weighing 5.2 ounces. For those less-covert individuals, Mission makes a steel-blade version, weighing slightly more.

Mission Knives & Tools

The All-Titanium Mission Knives Multi Purpose Folder 1 (MPF) features a tanto blade that reaches 4 inches in length, and 9 inches fully open. The blade is available with a partly serrated edge, if desired. The final design was done with the help of custom knifemaker Allen Elishewitz. Everything is titanium, including the blade, handles, screws, pins, studs and the removable belt clip. The knife weighs 5.2 ounces, is non-magnetic and non-conductive. Other models from Mission Knives are available with steel blades, weighing slightly more.

Outdoor Edge

Another past winner of a BLADE Magazine® Knife-Of-The-Year Award, the Outdoor Edge Field-Lite

In two blade lengths and two edge styles, the clip-point Outdoor Edge Pocket-Lites exude a tactical folder flavor in black, textured Zytel® handles and AUS-8A blades.

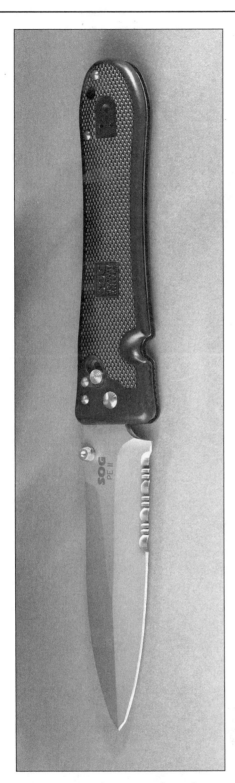

The longest folder SOG has produced, the PE18 Pentagon Elite II features a full 5-inch AUS-8A blade with a Kevlar®-reinforced Zytel® handle and a skeletonized stainless-steel pocket clip.

Spyderco certainly was a pioneer in pocket-clip knives that could be opened with one hand, such as the Military Model with a 4-inch CPM-440V blade, a G-10 handle and the Spyderco trademark hole in the blade.

folder is available in two blade lengths and two edge styles. The blades are AUS-8A stainless steel with either plain or half-serrated edges. A pocket clip makes for easy knife access, and the thumb stud is quickly employed for smooth one-hand operation. Handle material is contoured non-slip, textured Zytel®.

SOG Specialty Knives

Spencer Frazier of SOG has long been known for his innovative combat and law enforcement type knives. The new PE18 Pentagon Elite II that features a 5-inch AUS-8A stainless steel blade is the longest folder SOG has produced. The handle is Kevlar®-reinforced Zytel®, and the knife weighs only 6.8 ounces. When open, it is 10 3/4 inches long. The skeletonized pocket clip is stainless steel.

The knife is ambidextrous and features the company's Arc-Lock. The mechanism tests strong, with fast opening and closing. The spring-action ensures that the blade is safely secured within the handle when closed. The Arc-Lock is self-adjusting over time and easily cleaned for long-term performance. A smaller version, the Pentagon Elite I, is available with a 3.9-inch blade.

Spyderco

Spyderco certainly was a pioneer in pocket-clip knives that could be opened with one hand. The trademark hole in the blade for fast and easy opening may be found in many pockets around the world.

The Military Model features a 4-inch blade made of flat-ground CPM-440V stainless steel with slender G-10 handles. The locking liner is recessed into the handle for a thin profile. When open, the knife will measure 9 1/2 inches long, but weighs only 4 ounces. Spacers between the handle scales make it possible to rinse away accumulated dirt and grime. The enlarged opening hole and machining on the blade spine are an added advantage when wearing gloves. The black pocket clip is held onto the handle with three screws for tip-down carrying. The blade is available with plain or partially serrated blades in what Spyderco calls a "SpyderEdge" serration pattern.

Timberline

Timberline is part of the Great American Tool Co. (GATCO), known for its fine knife-sharpening

Getting a grip on the Timberline Envoy is easy with a textured G-10 handle, pocket clip and grooved thumb wheel. The piece is available in a plain or partially serrated AUS-8 blade.

systems. The Timberline Envoy uses the familiar locking liner and a 3.2-inch blade of AUS-8 stainless steel with a bead-blast matte finish. The handle scales are black, textured G-10 with a pocket clip. The grooved thumb wheel permits opening with either hand, and the blade edge is available plain or partially serrated.

TOPS Tactical-Ops USA

The TOPS Thunder Hawke No. 303 is designated a "close quarters tactical knife," and there is no mistake about that. The knife is available in either a tanto point or what is termed a "hunter's point." The blade is made of 154 CM (similar to ATS-34) stainless steel, with the blade measuring 3.6 inches. The handle material is machined aluminum with a reversible pocket clip. Locking mechanism is the spring liner.

The Thunder Hawke No. 303 from TOPS is a "close quarters tactical knife" in all black with a 154 CM blade and a machined-aluminum handle.

The Factory/ Custom Collaborations

By Roger Combs

The newest fixed-blade offering from the design team of Benchmade Knife Co. and Allen Elishewitz is the Model 100 River/Rescue Fixed Blade with a 3.23-inch GIN-1 stainless steel, modified-sheepsfoot blade.

THERE WAS A time when custom knifemakers jealously guarded their designs and knifemaking secrets. Sometimes they did so for good reason. Way back when Jimmy Lile made the original "First Blood" movie knife design, it was but a short time until unknown persons in Taiwan were producing unauthorized knockoffs at a fraction of the price Lile was getting for his handmade originals. Unfortunately, this sort of thing happened way too many times in those bad old days.

Most factory knives were designed in-house by owners of the company or by gifted employees within the firm. Usually, the designer went unrecognized and underappreciated.

Times have changed for the better. Factory cutlery manufacturers have come to realize the value of using designs from some of the most innovative custom makers in the industry. Today, most manufacturers actively seek out some of the better custom knifemakers to collaborate with the factory producers. Everybody benefits.

The consumer, most of all, can buy custom-designed knives at prices far below what an original handmade knife would cost from the same knifemaker. The custom designer has added exposure for his skills, helping him sell more of his hand-produced knives, and the factory makers have a wider range of designs to sell to the public.

The trend is growing. Each year, these collaborations are introduced to the public, offering us a chance to see and buy designs that we otherwise might not have an opportunity to enjoy. The following examples represent only a few of the designs that are available. Many manufacturers will utilize the designs of dozens of custom knifemakers, and their marketing success will lead to more in the future.

Benchmade Knife Co.

Benchmade has used custom knifemakers' designs for several years. Some time back, Jody Samson was living in Oregon and doing some design work for Benchmade, as well as for himself. Samson, you may remember, is the maker who designed and made the sword for the original "Conan the Barbarian" movie. He also came up with the Wee-hawk blade, still found on Benchmade's Bali-Song folding knife. Today, the company features knives designed by a half-dozen great custom knifemakers such as Allen Elishewitz, Mel Pardue, Bob Terzuola, Bill McHenry, Jason Williams and Warren Osborne.

Benchmade is best known for its many tactical folders, but now has some fixed-blade designs such as the Model 100 River/Rescue knife that is attributed to Allen Elishewitz. The M-100 has a full tang and a modified sheepsfoot blade of GIN-1 stainless steel that measures 3 1/4 inches long. The handle material is G-10 with a textured, non-slip grip. Overall, the knife reaches 7 1/2 inches and weighs a mere 6.4 ounces. A Kydex® sheath with a removable clip makes for a number of carry options, and a thumb-toggle latch/release permits the knife to be clipped to a belt or life jacket in the inverted or upright positions.

Beretta

As one of the oldest, continuously operating companies in the world, Beretta employs the design expertise of modern custom knifemaker Bob Loveless. Loveless is still making knives, but it was his efforts four decades ago that brought considerable public attention to what could be done with steel, skill and imagination.

Beretta's Master Knifemaker Series features a Loveless-designed skinner. The 3 3/4-inch ATS-34 stainless steel fixed blade with a sambar stag handle is all Loveless from butt to tip. The knife, which stretches 8 inches overall, is being produced in a limited edition of serial-numbered pieces for serious collectors.

Another Beretta project with custom knifemaker Warren Thomas resulted in the Avenger locking-liner folder with a carbon fiber handle and more carbon fiber laminated to the top half of a tanto-tip

Bob Loveless is known worldwide for his skinning knives, and Beretta took advantage of that fact with a Loveless-designed skinner, part of the company's Master Knifemaker Series. It features a 3 3/4-inch ATS-34 blade and a sambar stag handle.

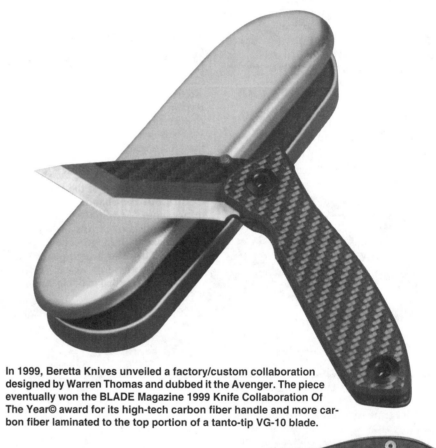

In 1999, Beretta Knives unveiled a factory/custom collaboration designed by Warren Thomas and dubbed it the Avenger. The piece eventually won the BLADE Magazine 1999 Knife Collaboration Of The Year© award for its high-tech carbon fiber handle and more carbon fiber laminated to the top portion of a tanto-tip VG-10 blade.

A lightweight carbon fiber handle and titanium liners pair up on the KLWT1 Walker Taos locking-liner folder designed by Michael Walker and made by Switzerland's H.P. Klotzli. The knife, with a 2 1/2-inch 440C blade, is available from Boker USA.

VG-10 blade. The piece took the BLADE Magazine 1999 Knife Collaboration Of The Year© award.

Boker USA

Boker, which traces its ancestry to Solingen, Germany for more than 130 years, casts its designer net across many knifemakers. The Model KLWT1, known as the Walker Taos, is a collaboration between New Mexico's Michael Walker and Switzerland's H. P. Klotzli.

The Walker Taos displays a 2 1/2-inch 440C stainless steel drop-point blade that opens and closes with a smooth, fluid motion, the same slick operation said to define the finest Swiss-made cutlery. Blade edge is partly serrated. The handle is of black carbon fiber and the liners are of titanium. Naturally, the knife utilizes the Walker LinerLock® blade locking system. It weighs less than 2 ounces and is 3 5/8 inches long when closed in its black pouch.

Neither rough terrain nor rapid waters will stop the Buck Tiburon, designed by Ed Gillet, who owns Southwest Kayaks of San Diego. Gillet employed 17-7PH stainless steel said to offer superior resistance to saltwater corrosion.

Twin Talonite specials are the result of a pairing between Camillus Cutlery and custom maker Robert Simonich. A hard-facing cobalt alloy, Talonite 6BH will not rust, and when complemented by a G-10 handle, it makes for a nearly indestructible combination.

Buck Knives

Ed Gillet, who owns Southwest Kayaks of San Diego, has paddled his kayak solo from California to Hawaii and from the tip of South America to Panama. Those feats may not qualify him as a custom knifemaker, but he knows something about what a kayaker or water sports enthusiast needs in the way of a knife.

Gillet developed and field tested the Buck Tiburon, now in production. The knife has a partially serrated 3 1/4-inch chisel-point blade of 17-7PH stainless steel, which is said to offer superior resistance to saltwater corrosion. The skeletonized piece may be used to pry, chop and hammer, if needed.

Other features include a multi-hex wrench that fits five sizes of bolts and nuts, and a hex hole that will accept a variety of tool bits. The Tiburon is 8 1/2 inches long and weighs 5.2 ounces. The sheath, with drain holes, features a clip that attaches to standard pouches on backpacks and life vests, plus a snap closure that secures the knife safely in the sheath — important to kayakers and others in rough water or on rough terrain.

Camillus Cutlery

The Talon and Mini Talon fixed blades from the CUDA division of Camillus Cutlery were designed by custom knifemaker Robert Simonich. The blade material is a hard-facing cobalt alloy, specifically Talonite 6BH, touted as one of the most revolutionary blade materials available. The 2 1/2- and 3 3/4-inch blades will not rust or corrode, and each model sports a black G-10 handle, textured and grooved for a firm grip. Kydex® and Concealex® sheaths complete the packages.

REPORTS FROM THE FIELD

Tony Bose has designed three knives for Case: a Slimline Trapper in 1999, a Bullnose Trapper in 2000, and his most recent offering, a Sowbelly pattern for 2001. Here is Bose at the grinder.

W. R. Case & Sons Cutlery

I guess that Case knives are the most collected knives in North America. Case realizes that, supporting collector clubs and turning out many knives intended to wind up in collections. I know collectors who have hundreds of specimens in their Case collections without duplications. Some years ago, a visit to the Case factory in Bradford, Pa., was, and still is, considered to be a "trip to heaven."

Custom knife designer Tony Bose started out

In 1973, Cold Steel president Lynn Thompson bought the first knife that custom maker Lloyd Pendleton ever made. Now the two friends have collaborated to make the Lloyd Pendleton Hunter and Mini Hunter with hollow-ground AUS-8A blades, Kraton® handles and Secure-Ex sheaths.

his knife collection with a Case Folding Hunter 30 years ago. He later began making his own knives and has won BLADE Handmade© awards for folding knives in 1995 and 1998. The year 2001 ushered in a collaboration between Bose and Case on the multi-blade Sowbelly. At least four versions of the three-blade folder are available, each measuring 3 7/8 inches closed and weighing 3.8 ounces. The blade shapes are clip, spey and sheepsfoot, and variations on handle slab materials and Case logos are available. Handle choices include Case's Vintage Bone, Pocket Worn Black Bone, Golden Amber Bone, Natural Bone and the new Cranberry Bone with the Case silver script logo. We might call these collectible collaborations.

The Sowbelly pattern was a famous pattern in the Case line for more than 80 years, and has been sought ever since. That was then, and this is now. Case teamed with custom knifemaker Tony Bose on the Case Sowbelly, a three-blade folder with a choice of handle materials and Case logos.

Cold Steel

Lloyd Pendleton, a long-time custom knifemaker, designed two new knives in the Cold Steel line, namely the Pendleton Mini Hunter and the Pendleton Hunter. Both incorporate 3- to 3 1/2-inch AUS-8A stainless steel blades and Kraton® handles. Each model sits comfortably in its respective Secure-Ex sheath.

Columbia River Knife & Tool

Columbia River Knife & Tool is an Oregon-based knife company that seems to employ many of the best-known custom designers. The company has teamed with many. One such entrepreneur is Steve Ryan, and the relationship has resulted in the Ryan Model Seven. A California knifemaker, Ryan specializes in tactical folders, and is a student of Okinawa Go Gyo martial arts. The Model Seven is inspired by the Filipino barong, a strong and powerful work knife. A deep finger choil presents an exceptional grip, while the deep-bellied blade has plenty of cutting power.

The knife has a 3 1/2-inch AUS-6M stainless steel blade and 420J2 stainless steel liners. Torx fasteners are used throughout, while a black, textured Zytel® handle is skeletonized in Ryan's trademark zigzag pattern. CRKT has added the patented Ron Lake and Michael Walker LAWKS safety locking mechanism,

The most appealing aspect of the Ryan Model Seven from Columbia River Knife & Tool has to be the textured Zytel® handle, designed, as is the rest of the knife, by custom maker Steve Ryan.

so when locked open, the blade will not accidentally close under stress. The Ryan Model Seven weighs 5.7 ounces.

Crawford Knives

Pat Crawford's Carnivore folder does not exactly fit the "custom collaborations" category we are discussing here, but perhaps it does. Crawford, one of the premier custom knifemakers, designed his Carnivores for Round Eye Knife & Tool and has a license from them to make the knife

himself and use the company's patented Rolling Lock mechanism.

The 3.9-inch blade is available in damascus or ATS-34 stainless steel, the handle is Micarta®, and the liners are stainless steel. The knife is 8 inches long overall, and some models by Crawford feature ivory handle inlays.

Emerson Knives

Can a designer put his own knife into his own production line and draw attention to it? Ernest Emerson has accomplished that feat many times. The latest design from Emerson recently won the Overall Knife of the Year© award at the BLADE Show in Atlanta, Georgia. The Commander has a 3 3/4-inch 154CM stainless steel blade and a black or green G-10 handle. The knife measures 8 3/5 inches and weighs 5 1/2 ounces. The handle liners are titanium, and the blade may be ordered with either a satin finish or a "Black T" non-reflective coating. The Commander is already in use around the world by certain elite military organizations. It features

Here is what can happen when makers and manufacturers work as a team: The consumer is given the choice of an original, handmade knife, like the Pat Crawford models above, in a variety of styles and materials, such as ivory handle inlays (above at bottom); or a factory-made piece, as is the case with the Round Eye Knife & Tool Carnivore model, right, designed by Crawford for mass production.

The Emerson Knives Commander model commands attention for its hefty 5 1/2 ounces of G-10 and 154CM stainless steel combined with "Dragon's Teeth" blade serrations and a fast-opening "Wave" mechanism. Though relatively new, the knife is already in use around the world by certain elite military organizations.

the patented "Wave" opening mechanism and "Dragon's Teeth" blade serrations.

Gerber Legendary Blades

When Joseph Gerber founded Gerber Legendary Blades in 1939, the company made kitchen cutlery exclusively. Today, sporting knives are part of the regular fare, and like its competitors, Gerber has teamed with talented custom knifemakers to bring innovative designs. One such piece is the Gerber Harsey AirFrame, a collaborative effort with William Harsey on a locking-liner folder with a contoured cast-titanium handle, titanium liners and a 154CM blade. A removable titanium pocket clip completes the piece that comes in regular or serrated edges.

Gutmann Cutlery

Gutmann Cutlery has chosen the designs of Japanese maker Tak Fukuta for a lineup of outdoor-use knives including the Tak Fukuta Hunters. Three Hunter models rely on AUS-8 stainless steel blades in 3 1/2-, 4 1/8- and 5 1/4-inch lengths. Full tangs are complemented by a choice of textured sambar stag or dramatic ebony handles and leather

Gerber's version of a locking-liner folder is the AirFrame, designed by William Harsey to incorporate a contoured cast-titanium handle, a 154CM blade and a removable titanium pocket clip.

The Schrade SDH3 is the second D'Alton Holder-designed fixed blade offered by Imperial Schrade, this one with a stabilized maple burl handle, a BG-42 blade and a leather sheath in a basket-weave pattern.

sheaths. Fukuta's signature is on each blade and his trademark braided leather lanyard is included.

Imperial Schrade Cutlery

Imperial Schrade continues its relationship with longtime custom knifemaker D'Alton Holder and embarks on a new team effort with art-knifemaker Van Barnett. D'Holder is, among other things, a past president of The Knifemakers' Guild. The Schrade SDH3 begins with a polished BG-42 blade flowing in to a stainless steel bolster and a stabilized maple burl handle with forest green and gold accents. The piece fits nicely into a leather sheath in a basket-weave pattern

With over 50 knifemaking awards under Van Barnett's belt,

Take the design of Tak Fukuta, take a sambar stag or ebony handle and an AUS-8 blade, and put them together in a trio of hunters, and you have the Gutmann Tak Fukuta Hunters in three blade sizes, each fitted with a leather sheath and braided leather lanyard.

Schrade's teaming with the custom knifemaker wasn't as much of a risk as a challenge in attempting to reproduce the artist's fancy design. The Schrade/Barnett Knife has a stepped, natural-bone handle, maroon in color and accented by a 24-karat-gold-inlaid bolster with leaf-pattern engraving on a blued background. The ATS-34 blade and handle spine are fileworked and the blade lifter and shackle are also adorned with pure gold.

Joy Enterprises

The first Knifemakers' Guild show I attended was 25 years ago in Kansas City. The first custom knifemaker I met at the show was Mike Franklin, already a member of the Guild and a pioneer in designs and blade materials.

Joy Enterprises has joined with Franklin to produce his Hawg folders, knives with the most aggressive and awesome serrations of any knives I have seen. Each serration on the blade of the patent-pending design is like a blade in itself.

The Hawg features 440A stainless steel blades with titanium liners in colorful anodized aluminum, and Micarta® handles. The 4 1/4-inch blades are bead blasted or Teflon® coated with Franklin's signature and his HAWG logo. The knife design includes a lanyard hole and a pocket clip.

For those looking for something smaller, the Hawg Tooth folders include a lanyard so the knife can be worn on the neck or in the pocket. The 2-inch concave, curved blade is of 440A stainless steel, and the curved handle may be anodized aluminum or titanium in various colors with Micarta overlays.

Kershaw

Kershaw and Ken Onion go together, it seems, like, well, hamburgers and fried onions.

The Schrade/Barnett knife designed by art-knifemaker Van Barnett catches the eye with pure gold accents, an engraved bolster and a stepped natural bone handle.

The Mike Franklin-designed Joy Enterprises Hawg folders have the most aggressive and awesome serrations of any folding knives I have seen.

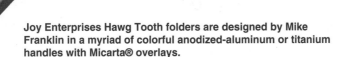

Joy Enterprises Hawg Tooth folders are designed by Mike Franklin in a myriad of colorful anodized-aluminum or titanium handles with Micarta® overlays.

The Onion-designed Random Task folder won the 1998 BLADE Magazine American Made Knife of the Year© award. The Random Task utilizes the Speed Safe mechanism, incorporating torsion bar technology for safe, assisted opening.

New to the scene this year is another, as Kershaw puts it, "fresh Onion," the Onion-designed Scallion with a textured Polyamide handle and a 2 1/4-inch 420 stainless steel blade. This piece, though smaller, also incorporates the Speed Safe assisted-opening mechanism.

Meyerco

One of the many Blackie Collins-designed knives from Meyerco is the Big Rascal folder. The knife uses a patent-pending locking-liner system and a lightning-fast, one-hand opening and closing mechanism. The Big Rascal has a 3 1/8-inch AUS-8 blade and a Fiberesin handle said to be "unbreakable," thus carrying a lifetime warranty on the folder. The knife is 7 3/8 inches overall and weighs 2.9 ounces. Blackie Collins, by the way, holds more than 60 patents on knife mechanisms.

Outdoor Edge

David Bloch of Outdoor Edge relies on several noted custom knife-makers as well as his own abilities for the Outdoor Edge designs. One such maker is Kit Carson, who made his first knife almost 30 years ago. The new Outdoor Edge Magna

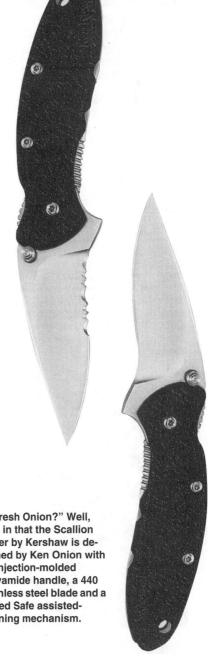

A "fresh Onion?" Well, yes, in that the Scallion folder by Kershaw is designed by Ken Onion with an injection-molded Polyamide handle, a 440 stainless steel blade and a Speed Safe assisted-opening mechanism.

A tough handle and an AUS-8 blade compose the bulk of the Meyerco Big Rascal designed by Blackie Collins, who holds more than 60 patents on knife mechanisms.

Kit Carson retired as a First Sergeant from the U.S. Army in 1993 and has been pounding out knives since the 1970s. His designs for Outdoor Edge include the Magna series of folders showcasing 4-inch AUS-9A blades and anodized-aluminum or black Zytel® handles.

series of folders features 4-inch AUS-9A blades and handle options of 6061-T6 anodized aluminum or black Zytel®.

The Magna knifes feature easy one-hand opening from either side, and a positive locking liner. The clothing clip sets flush in a recessed part of the handle to offer comfort when worn or carried in the pocket. Options include plain or half-serrated edges.

Spyderco

Spyderco for many years has combined the designs of dozens of well-known custom knifemakers from around the world with its factory production capabilities. Bob Lum has been producing fine custom knives for more than 25 years, bringing Oriental blade shapes to the forefront.

Spyderco's Bob Lum Chinese Folder features a 3 1/8-inch blade that is tapered like a leaf: broad, flat and thin along the edge. This leaf shape has been around for centuries in China and is ideal for general cutting chores at home or in the field. The blade is made of VG-10 stainless steel with an imperial jade green Almite-coated aluminum handle.

The blade of Spyderco's Bob Lum Chinese Folder is tapered like a leaf: broad, flat and thin along the cutting edge.

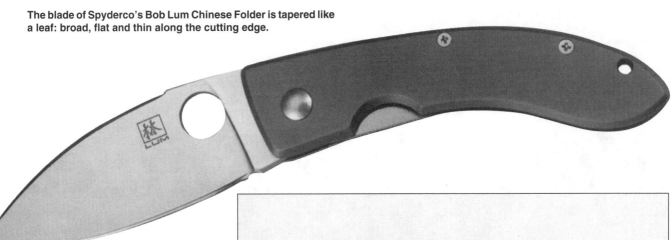

The nested LinerLock is plenty tough. The pivot pin is eccentric and adjustable for wear. The knife weighs 2 3/4 ounces and the blade edge may be all plain or serrated. The pocket clip may be moved to either end of the knife for tip-up or tip-down carry.

Timberline Knives

Timberline of New York has joined with Butch Vallotton of Oregon for the Millennium Lock folder. The 3.2-inch blade is AUS-8 stainless steel and the handle material is machined from a solid bar of 6061-T6 aluminum. The handle scales are hard-coat anodized gray. The knife body is assembled with Torx fasteners for easy disassembly and cleaning. The knife weighs 3 1/2 ounces.

The Millennium Lock is a spring-assisted opening mechanism that requires but a touch of the thumb to open with either hand. To unlock, the lock button is retracted and the blade will close. It is fast and smooth.

United Cutlery

United Cutlery debuts a full line of six locking-liner folding knife patterns by renowned custom knifemaker Fred Carter. The FC1 and FC2 folders have tempered stainless steel and T6 aircraft aluminum handles, respectively, and both make use of 440 stainless steel blades.

United Cutlery has teamed up with Fred Carter on numerous knives in the past, and the latest offerings are not disappointing. The FC1(top) and FC2 locking-liner folders give the consumer a choice of stainless steel or aircraft aluminum handles, and both have 440 stainless steel blades and skeletonized pocket clips.

Taking On Multi-Tool Knives

By Durwood Hollis

AS A CHILD, I remember my father saying he could fix "darn near anything" with a knife, pliers, a couple of screwdrivers, some electrical tape and a length of bailing wire (he might have wanted to include a sledge hammer for good measure). There wasn't a camping, hunting or fishing chore this basic set of tools couldn't handle. Sure, the tool assortment required a box for containment and made more noise in the automobile trunk than a rattlesnake with a bad attitude, but on more than one occasion, the old man put his basic tools to work solving a problem.

If Father were here today, he would appreciate the current lineup of factory-produced multi-tools. Each is decades beyond what Dad could have imagined, and every one of these unique units can handle as many tasks as a noisy box of pliers, knives and screwdrivers. The multi-tools of the new millennium depart dramatically from the tools of old in one particular department: compact packaging (no box required).

A new generation of tools has the ability to do it all in single, hand-held, fold-up, self-contained units that can be slipped onto a belt, clipped to a pocket and toted anywhere. Take a look at a sampling of this year's multi-tool lineup and see if there's something that tickles your fancy.

Small in stature but big in the tools category is the Boker Small Jaws Mini Tool that attaches to a key chain and features pliers, rulers, screwdrivers, bottle opener, plain and serrated knife blades, a fingernail file and a lanyard attachment loop. An equally small flashlight is optional.

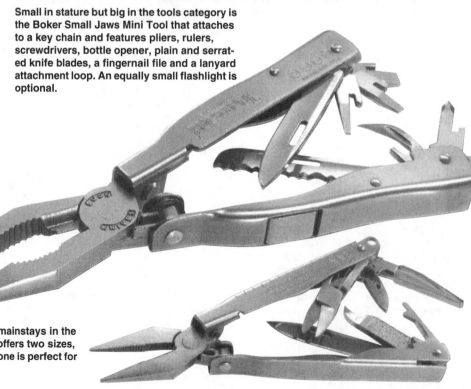

The BuckTool and MiniBuck Tool are two mainstays in the Buck line of knives and multi-tools. Buck offers two sizes, each housing 10 implements. The smaller one is perfect for key-chain carry.

Boker USA

This forward-thinking company debuts the Small Jaws Mini Tool (Model W12101) that can be attached to a key chain. Featuring 12 functions, this little wonder can fix "darn near anything." It includes pliers; English and metric rulers; large, small, standard and micro screwdrivers; Phillips screwdriver; bottle opener; plain and serrated knife blades; fingernail file; and lanyard attachment loop.

Measuring just 2 1/2 inches closed and weighing a mere 1.7 ounces, the Small Jaws Mini Tool is available with an optional and equally small flashlight (with battery). The number of times I've had to adjust loose eyeglass screws or fix computers, calculators and business office machines has been legion. In almost every instance, a little multi-tool like this would have resolved the matter in seconds.

Buck Knives

The BuckTool (Model 360) is a testimony to the enduring nature of a good design. Originally debuted in 1996, this multi-tool has remained virtually unchanged to date. Designed with 10 implements (needle-nose pliers, wire cutters, can and bottle opener, three flat screwdrivers, one Phillips screwdriver, non-serrated drop-point knife blade, fully serrated sheepsfoot knife blade and lanyard loop) incorporated into a versatile and reliable configuration, this tool continues to garner its share of the market.

Measuring 4 1/8 inches closed and weighing 7 ounces, the BuckTool is easily carried in a heavy-duty, black-nylon belt pouch. The MiniBuck Tool (Model 350), the smaller sibling, also employs 10 implements (needle nose pliers, scissors, drop-point knife blade, Phillips screwdriver, tweezers, nail file, bottle opener and cap lifter, metric and fractional scales and a lanyard loop), but the tool measures a mere 2 1/2 inches and weighs only 1 1/2 ounces.

Buck pushed the multi-tool envelope with the addition of an implement and blade locking system, and a more user-friendly handle design. I expect the design to remain a strong contender in this market.

W.R. Case & Sons Cutlery Co.

Well known for its extensive line of pocketknives, Case carries several models that could be classified as

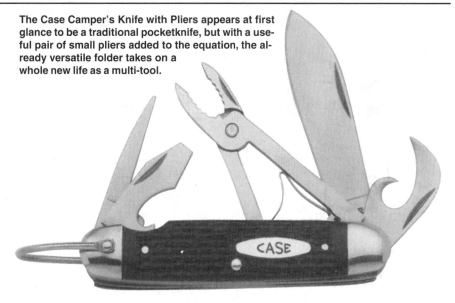

The Case Camper's Knife with Pliers appears at first glance to be a traditional pocketknife, but with a useful pair of small pliers added to the equation, the already versatile folder takes on a whole new life as a multi-tool.

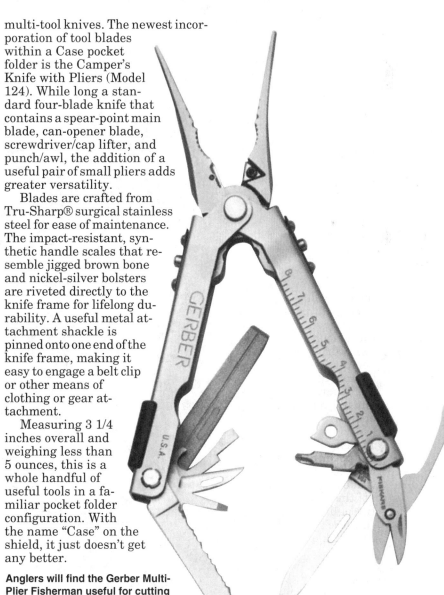

multi-tool knives. The newest incorporation of tool blades within a Case pocket folder is the Camper's Knife with Pliers (Model 124). While long a standard four-blade knife that contains a spear-point main blade, can-opener blade, screwdriver/cap lifter, and punch/awl, the addition of a useful pair of small pliers adds greater versatility.

Blades are crafted from Tru-Sharp® surgical stainless steel for ease of maintenance. The impact-resistant, synthetic handle scales that resemble jigged brown bone and nickel-silver bolsters are riveted directly to the knife frame for lifelong durability. A useful metal attachment shackle is pinned onto one end of the knife frame, making it easy to engage a belt clip or other means of clothing or gear attachment.

Measuring 3 1/4 inches overall and weighing less than 5 ounces, this is a whole handful of useful tools in a familiar pocket folder configuration. With the name "Case" on the shield, it just doesn't get any better.

Anglers will find the Gerber Multi-Plier Fisherman useful for cutting leaders, wire and fishing line, and a needle-nose pliers helps retrieve hooks from hard-to-reach places.

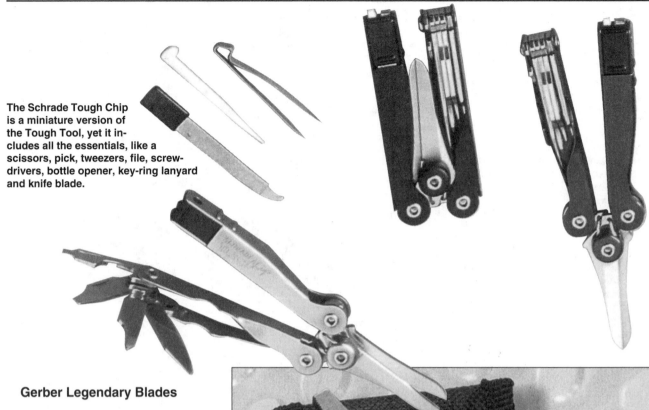

The Schrade Tough Chip is a miniature version of the Tough Tool, yet it includes all the essentials, like a scissors, pick, tweezers, file, screwdrivers, bottle opener, key-ring lanyard and knife blade.

Gerber Legendary Blades

Taking its famed Multi-Plier tool the next step, Gerber recently introduced the Multi-Plier Fisherman (Model 07572). The patented one-hand-opening pliers design is now configured into slender fisherman's needle-nose pliers. Within the jaws of the pliers are situated sets of tungsten-cobalt, steel-carbide wire cutters for maximum power when severing all types of steel fishing leaders.

Housed within the handles is a hook sharpener, a Fiskars scissors that cuts through both braided and fused fishing lines, and several other knife and tool blades that anglers will find useful. All tools feature independent rotation (only one component comes out at a time), and all implements lock open for safety. With all-stainless-steel construction, this multi-tool is an angler's dream come true.

Imperial Schrade Corp.

A compact, 10-function version of Schrade's larger Tough Tool, the new Tough Chip is a palm-size toolbox all by itself. The head is a set of heavy-duty scissors with reliable spring action for cutting ease. A pick, tweezers and file are housed in one handle and are designed for easy removal. The other handle holds flathead and Phillips screwdrivers, as well as a knife blade.

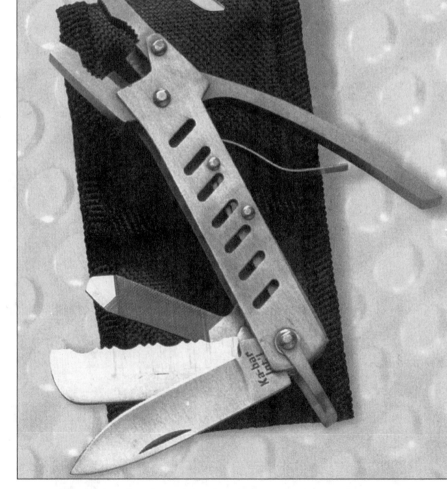

A stainless steel tool/knife, the Ka-Bar Multi-Tool is packed with useful implements, including drop-point and sheepsfoot knife blades, pliers, wire cutter, screwdriver, file and attachment shackle.

Additional implements include a small flathead screwdriver, bottle opener and key ring lanyard. Black, red, blue and green Tough Chips handles are also available to complement the standard stainless steel model. Personally, I keep one of these little "fix-it" tools attached to my fishing vest all the time, and I can't think of a better purse tool for the ladies. Indeed, this is a "chip off the old block."

Ka-Bar

Ka-Bar catalogs a Multi-Tool (Model 1307) that offers a number of useful features (pliers, wire cutter, screwdriver, drop-point knife blade, fully serrated sheepsfoot knife blade, file and attachment shackle). Made entirely from stainless steel, the tool measures 3 3/4 inches closed and can be carried easily in a Velcro® nylon belt pouch. A rugged performer, this tool can handle everything from minor auto adjustments to household repairs.

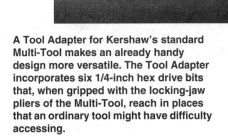

A Tool Adapter for Kershaw's standard Multi-Tool makes an already handy design more versatile. The Tool Adapter incorporates six 1/4-inch hex drive bits that, when gripped with the locking-jaw pliers of the Multi-Tool, reach in places that an ordinary tool might have difficulty accessing.

Kershaw

The recent addition of a tool adapter and a bit assortment to Kershaw's standard Multi-Tool enhances the functional capabilities of an already outstanding design. The Multi-Tool features 10 handy functions all contained in a tool configuration that measures 6 3/4 inches in length and weighs 8.6 ounces.

A drop-point partially serrated knife blade, hacksaw blade, wire cutter, two-sided file, slotted screwdriver, Phillips screwdriver, and can and bottle opener could only be complemented by one thing: a tool adapter. The Tool Adapter features six different 1/4-inch hex drive bits and can be purchased with the tool or separately.

By using the locking-jaw pliers function, the adapter adjusts for horizontal, 45-degree or 90-degree angle grips to reach places that an ordinary tool might have difficulty accessing. The entire tool is crafted from 440A stainless steel and supplied with a nylon or harness-leather sheath.

The adapter sheath hooks directly to the multi-tool sheath, or can be carried separately. With the new companion tool adapter, Kershaw's multi-tool is even more versatile. If you can't handle the problem with this multi-tool, there's a good bet that you'll need a mechanic and an entire workshop full of tools.

Leatherman

The colorful Leatherman Juice multi-tools pack a plethora of handy implements into 3 1/4-inch, color-anodized aluminum handles. The smallest model, the Juice C2,

Built in a rainbow of colors, five Leatherman Juice multi-tools are small enough to fit in a brief-case or backpack and come with a wide variety of tools, including screwdrivers, pliers, saws, awls, files, scissors, can and bottle openers, corkscrew and plain and serrated blades.

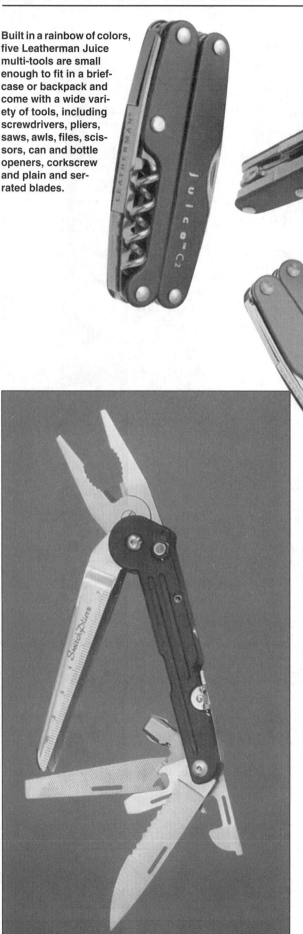

Here's a switch: the SOG SwitchPlier automatic pliers tool that springs forth with the push of a button and houses an assortment of tools, including a can opener, knife blade, file, screwdrivers, bottle opener and 1/4-inch drive.

combines the standard Leatherman needle- nose pliers with four screwdrivers, a can and bottle opener, knife blade and a corkscrew in a set of fiery red handles. A lanyard attachment allows this tiny tool to be easily joined to a zipper or key chain.

Next in size, the Juice S2 has a distinctive burnt-orange handle, and in addition to the pliers, comes with serrated scissors, can and bottle opener, four screwdrivers, and a knife blade. Also included is a lanyard attachment for ready access.

The luminescent yellow handle of the Juice KF4 sets it apart from its siblings. Within the handle scales of this tool, you'll find four screwdrivers, a saw, awl and diamond-coated file. It is provided with a choice of a plain or serrated knife blade, and of course, all of these tools are adjuncts to the rugged pliers that folds into a colorful handle.

Not to be left out, the glacier-blue handle slabs of the Juice CS4 contain four screwdrivers, saw, awl, serrated scissors, knife blade, can and bottle opener, and a corkscrew. Coupled with the pliers, this is a handful of useful tools.

The Outdoor Edge Sportsman's Multi-Tool is a dream come true for hunters who prefer to repair their own guns and bows, or for those who field dress game.

The final entry, the lovely purple Juice XE6, is jammed full of tool options in addition to the pliers, which include four screwdrivers, saw, awl, file, plain and serrated knife blades, serrated scissors, can and bottle opener, and a corkscrew.

The five Juice models have something that fits nearly everyone's lifestyle, and their small size and abundance of color allow the line of multi-tools from Leatherman to fit in anywhere, from briefcase to backpack.

Outdoor Edge

For the first time, this innovative cutlery company is entering the multi-tool market with its Sportsman's Multi-Tool (Model ST-100). The versatile tool features a heavy-

Don't take your eyes off the Spyderco SpydeRench: It might change into a new tool, including a knife, an adjustable wrench, a pliers, screwdriver and more.

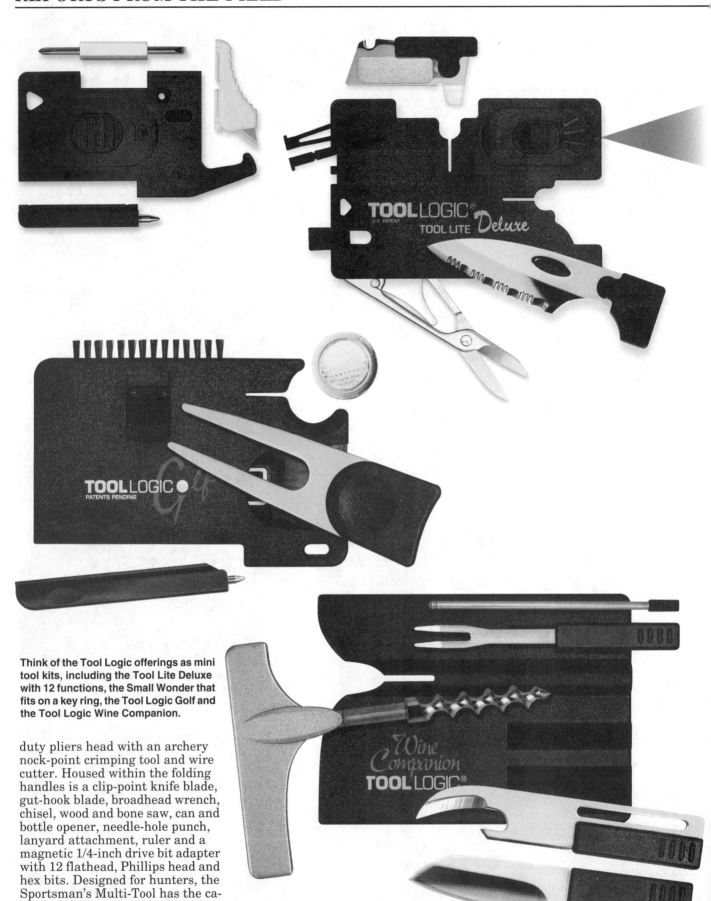

Think of the Tool Logic offerings as mini tool kits, including the Tool Lite Deluxe with 12 functions, the Small Wonder that fits on a key ring, the Tool Logic Golf and the Tool Logic Wine Companion.

duty pliers head with an archery nock-point crimping tool and wire cutter. Housed within the folding handles is a clip-point knife blade, gut-hook blade, broadhead wrench, chisel, wood and bone saw, can and bottle opener, needle-hole punch, lanyard attachment, ruler and a magnetic 1/4-inch drive bit adapter with 12 flathead, Phillips head and hex bits. Designed for hunters, the Sportsman's Multi-Tool has the capabilities to repair a bow or rifle, as well as field dress game. The tool and all bits are stored in a compact nylon case that fits on the belt. For hunters, especially bow hunters, it doesn't get any better than this handy toolbox for a belt.

SOG Specialty Knives

Touted as the "world's first automatic pliers," the jaws of the SOG SwitchPlier (Model SWPL76) spring into action with the push of a button. Just 4.2 inches overall when closed, this is the ultimate one-hand-opening multi-tool for a host of light to moderate "fix-it" assignments. The pliers are nestled within an aircraft aluminum handle, and the handle works off spring tension so when gripped along with the frame of the tool, each acts as opposite handles for the pliers.

Within the frame are five locking tool components (a can opener/small screwdriver, half-serrated knife blade, bottle opener/medium screwdriver, three-sided file/large screwdriver, and a 1/4-inch drive). All tools and blades, including the automatic-opening pliers, are made of stainless steel. Supplied with a form-fitted nylon pouch sheath and an attachment clip, the tool weighs just 5 1/2 ounces. An extraordinary tool for ordinary chores, the SwitchPlier is definitely a friend when you're in need.

Spyderco, Inc.

Recently, the folks at Spyderco entered the multi-tool market with the new SpydeRench (Model T01). This is a full-size, locking, one-hand opening and closing knife with a 440C stainless steel blade, a pocket clip and much more. The tool can be configured as an adjustable wrench, or as a two-setting, slip-joint pliers. Tucked inside is a set of four screwdriver bits that can be inserted into the 1/4-inch drive port. The SpydeRench includes an extended bit with a flat and Phillips head screwdriver for access into tight places. Available in a PlainEdge, SpyderEdge or a combination blade, this is truly a revolutionary multi-tool.

Tool Logic

Typically, we think of multi-tools as something based on a set of pliers, or integrated into a knife frame. Realizing that tools are a vital part of our everyday life, the folks at Tool Logic have come up with a way to miniaturize tools and combine them in an easily carried configuration.

In the mid-1990s, Tool Logic created the first fully functional credit-card-size tool kit. Now, an entire line of compact multi-tools is being intro-

duced. Every imaginable tool grouping, from the tiny Small Wonder (Item KR1B) that fits on a key ring, to the Tool Lite Deluxe (Item SC25B) with 12 separate tool functions, is now available for customers.

The Tool Logic Golf (Item GT1SB) tool combines a stainless divot tool, ball marker, groove cleaner, nylon brush and grip rest into credit-card-size containment. For the wine taster, the Wine Companion (Item WC1B) places a stainless corkscrew, foil cutter, olive fork and can and bottle opener in a similar wallet-size package. The super-thin tool containment offers maximum utility with the use of minimum space. Weighing just a tad over 1 ounce and easily carried in a wallet or purse, there is no excuse for not making one of these Lilliputian tool kits part of your own personal accouterment.

United Cutlery

New for this year, United has added the Pocketech (Model UC1247) multi-tool to its

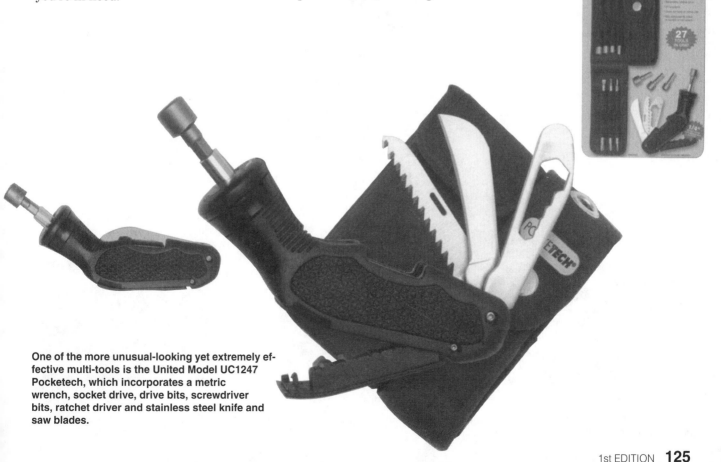

One of the more unusual-looking yet extremely effective multi-tools is the United Model UC1247 Pocketech, which incorporates a metric wrench, socket drive, drive bits, screwdriver bits, ratchet driver and stainless steel knife and saw blades.

knife lineup. Featuring 27 functions and an assortment of blades and other tools, this pocket tool has more applications than imaginable in a small package. Included are a metric wrench with a ruler on the side and a prying tip, seven socket drive bits, three Phillips screwdriver bits, two standard screwdriver bits, sheepsfoot knife blade, saw blade and reversible ratchet driver that mates with all of the tool bits. For ready access, the tool bits are contained inside an angled Zytel® handle. Blades are made from 420 stainless steel, so it shouldn't rust. Obviously, the designers of this multi-tool took a good idea and pushed it well beyond the ordinary.

Victorinox

New for 2001, the Victorinox SwissCard® is available in several colors, including translucent green, blue and black models. No larger than a credit card, the multi-tool contains a tiny fixed-blade knife, scissors, nail file, toothpick, tweezers and ball-point pen. All tools, including the knife blade and scissors, are stainless steel, and each is replaceable if lost. A tool for a shirt pocket or wallet, for the backcountry or boardroom, the tiny SwissCard is indispensable for everyday life. One of many specialty tools and knives made by "The Original Swiss Army Knife" company, the SwissCard is one credit card that doesn't come with a monthly fee, headache or bill.

Wenger

Most multi-tools are centered around a pair of pliers, with the handles carrying the accessory tool assortment. Taking a different approach, Wenger uses the basic Swiss Army Knife frame to create its own MiniGrip and SwissGrip tool

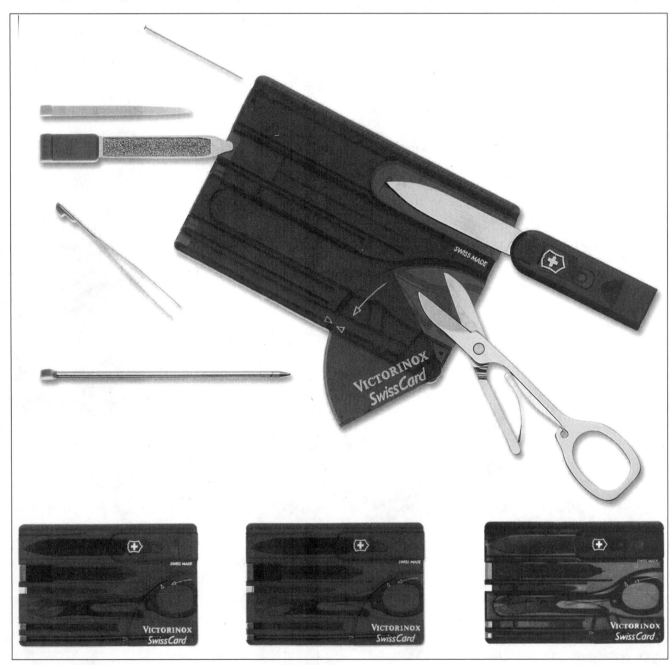

A credit card with no monthly fee, the Victorinox SwissCard more than pays for itself, incorporating a tiny fixed blade, scissors, nail file, toothpick, tweezers, straight pin and ball-point pen.

knives. The MiniGrip comes in two configurations—flat (Model 16467) and needle-nose pliers (Model 16466).

Both designs offer 15 implements with 24 functions (large serrated knife blade, pliers, wood saw, straight edge ruler, three magnetized Phillips head and three flathead screwdrivers, a removable screwdriver bit adapter extension, recessed bit adapter, metal file, metal saw, locking screwdriver, cap lifter, wire stripper; can opener, reamer and awl).

Made from stainless steel with the traditional red Swiss Army Knife handle, either configuration is its own hand-held tool kit. The somewhat larger SwissGrip® (Model 16568) has 13 implements (a 4-inch locking clip-point knife blade, flat-nose pliers with wire cutter, wood saw with straight edge, screwdriver/socket adapter for 1/4-inch bits, two Phillips head extra-hard bits, slotted power screwdriver bit, socket adapter for the 1/4-inch adapter, recessed bit adapter, Phillips head screwdriver, metal file/saw, locking screwdriver with cap lifter and wire stripper, and reamer/awl with sewing eye). Supplied in a ballistic-nylon pouch, this is a multi-tool with serious intentions. Leave it up to the Swiss to come up with a solution to the world's problems, especially those needing a little fixing. Any one of these tools will be a welcome addition to the tackle box, glove compartment or hunting gear kit.

The Bottom Line

Many of the small problems of daily life just don't seem to get fixed. Away from the convenience of home and the local hardware shop, where tools are readily available, what's at hand must be used to resolve the situation. If that solution is a multi-tool, then most minor fix-its can be handled with ease. If not, then one can resort to my father's old knife, pliers, screwdrivers, tape and bailing wire assortment. It comes down to a choice of a boxful or handful of tools. Personally, I've already done the boxful-of-tools routine once too many times.   ●

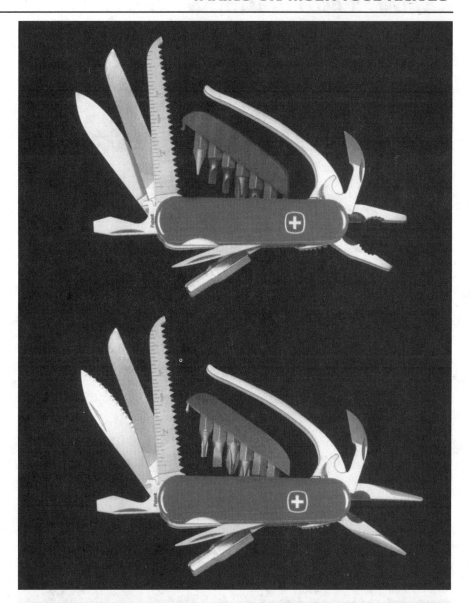

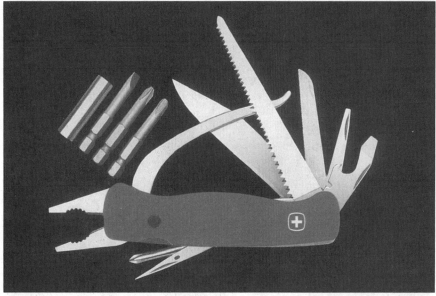

Wenger hopes you'll grip on to the MiniGrip Flat-Nose (with a flat-nose pliers, top), Mini-Grip Needle-Nose (center), or the slightly larger SwissGrip, which has 13 implements, including a 4-inch clip-point blade with a safety lock.

Sporting Folders

By Durwood Hollis

IN A CUTLERY era focused heavily on "tactical" knife design, it is gratifying that we outdoor sports enthusiasts haven't been totally forgotten. Moreover, much of the leading-edge technology witnessed in tactical folders has finally made its way into the sporting folder market. New blade steels offer enhanced resistance to harmful elements, and the use of rugged thermoplastic handle materials has gained acceptance with many traditional sporting knife users. Design features—one-hand-opening thumb studs for sporting folders, full and partial blade serrations, and heat-molded synthetic sheaths—have all made significant inroads in the sporting knife market. A look at a selection of this year's new sporting folders should stimulate even the most conservative knife user to have a serious case of the "got-to-have-its."

Knife writer and hunter Durwood Hollis gives his sporting folder suggestions for outdoor enthusiasts, with a tendency toward those folders that will "enhance the hunt."

Boker USA

Always on the leading edge of production, Boker introduces the Gemini Badger (Model 90X) to the sporting folder market for 2001. Sportsmen have something to celebrate in X-15 stainless steel, appar-

Lightweight and durable, the Boker Gemini Badger features a black handle with a black Kraton® insert, a partially serrated X-15 stainless steel blade and a belt clip.

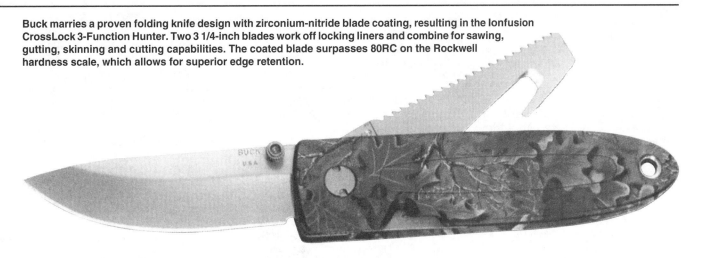

Buck marries a proven folding knife design with zirconium-nitride blade coating, resulting in the Ionfusion CrossLock 3-Function Hunter. Two 3 1/4-inch blades work off locking liners and combine for sawing, gutting, skinning and cutting capabilities. The coated blade surpasses 80RC on the Rockwell hardness scale, which allows for superior edge retention.

ently a more stain-resistant alternative to the "wonder steels" available today, yet it maintains the same cutting power of 440C and ATS-34 stainless.

The blade features an elongated clip pattern with a slight wedge on the back. A portion of the blade near the base has been serrated for added cutting enhancement, and a thumb stud permits rapid one-hand blade access. The durable molded handle has a Kraton® insert for enhanced grip, and the side lock secures the blade in the open position. Measuring just 4 3/4 inches closed, the knife weighs a slight 3.2 ounces. An excellent choice for hunting needs, from basic field care to skinning, this Boker offering is right on target.

Buck

Combining advanced technology with a functional outdoor design is manifest in Buck's Ionfusion Cross-Lock 3-Function Hunter. The hollow-ground, drop-point main blade is 420HC stainless steel, stretches 3 1/4 inches, and works off a locking-liner system. The companion blade of the same length operates on a second locking liner, showcases gutting and skinning features, and exhibits a saw-tooth blade spine for cutting through bone and cartilage.

The handle design makes it easy to roll the closed knife in the hand to access either of the two blades, one recessed in one side of the handle, and the other in the opposite side. Pegs on both blades facilitate one-hand opening with slight thumb pressure. The Advantage Classic Camo handle has a rubber insert for superior control.

Best of all, Buck has fused zirconium nitride to the 420 HC stainless

steel blades, resulting in surfaces so hard they surpass 80RC on the Rockwell hardness scale. This process allows the blades to retain their edges, according to Buck, for at least five times longer than blades without the coating.

The slick nature of the Ionfusion allows blades to slide through any cutting medium with little resistance. Working off a proven folding hunter design and combined with this new blade coating, the Ionfusion CrossLock Hunter has even more of the "right stuff."

W.R. Case & Sons Cutlery Co.

Yellow-handle knives are a classic tradition with Case Cutlery. In fact, Case has been producing pocket folders with brightly colored handle scales almost as long as the company has been in business. New for 2001 is the Model 120 Fishing Knife with brilliant yellow scales.

This handy angler's folder contains two blades — an elongated (Turkish) clip and a scaler/hook remover blade — both of which are crafted from Tru-Sharp stainless steel. Based on a medium Texas Toothpick design, the

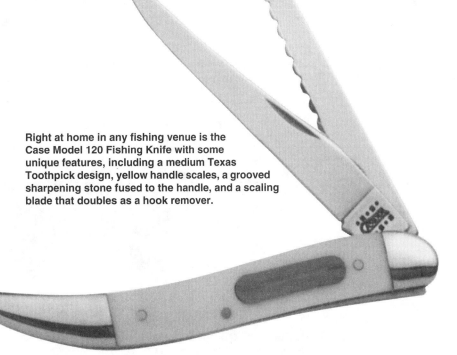

Right at home in any fishing venue is the Case Model 120 Fishing Knife with some unique features, including a medium Texas Toothpick design, yellow handle scales, a grooved sharpening stone fused to the handle, and a scaling blade that doubles as a hook remover.

knife measures 4 1/4 inches closed and weighs just 2.6 ounces.

To ensure fishhooks are always sharp, a grooved abrasive stone has been fused to one of the yellow handle scales. Additionally, should the Fishing Knife fall into tall grass or brush alongside a favorite fishing hole, the handle will stand out like a beacon. Definitely a hardworking design, it's right at home in any fishing venue.

Cold Steel

Newly redesigned, Cold Steel's Voyager series of Zytel®-handle lock-back folders incorporates at least one model hunters will enjoy. The Large Voyager® features a 4-inch, hollow-ground, clip-point blade, with a plain or partially serrated edge that is slightly wider than most blades, and ground extremely thin at the edge for added shearing potential.

The cutting surface is continuously curved along its entire length for the best possible slicing action. A double thumb stud positioned at the base of the blade provides ambidextrous one-hand-opening capabilities.

The molded Zytel® handle is more oval-shaped and thicker than other folders, allowing for increased strength and stiffness, and the aggressive handle texture ensures integrity and better blade control. A handle-mounted, stainless steel clip gives users the option of wearing the Large Voyager on the belt, or at the edge of nearly any article of clothing. An appropriate design for the hunter, the improved ergonomics of this handy folder are hard to beat.

Gerber Legendary Blades

Riding a wave of enthusiasm for the well-received Gator folders, Gerber introduces the Stud Gator (Model 06909). The 3 3/4-inch, ATS-34 blade is outfitted with a one-hand opener for easy access. A soft Kraton® handle is wrapped around a rugged Zytel® frame, and the molded handle material provides a secure grip, even when covered in grime. In keeping with the advanced design, the blade pivot pin and handle fasteners are precision machined for a tight and long-lasting fit. Combining the best features of previous Gator folders with partial edge serration and a convenient one-hand-opening thumb stud, the Stud Gator excels in design, performance and user comfort.

Imperial Schrade Corp.

Collaborating with knifemakers Ron Lake and Michael Walker in the new millennium, Schrade has introduced the Schrade Lake & Walker folder, and perhaps with more fanfare, the Tough Lock. Schrade touts the Tough Lock as the safest, most reliable locking system extant. The arc-shaped lock is built to provide maximum surface contact with the blade tang, which in theory offers the ultimate in strength. Even after years of use,

Cold Steel's Large Voyager offers sportsmen a 4-inch hollow-ground, clip-point blade ground extremely thin for added shearing potential.

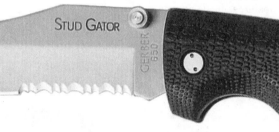

The "stud" of the Gerber Gator line may well be the Stud Gator, a departure from earlier Gators with the addition of a thumb stud for blade-opening ease, and partial edge serrations.

a precision bevel in the tang should ensure the lock's integrity. As an additional safety feature, the knife has a secondary sliding safety switch.

The Lake & Walker folder delivers a 2 7/8-inch, drop-point BG-42 blade, and BG-42, I might point out, is a steel initially employed in jet engine bearings. Reaching 60-62 RC on the Rockwell hardness scale, the high-tech steel has enhanced edge-holding capabilities to handle a variety of field chores, including primary field dressing and skinning of big game.

All pins and screws, as well as the back spacer, ferrule and pocket clip, are crafted from titanium for lightweight and dependable performance. The handle scales are a new material, Zylite®, which is a combination of Zytel® and Kevlar®.

In this writer's opinion, the sophisticated blending of materials produces one of the best high-performance folding knife handles on the market. The blending of the creative genius of two known and respected knifemakers with the production capability of a leading cutlery manufacturer, has produced one of the most innovative and unique pieces of sporting cutlery I've seen in a long time.

Ka-Bar Knives, Inc.

New for 2001, the Ka-Bar D2 Extreme folder incorporates many proven military and tactical knife features into a user-friendly sporting knife theme. Utilizing D-2 carbon steel for maximum toughness and edge retention, the blades in this knife series have been hardened to a Rockwell of 59-60RC. The lightweight, hard-anodized handle scales are crafted from aircraft-grade aluminum with horizontal handle grooves positioned for enhanced control.

While there are several different blade options, my pick for hunting use would be the drop-point (Model 4051) blade configuration. The 3-inch blade is fully hollow-ground, featuring 1 1/4 inches of serrations near the base. A removable pocket clip provides for a variety of carrying positions.

D-2 carbon steel is a great choice for tough work assignments and is often overlooked by many unfamiliar with its performance features. While this blade steel takes a little more care than stainless, nevertheless, it is tough to beat in a field knife.

Kershaw Knives

It's hard to know where to start when reviewing Kershaw's lineup of new products. If I had to select a single knife, however, it would have to be the new Elk (Model 1560RM) lock-back folder. Designed by custom knifemaker Ken Onion, this piece features a 440A, black, titanium-nitride-coated blade. A utilitarian-sized, 3 1/4-inch clip-pattern

blade sports a thumb stud at the base for easy opening, and the molded Polyamide handle is molded with integral positive texturing for a better grip. A handle-mounted pocket clip eliminates the need for a sheath or carrying case. Specially designed to help benefit the Rocky Mountain Elk Foundation, a portion of each sale of the Elk goes toward facilitating the habitat conservation projects of the organization. A fine,

The Schrade Lake & Walker is born from the minds of knifemakers Ron Lake and Michael Walker in cooperation with Imperial Schrade. The resulting high-tech folder premieres the Tough Lock to keep the blade open under extreme pressure, and an additional safety switch in the unlikely case of blade disengagement.

big-game blade with a special purpose: Kershaw can well be proud of this folder.

Knives of Alaska

Big-game trophy hunters like myself have often speculated about how nifty it would be to have a folding caper. Well, that dream has finally come true. Recently introduced by Knives of Alaska, the Alaskan Super Cub was, according to company president Charles Allen, "designed specifically to provide the hunter with a folding caping knife."

The 2 1/2-inch VG-10 stainless steel blade is built in a delicate, scalpel-like drop-point pattern. Double finger choils, top and bottom, provide an alternative gripping surface for delicate work.

The knife itself measures just 4 1/4 inches closed and employs a locking liner to secure the blade in the open position. A blade-mounted opening stud provides ready access and can be switched to either side for right- or left-hand use.

The space between the frame liners is completely open, making it easier to clean off by-products like blood, fat and sinew after the caping work is completed. Knives of Alaska gives a choice of a G-10, carbon fiber or rubber "Suregrip" handle.

The nice thing about VG-10 steel in this folding caper, compared to many other stainless steels, is that it offers enhanced edge retention and solid toughness. Trophy work is tough on any blade edge while constantly butting up against bone. Edge corrosion is an omnipresent threat.

Furthermore, VG-10 is tough enough to handle the intense pressure that's often applied to the cutting edge when removing the skin from an animal skull. Personally, this design leaves other caping knives far behind in functional application and cutting performance. Need I say more?

Kopromed USA

While on a church mission in Poland, Ray Simonson discovered the Kopromed cutlery factory. At the time, it was a small manufacturing facility with only a handful of cutlers, but the knives they produced were striking in appearance and remarkable in performance.

Made from 440C stainless, with a Rockwell hardness of 56-58RC, modern Kopromed blades are manually ground and mirror polished.

Though the Ka-Bar D2 folder is available in four blade shapes, including clip-point, drop-point, tanto and spear-point, hunters will no doubt gravitate toward the drop-point, hollow ground blade of high-carbon D-2 steel with 1 1/4 inches of serrations near the base.

A folding caper is an unusual but sought-after knife pattern, and Knives of Alaska has built a winner with a VG-10 partially serrated blade and a choice of a G-10, carbon fiber or rubber "Suregrip" handle.

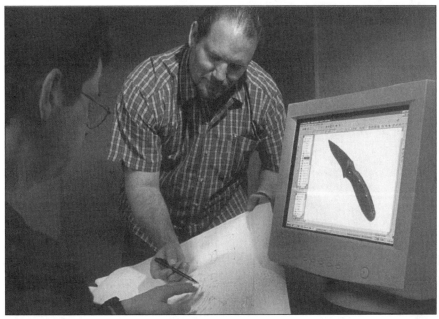

Custom knifemaker Ken Onion teamed with Kershaw Knives on the Elk model specifically designed to benefit the Rocky Mountain Elk Foundation. With a titanium-nitride-coated blade and a Polyamide handle, the Elk also benefits hunters and outdoorsmen.

Typically European in design, most of the company's Polish-made knives are fixed blades.

My pick of the lot would have to be the sole lock-back folding design (Model 23). Featuring a drop-point blade mated with stainless bolsters and a beautiful set of red stag handle scales, this folder speaks loudly of its hunting heritage. The same knife is available with African hardwood handle scales, and with or without stainless bolsters. While Kopromed has been specializing in the exclusive manufacture of hunting knives for many years, the recent entry of these fine knives into our domestic cutlery market is a welcome event.

Outdoor Edge

Designed by custom knifemaker Kit Carson, the new Outdoor Edge Magna line (Models MA-10/10S and MZ-10/10S) of lock-back folders offers the choice of cold-forged alumi-

The Kit Carson-designed Outdoor Edge Magna is defined by a 4-inch AUS-8A, clip-point blade, a double thumb stud and an ergonomically designed handle.

num or molded-Zytel® handles. Each Magna is a robust, full-size folder that can tackle all game cares and outdoor needs with ease. The AUS-8A stainless steel, clip-point blade reaches 4 inches and opens easily by means of a double thumb stud. Available with a plain or partially serrated edge, each Magna model features an inner-frame blade locking mechanism. The grooved, ergonomically designed handle provides user comfort and blade control. An outstanding choice for hunters, the high-tech design has distinct advantages that make it just right for field use.

Remington

Interestingly enough, during the first part of the last century, Remington was this country's leading manufacturer of cutlery. However, its knifemaking efforts gave way during World War II to the production of military hardware, and the Remington mark continued to be absent from the cutlery market until recently.

Now, using modern materials and production methods, this famed manufacturer of firearms is once again in the knife business. Introduced this year as a continuing part of its "Bullet" knife reproductions, the 2001 Mariner Bullet Knife is one of the most unique in the series.

The only lock-back folder in the Kopromed line, the Model 23 red-stag-handle, drop-point hunter provides stainless bolsters and a 440C stainless steel blade for an altogether polished look.

The slender folder begins with a single, 3 1/2-inch locking, elongated clip-point, stainless steel blade flowing into a celluloid tortoiseshell handle, striking in appearance, and offset by the nickel-silver bolsters, liners, pins, and the hallmark "Bullet" shield. Measuring just 5 inches closed, this trim beauty is an angler's dream come true. If you want one, better hurry. Collectors are sure to see the value in this recent Remington release.

Spyderco

Spyderco joined forces with custom knifemaker Bob Terzuola to come up with a lock-back folder that serves a broad user base, including big game hunters. The Starmate (Model C55G) features a blade crafted from CPM 440V stainless steel with a modified clip-point pattern and a top swedge. This hollow-ground blade offers a 3 5/8-inch cutting edge, which is just the right length for basic big-game field chores.

Of course, the trademark Spyderco hole in the blade is part of the overall design, and slim handle scales are made from molded, premium black G-10 for enhanced strength and a positive grip. Interestingly, the lock incorporates a precision ball bearing detent to se-

cure the blade open and closed. Extremely powerful, yet lightweight, this knife fits well into any hunting venue.

United Cutlery

New for 2001, United brings the Henckels pocketknife line to American shores. Since 1731, the Henckels Zwilling (Twin Brand) has been a symbol of handcrafted cutlery. Made with strict quality control standards, these knives are the "best of the best" German-made pocket folders.

My pick of the sporting models would have to be the Premium Lockback Series (Model HK120). There are three knives in this series, each with different handle scales (European gunstock walnut, red jigged bone, or green jigged bone).

The 3 1/8-inch, clip-point 420 stainless steel blades lock open for

safety, while double-end bolsters and liners are made from gleaming brass. The familiar Henckels twin mark can be found on circular nickel-silver shields. Each knife is serially numbered and comes with a black felt storage pouch. A proven hunting knife design, the smooth lines of this lock-back folder will bring grace and dignity to hunting camps everywhere.

The 2001 Remington Mariner Bullet Knife is the latest in a series with Remington's hallmark "Bullet" shield. A slender folder, the Mariner Bullet Knife sports an elongated clip-point, stainless-steel blade and a celluloid tortoiseshell handle.

A hollow-ground CPM 440V stainless steel blade with a top swedge anchors the Spyderco Starmate designed by Bob Terzuola in a modified-clip-point pattern and complemented by a G-10 handle for strength and positive grip.

United Cutlery offers three Henckels German lock-back folders in European gunstock walnut (top), and red or green jigged bone handles. Each features brass bolsters, a nickel-silver handle shield and a 420 stainless steel, clip-point blade.

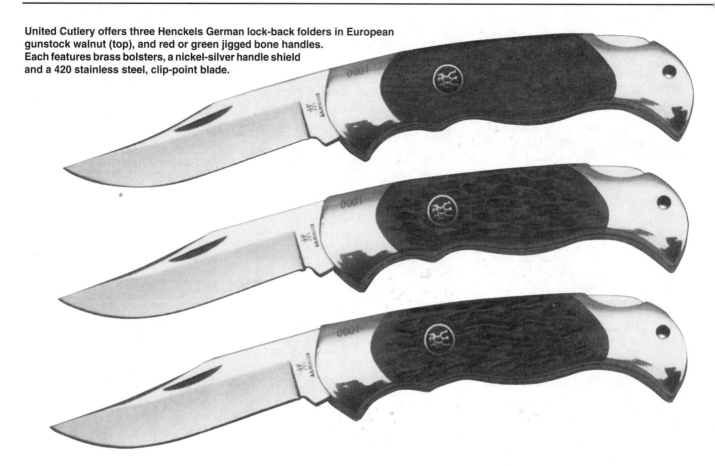

Wenger

The famed "Genuine Swiss Army Knife" company has always offered a welcome handful of useful edges and tools for the sportsman. In its extensive line, Wenger showcases models that are applicable to most popular forms of outdoor recreation. In-line skaters, snowboarders, skiers, backpackers, fishermen, travelers and even cigar smokers (definitely an outdoor sport!) all have their pick of edged tools. My own selection would have to be the Serrated Mountaineer knife that features seven implements with 10 functions.

The main clip-pattern blade is 4 inches long, locks open for safety, and features a serrated portion that is useful in difficult cutting mediums. A double-cut wood saw, can opener, locking screwdriver, Phillips head screwdriver, wire stripper, reamer and awl with a sewing eye are also part of the package.

Rather than the traditional red handle, this oversize model has black thermoplastic handle scales. Capable of handling nearly everything—from gutting a buck to tightening a fishing reel screw — this knife is my idea of an invaluable outdoor tool.

The Final Cut

Like many sporting knife users, I am always looking for a better "way to go." As knife designs and materials evolve, the "better way" results in stronger, lighter and more user-friendly cutting tools. Such advancements have emerged into a competitive marketplace that combines quality craftsmanship with superior materials at an affordable consumer price point. In truth, the new millennium has begun with premier sporting knife introductions. What the future holds is sure to set the market ablaze with even more revolutionary cutlery developments. •

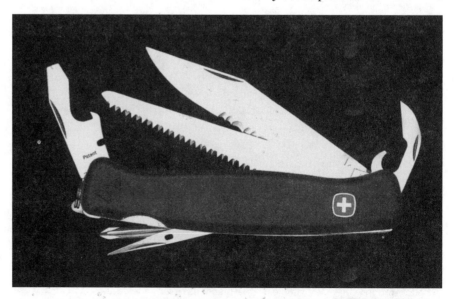

The Serrated Mountaineer is a welcome addition to the Wenger knife line of "Genuine Swiss Army Knives" with a clip-point blade, double-cut wood saw, can opener, locking screwdriver, Phillips head screwdriver, wire stripper, reamer and awl.

Sporting Fixed Blades for the New Millennium

By Jack Edmondson

AMID A SPATTERING of hunters, the dominant trend in sporting fixed blades for 2001 (as with folders) is toward tactical, personal-defense knives, often designed by some prominent knifemaker in collaboration with a knife company.

Al Mar Knives

Some two decades ago, former Green Beret and martial artist Al Mar revolutionized the knife industry when he introduced his massive S.E.R.E. (Survival-Evasion-Resistance-Escape) folding knife, perhaps one of the first, if not the first, tactical folders. Mar also offered several scaled-down models of the folder and two sizes of fixed blade SERE fighters. Since Mar's death in 1992, the Al Mar Knives line has undergone significant changes, the focus shifting from fixed-blade fighters to a dominant emphasis on lightweight folding knives.

Last year saw the introduction of the SERE 2000 folder, and new for this year, AMK has continued to meld old and new traditions with the release of the SERE Operator. Like the new SERE folder, the fixed-blade Operator essentially qualifies as a streamlined reincarnation of its SERE ancestors. It maintains the distinctive SERE profile, scaled down to just over 10 inches and weighing only 6 ounces. The 5-inch spear-point blade is manufactured from ATS-34 steel with a 59-60RC Rockwell hardness rating.

Textured G-10 serves as the material for the handle scales attached to and covering a full tang. This new SERE fixed blade is intended for the personal defense market, but its universal styling lends itself to almost any general purposes.

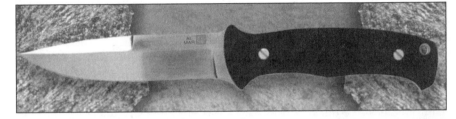

Fixed to cut is the Al Mar SERE Operator, a meld of old and new traditions into a streamlined profile, scaled down to just over 10 inches and weighing only 6 ounces. The spearpoint ATS-34, full-tang blade is anchored by a textured G-10 handle.

This year, AMK will introduce a second fixed blade, the Nomad, designed for the hunter. The result of a collaboration with American Bladesmith Society master smith Kirk Rexroat, the Nomad will feature a 4 1/4-inch drop-point blade of AUS-8A steel, and an ergonomically styled handle.

Bear Cutlery

For 2001, Bear Cutlery has released new variations of four of their popular fixed-blade patterns: the small Upswept Hunter and Drop Point Hunter, both 6 1/2 inches in overall length; the 8-inch Professional Guthook Hunter; and the 9 1/2-inch Professional Hunter with an upswept

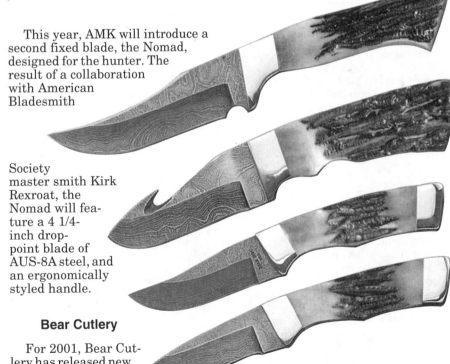

"Unique as a thumbprint," claims Bear Cutlery of each damascus blade of the deluxe models of four fixed blades with red-stag handles. From top are the Professional Hunter with an upswept blade, the Professional Guthook Hunter, the small Upswept Hunter and the Drop Point Hunter.

blade. These full-tang hunting knives are still manufactured using original specifications, with 5/32-inch-thick blades of high-carbon, 440 rust-resistant steel, nickel bolsters and oak handle scales. However, this year they are offered with Camo Wood and Genuine Red Bone Stag handles.

Moreover, all four models are now available in deluxe versions with damascus blades, all hafted with Red Bone Stag scales, and produced in limited quantities. The folks at Bear Cutlery proclaim the damascus process to be a combination of steels in different properties to produce blades with extraordinary toughness and edge-holding ability. The pattern on each is said to be "as unique as a thumbprint."

Benchmade

The latest fixed blade resulting from the collaboration between Benchmade and knife designer Allen Elishewitz is the Model 100 R&R. A cousin to last year's drop-point Model 140 Nimravus, the Model 100's initials stand for "River Rescue," and it incorporates a modified sheepsfoot blade for safe tip control on the water. The GIN-1 stainless blade measures 3.23 inches and is hardened to 58-60RC on the Rockwell hardness scale. The knife is balanced by a rugged, black G-10 handle and a full tang, and equipped with a form-fitting, Kydex® thermoplastic sheath with an innovative thumb-toggle release that can be worn inverted if desired.

Boker USA

Boker has introduced several new fixed blades for 2001, including the fourth in a series honoring the late Col. Rex Applegate. With a limited production of 300 pieces, the Damascus Applegate Mini Smatchet sports a 4 3/4-inch double-edge blade crafted from 180 layers of stainless damascus. The blade is mounted with a nickel cross-guard and grooved rosewood scales, and the knife is packaged in a wood presentation box with a certificate of authenticity.

For those who want a using Smatchet, Boker has a new, full-size version with a 10-inch, satin-finished 420 Solingen stainless steel blade, an integral guard and tang, and a lightweight, polycarbonate handle. It fits in a Cordura® sheath.

Col. Applegate is again remembered in the new Operation Leopard

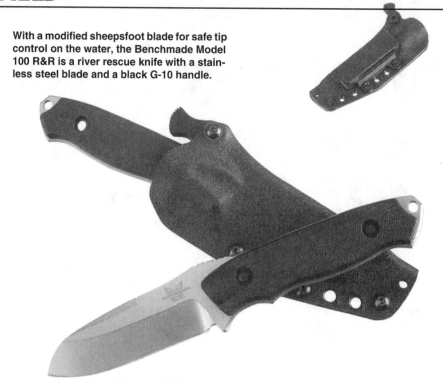

With a modified sheepsfoot blade for safe tip control on the water, the Benchmade Model 100 R&R is a river rescue knife with a stainless steel blade and a black G-10 handle.

fighter based on an original Applegate-Fairbairn combat design. The knife, limited to 999 pieces, commemorates the French Foreign Legion's 2nd Parachute Regiment and its 1978 rescue of 3,000 Europeans held hostage in Zaire. It features an etched 6-inch double-edged Solingen stainless steel blade, an olive-drab Delrin® handle and a stainless cross-guard.

The Orca Dive Knife was made according to recommen-

dations from the German Special Forces with a 3 3/8-inch clip-point, virtually rustproof, black-titanium-coated X15 T.N steel blade that reportedly withstands even the corrosive effects of seawater. The back edge is serrated, and

Only 300 Damascus Applegate Mini Smatchets will be produced by Boker to honor the late Col. Rex Applegate. Each features a 4 3/4-inch double-edge, 180-layer damascus blade, a nickel cross-guard and a grooved rosewood handle.

Boker's Operation Leopard fighter is based on an original Applegate-Fairbairn combat design and honors the French Foreign Legion's 2nd Parachute Regiment and its 1978 rescue of 3,000 Europeans held hostage in Zaire.

there is a false edge along the back of the blade for chopping. With an injection-molded handle and a tactical sheath, it is equally effective for land or sea operations, and is being considered as standard issue for the German GSG-9 elite forces.

Buck Knives

This year, Buck's most significant addition to its regular catalog is the DiamondBack, a universal drop-point fixed blade showcasing a 420HC stainless steel blade, and a synthetic black handle textured to replicate the pattern of a diamondback rattler's skin. The DiamondBack is available in two sizes sporting either a 4 1/4-inch or 3 1/4-inch blade. Both are equipped with a heavy-duty nylon sheath.

Several exciting new fixed blades have been added to Buck's Limited Edition line. The Chuck Buck Signature Knife is a traditional outdoor and hunting knife with a sleek, 4-inch blade of ATS-34 steel hardened to 59-61RC and showcasing the signature of Chuck Buck. The full-tang knife features a single quillon guard and handle scales of resin-impregnated Obechee wood stained to an oak finish. It comes with a genuine leather sheath, a limited edition box, and a certificate of authenticity. The first 2,000 are serial numbered.

The Damascus Dagger utilizes a 3-inch, double-edged blade exhibiting a swirling damascus pattern. The full-tang model is mounted with Bahama Cherrywood handle scales, and the knife is displayed in a glass-top, blackwood box and is accompanied by a certificate of authenticity. The first 500 are serialized.

Two more limited edition knife models are aimed at the sportsman and collector. The Vanguard Deer Profile features a 24k-gold deer laser cut into and through the 4 1/8-inch, hollow-ground, drop-point blade of Buck's popular Vanguard knife model. The box elder handle is mounted with a brass guard and pommel, and the butt is decorated with a laser cut deer head. The knife comes with a brown leather scabbard, also embossed with a deer head, a limited edition box, and a certificate of authenticity. The first 1,000 are serialized.

In that same vein, the Mini-Mentor Elk Profile displays the laser cut profile of an elk within its 3 1/2-inch

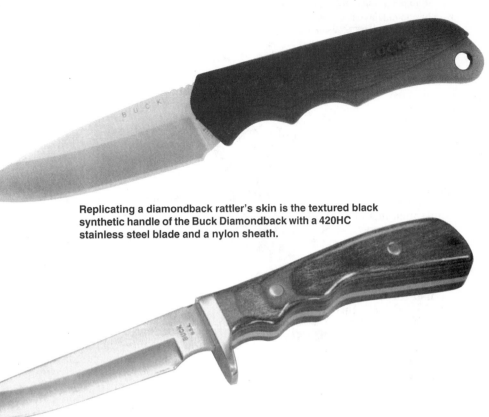

Replicating a diamondback rattler's skin is the textured black synthetic handle of the Buck Diamondback with a 420HC stainless steel blade and a nylon sheath.

The Chuck Buck Signature Knife is a traditional outdoor and hunting knife with a sleek, 4-inch ATS-34 blade showcasing the signature of Chuck Buck (not shown), and an Obechee wood handle.

Two new Buck fixed-blade hunters, the Vanguard Deer Profile and Mini-Mentor Elk Profile, incorporate blades laser cut in the likeness of deer and elk profiles. Wood handles and brown leather sheaths complete the packages.

As the name implies, the Camillus Bush Hog is one massive knife with a 14-inch blade and a molded, glass-filled thermoplastic handle. The piece is part of the Becker Knife & Tool division of Camillus.

drop-point blade, and an elk scene is lasered into the oak scales. It comes with a brown leather sheath embossed with the full body of an elk, and a limited edition box.

A rosewood-handle version of the Vanguard is one of two fixed blade knives that Buck has just added to their Ionfusion series. The other is Buck's most popular sheath knife, the bowie-like Model 119 Special. This version of the Special sports a 6-inch clip-point blade with a blood groove, a brass cross-guard and pommel, and a rosewood handle.

In the Ionfusion process, zirconium nitride is molecularly bonded to the 420 blade steel to create an edge surface that surpasses 80RC on the Rockwell hardness scale, the top rating on the scale. Buck boasts that the treatment allows the knife to hold an edge at least five times longer than a standard blade.

Camillus

"CUDA," which stands for Camillus Ultra Design Advantage, is the name Camillus gave to its deluxe knives, and under that banner, the company debuts two knives in the Talonite series. Talonite is a high performance, cobalt-chromium alloy designed for extreme high-stress applications, as in saw tips, deep earth drills, and high-speed scraper blades. Camillus boasts that it is the "finest knife blade material available" because the edge holding ability is unparalleled and it will never rust or corrode.

Custom knifemaker Robert Simonich, a pioneer in the application of Talonite as a blade material, designed the Talonite series for the CUDA division of Camillus. The Talon features a 3 3/4-inch, flat-ground, drop-point blade hand finished in the Camillus custom shop. The ergonomic handle bears contoured and grooved G-10 scales. A hand-molded, multi-position Concealex® pouch sheath accompanies the knife. Although it has a tactical appearance, Camillus pragmatically promotes the Talon as the "ultimate personal fixed blade knife" whose design and profile lend it to a myriad of work-knife chores like skinning, boning, and light utility work.

The Mini Talon retains all the same features scaled down to a 2 1/4-inch blade. It is supplied with a molded Kydex® necklace sheath.

Becker Knife & Tool is another division of Camillus. Wilderness survival instructor and tactical trainer Ethan Becker designed this award-winning series of sturdy- yet-economical outdoor edged utensils. The newest addition is the Bush Hog, a massive machete with a deceptively lightweight 14-inch blade of 0170-6C high-carbon steel. The ergonomic handle is molded Swiss GV6H, a 60 percent glass-filled, thermoplastic polymer alloy for the ultimate in strength and durability. The Bush Hog comes with a Kydex® multi-carry sheath with a rugged black epoxy finish.

Cold Steel

The folks at Cold Steel have been busy releasing new models and revamping

The SafeKeeper II and SafeKeeper III push daggers from Cold Steel combine Kraton® handles, bead-blasted blades and Secure-Ex sheaths with belt and boot clips.

Pared down to its bare essentials is the Cold Steel Spike with a sub-zero-quenched 420 stainless steel blade and a cord-wrapped handle.

Cold Steel's ODA and OSS fixed blades take advantage of classic knife designs with modern materials, including integral Kraton® handles, guards and sub-hilts, and 420 stainless, sub-zero-quenched blades.

Cold Steel re-issues the Outdoorsman, an 11-inch AUS-8A fixed blade with a Kraton® handle and a leather sheath. This newest version of a proven design incorporates two improvements: a chopping edge on the blade spine, and a grooved thumb and finger rest for better indexing and control.

old ones. One of the newest, the Spike, is designed by Barry Dawson with a 4-inch, 420 stainless steel blade that is sub-zero quenched. Flat ground to a zero edge, the Spike reportedly provides a cutting ability previously unknown in such a thick, narrow blade. The knife comes with a Secure-Ex sheath and a steel-bead lanyard for securing it to the neck, body or equipment. A tanto blade version is also available.

While Cold Steel continues to utilize a black-epoxy-powder coating to protect many of its Carbon V blades, the 420 sub-zero-quenched stainless steel models are made with a bead-blast finish. These include the serrated 5-inch clip-point Desperado with an innovative egg-shaped Kra-

ton® handle that allows the knife to perform as either a push dagger or a conventional boot knife. It comes with a "Quick Draw" Secure-Ex sheath with a boot and belt clip.

The SafeKeeper series of modern push daggers also features the new bead-blast finish, including the Safe-Keeper II, which employs a 3 3/4-inch double-edged blade, and the Safe-Keeper III, with a 2 1/2-inch single-edged blade. Both come with Kraton® handles and Secure-Ex sheaths with belt and boot clips.

Two economical variations of Cold Steel's premium fighters were added this year. The R1 Military Classic was Cold Steel's homage to the Randall Model 1. The new ODA possesses virtually the same profile,

but whereas the 7-inch, satin finished, clip-point blade on the R1 was AUS-8A stainless, the ODA utilizes bead-blasted 420 stainless steel. The R1's stainless cross-guard and black Micarta® handle have been replaced on the ODA with an integral Kraton® handle and guard. Although these modifications were done to produce a less expensive knife, the Kraton® handle is more comfortable and more secure in the hand, especially under adverse circumstances.

Cold Steel's OSS is a similarly economized version of the Black Bear Classic, Cold Steel's replica of a Bob Loveless Big Bear Bowie. As on the Black Bear, the double-edge, clip-point blade of the OSS measures 8 1/4 inches, and the characteristic sub-hilt is incorporated into the integral Kraton® handle.

A third knife in this series of bead-blasted 420 stainless fighters with Kraton® handles, the UWK re-

Columbia River Knife & Tool employed the design skills of knifemaker Al Polkowski, best known for tactical fixed blades, on the Polkowski/Kasper Companion with an injection-molded polyoxymethylene acetal handle ergonomically sculptured and textured for a non-slip grip.

Ideal for general use is the Gerber Gator XCP with a traditional clip-point blade (left), and a perfect candidate for field dressing large game is the Gerber XGH with a gut hook.

interprets the famous SOG knife design from the Vietnam era. The distinctive triple-ground, concave, clip-point blade measures 6 1/2 inches. All three knives in the series come with Secure-Ex sheaths.

From its outset, Cold Steel was a company that concentrated on combat and survival knives. Its earliest concession to the general sportsman was the Outdoorsman tanto. This year, in

response to popular demand, Cold Steel has resurrected that model and added a few refinements. It still features a 6-inch AUS-8A blade, a nickel guard and pommel, and checkered Kraton® handle; however the blade spine of the Outdoorsman is grooved near the handle for better indexing and control. There is also a chopping edge ground into the blade spine so the primary edge can be reserved for basic

slicing. As with the original issue, the new Outdoorsman is supplied with a black leather sheath.

Also for the sportsman, Cold Steel has introduced the Pendleton Hunter, which faithfully reproduces the design and flowing lines of custom knifemaker Lloyd Pendleton. The Lloyd Pendleton Hunter features a 3 1/2-inch, hollow-ground, drop-point blade of AUS-8A, and a

▶Gutmann Cutlery releases the Junglee Special Forces knife, blending a matte Teflon®-coated AUS-8A blade with a black Kraton® rubber handle for an all-black, stealth look.

▲ A sleek, black oxide-coated blade and a black-canvas-Micarta handle team for an all-black, stealth look on the Gerber Yari with a molded Concealex sheath.

checkered Kraton® handle. It comes equipped with a Secure-Ex sheath. The Lloyd Pendleton Mini Hunter is virtually identical but scaled down to a 3-inch blade.

Columbia River Knife & Tool

"I wanted a knife that the average person could carry," proclaims knife-maker Al Polkowski, best known for tactical fixed blades that have result-ed from his collaboration with writer and instructor Bob Kasper. Their lat-est fixed blade, just released by Co-lumbia River Knife & Tool, is the Polkowski/Kasper Companion.

Its dimensions were chosen for convenience, utility, and strength. The full-tang, AUS-6M blade is 3.56 inches long, 1/4-inch thick, and hardened to 55-57RC. It comes plain or serrated and flows into an in-jection-molded, polyoxyme-thylene acetal handle ergonomically sculp-tured and textured for a comfortable, non-slip grip.

The Companion comes with two injection-molded Zytel® sheaths, one for pants or trouser carry with a clip, and the second multi-purpose sheath with slots and holes that per-

Defining versatility is the Walther Hammerhead by Gutmann Cutlery. It has a pommel built for hammering, a blade spine with saw teeth for sawing, and a straight 440A cutting edge. The handle is fashioned from textured Kraton® for a secure grip.

Gutmann offers the Walther Tactical Knife with a fierce spear-point blade, a partially serrated spine, and a textured Kraton® handle. The knife is packaged with a rapid-deployment sheath.

mit the knife to be lashed to packs and equipment in various ways.

Gerber Legendary Blades

This year, Gerber has expanded its Gator series to include three fixed-blade hunters. The Gator XDP features a shallow drop-point design, perhaps the most popular blade style among hunters today. A traditional clip-point blade, ideal for general use, defines the Gator XCP, and the Gator XGH sports a gut hook that makes it an effective field dressing tool for large game.

All three fixed-blade Gators have high-carbon stainless steel blades, and molded rubber handles with glass-filled polypropylene cores, creating a grip that remains soft and tacky, even when wet. The Gator sheaths are constructed of ballistic nylon with molded inserts for safety.

Continuing its long tradition of producing fine fixed-blade tactical and survival knives, Gerber has introduced the Yari. The sleek, single-edge 154CM blade stretches 4.87 inches and is heat treated to 59-61RC. The black oxide-coated blade is bead-blasted for a non-reflective finish, and complemented by a black canvas Micarta handle. The Yari comes with a molded Concealex sheath designed to provide multiple carrying options.

Gutmann Cutlery

The Junglee Special Forces Knife is Gutmann's new fixed blade aimed at the tactical and personal defense market. A matte-gray Teflon® coating covers a 4 3/4-inch, AUS-8A, clip-point blade with a partially serrated edge. Fabricated from soft Kraton® and symmetrical in shape, the handle provides a comfortable, secure, and versatile grip. The ballistic nylon scabbard can be clipped to the boot or belt or attached to a shoulder harness.

Gutmann has modified and expanded its graceful Junglee Tak Fukuta line of signature hunting knives. The Tak Fukuta Hunter, with its slim 4 1/8-inch blade, has proved so popular for Gutmann that the company has added a small and large version. The Tak Fukuta Small Hunter features a 3 1/2-inch blade, and the Tak Fukuta Large Hunter boasts a 5 1/4-inch blade. All three Fukuta knives utilize AUS-8 steel and are handled in elegant ebony with brushed nickel bolsters. Each is delivered with a full-grain leather sheath and Tak Fukuta's trademark braided lanyard.

As part of its new Walther line of knives, Gutmann introduces the Hammerhead. Named for its flat, hammer-shaped pommel, the Hammerhead strives to match the ferocity of its namesake with a 4-inch 440-A blade with a reinforced nose/tip and sinister saw teeth lining the clip-point. Behind the bead-blasted cross-guard extends an ergonomic handle made of textured Kraton® to afford a secure grip whether working with the blade or the ham-

Ka-Bar's Black Recurve and Black Tanto fixed blades remain faithful to the original Short Ka-Bar designs, but the Black Tanto features a 5 1/4-inch tanto-shaped blade ideal for penetration, and the Recurve, an S-curved edge that facilitates slicing.

The Black Warthog and Black Tanto from Ka-Bar are all-black, hollow-ground fixed blades with contoured Zytel® handles and ballistic nylon sheaths.

mer pommel. The knife is available in two blade variations: satin finished or gray Teflon® coated. It comes with a ballistic nylon sheath rigged for the boot, belt, or shoulder harness.

The Walther P99 Tactical Knife sports a 5 1/2-inch 440C spear-point blade with a steel cross-guard and Kraton® handle. The knife is equipped with a sheath specially designed for rapid deployment.

Those who favor a small, lightweight, slender knife for easy concealment may prefer the Walther Solace. Flat and simplistic, the Solace has a 3 1/2-inch 440A blade with thumb serrations on the back and a para-cord-wrapped handle. It comes in a Kydex® sheath with a belt and boot clip and more para cord for securing the knife to gear or around the neck.

Going on safari? Take the Walther Jungle Tool. The double-stitched 8-by-4 1/2-by-2-inch ballistic nylon pouch contains almost everything necessary for a trek up the Amazon or into darkest Africa. There is a stainless steel shovel and pick (17 1/2 inches long when attached to the aluminum shaft and Kraton handle), a knife with a 4 5/16-inch spear-point blade with saw teeth along the blade spine, and stored within are a fishing line and hooks, slingshot, bandages, razor blade, matches, sinkers, finger splints, sewing needle, safety pins, cutting cable and pencil.

Ka-Bar Knives

Ka-Bar has introduced seven new fixed-blade knives. The Korean War 50th Anniversary Commemorative is a deluxe version of the military knife that became synonymous with the company name. All the original features are there. The 7-inch clip-point blade with blood groove is manufactured from 1095 high-carbon steel and epoxy powder coated to provide a matte-black surface. The oval handle is fabricated from polished and grooved leather washers and framed by a blackened cross-guard and butt cap. However this anniversary model features a special "Lest We Forget" logo that has been pad printed onto the blade. The knife is available with either a U. S. M. C. or U. S. Army-embossed brown leather scabbard.

Ka-Bar has added two new knives to its Short Ka-Bar series of scaled-down variations of its namesake knife. Both retain the black epoxy powder coating on blade, cross-guard, and butt cap, as well as the grooved, oval handle, but with Kraton® G thermoplastic elastomer substituted for the stacked leather washers. The Black Tanto features a 5 1/4-inch, tanto-shaped blade that is ideal for penetration. And the Black

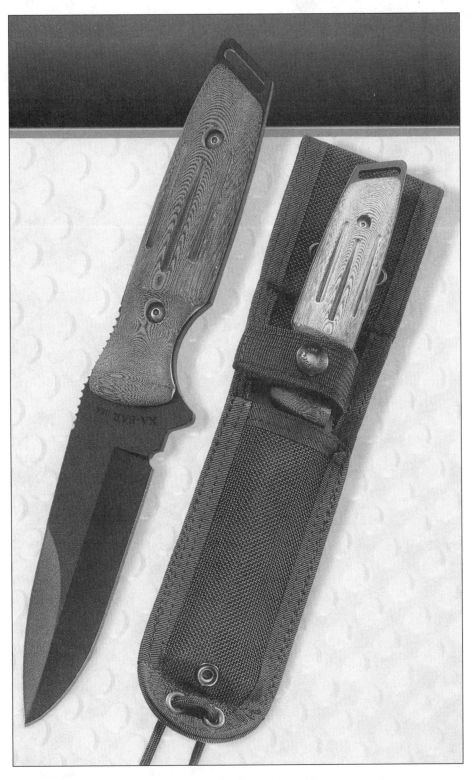

A member of Ka-Bar's Impact series is the D-2 Spear Point with a heat-treated, deep frozen and double-draw tempered D-2 tool steel blade and a contoured Micarta® handle.

The curve on the AUS-8A blade of the Kershaw Echo leads nicely into an ergonomic, contoured and checkered Polyamide handle.

The fully serrated blade of the Kershaw Barramundi Fillet Knife is a bit stouter than most fillets, and slides into a black sheath that matches the grooved, non-slip handle.

Recurve has an S-curved edge that facilitates slicing. Each model is available with a choice of a black leather scabbard or a black Kydex® sheath.

For the sportsman, Ka-Bar has introduced its Impact Series, consisting of the 3 7/8-inch Spear Point, the 4 5/8-inch Tanto, and the 3 5/8inch Warthog, a chunky clippoint. All three have 1095 high-carbon steel blades heat-treated to 56-58RC, contoured Zytel® handles, and ballistic nylon sheaths with molded blade inserts.

The versatile spear point model also comes in a deluxe version, manufactured from D-2 steel that has been heat treated to 59-60RC, deep frozen to 120 degrees Fahrenheit, and then double draw tempered. This model is mounted with gray Micarta® scales.

Kershaw Knives

The Echo is a nifty new drop-point hunter designed for Kershaw Knives by custom maker Ken Onion. The 4-inch, AUS-8A, recurved blade leads into an ergo-nomic, contoured and checkered Polyamide handle. The whole works fits into a leather harness sheath.

The Barramundi Fillet Knife expands Kershaw's products for the angler. The 6-inch, 420-J2 blade, a bit stouter than on most fillet knives, is fully serrated and slides into a

Puma releases a fearsome foursome of hunting knives with full tangs, integral guards and stag handles.

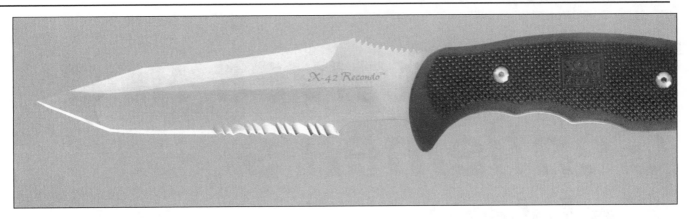

The SOG X-42 Recondo blends elements of a tanto, a clip-point fighter and a hunter into its 5.3-inch blade for a radically modern design.

black sheath that matches the grooved, non-slip handle.

For heavier chores, the new Camp Axe is made from one solid piece of drop-forged, high-carbon steel. It has a Kraton® handle and comes with a leather sheath.

Puma

This year, Puma introduced a new generation of full-tang, integral-guard, stainless hunting knives mounted with stag horn handles that straddle the line between traditional and modern design. The Buddy features a laser-cut design through the thumb ramp portion of a 3-inch, trailing-point blade. The Skinner II retains the same lines, and cutout, expanded to a 4 3/4-inch blade. A slender 6-inch clip-point blade characterizes the Bowie II, while the Hunter's Pal II has a 4-inch flaring spear-point blade.

Aimed for the collector, Puma promotes its new Golden Stag as "Knife of the Year" for 2001. The deluxe hunter has a 3 1/2-inch stainless damascus blade, a cutout pattern at the ricasso of an elk antler, brass bolsters and a stag handle.

SOG Specialty Knives

The Scuba/Demo, the latest addition to SOG's tactical line, also harks back to the traditions of the military elite Studies and Operation Group from which the company derived its name. The Scuba/Demo was the rarest of the Vietnam SOG knives. Only one original is known to survive today! The SOG knife company has replicated that lone survivor, adding just a few improvements to enhance quality and functionality.

The 7 1/4-inch blade — .230-inch thick! — is made from AUS-8A steel with a Rockwell hardness rating of 57-58RC. The spear-point blade is double-edged with a serious serration extending along most of the back. Stacked-leather washers form a handle wedged between a brass cross-guard and pommel. A black leather sheath with sharpening stone, lanyard and a letter of authenticity accompany the knife. The first 250 will bear serial numbers.

Although named for the MACV Recondo School established during the Vietnam War to train Special Forces units, the new X-42 Recondo blends elements of a tanto, a clip-point fighter, and a hunter into its 5.3-inch blade to produce a radically modern design. The BG-42 blade with a Rockwell hardness rating of 62-64RC incorporates cutting serrations along the rear half of the edge and thumb serrations on the back for control. The checkered Zytel® handle scales attach to a full tang and contribute to a handle designed for maximum control. The Recondo is supplied with a Kydex® sheath that is military-belt and jump rated, as well as being quiet, self-draining, and secure. ●

Pocketknives and Gentlemen's Folders

By Jack Edmondson

THE TREND OVER the past decade in folding knives has been in the tactical genre, with one-hand locking-liner folders dominating the field. Poor old Daddy's pocketknives were relegated to a corner. Sooner or later, the tides had to turn, and turn they did toward "higher-end tacticals." What does that mean? Well, instead of all-black tactical folders with indestructible handles, more modern versions were appearing with pieces of pearl or ivory added to black handles, gems set in thumb studs, or filework cut into blade spines. The term "gentlemen's folder" became readily accepted, and lo-and-behold, regular old working pocketknives, though fancied up a bit, seemed desirable again. Or, perhaps they always were desirable, just not fashionable. By the looks of the following, they're back in fashion.

Bear Cutlery

Never having given up on pocketknives is Bear Cutlery, which made its fair share of black-handle folders, but also stuck to tried, true and traditional designs. Bear presents a high-tech, 4-inch Side Liner Lock with an ATS-34, clip-point blade, and the most impressive feature, a colorful, lightweight, metal handle with a skeletal stainless steel overlay and attached pocket clip.

Premiered for the pocket is a series of Camo Wood Lockbacks. The five single-blade folding hunters in

A colorful, lightweight metal handle with a skeletal stainless steel overlay and attached pocket clip dress up a Bear Cutlery ATS-34 folder named Side Liner Lock.

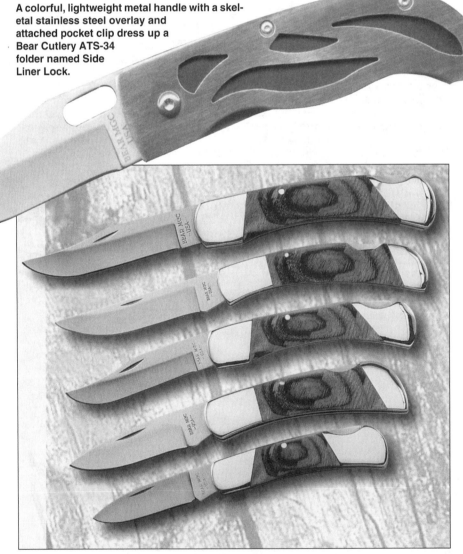

Traditional Bear Cutlery lock-back folders are fancied up a bit with the company's laminated Camo Wood handle material.

this series have laminated Camo Wood scales mounted between nickel silver bolsters. They range in size from 3-5 inches.

Another new handle material is genuine Red Bone Stag. Bear has utilized it on most of the knife patterns it makes, from the tiny 2 3/4-inch, two-blade Peanut, to the 5-inch single-blade Professional Lockback folding hunter.

The genuine Red Bone Stag is the only handle material available on every one of Bear's deluxe limited series of Damascus Steel folders, which encompasses most of Bear's patterns. However, three of the smaller single blade damascus lockbacks can be acquired with mother-of-pearl scales.

Benchmade

Best known for tactical knives, Benchmade has utilized the talents of several prominent knifemakers to boldly venture into the gentleman's knife market. The elegant Model 335 Big Spender Money Clip Gent Folder, designed by Mel Pardue, is intentionally thin with no added scales on the 3.4-inch 410 stainless steel liners.

The comfortably flat side clip is intended to hold money rather than fasten to the pocket. The Model 335 features a 2.3-inch drop-point blade with thumb stud. Blade steel is ATS-34 hardened to 59-61RC on the Rockwell hardness scale.

Bob Terzuola designed the Model 450 Park Avenue Gent Folder, a distinguished locking-liner that sports a 2.68-inch BCI (boron carbide) charcoal-color blade with thumb stud. The blade is 154CM stainless steel, and a 6061 T-6 aluminum handle, anodized to an industrial gray, rounds off the piece. A classy silver chain with lapel hook is attached to the handle.

The Model 770 Axis Gent Folder, designed by Warren Osborne, incorporates Benchmade's ultra-smooth AXIS locking mechanism. The 2.8-inch drop-point blade with dual thumb studs is made from 154CM stainless hardened to

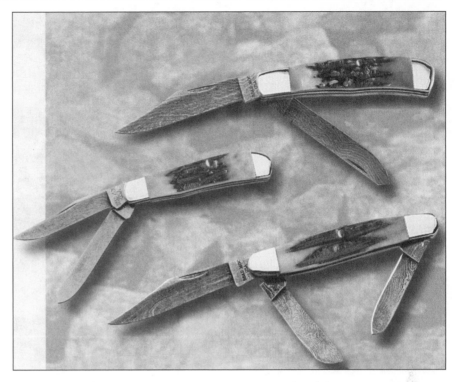

Genuine Red Bone Stag is the only handle material available on every one of Bear's deluxe Damascus Steel folders.

59-61RC. The 3.75-inch handle displays textured scales of black carbon fiber with a removable belt clip.

The distinctive Model 690 Folder, an Allen Elishewitz design, showcases a 4.12-inch handle with black carbon fiber bolsters, stabilized rosewood scales, double blue-anodized titanium liners, and removable pocket clip. The 154CM blade is two-toned with thumb stud but also available in a gray boron-carbide coating for dramatic effect and corrosion resistance.

A classy silver chain and lapel hook help hold the Benchmade Model 450 Park Avenue Gent Folder. It has a charcoal-color boron carbide blade and 6061 T-6 aluminum handle, anodized to an industrial gray. Bob Terzuola designed the Model 450.

Rosewood handle scales bounce off the stark-black carbon fiber bolsters of Benchmade's Model 690 Folder designed by Allen Elishewitz.

Boker USA

Boker's annual 2001 Damascus Knife combines the talents of master forger Manfred Sachse with the classic lines of a Boker lock blade. The 3 1/4-inch drop-point blade, made from 300-layer, hand-forged damascus steel, is set off by exotic Amboyna scales mounted with nickel silver bolsters. Limited to 999 serialized pieces, the knife comes with presentation case and certificate of authenticity.

The 2001LTD A Space Odessey locking-liner folder is another limited edition from Boker with a planetary scene etched on a striking blue, anodized-aluminum handle. A 2 3/4-inch, 440C, drop-point blade is etched with the name of the knife and supports a thumb stud. The knife comes in a presentation box.

Boker breaks through the clouds with the 2001LTD A Space Odyssey locking-liner folder with a planetary scene etched on a striking blue, anodized-aluminum handle.

The new Gemini Badger locking-liner folder utilizes a 3 3/8-inch drop-point blade with partial serration and thumb stud. As with the other knives in the Gemini series, the XI 5 T.N surgical tool steel blade is reportedly more rust-resistant than any other stainless steel on the market. Boker pledges it still yields the same cutting power as 440C or ATS-34 steels. The blade folds into a 4 3/4-inch handle with Kraton® insert and pocket clip.

Buck Knives

Buck has provided a wide variety of new offerings for 2001. For the outdoorsman, the company has expanded its NXT series of high-tech locking liners by adding a partially serrated version. The NXT knives feature 2 3/4-inch drop-point blades with thumb slots for one-hand opening. The 3 1/2-inch handles are composed of black, skeletonized Dynaflex rubber secured to a glass-reinforced nylon base colored blue, red or cobalt.

The Bucklite line has grown with the addition of the new BuckLite II lock-back folder featuring thermoplastic handles in aqua, cobalt or red. All three lightweight outdoor knives have 2 3/4-inch drop-point blades with partial serrations and thumb buttons.

With the new little Hitchhikers, Buck has adapted the mountain climber's carabineer to a practical use on a small folding tool. The carabineer clip allows the 2-inch, two-tone stainless steel frame to be attached to a belt loop, purse strap, or backpack. One version holds a 420J2 stainless drop-point knife blade. A second has a pair of scissors. And the third model houses a nail file and tiny cuticle blade.

Buck has introduced several new folders intended for everyday use. The smaller of the two new Access lock-back models features a 2 1/4-inch, high-tech, modified drop-point blade made from Buck's standard 420HC steel. It folds into a sweeping, contoured handle of injection-molded, glass-filled thermoplastic. The larger Access boasts a 3-inch blade and has a pocket clip added to the handle.

The Odyssey locking-liner series provides a 3 7/8-inch 420HC drop-point blade with either straight or partially serrated edges. A slot in the blade allows for one-hand open-

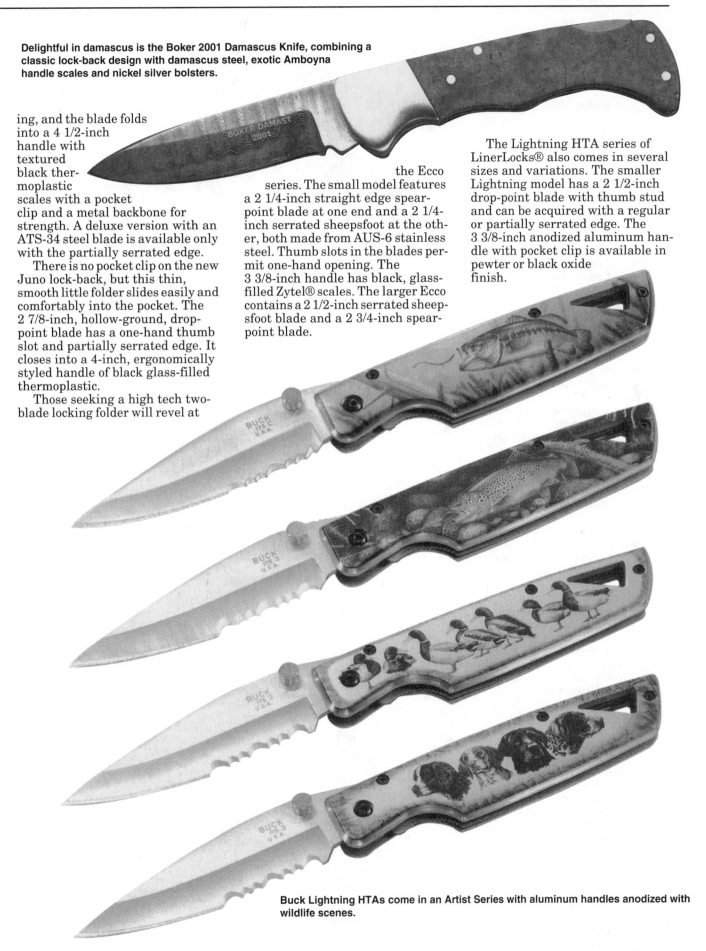

Delightful in damascus is the Boker 2001 Damascus Knife, combining a classic lock-back design with damascus steel, exotic Amboyna handle scales and nickel silver bolsters.

ing, and the blade folds into a 4 1/2-inch handle with textured black thermoplastic scales with a pocket clip and a metal backbone for strength. A deluxe version with an ATS-34 steel blade is available only with the partially serrated edge.

There is no pocket clip on the new Juno lock-back, but this thin, smooth little folder slides easily and comfortably into the pocket. The 2 7/8-inch, hollow-ground, drop-point blade has a one-hand thumb slot and partially serrated edge. It closes into a 4-inch, ergonomically styled handle of black glass-filled thermoplastic.

Those seeking a high tech two-blade locking folder will revel at the Ecco series. The small model features a 2 1/4-inch straight edge spear-point blade at one end and a 2 1/4-inch serrated sheepsfoot at the other, both made from AUS-6 stainless steel. Thumb slots in the blades permit one-hand opening. The 3 3/8-inch handle has black, glass-filled Zytel® scales. The larger Ecco contains a 2 1/2-inch serrated sheepsfoot blade and a 2 3/4-inch spear-point blade.

The Lightning HTA series of LinerLocks® also comes in several sizes and variations. The smaller Lightning model has a 2 1/2-inch drop-point blade with thumb stud and can be acquired with a regular or partially serrated edge. The 3 3/8-inch anodized aluminum handle with pocket clip is available in pewter or black oxide finish.

Buck Lightning HTAs come in an Artist Series with aluminum handles anodized with wildlife scenes.

Though they could qualify as tactical folders, the Buck Odysseys have such alluring contoured handles that they appeal to more than just the tactical crowd.

The larger Lightning II retains the same features and variations applied to a 3-inch blade with 4 1/8-inch handle. And again, there is an upscale version with ATS-34 steel and a combination Kevlar®/carbon-fiber handle.

Nor has Buck forgotten the collector, adapting the Lightning II model into an Artist Series with anodized aluminum handle scales decorated with a wildlife scene. Currently depicted are images of a bass, a brown trout, a flock of ducks, four hunting dogs and two deer.

For the gentleman, sportsman or collector, there is the Memory Series of small, 1 7/8-inch drop-point blades, aluminum handles and anodized images of deer or Labrador retrievers.

The Folding Hunter Tribute is a version of Buck's legendary model 110 lock-back Folding Hunter paying homage to two legends of the Wild West. Depictions of Wyatt Earp or Wild Bill Hickock are displayed in 24k-gold acid etching on the familiar 3 3/4-inch clip-point blade. The 4 7/8-inch handle has oak scales framed between brass bolsters. The knife is supplied in a limited edition box, acrylic knife holder, and a biography of Earp or Hickock. The first 500 are serialized.

Buck also has reissued two of the popular lock-back SlimLine models in special limited editions. The Poly-Pearl/Bonded Stone Prince, with its 2 1/2-inch drop-point blade and nickel bolsters is being released with scales of either cast resin Poly-Pearl in sea blue or red, and white

Bucklite II lock-back folders from Buck Knives feature thermoplastic handles in aqua, cobalt or red, and all three lightweight outdoor knives have 2 3/4-inch drop-point blades with partial serrations and thumb buttons.

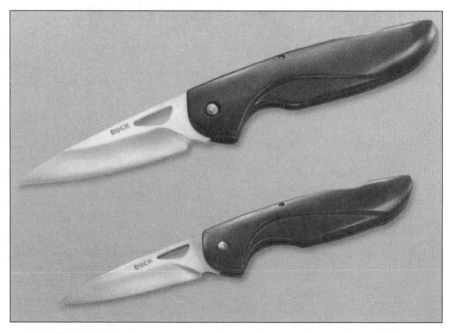

Buck has introduced several new folders intended for everyday use, including two new Access lock-back models with sweeping, contoured handles and modified drop-point blades.

spiny bonded stone. The scaled-down Poly Pearl/Bonded Stone Knight showcases cast resin Poly-Pearl in snow leopard or malachite-bonded stone.

The serious collector may prefer the Koji Folder, an elegant collaboration with Koji Hara, one of Japan's finest custom knifemakers. This one-hand locking liner features a hollow-ground, 2 1/4-inch drop-point ATS-34 blade with thumb stud. The 3 1/8-inch handle has scales of

The serious collector may prefer Buck's Koji Folder, an elegant knife named after its designer, Koji Hara, featuring a dark, hardwood handle with a swirling grain pattern and Koji's trademark "stone step" contoured bolster.

quince-wood, a dark hardwood with a swirling grain pattern which contrasts nicely with the unique "stone step" design Koji imparts to the bolster. The knife is issued with a limited edition box and a certificate of authenticity.

Camillus

Continuing its longstanding tradition of providing the official knives for the Boy Scouts of America, Camillus has just introduced this year's BSA Norman Rockwell commemorative, the Adventure Trail. On one side of the 3 5/8-inch handle is a full-color reproduction of Rockwell's "Adventure Trail" scene preserved under clear Lexan®. The Boy Scout oath is reproduced on the opposing handle scale. The knife includes all the appropriate utensils: a 2 3/8-inch, high-carbon stainless steel blade, can opener, punch and combination screwdriver/cap lifter. A shackle is attached to the nickel silver bolsters. Available in a limited edition, the Adventure Trail comes in a decorative box.

Inspired by the past, Camillus has reintroduced three traditional pocketknife patterns and labeled them the "Carbon Series." The Stockman houses its clip-point, sheepsfoot, and spey blades in a 3.9-inch handle. The 4.125-inch Trapper has the appropriate clip and spey blades. And a single drop-point blade folds into the 3.25-inch Gent's Lockback. All three models feature highly

polished, 1095 carbon steel blades and durable imitation stag scales mounted with nickel silver bolsters and shields.

Cold Steel

Another company best known for it tactical and combat models, Cold Steel has surprised the industry with the introduction of three traditional multi-blade pocketknives. The 4-inch Classic Stockman features the three blade patterns

associated with stockman knives: clip point, sheepsfoot and spey, as does its pint-size cousin, the Classic Junior Stockman, measuring 3 1/4-inches. The 4 1/8-inch Classic Trapper incorporates long, slender clip point and spey blades, both opening from the same end. All three models utilize Cold Steel's famous Carbon V steel for both the blades and

Next up are the Buck NXTs with ultra-high-tech, glass-reinforced nylon handles covered with skeletonized black rubber for an altogether modern look.

springs, nickel silver bolsters, and scales of faux jigged bone.

Gerber Legendary Blades

When Gerber introduced the Gator in 1991, it won Blade Magazine's Most Innovative Knife of the Year Award©. This year, Gerber has added yet another folding knife to the Gator series, the Gator GH, integrating the field dressing abilities of a gut hook on a 3 3/4-inch, stainless drop-point blade. As with all Gators, the handle is soft Kraton® molded around a hard inner core of glass-filled nylon to provide a comfortable and nearly indestructible grip. The knife comes with a ballistic cloth sheath.

Gutmann Cutlery

Distributed by Gutmann Cutlery, the new Walther knife division is resurrecting the ancient art of scrimshaw on a series of small, potentially collectible folders. The Scrimshaw Collection currently consists of three knives with skeletonized 1 5/8-inch drop-point, locking blades of 440C. Black, Zytel® handles are overlaid in synthetic ivory, each scrimmed in the likeness of one of several handguns that made the Walther name famous.

Currently available are the classic P38; the PPK made famous by James Bond; and the brand new P99, dubbed "the first pistol for the next century." The knives are manufactured by the skilled cutlers in Seki City, Japan, and the scrimshaw is handcrafted in the United States.

A wolf pack is scrimmed onto the synthetic ivory overlay adorning the 3 5/16-inch handle of the new Walther Belize. The sleek 2 9/16-inch clip-point blade of 440A steel has an ambidextrous thumb stud, and a pocket clip is attached to the opposite side of the black Zytel® handle.

The new Walther P99 handgun is commemorated again in the Walther P99 Silhouette Folder. The gun appears in a cutout on the 2 13/16-inch tanto-shaped blade. The 440C blade bears a reversible thumb stud, and folds into a black, checkered Zytel® handle using a blade tension screw and push-button lock release.

Known for tactical folders and fixed blades, Cold Steel shocked the knife industry with the introduction of three traditional multi-blade pocketknives known as (from top): the Classic Jr. Stockman, Classic Stockman and Classic Trapper.

The excellent field-dressing qualities of a gut hook are captured in the Gerber Gator GH with a 3 3/4-inch, stainless steel, drop-point blade and a Kraton® handle.

The Walther Tiger Eye is named for an amber stone embedded in a 4 1/4-inch, bead-blasted aluminum handle. The handle also holds a Kraton® insert to provide a secure grip, a locking liner and a pocket clip. The 3-inch clip-point blade of 440A steel bears an ambidextrous thumb stud. The knife comes in two colors, champagne or black, the latter possessing a blackened blade. A razor or semi-serrated edge is available with either color. As with all the Walther folders, the emphasis is on lightweight but sturdy.

Imperial Schrade

Schrade's most exciting new knife is appropriately christened the "Schrade/Barnett Knife," which extends a tradition of collaborations initiated last year with the introduction of the fixed blade Millennium Knife designed by D'Alton Holder. This new folder is in association with custom knifemaker Van Barnett, whose art knives have won "Best of Show" awards from Orlando to New Orleans to Solvang. The knife features a plain-edge blade of

ATS-34 held securely open by a new "V" lock design. The stepped handle scales are crafted from genuine bone. The centerpiece of the knife is the bolster, which displays an elaborately engraved leaf pattern with 24-karat gold inlay contrasted against a blued background. Intricate filework extends from the back of the blade along the handle, and both the thumb stud and shackle are adorned with 24-karat gold. Limited to 1,000 serialized pieces, the knife is issued with a custom sharkskin sheath.

Kershaw

With its new Double Cross and Double Duty folders, Kershaw has shrewdly blended modern technology into traditionally styled two-blade pocketknives. The Double Cross exhibits a 3 1/2-inch handle with sandalwood scales and nickel silver bolsters. A 2 3/8-inch clip-point blade opens from one end, and a 1 7/8-inch wharncliffe works off the other. Departing from the traditional, both AUS-6A blades incorporate thumb studs for one-hand opening, and both are secured open by a single locking liner.

Similar but larger, the Double Duty has a 4 1/8-inch handle with a 2 3/4-inch clip-point blade, and the wharncliffe has been replaced by a spey blade.

The Shotgun Shell is a premium-grade novelty knife. The 2 5/8-inch handle of sandalwood with brass bolsters replicates a 12-gauge shotgun shell. A drop-point blade and combination file and screwdriver fold out of the brass-mounted end.

A wolf pack is scrimshawed onto a synthetic ivory overlay adorning the 3 5/16-inch handle of the new Walther Belize from Gutmann Cutlery.

For the hunter who starts too early or lingers too late, Kershaw has coupled its popular Black Horse 11 lock-back folding hunter with a Mini Mag-Lite in a nylon sheath to create the new Black Horse/Mag-Lite Combo. The knife has a 3 3/4-inch clip-point blade of 440A that folds into a finger-contoured co-polymer handle. Batteries are included.

The Elk is a folding hunter with a locking liner and a tactical influence. Yet, the heart of this knife remains in the woods. A portion of the proceeds from the sale of the Elk goes to benefit the Rocky Mountain Elk Foundation and its habitat conservation projects. The 3 1/4-inch clip-point blade of black, titanium nitride-coated 440A steel has a thumb stud and Speed-Safe torsion bar-assisted opening for one-hand convenience. It folds into a

4 1/2-inch textured polyamide handle with pocket clip.

Designed by custom knifemaker Ken Onion, the Scallion locking-liner folder brings the tactical influence into a small personal using knife. The 3 1/4-inch handle features high-tech, black, textured Polyamide scales, and the 2 1/4-inch drop-point blade of 420 high-carbon stainless steel has a thumb stud and Speed-Safe mechanism for one-hand opening. The knife is available with plain or semi-serrated edges.

Scale the Scallion down to 2 7/8-inches (with a 1 15/16-inch blade), replace the black Polyamide with 410 stainless steel, and the result is a gentleman's knife with tactical overtones. Kershaw has named it the "Chive."

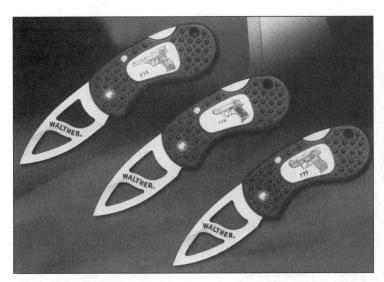

The Gutmann Scrimshaw Collection is made up of three lock-back folders with skeletonized blades and black Zytel® handles. Each of the handles features a synthetic ivory overlay scrimshawed in the likeness of one of several handguns that made the Walther name famous.

You even get a custom sharkskin sheath with the Schrade/Barnett Knife designed by Van Barnett in a plain-edge ATS-34 blade, a stepped, genuine bone handle, and the centerpiece, an elaborately engraved bolster with 24-karat gold inlay on a blued medium. Fancy filework extends the entire length of the piece.

REPORTS FROM THE FIELD

Klotzli

Klotzli, a Swiss company, has been making knives for more than a century-and-a-half, but its newest products keep pace with the current trends. The Walker Taos, a collaboration between traditional Swiss craftsman H.P. Klotzli and innovative custom knifemaker Michael Walker, is a small, sleek, LinerLock. The 2 1/2-inch hollow-ground, drop-point blade of 440C has a thumb stud and partial cutting serrations. It folds smoothly into a 3 5/8-inch handle with titanium liners, scales of black carbon fiber, and an attached pocket clip.

Walker also designed the similarly sized KLM200 series of compact folders with titanium LinerLocks. All feature hollow-ground, clip-point blades of 440C with thumb studs and partial serrations along the edges. The newest models in this series are available with handle scales of red, blue, or black G-10 material. They come with both pocket clips and belt pouches, but a variation of the black-handle model is available without the clip.

Timberline

Last year, Timberline introduced the semi-serrated Locking Liner designed by Pacific Northwest knifemaker Butch Vallotton to withstand the rigors of daily hard use. This year, Timberline has added a plain-edge version of the sturdy folder. The 3 1/2-inch clip-point blade is manufactured from AUS-8 stainless steel with a Rockwell hardness of 58RC. It has a bead-blast finish and an ambidextrous thumb stud. The locking blade folds securely between dual 420J stainless steel liners housed in a Zytel® handle. Inserts of soft, checkered Kraton®

provide a comfortable, secure grip, even under wet conditions. Stainless Torx® screws in the handle can be removed to disassemble the knife for cleaning. A stainless steel pocket clip allows for easy carrying.

United Cutlery

United has teamed with two of the best known of all custom knifemakers. Gil Hibben started making knives before some of the newer knifemakers were born, and long enough, certainly, to establish himself as one of the few real legends in the industry. His latest folder design produced by United is the Generation 2 Pro-Folder. The 3 1/4-inch 440 blade features an ambidextrous thumb stud. It folds into a precision CNC-machined, 6061-TG aircraft aluminum frame that measures 4 1/2 inches. This locking liner has a pocket clip. The handle is bead blasted with a contrasting color-anodized finish.

Having served two terms as president of The Knifemakers' Guild, Fred Carter is another legitimate giant in his field. In partnership with United, he has developed a full line of six LinerLock folding knife patterns:

The FC1 has a 3 1/8-inch 440 blade that closes into a 4 5/16-inch tempered stainless steel handle. A slot in the blade facilitates one-hand opening.

The FC2 features a 5 1/16-inch handle of 6061-T6 aircraft aluminum and a 3 3/4-inch 440 stainless tanto blade with thumb stud.

Locking liners pull double duty on the Kershaw Double Cross (top) and Double Duty two-blade folders with sandalwood handles and nickel silver bolsters.

The FC3 series utilizes a 3 1/16-inch 440 stainless blade with thumb stud. A 6061-T6 aircraft aluminum handle is available in black, blue, red or silver finishes.

The FC4 series adds a diamond texture to the four knives in the previous series.

The FC5 series repeats the same four colors and materials in a 4 1/2-inch skeletonized handle and 3 1/8-inch blade with thumb stud.

The FC6 is a titanium-handle version of the FC5. The blade steel is ATS-34.

The FC7 features a 3 5/8-inch 440 blade with thumb stud and slots. It

Kershaw has coupled its popular Black Horse 11 folding lock-back hunter with a Mini Mag-Lite in a nylon sheath to create the new Black Horse/Mag-Lite Combo.

closes into a 4 15/16-inch skeletonized handle of 6061-T6 aircraft aluminum.

W.R. Case & Sons Cutlery Co.

The folks in Bradford, Pa., still
make what we used to call pocketknives, and they make a lot of them.
This year, Case is offering new handle materials and resurrecting some
popular old styles.

Case discontinued the Sowbelly
some 80 years ago, and the heavy-
duty stockman became one of the
most desired prizes among collec-

W.R. Case & Sons Cutlery resurrects a
favorite pattern in the Doctor's Knife, which
has a slender 3-inch spear-point blade,
originally used for cutting pills or as an
emergency scalpel. The flat butt of the knife
easily ground medicine into powder.

tors. Now, in collabora-
tion with custom knifemaker Tony
Bose — who won the Best Folding
Knife Award© at both the 1995 and
1998 Blade shows — Case has
reintroduced this classic pattern.
Measuring 3 7/8 inches, the Sowbelly features the three traditional
stockman blades — clip, spey, and
sheepsfoot — manufactured from
Case's Tru-Sharp surgical steel. A
special edition, handled in Natural
Bone, is only available in a new oval
collector's tin. Also available on the
Sowbelly are the four other new handle materials.

According to Case, Vintage Bone
has the "look of an heirloom that's
aged gracefully as it's been handed
down for generations."

A little extra hand-finishing produces the new "Pocket Worn Black
Bone" that "feels right, right away,
as comfortable and dependable as
an old pair of jeans."

The deep golden Amber Bone
possesses dark, rich
brown grooves.

And then there is
the dramatically new
Case Silver Script that
replaces the nameplate
shield with a fine silver line
of cursive handwriting. Combining modern technology with hand-
craftsmanship, the script logo is cut
from nickel silver and inlaid into

double-dyed Cranberry Bone scales,
the only handle material in which it
appears. Along with
the Sowbelly, Case is
offering this handle
on all of its popular
larger knives.

Another resurrected
favorite is the Doctor's
Knife, a pattern that harks
back to a time when physicians
made house calls in their horse-
drawn buggies. In those days, the
slender 3-inch spear blade would cut
pills in half or serve as an emergency
scalpel, while the flat butt was used
to grind medicine into a powder. Case
is producing the new Doctor's Knife

in two versions: a Tru-Sharp surgical
steel blade with genuine Vintage
Bone scales; and a chrome vanadium
blade that closes into a synthetic
yellow handle.

Another new product is the Medium Texas Toothpick, available in
several versions. The slender, gracefully curved and tapered 4 1/4-
inch handle can be scaled in
either Amber Bone or
Rosewood. The knife
can feature a single,
long clip blade of
Tru-Sharp surgi-
cal steel, or the
two-blade
model can add
a short pen
blade. Anglers
will appreciate
the Fishing Knife varia-
tion, with a scaling blade ac-
companying the long clip
and a fish hook
sharpening stone
embedded into the
yellow handle.●

Case blends slender, gracefully
curved and tapered handles with
clip-point, pen and scaling
blades in three versions of
Medium Texas Toothpick knives.

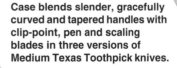

Traversing Swords and Fantasy Knives

By Butch Winter

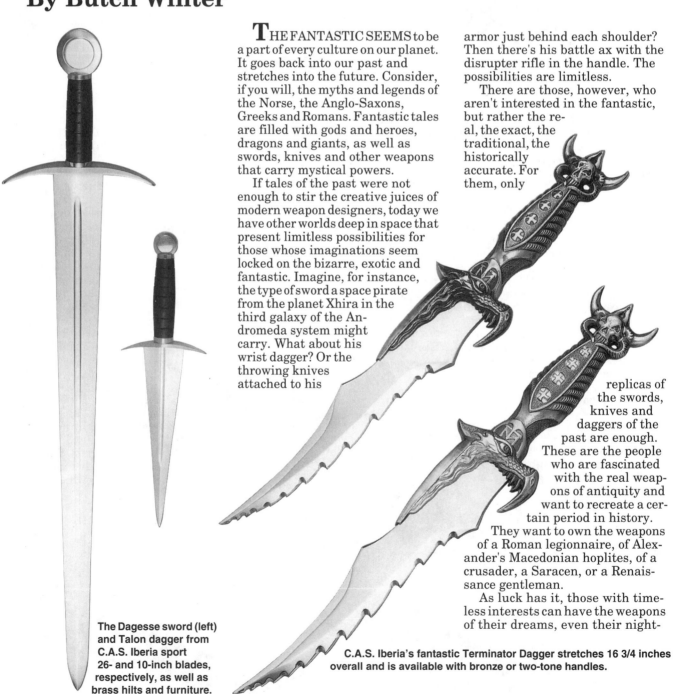

THE FANTASTIC SEEMS to be a part of every culture on our planet. It goes back into our past and stretches into the future. Consider, if you will, the myths and legends of the Norse, the Anglo-Saxons, Greeks and Romans. Fantastic tales are filled with gods and heroes, dragons and giants, as well as swords, knives and other weapons that carry mystical powers.

If tales of the past were not enough to stir the creative juices of modern weapon designers, today we have other worlds deep in space that present limitless possibilities for those whose imaginations seem locked on the bizarre, exotic and fantastic. Imagine, for instance, the type of sword a space pirate from the planet Xhira in the third galaxy of the Andromeda system might carry. What about his wrist dagger? Or the throwing knives attached to his armor just behind each shoulder? Then there's his battle ax with the disrupter rifle in the handle. The possibilities are limitless.

There are those, however, who aren't interested in the fantastic, but rather the real, the exact, the traditional, the historically accurate. For them, only replicas of the swords, knives and daggers of the past are enough. These are the people who are fascinated with the real weapons of antiquity and want to recreate a certain period in history.

They want to own the weapons of a Roman legionnaire, of Alexander's Macedonian hoplites, of a crusader, a Saracen, or a Renaissance gentleman.

As luck has it, those with timeless interests can have the weapons of their dreams, even their night-

The Dagesse sword (left) and Talon dagger from C.A.S. Iberia sport 26- and 10-inch blades, respectively, as well as brass hilts and furniture.

C.A.S. Iberia's fantastic Terminator Dagger stretches 16 3/4 inches overall and is available with bronze or two-tone handles.

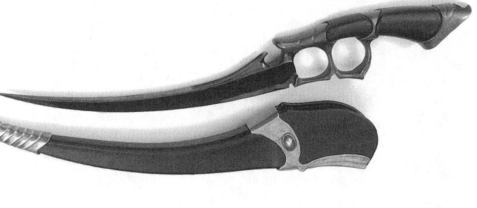

mares. There are a number of companies in business today who supply weapons and accoutrements to fill almost any dreamer's order. As was the case in the past, quality and workmanship span from the finest pieces fit only for a knight or prince of the blood, to the barely adequate to arm the peasant or serf forced to serve his master in time of war.

It is customary for manufacturers to unveil their latest products at the annual Shooting, Hunting, Outdoor Trade (S.H.O.T.) Show in January each year. This year, the following manufacturers were in attendance at the show in New Orleans, and both the real and fantastic were on display.

C.A.S. Iberia, Inc.

C.A.S. Iberia specializes in swords, knives, armor, helmets and ornamental items. With a name derived from the famous Iberian Peninsula, comprised of Spain and Portugal, most of the company's swords and edged weapons are made in Toledo, Spain, the city of swords.

Those seeking top-of-the-line craftsmanship should consider the C.A.S. Iberia inventory. C.A.S. can furnish a sword for a space pirate, a Roman gladius sword for a gladiator, or a saber for an American Civil War re-enactor. Swords from C.A.S. Iberia range in quality from the wall-hanger, or showpiece, to the serious working blade for those who want a little more realism in their fantasy life.

New in 2001 from C.A.S. Iberia are armored helmets designed by custom knife and sword maker Virgil England. England is recognized in the custom knife world as one of the most imaginative artists working in the craft. England creates the most exotic and fantastic items possible.

There are four profusely illustrated, four-color, top-quality paper catalogs available from C.A.S. featuring a wide range of products. It is nothing but pure pleasure to flip through the pages.

Deepeeka Exports Pvt., Ltd.

The India firm of Deepeeka Exports Pvt. Ltd. is founded on the belief that warfare has been a recurring phenomenon since the dawn of civilization. It is with that

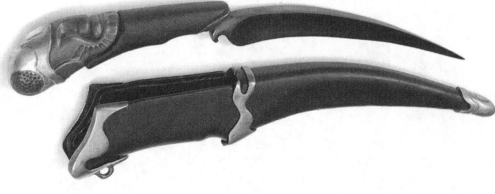

New in 2001 from C.A.S. Iberia are several rakish knives designed by custom knife and sword maker Virgil England.

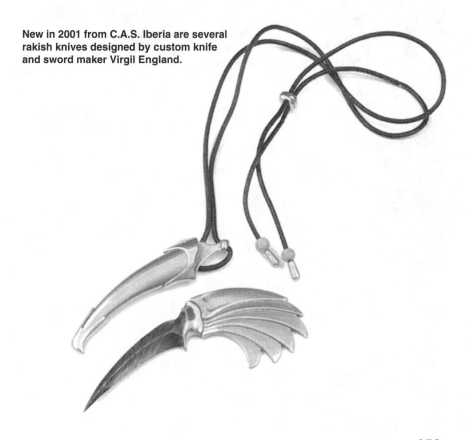

premise that the company's edged weaponry inventory has been separated into Roman, gladiator, medieval, renaissance, British and French, and American offerings, including knives, swords, daggers,

armor, tomahawks and axes, spears, pole arms, and period attire.

Replicas in the Deepeeka collection are derived from studying originals in private collections, museums and antique inventories. Deepeeka offers nothing from the fantasy world unless one's fantasy is rooted in history, and the company stocks everything from a Roman soldier's gladius to a Viking helmet. Full sets of armor fit every body type, and frocks for milady are available from almost any time period.

Contact Deepeeka Exports, in care of Gift International Company 8001 Falstaff Rd. McLean, VA 22102 (703) 827-8978.

Matthews Cutlery

Matthews Cutlery has perhaps the largest selection of sword and fantasy knives. In addition to major American brands of knives, Matthews carries most American swords and fantasy knives and several European brands.

Of particular interest are pieces made by the German manufacturer, Linder. This company produces a complete line of fancy daggers, some rooted in traditional designs, others

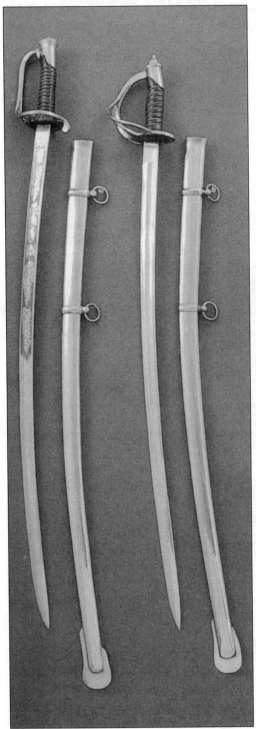

The C.A.S. Iberia DG-A18 Foot Officer's Sword (left) features an elaborately etched carbon-steel blade, a wire-bound leather grip and a steel scabbard with brass fittings. The DG-A2 U.S. 1860 Cavalry Sabre is a reproduction of a standard issue Union cavalry sword with a blade fuller, a spiral-bound leather grip and a steel scabbard.

Something for everyone, Deepeeka Exports offers up (from left) the Lord of Ring sword, Great Sword, Baby Prince Sword, Frankish Sword, Medieval Decorative Sword and Thomas Sword.

combining the traditional with the exotic, particularly the Linder Solingen Fancy Kris Daggers. These daggers have more or less traditional European handles of stag, sheep horn, wood or ivory combined with the wavy blades of the West Indian kris daggers.

With such a large supply house, Matthews provides the fantasy items from C.A.S. Iberia as well as United Cutlery, and the company catalog is not only a guide to what is available today, but lists the suggested retail prices of each item.

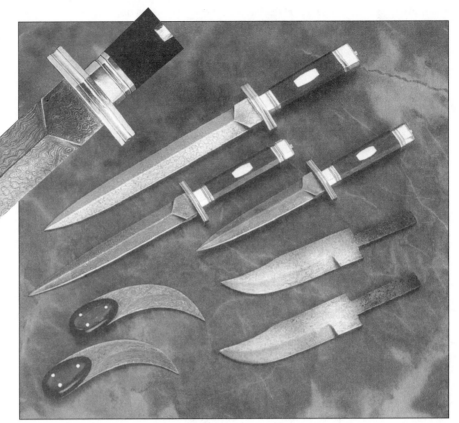

Deepeeka Exports' damascus offerings include boot knives, hunting blades and "Tiger Claws."

Any knight would be brave in Full Body Maxmillan Armour, holding a Celtic sword and a Lion Shield, each available from Deepeeka Exports.

The Scorpion is the newest member in United's Gil Hibben custom design series, incorporating 420 J2 stainless steel blades and a solid metal handle with a black chrome finish.

Museum Replicas, Ltd.

Museum Replicas brings historically accurate, battle-ready swords, daggers, axes and helmets to the forefront, plus shields, period clothing, jewelry, sculpture, and books.

New this year is the Winged Griffin Axe, a double-bit beauty fit for the bravest warrior. For those interested in the Oriental warrior, there is the coiled dragon Katana and Aikuchi that have to be seen to be appreciated. For the crusader, medieval knight or man-at-arms ready for battle is the Knightly Hand-and-a-Half Sword with its companion dagger.

Museum Replicas products are aimed at the historical re-enactor. There are daggers, swords, armor and accoutrements from almost any period of history, with a few fantasy pieces based on weapons mentioned in the "Wheel Of Time" series of books.

Most of Museum Replicas' weapons are made in India, with a few from China. Prices can be expensive for such items as swords with genuine damascus blades, or more reasonable for replicas of Scottish daggers.

Anyone interested in re-enacting medieval, renaissance or ancient

Whether a Cinquedea Venetian sword (left) or a Roman Cavalry sword are up your alley, Deepeeka Exports has them.

times should contact Museum Replicas.

United Cutlery

United Cutlery has one of the most extensive knife lines in the United States today. They also have two of the most talented fantasy knife designers, Gil Hibben and Kit Rae, currently producing knives.

Don't go here looking for a blade for the Roman soldier or Greek hoplite. Here is where you outfit that Xhira pirate with a blade, or blades, whose descriptions will challenge your imagination. New this year are Hibben's "Scorpion" and Rae's "Medusa Dagger" which should fit the bill for the most discriminating pirate. Should there be a corsair from the deserts of Zhusa searching for a suitable blade, Kit Rae's "Shadow Slayer" should fill the bill. Gil Hibben's "Griffyn" will serve as any earthman's 23rd-century survival knife.

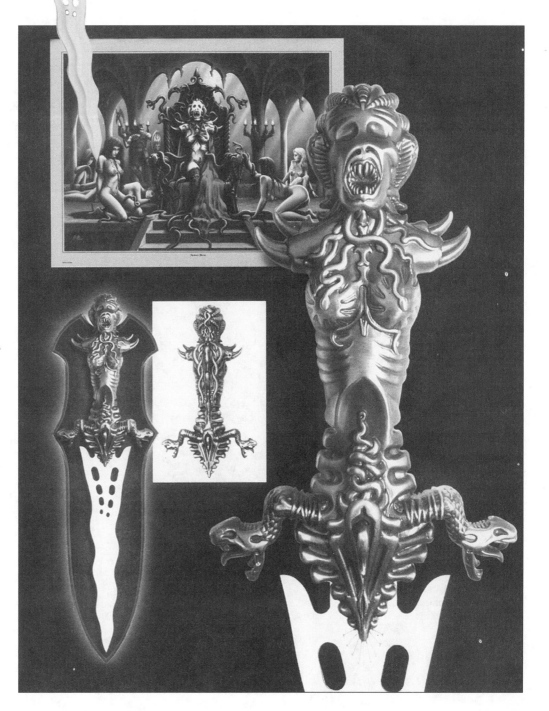

Kit Rae of United Cutlery designed the Medusa Dagger, aptly named for a cast-metal handle in the form of the Greek mythological creature, Medusa. A kris-style 420 J2 blade completes the piece.

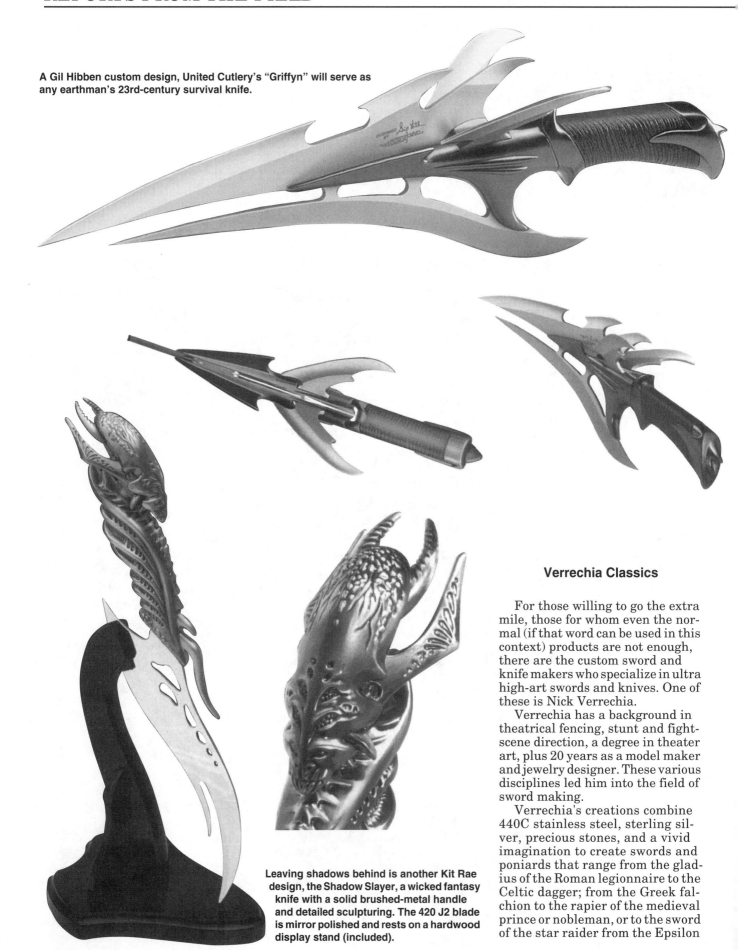

A Gil Hibben custom design, United Cutlery's "Griffyn" will serve as any earthman's 23rd-century survival knife.

Leaving shadows behind is another Kit Rae design, the Shadow Slayer, a wicked fantasy knife with a solid brushed-metal handle and detailed sculpturing. The 420 J2 blade is mirror polished and rests on a hardwood display stand (included).

Verrechia Classics

For those willing to go the extra mile, those for whom even the normal (if that word can be used in this context) products are not enough, there are the custom sword and knife makers who specialize in ultra high-art swords and knives. One of these is Nick Verrechia.

Verrechia has a background in theatrical fencing, stunt and fight-scene direction, a degree in theater art, plus 20 years as a model maker and jewelry designer. These various disciplines led him into the field of sword making.

Verrechia's creations combine 440C stainless steel, sterling silver, precious stones, and a vivid imagination to create swords and poniards that range from the gladius of the Roman legionnaire to the Celtic dagger; from the Greek falchion to the rapier of the medieval prince or nobleman, or to the sword of the star raider from the Epsilon

Verrechia Classics premieres the Etruscan Gladius (left), primarily a thrusting weapon, and its counterpart, the Celtae, a 28-inch slashing broadsword. All Verrechia bronzes contain sterling silver highlights and come with a soft brown leather, fur-lined sheath.

cluster. Verrechia's swords and daggers are not for the budget-challenged.

So there it is: what's available to the re-enactor and lover of exotic cutlery of all sizes. There's something here for almost any budget and almost any enthusiasm. ●

◄ The Verrechia Classics model Pericles is named for the man who ruled Athens during its golden age of democracy. The 24-inch sword is hilted in 14-karat gold and sterling silver. Its 440C blade is entirely engraved, and the sword is balanced to stand up on its pommel.

► Verrechia's Stormlord is edge-hardened 4140 steel, structurally relieved for shock dispersion. Styled in cloud motifs, it showcases an engraved Florentine finish. The sword employs more than 4 pounds of sterling silver and 1.8 ounces of 14-karat gold in the hilt.

WEB DIRECTORY

MANUFACTURERS OF PRODUCTION & SEMI–PRODUCTION KNIVES

A

A.G. Russell Knives — http://www.agrussell.com
Al Mar Knives — http://www.almarknives.com/
Antoni Diving Knives — http://www.italpro.com/antoni/index.htm

B

Benchmade Knife Co. — http://www.benchmade.com/
Blade Rigger — http://www.bladerigger.com/
Blue Grass Cutlery (Winchester Knives and John Primble Knives) — http://bluegrasscutlery.com/
Boker (Germany) — http://www.boker.de
Boker (USA) — http://www.bokerusa.com/
Browning Knives — http://www.browning.com/products/catalog/knives/knives.htm
Buck Knives — http://www.buckknives.com/
Busse Combat Knife Co. — http://www.bussecombat.com/

C

Camillus Cutlery Co. — http://www.camillusknives.com
C.A.S. Iberia — http://www.casiberia.com/
W.R. Case & Sons Cutlery — http://www.wrcase.com/
Chris Reeve Knives — http://chrisreeve.com/
Cold Steel — http://www.coldsteel.com/index.html

D

Delta Z Knives — http://www.deltaz—knives.com/
Duel Knives — http://www.duelknives.co.nz/

E

Eickhorn — http://www.eickhorn-solingen.com/
Emerson Knives, Inc. — http://www.emersonknives.com/

F

Fallkniven — http://www.fallkniven.com/
Fox Cutlery — http://www.italpro.com/fox/

G

GT Knives — http://www.gtknives.com/
Gerber Legendary Blades — http://www.gerberblades.com/
Gigand Knives — http://www.gigand.com/
Grohmann Knives — http://www.grohmannknives.com/pages/index2.html
Gutmann Cutlery and Junglee Knives — http://gutmanncutlery.com/

I

Imagical Design — http://www.imagical—design.com/
Imperial Schrade — http://www.schradeknives.com/

K

KA—BAR Knives — http://www.ka—bar.com/
Kershaw Knives — http://www.kershawknives.com
Klotzli — http://www.klotzli.com/
Knives of Alaska — http://www.knivesofalaska.com/
Kopromed — http://www.kopromed.com.pl/

L

Laguiole — http://www.laguiole.com/
Leatherman Tool Group — http://www.leatherman.com/

M

Marttiini — http://www.marttiini.fi/
Maserin — http://www.italpro.com/maserin/index.htm
Meyerco USA — http://www.meyercousa.com/
Micro Technology — http://www.microtechknives.com/
Mission Knives & Tools — http://www.missionknives.com/

P

P.J. Turner Knife Mfg. — http://dns1.silverstar.com/turnermfg/

R

Randall Made Knives — http://www.randallknives.com/
Round Eye Knife & Tool (REKAT) — http://www.rekat.com/

S

SOG Specialty Knives — http://www.sogknives.com/home.htm
Spyderco, Inc. – http://www.spyderco.com

T

TiNives, Inc — http://www.tinives.com/tinives/html/index.asp
TOPS Knives — http://www.topsknives.com/

U

United Cutlery — http://www.unitedcutlery.com/

V

Victorinox — http://www.victorinox.ch/

W

William Henry Fine Knives — http://www.williamhenryknives.com/

KNIFE RETAILERS AND PURVEYORS

A

AKO4U — http://www.ako4u.com
A.G. Russell Knives — http://www.agrussell.com/
Arizona Custom Knives — http://www.arizonacustomknives.com/
Arrow Dynamics — http://www.arrow—dynamics.com/
Atlanta Cutlery — http://www.atlantacutlery.com/sys—tmpl/door/

B

Bayou Knife Works — http://www.bayouknifeworks.com/
Bayou LaFourche — http://www.knifeworks.com/
Beck's Cutlery — http://www.beckscutlery.com/
BladeArt — http://www.bladeart.com/
Blade Runner Knives — http://www.brknives.com/
Blades For Less — http://www.uws.com/blades4less
Blowout Knives — http://www.blowoutknives.com/
Brigade Quartermasters — http://www.actiongear.com/
Bud K Worldwide — http://www.budkww.com/
Bullman Cutlery — http://www.bullmancutlery.com/

C

Cascade Blades — http://www.teleport.com/~jawilson/cascade-blades.shtml
Chesapeake Knife & Tool — http://www.chesapeakeknifeandtool.com/
Confederate Cutlery — http://www.confederatecutlery.com/
Cove Cutlery — http://www.covecutlery.com/
C.R. Specialties — http://www.geocities.com/crspecialties
Cumberland Knives — http://www.cumberland—knives.com/
Cutlery Shoppe — http://www.cutleryshoppe.com/
Cutlery To Go — http://www.cutlerytogo.com/
Cutting edge Swords — http://www.cuttingedgeswords.com/

D

Dantes Knife Works — http://www.dantesknife.com/
Denver Cutlery — http://www.denvercutlery.com/
Discount Knives — http://www.discountknives.com/

E

Edge Pro Sharpeners — http://www.gorge.net/business/edgepro
Excalibur Cutlery — http://www.excaliburcutlery.com/
Extremely Sharp — http://www.extremely—sharp.com/

F

Fantasy Cutlery East — http://www.fantasycutlery.com/

G

Gurkha House — http://www.cystern.com/khukuri/

H

Historical Weapons — http://www6.bcity.com/nitrodriver/

I

IMS-Plus — http://www.imsplus.com/

K

Knife.com — http://www.knife.com
KnifeArt.com — http://knifeart.com/
KnifeCenter of the Internet — http://www.knifecenter.com
Knife Outlet — http://www.knifeoutlet.com/
The Knife Professional — http://www.knifepro.com/
Knife Shop — http://www.knifeshop.com

M

Maxon Systems — http://www.maxonsystems.com/

N

NorthWest Cutlery — http://www.nwcutlery.com/

O

1 Stop Knife Shop — http://www.onestopknifeshop.com/
Online Knives — http://www.onlineknives.com/
Otto-Corrado — http://www.otto—corrado.com/

P

Phil's Fine Cutlery — http://www.philfine.com/
Pioneer Valley Knife & Tool — http://www.pvknife.com/
Premium Knives — http://www.premiumknives.com/

R

Rayjay Knives — http://members.home.net/rayjay/rayjayknives.html
Robertson's Custom Cutlery — http://www.robertsoncustomcutlery.com/
RP Sports — http://www.networksplus.net/rpsports/

S

Safe & Knife Company — http://www.safe—knife.com/
Santa Fe Stoneworks — http://www.santafestoneworks.com/
Sharpknives.com — http://www.sharpknives.com/
Skylands Cutlery — http://www.skylandscutlery.com/
Stidham's Knives — http://www.kmg.org/stidham/index.html
Straight River Knife Inc — http://www.srknife.com/

T

Tool Shop — http://www.tool—shop.com/
Top of Texas Knives — http://www.toptexknives.com/
Triple Aught Design — http://www.tripleaughtdesign.com/

Y

Yukon Bay – http://www.yukonbay.com

KNIFE CARE & ACCESSORIES

B

Buck Knives — http://www.buckknives.com/

C

Chef's Choice Sharpeners — http://www.chefschoice.com/

D

Diamond Machining Technology (DMT) — http://www.dmt-sharp.com/

E

Edge Pro Sharpeners — http://www.gorge.net/business/edgepro

F

Flitz Metal Polish — http://www.flitz.com/

L

Lansky Sharpeners— http://www.lansky.com/

M

Meyerco USA — http://www.meyercousa.com/
Mission Knives & Tools — http://www.missionknives.com/

N

Normark – http://www.normark.com

R

Razor Edge Systems — http://www.razoredgesystems.com/

S

Sentry Solutions — http://www.sentrysolutions.com/
Smith Abrasives — http://www.smithabrasives.com/
Spyderco, Inc. – http://www.spyderco.com

T

Tomway Products – http://www.ultimatehumidor.com
Tru Hone — http://www.truhone.com/

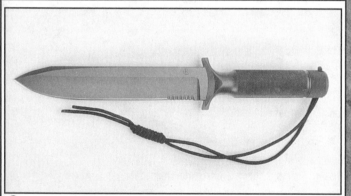
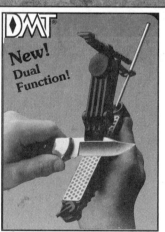

KNIVES MARKETPLACE

CUSTOM KNIVES

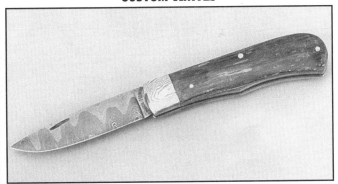

Knife pictured has Damascus blade made of 480 layers of 1095-203E steels in Mr. Hawes' shimmed ladder pattern. Bolster made of mokume from Sakmar. Handles are mammoth ivory. Truly a one-of-a-kind gem that will also function as a utility knife if you desire.

Hawes Forge specializes in high carbon, Damascus steel that are not just for show, they are made to stand up to use and will hold a superior edge. Let Hawes Forge provide you with a knife you can be proud of from their designs or yours.

HAWES FORGE

P.O. Box 176, Weldon, IL 61882

Phone: 217-736-2479

WORDEN TACTICAL

Possibly the best folding tactical knife in production today is the only way to describe the new Kelly Worden designed knife from Timberline Knives. Taking the positive locking security of a liner-lock design and melding that with a comfortable and secure grip profile handle, the Worden Tactical will meet and exceed the demands of the serious knife owner.

Made from AUS 8 steel, this drop-point style blade has 58 hardness rating on the Rockwell scale. Available in two sizes: medium, with a 2.9-inch blade or large with a 3.9-inch blade, both have bead blasted finish. Mated with 420J stainless liners and a glass-filled nylon handle, this knife feels right from the first time you pick it up.

The MSRP for the medium Worden Tactical is $44.99, the large Worden Tactical is $59.99.

TIMBERLINE KNIVES

P.O. Box 600, Getzville, NY 14068-0600

Phone: 1-800-LIV-SHARP™ • 716-877-2200 • Fax: 716-877-2591

E-mail: gatco@buffnet.net • www.greatamericantool.com

A. G. RUSSELL™ KNIVES

As an industry leader for the past 37 years, A. G. Russell Knives continues to offer the finest quality knives and accessories worldwide. Lines include Randall, Dozier, Leatherman, Case, Gerber, SOG, Ka-Bar, Kershaw, Columbia River, Al Mar, Klotzli, Boker, Marble's, Schatt & Morgan, A. G. Russell, and more. Call for a free catalog, or shop online to see the entire inventory of products at agrussell.com.

A. G. RUSSELL KNIVES

1705 North Thompson Street, Dept. SKA02
Springdale, AR 72764-1294
Phone: 501-571-6161 • Fax: 501-751-4520
Email: ag@agrussell.com

KNIVES MARKETPLACE

CURRENT RIVER SKINNERS

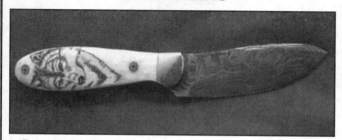

Current River Skinners evolved from the designs favored by the hunters and trappers of the Current River region in the mountains of the Missouri Ozarks. These knives are offered in damascus and ATS-34 and come with handmade sheaths. Many have ivory inserts and scrimshaw. Prices are $100.00 to $200.00. They also sell custom knives from recognized makers and custom zippered knife cases.

CURRENT RIVER KNIFE

827 Ridgetop Circle
Saint Charles, MO 63304
Phone: 636-441-8204
Email: crknives@aol.com

MARBLE'S HISTORY

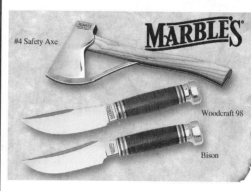

#4 Safety Axe

Woodcraft 98

Bison

Marble's® of Gladstone, Michigan, U.S.A. has been making high quality sporting specialty products since 1898. Their founder, Webster L. Marble literally designed and manufactured America's first true fixed blade hunting knives. His "Ideal®", "Expert®", "Woodcraft®" and "Trailmaker®" knives have become famous with true sportsmen and collectors all over the world. Marble's® sporting knives are all razor sharp and have unmatched edge holding ability. Every Marble's® knife is still hand finished in the traditional way, just like their vintage knives. Marble's® axes and "safety axes®" are all forged from high carbon American steel. These distinctive "pure Marble's®" axes will outchop any other axes of their size or type. Marble's® line of traditional multi-blade pocket knives are exactly the same American patterns they introduced in 1904. These pocket knives are genuine works of art. For more information send $3.00 for their full line 48-page catalog.

MARBLE ARMS

P.O. Box 111, Gladstone, MI 49837
Phone: 1-906-428-3710 • Fax: 906-428-3711

DuoSharp™
A superior two grit diamond sharpening system

8" x 2 5/8" (203mm X 67mm)

10" x 4" (250mm X 100mm)

TECHNICAL BREAKTHROUGH

First Double-Sided Diamond Bench Stones!

- ◆ sharpens, hones, laps knives & tools fast
- ◆ precision flatness for precision sharpening
- ◆ extends carbide tooling life 5 to 7 times
- ◆ flattens conventional stones & waterstones

AMERICA'S FINEST KNIFE AND TOOL SHARPENERS

DIAMOND MACHINING TECHNOLOGY INC.

85 Hayes Memorial Drive
Marlborough, MA 01752
Phone: 1-800-666-4368 • Web: www.dmtsharp.com

Photo Catalog: $5.00, $7.00 Overseas

Arizona Custom Knives

Koji Hara

Jay & Karen Sadow
Arizona Custom Knives
8617 E. Clydesdale Trail
Scottsdale, AZ 85258

480.951.0699

VISA MasterCard DISCOVER

Your collection is our first priority

www.arizonacustomknives.com

Established in 1992, Arizona Custom Knives (AZCK) has become a market leader in bringing you the finest handmade knives. From one-of-a-kind, investment-grade knives to your everyday carry knife, Arizona Custom Knives tries to "custom fit" the customer with the right knife at the right price. The company brings to you the best of the top makers, along with the latest from the up-and-comers. Years of established relationships with hundreds of custom knifemakers assures you of obtaining those rare gems you seek.

Your collection is their first priority!
Color Catalog: $5.00 U.S.; $7.00 overseas

ARIZONA CUSTOM KNIVES

Jay & Karen Sadow
8617 E. Clydesdale Trail, Scottsdale, AZ 85258
Phone: 480-951-0699 • Fax: 480-951-0699
Web: http://www.arizonacustomknives.com
Email: sharptalk@aol.com

Titanium will make a superior knife blade - Absolutely! You must obtain the right alloy. Like most good products you have to use the best raw materials. Mission uses Beta Titanium that undergoes a complicated heat treatment to make the most durable blade in the world. The knives are so tough they will last through many generations. They are easily field sharpened and hold an edge, even under wet and searing conditions. Mission's titanium knives are difficult to break. In fact, the MPK's used by Navy SEAL/EOD teams have never been broken. They have been shot at, run over by tanks, left in ocean water and subjected to the worst use you can imagine. Titanium is forty percent (40%) lighter than steel, and will not break or chip in the arctic cold. Mission welds a good design with quality mechanical and material engineering. The handles on their products are made for the human hand and designed for long-term comfort. As they say, "Look sharp, be sharp, and stay sharp!" That's a Mission knife!

www.missionknives.com

MISSION
Knives & Tools, Inc.

13805 Alton Pkwy Ste D
Irvine CA 92618
949-951-3879 orders
949-598-0258 fax
info@missionknives.com

DIAFOLD DIAMOND WHETSTONE™

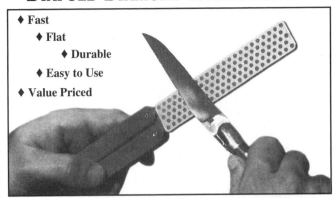

- ♦ Fast
  - ♦ Flat
    - ♦ Durable
- ♦ Easy to Use
- ♦ Value Priced

A versatile 4-inch Diamond Whetstone housed in a self-storing fold away handle that remains permanently attached. The convenient handle folds to become a compact storage case that slips into a tackle box, fanny pack, backpack or pocket. Easy, clean, durable and fast-sharpening. Hones any hard material, even carbides. Available in extra-coarse, coarse, extra-fine or fine.

AMERICA'S FINEST KNIFE AND TOOL SHARPENERS

DMT®

DIAMOND MACHINING TECHNOLOGY INC.

85 Hayes Memorial Drive
Marlborough, MA 01752
Phone: 1-800-666-4368 • Web: www.dmtsharp.com

MUELA HUNTER

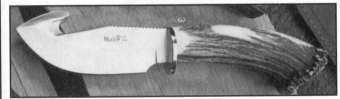

The Muela Hunter shown is made in Spain to the specifications of Joy Enterprises. This beautiful knife features 440 stainless with molybdenum vanadium. The overall length is 9-1/2" with a 4-1/2" blade. This is complimented with a rare Spanish crown stag handle of 5" that is contoured for a full-sized grip. The spine of the blade has nicely done serrations and the choil is extended for your safety and comfort. It also has a gut hook built into a dramatically upswept blade tip that is perfect for skinning. The Muela Hunter comes with a superb leather sheath. This is a knife that is functional, beautiful and very affordable.

Joy Enterprises searches worldwide for quality blades that meet their stringent standards. They import hundreds of truly fine knives at prices that are hard to believe. You can also purchase wonderful collector pieces from various sources. Some of the brands include Muela, Fury™, Mustang™, HAWG!, Herbertz®, Cudeman, and Sotoca. They are sure to have a knife that will satisfy your tastes.

To order the Muela Hunter ask for Joy #90082 or call for information on other models.

JOY ENTERPRISES

7516 Central Industrial Drive, Riviera Beach, FL 33404
Phone: 561-863-3205 • Fax: 561-863-3277
E-mail: mail@joyenterprises.com • www.joyenterprises.com

GATCO 5-STONE SHARPENING SYSTEM

The GATCO 5-Stone Sharpening System is the only fixed-angle sharpening kit needed to restore a factory perfect edge on even the most well-used knives.

Instructions are permanently mounted inside the storage case to make the job easy.

Just secure the blade in the polymer vise, select the proper angle guide, insert one of the five hone-stone angle guide bars into the guide slot, then put a few drops of mineral oil on the stone and start sharpening.

The GATCO 5-Stone Sharpening System includes extra coarse, coarse, medium and fine honing stones that are made from high-density aluminum oxide for long wear. The fifth, triangular-shaped hone is used for serrated blades.

All stones are mounted in color-coded grips.

To locate a GATCO dealer, call 1-800-LIV-SHARP.

GATCO SHARPENERS

P.O. Box 600, Getzville, NY 14068-0600
Phone: 716-877-2200 • Fax: 716-877-2591
E-mail: gatco@buffnet.net • www.greatamericantool.com

Commercial Knife
Manufacturers and Distributors

(Companies that manufacture or are the primary importer of a knife brand)

A.G. Russell Knives Inc.

1705 N. Thompson St.
Springdale, AR 72764
800-255-9034
Fax: (501) 872-5209
www.agrussell.com
E-mail: ag@agrussell.com

Styles: Fixed blade and folding knives for hunting, camping and general use.

Sheaths: Leather and fiberglass-reinforced nylon.

Handles: Black pearl, mother of pearl, white bone, India stag, stainless steel, quince burl, carbon fiber, black Micarta® and fiberglass-reinforced nylon.

Features: Traditional designs with high-grade steel blades. Deer Hunter and Bird & Trout models feature extremely thin AUS 8A steel blades for precision cutting.

Retail price: $29.95 to $225.00

The Jess Horn-designed folder has a 3 1/8-inch ATS 34 blade with black linen Micarta® handle. Also offered with a 2 5/8-inch blade. **$99.00**

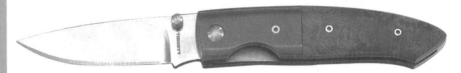

Walker-Lock has a 3 1/8-inch drop-point blade of ATS 34 steel, sky-blue titanium bolsters and a handle of Chinese quince burl. Also offered with carbon fiber handle. **$195.00**

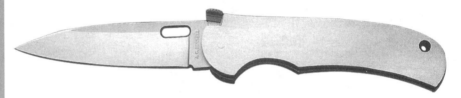

The One Hand Knife has a 3 1/8-inch AUS 8A blade with a hole and top lock-release button for one-hand opening and closing. Blade offered in a bowie or general-purpose shape. **$49.95**

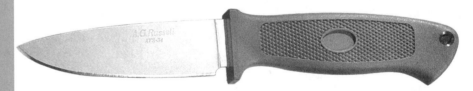

Deer Hunter has a thin-ground, 4-inch drop-point blade of AUS 8A stainless steel with a handle and sheath of fiberglass-reinforced nylon. Knife locks into sheath. **$44.95**

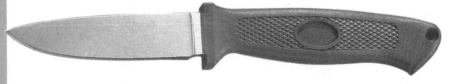

Bird & Trout has a 3-inch drop-point blade of AUS 8A steel with a handle and locking sheath of fiberglass-reinforced nylon. **$29.95**

SERE 2000 liner lock has a 3.6-inch VG-10 steel blade and G-10 handle. Includes pocket clip. **$189.00**

Eagle Ultralight front lock has a 4-inch AUS-8 stainless steel blade with dual thumb studs and black linen Micarta® handle with pocket clip. Offered with satin (shown) or mirror finish and plain, 40 percent serrated or fully serrated edges. **$108.00 (mirror finish, $138.00)**

Falcon Ultralight front lock has a 3 1/4-inch AUS-8 stainless steel blade with dual thumb studs and black linen Micarta® handle with pocket clip. Offered with satin or mirror finish (shown) and plain, 40 percent serrated or fully serrated edges. **$118.00 (satin finish, $98.00)**

Hawk Ultralight front lock has a 2 3/4-inch AUS-8 stainless steel blade with dual thumb studs and black linen Micarta® handle with pocket clip. Offered with satin or mirror finish (shown) and plain, 40 percent serrated or fully serrated edges. **$98.00 (satin finish, $87.00)**

Al Mar Knives Inc.

P.O. Box 2295
Tualatin, OR 97062
(503) 670-9080
Fax: (503) 639-4789
www.almarknives.com
E-mail: info@almarknives

Styles: Folding knives for tactical and general use.

Sheaths: N/A.

Handles: Micarta®, aluminum and G-10.

Features: All models have pocket clips; most have thumb studs for one-hand opening.

Retail price: $87.00 to $270.00

Bear
MGC Cutlery

1111 Bear Blvd.
Jacksonville, AL 36265
800-844-3034
or (256) 435-2227
Fax: (256) 435-9348
Web site: N/A
E-mail: N/A

Styles: Fixed blade and folding models and multi-tools for hunting, fishing, camping and general use.

Sheaths: Leather and ballistic nylon.

Handles: India stag horn, Kraton®, oak, cocobolo, Zytel®, laminated zebra wood, mother of pearl, Micarta®, metal alloy and stainless steel.

Features: Many models offered with damascus steel blades; some models with gut hooks and saw blades; several models of butterfly knives.

Retail price: $23.00 to $455.00

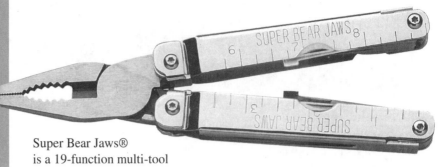

Super Bear Jaws®
is a 19-function multi-tool
with stainless steel construction and a lock for all blades. Overall length is 4 1/2 inches. Also available with coupler and screwdriver bits set. **$90.00**

Model 460GH has a hollow-ground, locking 440 steel blade, plus a 5 1/8-inch locking saw blade with gut hook. Handle is Kraton®. Includes nylon sheath. **Price unavailable.**

Model 408 Tactical has an ATS-34 blade with chisel point and bead-blasted finish, Micarta® handle. Includes nylon sheath. **$120.00**

The India stag horn handle accents this Model 585D Professional Hunter model with damascus blade. Overall length is 9 1/2 inches. Includes leather sheath. **$205.00**

Model 567 fillet knife has a 7-inch, high-carbon 440 steel blade and India stag horn handle. Includes leather sheath. **$57.50**

Allen Elishewitz-designed Model 690 folder has a 3.25-inch blade of 154CM stainless steel and black carbon fiber/rosewood handle. Also offered with boron carbide-coated blade and with straight or partially serrated edge. **$180.00**

Allen Elishewitz-designed Model 914 Rescue Stryker folder has a 3 1/2-inch blade of GIN-1 stainless steel with a downturned tip and G10 handle. Includes removable pocket clip. **$125.00**

Allen Elishewitz-designed Model 145 Nimravus Cub has a 3.6-inch fixed blade of 154CM or M2 steel and a G10 handle. Includes Kydex® sheath. Similar Model 140 Nimravus has a 4 1/2-inch blade. **$150.00**

Benchmade Knife Co.

300 Beavercreek Road
Oregon City, OR 97045
(503) 655-6004
Fax: (503) 655-6223
www.benchmade.com
E-mail: info@benchmade.com

Styles: Fixed blade and folding knives for hunting, rescue and tactical uses.

Sheaths: Kydex® and ballistic nylon.

Handles: Aluminum, G10, carbon fiber, stainless steel, rosewood/carbon fiber, titanium and Zytel®.

Features: Numerous collaborations with custom knifemakers Mel Pardue, Allen Elishewitz, Bill McHenry, Jason Williams, Warren Osborne and Robert Terzuola. Some models feature AXIS locking system, partially serrated blades, pocket clips, boron carbide or BT2® coatings and multi-colored or camouflage handles.

Retail price: $55.00 to $230.00

Benchmade Knife Co. (cont.)

Model 100 River/Rescue has a 3.2-inch fixed blade made of GIN-1 stainless steel and G10 handle. Includes Kydex® sheath with thumb-toggle lock. Straight or combo edge. **$80.00**

Model 160 TK-1 Tether Knife has a 2-inch GIN-1 stainless steel blade and skeletonized handle with thermoplastic coating. Includes Kydex® sheath and 64-inch chain. Offered in straight or partially serrated edge with black, green or gray handle. **$80.00**

Warren Osborne-designed Model 940 has a 3.4-inch blade of 154CM stainless steel and a green anodized aluminum handle with an AXIS lock. Similar Model 942 has a black handle. Offered with straight or partially serrated edge. **$170.00**

Avenger with 3 1/4-inch tanto-point blade (VG-10 steel) and carbon fiber handle. **$225.00**

Electra with VG-10 2 1/2-inch Wharncliffe blade and "circuit board" handle. **$130.00**

Tasca with AUS8 stainless steel blade and black Micarta, stainless steel or aluminum handle. **$85.95**

Airlight with skeletonized or solid AUS6 blade and handle available in black, camo or orange Zytel or black or silver aluminum. **$49.95 to $71.95**

International Guide series fixed-blade or folding knife with AUS8 straight-edge blade and green Micarta or cocobolo handle. **$79.95 to $109.95**

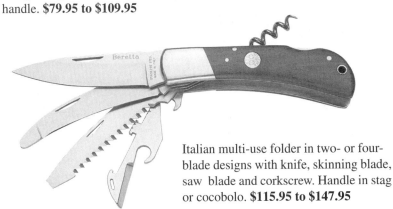

Italian multi-use folder in two- or four-blade designs with knife, skinning blade, saw blade and corkscrew. Handle in stag or cocobolo. **$115.95 to $147.95**

Beretta USA Corp.

17601 Beretta Dr.
Accokeek, MD 20607
(301) 283-2191
Fax: (301) 283-0189
Web site: N/A
E-mail: wrice@
berettausa.com

Styles: Tactical and multi-blade folders; fixed-blade hunting knives.

Sheaths: Tooled leather.

Handles: Camo or orange Zytel®, black or brushed aluminum, stainless steel, black or green Micarta®, carbon fiber, cocobolo and stag.

Features: Most folders feature thumb stud on blade for one-hand opening and handle clip. Some Airlight models feature skeletonized blades. Blades offered in straight-edge or 30 percent serrated versions. Italian multi-use models include two- or four-blade versions with main blade, saw blade with screwdriver tip, skinning blade and fold-out corkscrew.

Retail price: $49.95 to $469.95

Boker USA Inc.

1550 Balsam St.
Lakewood, CO 80215-3117
(303) 462-0662
Fax: (303) 462-0668
www.BokerUSA.com
E-mail:
bokerusa@worldnet.att.net

Styles: Wide range of fixed blade and folding knives for hunting, military, tactical and general use.

Sheaths: Leather and Cordura nylon.

Handles: Sambar stag, rosewood, bone, mother of pearl, cocobolo, titanium, stainless steel, Zytel® and Delrin.

Features: Distributor for Boker, Klötzli and Opinel knives. Blade materials include carbon steel, 440C stainless steel, damascus steel, titanium and ceramic. Some models have interchangeable blades. Collaborations with Michael Walker, Walter Brend, the late Col. Rex Applegate and others. Many models with decorative handles, faux scrimshaw or etched blades. Some limited editions.

**Retail price:
$7.95 to $485.00**

Model 2076 liner lock designed by Michael Walker has a 2 7/8-inch ATS-34 blade and cocobolo handle. **$110.00**

A-F 543DES Desert Storm is based on the original Applegate-Fairbairn A-F 12 fighting knife, with a 6-inch 440C stainless steel blade, forward-bending cross-guard and weighted Delrin® handle. Includes Kydex® sheath with desert camo finish. **$170.00**

Model 585AM is designed by U. Look of Germany, features 4 5/8-inch drop-point blade of 440C stainless steel, integral guard and pommel. Handle of Amboina wood. Includes leather sheath. **$340.00**

Opinel line imported from France by Boker includes this model with a 6 1/4-inch overall length (closed) and unique turning-ring design that locks the blade. All 12 models feature carbon-steel locking blades and pearwood or walnut handle. **$7.95 to $19.95 (model shown, $18.95)**

Smatchet, designed by Col. Rex Applegate, has a 10-inch double-edged blade made of 440C stainless steel with a Micarta® handle for a 1-pound chopping package. Includes Cordura nylon sheath. **$375.00**

Optima knife takes interchangeable blades, comes with 3 5/8-inch Solingen stainless steel clip point and saw blades, plus Cordura belt sheath. Available with Delrin® or gray bone handle. Blades offered include gut-hook, damascus steel, ceramic and drop point. **$170.00 (Delrin® handle).**

Browning

One Browning Place
Morgan, UT 84050-9326
800-333-3288
Fax: N/A
www.browning.com
E-mail: N/A

Styles: Fixed blade and folding hunting, fishing, camping and general-use knives.

Sheaths: Leather, nylon or Concealex®.

Handles: G-10 composite, carbon fiber, Zytel®, Zytel® with laminated-wood inserts, Zytel®/Kevlar® with checkered rubber, rosewood, cocobolo, quince, stag and mother of pearl.

Features: High-carbon, AUS-8A or ATS-34 blades.

Retail price: $25.00 to $152.00

Swivel-Lok Hunter has a 3 3/8-inch, AUS-8A steel blade with a gut hook that can be used in the T-handle or extended position. Handle is Zytel and rubber; includes nylon sheath. **$65.00**

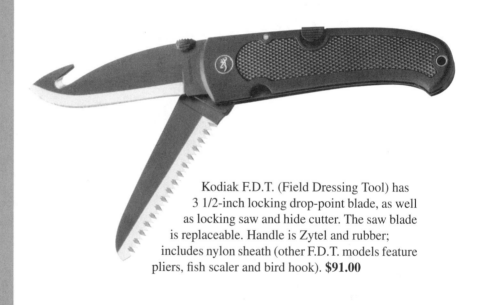

Kodiak F.D.T. (Field Dressing Tool) has 3 1/2-inch locking drop-point blade, as well as locking saw and hide cutter. The saw blade is replaceable. Handle is Zytel and rubber; includes nylon sheath (other F.D.T. models feature pliers, fish scaler and bird hook). **$91.00**

Expedition combines a fixed-blade knife with an AUS-8A 4 1/2-inch blade and a folding lockback knife that snaps inside the Micarta® handle. Includes leather sheath. **$132.00**

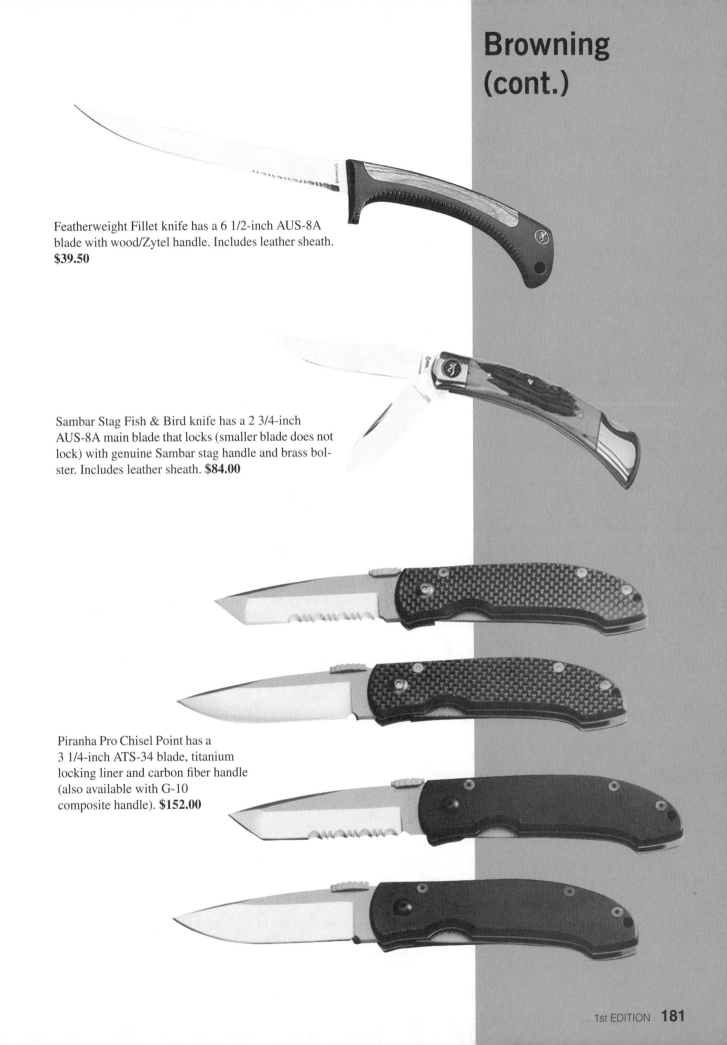

Featherweight Fillet knife has a 6 1/2-inch AUS-8A blade with wood/Zytel handle. Includes leather sheath. **$39.50**

Sambar Stag Fish & Bird knife has a 2 3/4-inch AUS-8A main blade that locks (smaller blade does not lock) with genuine Sambar stag handle and brass bolster. Includes leather sheath. **$84.00**

Piranha Pro Chisel Point has a 3 1/4-inch ATS-34 blade, titanium locking liner and carbon fiber handle (also available with G-10 composite handle). **$152.00**

Buck Knives

P.O. Box 1267
El Cajon, CA 92020
800-326-2825
Fax: 800-729-2825
www.buckknives.com
E-mail: N/A

Styles: Wide range of fixed-blade and folding knives and multi-tools for hunting, fishing, camping and general use.

Sheaths: Leather, plastic, nylon and Kydex®.

Handles: Thermoplastic, G10, stainless steel, nylon /rubber, nylon, resin-impregnated Obechee wood, glass-reinforced nylon with rubber, Kraton®, aluminum, Zytel®, cocobolo, phenolic, hardwood, rosewood, cast resin Poly-Pearl and bonded malachite stone inlay.

Features: Ionfusion™ zirconium nitride coating on some blades provides a hard, long-lasting edge; some limited editions with laser-cut blades featuring elk or deer figures; full-color artwork on some handles; damascus-blade dagger; Crosslock® two-bladed knives with one-hand opening and closing design; many folders feature pocket clips and holes or studs in the blade for one-hand opening.

Retail price: $26.00 to $230.00

CrossLock® 3-Function Hunter has a 3 1/4-inch gutting/skinning blade with saw on back edge, and a 3 1/4-inch drop-point blade, both designed to open, lock and unlock with one hand. Advantage Classic® Camo handle, metal pocket clip. **$80.00**

CrossLock® Yachtsman has a 3 1/8-inch, partially serrated sheepsfoot blade, 3 1/4-inch blade with spanner wrench, shackle wrench, paint can/bottle opener, screwdriver and wire stripper. Includes nylon sheath and wrist lanyard. **$70.00**

Strider™ tactical folder designed by Mick Strider and Duane Dwyer has a 4-inch ATS-34 stainless steel blade with tanto point, titanium lock and liners, G-10 handle. **$190.00**

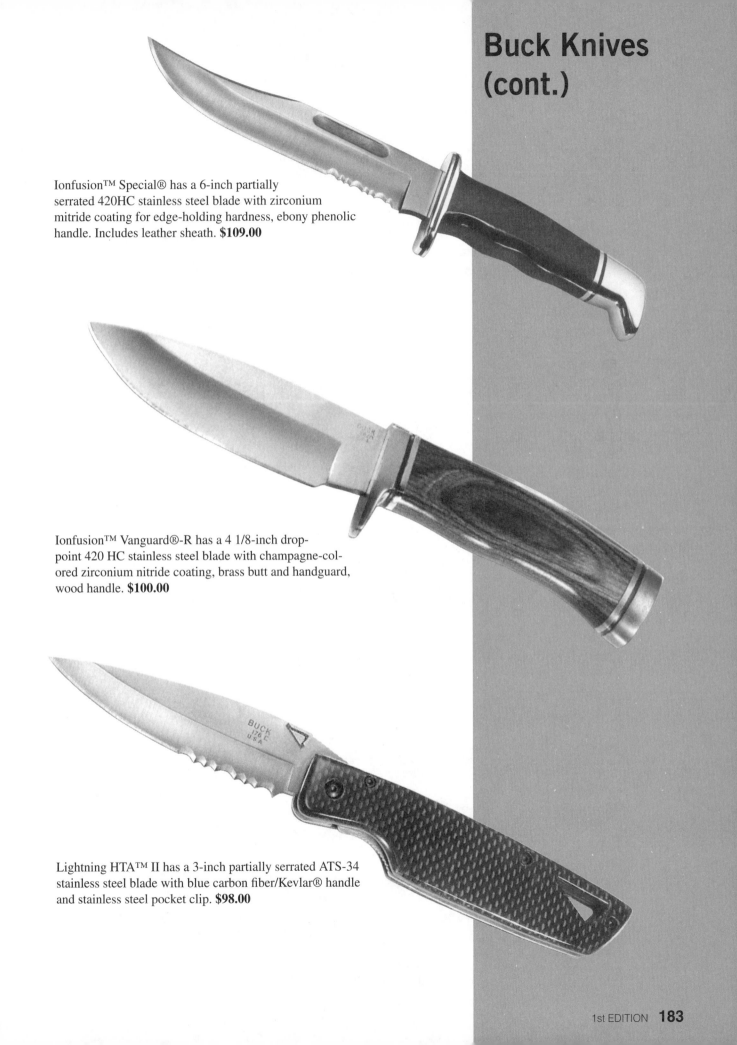

Ionfusion™ Special® has a 6-inch partially serrated 420HC stainless steel blade with zirconium mitride coating for edge-holding hardness, ebony phenolic handle. Includes leather sheath. **$109.00**

Ionfusion™ Vanguard®-R has a 4 1/8-inch drop-point 420 HC stainless steel blade with champagne-colored zirconium nitride coating, brass butt and handguard, wood handle. **$100.00**

Lightning HTA™ II has a 3-inch partially serrated ATS-34 stainless steel blade with blue carbon fiber/Kevlar® handle and stainless steel pocket clip. **$98.00**

Bulldog Brand Knives

P.O. Box 23852
Chattanooga, TN 37422
(423) 894-5102
Fax: (423) 892-9165
Web site: N/A
E-mai: N/A

Styles: Fixed-blade and folding knives for hunting and general use.

Sheaths: Leather.

Handles: Stag, hardwood, celluloid, other materials.

Features: Primarily traditional-design fixed-blade knives. Many blades have wildlife or other designs etched on them.

Retail price:
$15.95 to $124.95

Bird and Trout Skinner has a four-color etching of a Parker shotgun on the blade, stag handle. It was made for the Parker Gun Collectors Association. Includes leather sheath. **$55.00**

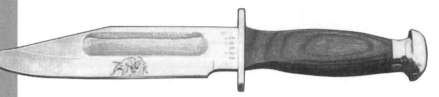

Clip-point Skinner has a 5 1/2-inch blade and a hardwood handle. Includes leather sheath. **$124.95**

Upswept Skinner has a 4 3/4-inch blade and hardwood handle. Includes leather sheath. **$119.95**

Baby Sunfish features a seven-color etching on the blade, "broken chain" celluloid handle. Overall length 3 inches (closed). Also offered in blue sapphire, India stag horn, oyster shell and pearl handles. **$99.99**

Double Doghead has a 4-inch, etched blade and India stag horn handle. Includes leather sheath. **$29.99**

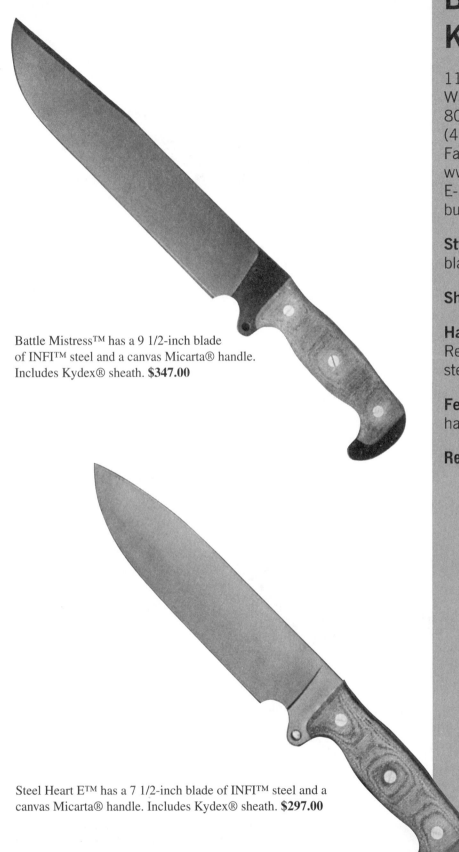

Busse Combat Knife Co.

11651-12
Wauseon, OH 43567
800-860-3622 or
(419) 923-6471
Fax: (419) 923-6471
www.bussecombat.com
E-mail: info@
bussecombat.com

Styles: Military-style fixed-blade knives and machetes.

Sheaths: Kydex®.

Handles: Canvas Micarta®, Resiprene C or skeletonized steel.

Features: Semi-production handmade.

Retail price: $150.00 to $347.00

Battle Mistress™ has a 9 1/2-inch blade of INFI™ steel and a canvas Micarta® handle. Includes Kydex® sheath. **$347.00**

Steel Heart E™ has a 7 1/2-inch blade of INFI™ steel and a canvas Micarta® handle. Includes Kydex® sheath. **$297.00**

CAS Iberia Inc.

650 Industrial Blvd.
Sale Creek, TN 37373
(423) 332-4700
Fax: (423) 332-7248
www.casiberia.com
E-mail: N/A

Styles: Extensive variety of fixed-blade and folding knives for hunting, diving, camping, military and general use.

Sheaths: Leather and nylon.

Handles: Thermoplastic, stag, various hardwoods, laminated wood and steel.

Features: Aitor and Muela knife lines made in Spain.

Retail price: $5.00 to $1,042.00

Aitor Gran Ranchero has everything needed for camping: knife, fork, spoon, can/bottle opener and corkscrew. Green polymer handle. Aitor offers a variety of multi-blade knives with blades that include saws, scissors, awls, files and more. **$31.00**

Aitor Vivac has a 5-inch blade with straight edge and serrations on top, plus a bottle opener and corkscrew in the handle. Includes polymer sheath. **$35.00**

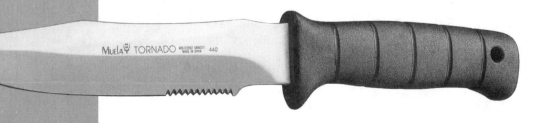

Muela Tornado has a 7 1/8-inch moly-vanadium-stainless steel blade with partially saw-toothed edge and a synthetic handle. Includes nylon sheath. Also offered in a black-coated blade. **$61.00**

Muela Rebeco Drop-Point
Hunter has a 3 1/2-inch
moly-vanadium-stainless steel blade and a
hardwood handle. Includes leather sheath. **$57.00**

Muela Small Game Knife has a 4 3/8-
inch moly-vanadium-stainless steel blade and a crown
stag handle. Includes leather sheath. **$41.00**

Aitor Jungle King II has a 5 1/2-inch
blade and a hollow cast-metal handle with threaded
cap that holds a variety of survival packets available from Aitor.
Included green polyamide sheath converts to a slingshot. Jungle
King models also offered in 4-inch and 8 7/8-inch blades with
black, satin stainless steel and camo finishes. **$88.00**

Camillus Cutlery Co.

54 Main St.
Camillus, NY 13031
(315) 672-8111
Fax: (315) 672-8832
www.camillusknives.com
E-mail: camcut2@aol.com

Styles: Wide variety of pocketknives for hunting and general use.

Sheaths: Nylon, Kydex® and leather.

Handles: Laminated wood, Kraton®, Delrin®, Zytel®, stainless steel, leather, Valox®, circuit board, celluloid abalone and Micarta®.

Features: Sells Camillus, Western, Becker Knife & Tool and Cuda® brands.

Retail price: $10.95 to $199.95

LEV-R-LOK® Piranha Blade has a partially serrated 2 7/8-inch clip blade with patented LEV-R-LOK® mechanical one-hand opening design, Zytel® handle. **$40.95**

Marine Corps Camp Knife is approved by the U.S. military and built to government specifications. High-carbon stainless steel blade is 2 3/8 inches. Also has a can opener, punch, screwdriver and cap lifter. Stainless steel handle, springs and shackle. **$19.49**

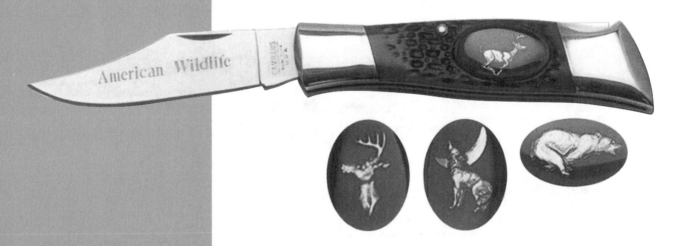

American Wildlife Series lockbacks have 3 1/8-inch high-carbon stainless steel clip blades with brown jigged Delrin® handles and a choice of running deer (shown), howling coyote, buck deer or charging bear gold-plated medallions in the handle. Includes leather sheath. Also offered in a two-blade trapper model. **$61.95**

Becker Knife & Tool TacTool has a 7-inch high-carbon steel blade with gut hook and a GV6H synthetic handle. Includes Kydex® multi-carry sheath system. **$149.95**

Cuda® Quik-Action Spear Blade has a 3 31/32-inch ATS-34 spear blade with bead-blasted finish that opens from its G-10 handle with the forward push of a button. Includes pocket clip. Cuda® models offered in a variety of blade lengths and points, as well as titanium nitride coating. **$169.95**

Cuda® Cyber has a 3-inch drop-point ATS-34 steel blade with thumb-stud opener and circuit-board scales. **$99.95**

Case, W.R. & Sons Cutlery Co.

Owens Way
Bradford, PA 16701
800-523-6350
or (814) 368-4123
Fax: (814) 368-1736
www.wrcase.com
E-mail:
consumer-relations@
wrcase.com

Styles: Vast variety of fixed-blade knives and pocketknives (including limited editions) for hunting, camping, general use and collecting.

Sheaths: Leather.

Handles: Rosewood, amber bone, red bone, black bone, cranberry bone, vintage bone, natural bone, Staminawood™, leather, mother of pearl, plastic, Pakkawood, stainless steel and Zytel®.

Features: Some models feature RussLock™ one-hand opening mechanisms, multiple blades, exchangeable blades and nickel-silver Case logo imbedded in handle.

Retail price: $17.50 to $249.30

Hobo™ Knife separates into a knife and fork with bottle opener when opened. Overall length 4 1/8 inches. Available in stag (shown) or chestnut bone. **$73.60**

Tony Bose-designed Sowbelly Model 5425 has clip, spey and sheepfoot blades with a cranberry bone handle and silver script shield. Also offered in amber bone, vintage bone or PocketWorn® black bone handles. **$80.00**

Slab Side Hunter Model 370 has a 5-inch surgical steel blade and a chestnut bone handle. Includes leather sheath. Slab Side Hunters also offered with a 3 1/2-inch blade and stag or rosewood handles. **$102.90**

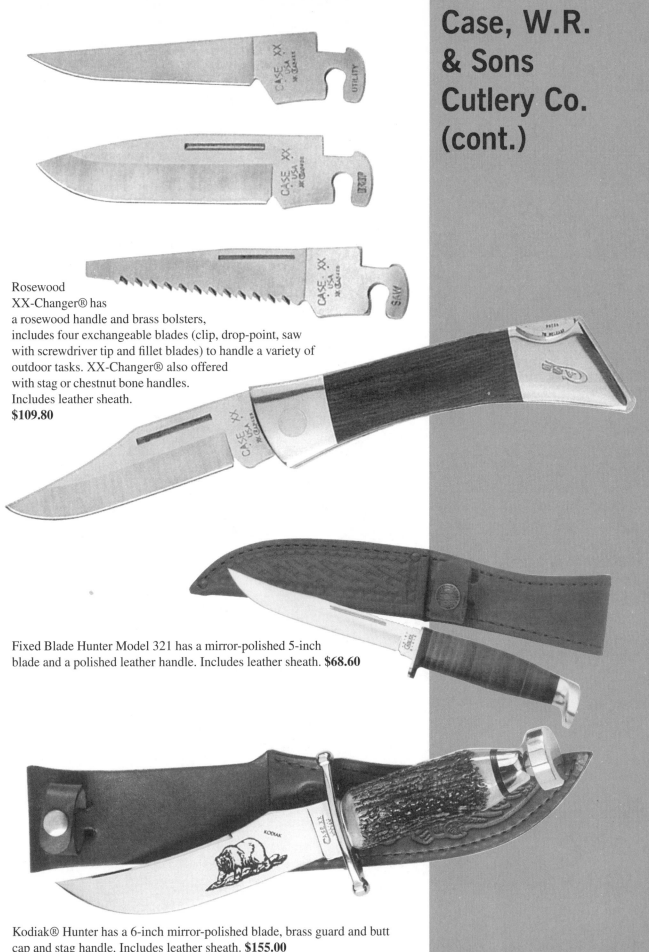

Rosewood XX-Changer® has a rosewood handle and brass bolsters, includes four exchangeable blades (clip, drop-point, saw with screwdriver tip and fillet blades) to handle a variety of outdoor tasks. XX-Changer® also offered with stag or chestnut bone handles. Includes leather sheath. **$109.80**

Fixed Blade Hunter Model 321 has a mirror-polished 5-inch blade and a polished leather handle. Includes leather sheath. **$68.60**

Kodiak® Hunter has a 6-inch mirror-polished blade, brass guard and butt cap and stag handle. Includes leather sheath. **$155.00**

Chris Reeve Knives

11624 W. President Drive
No. B
Boise, ID 83713
(208) 375-0367 or
(208) 375-0368
Fax: N/A
www.chrisreeve.com
E-mail: creeve@micron.net

Styles: Semi-custom fixed blade survival, hunting and skinning knives and high-tech locking folders.

Sheaths: Leather and Cordura nylon.

Handles: A2 steel, titanium, maple burl, curly maple, buckeye, box elder, desert ironwood, black walnut and redwood burl.

Features: Fixed-blade knives of one-piece design; integral-lock folders use a slotted titanium handle scale that serves to lock the blade.

Retail price: $185.00 to $705.00

Umfaan (Zulu for "little boy") has a 2.3-inch BG-42 stainless steel blade with the Sebenza Integral Lock© and titanium handle. **$295.00**

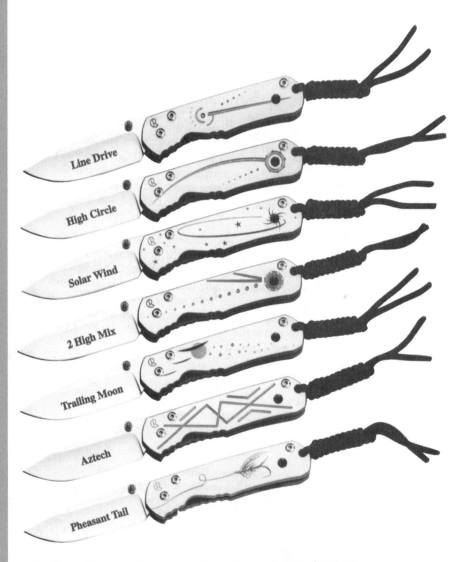

Umfaan with computer-generated graphics on handle. **$365.00**

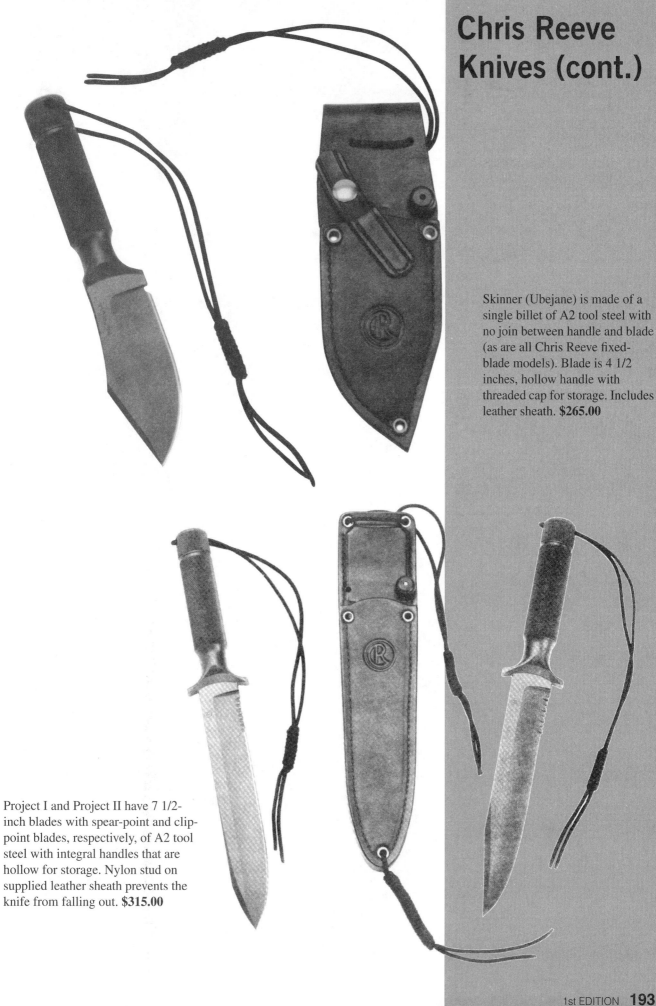

Skinner (Ubejane) is made of a single billet of A2 tool steel with no join between handle and blade (as are all Chris Reeve fixed-blade models). Blade is 4 1/2 inches, hollow handle with threaded cap for storage. Includes leather sheath. **$265.00**

Project I and Project II have 7 1/2-inch blades with spear-point and clip-point blades, respectively, of A2 tool steel with integral handles that are hollow for storage. Nylon stud on supplied leather sheath prevents the knife from falling out. **$315.00**

Chris Reeve Knives (cont.)

Aviator has an A2 tool steel, 4-inch blade with saw teeth and hollow handle with threaded cap for storage. Includes leather sheath. **$205.00**

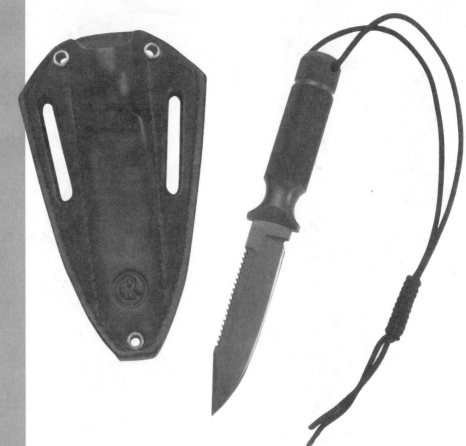

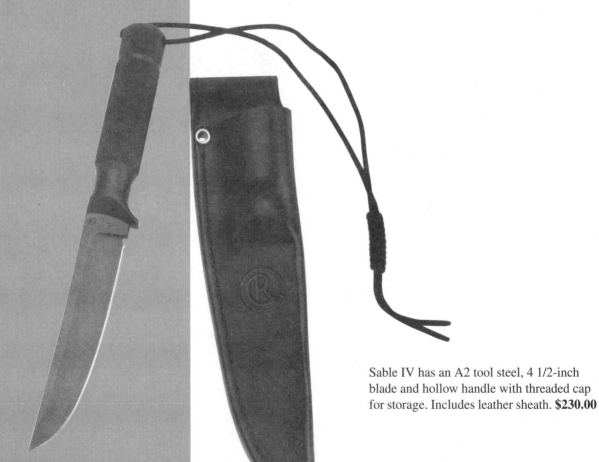

Sable IV has an A2 tool steel, 4 1/2-inch blade and hollow handle with threaded cap for storage. Includes leather sheath. **$230.00**

All Terrain Hunter with 4 1/2-inch Carbon V steel, black epoxy powder-coated blade and Kraton handle. Comes with polycarbonate sheath. **$41.99**

Bird and Trout knife with 2 1/4-inch Carbon V steel, black epoxy powder-coated blade. Comes with Concealex neck sheath and paracord lanyard. **$44.99**

Stag Trail Master with 9 1/2-inch Carbon V steel blade and sanbar stag handle. Comes with leather sheath. **$399.99**

Recon Scout with 7 1/2-inch Carbon V steel, black epoxy powder-coated blade. Comes with leather sheath. **$219.99**

Cold Steel Inc.

3036-A Seaborg Ave.
Ventura, CA 93003
800-255-4716 or
(805) 650-8481
Fax: (805) 642-9727
www.coldsteel.com
E-mail: custsvc@spyder-co.com

Styles: Wide variety of folding lockbacks and fixed-blade hunting, fishing and neck knives, as well as bowies, kukris, tantos, throwing knives and kitchen knives.

Sheaths: Concealex® (plastic), polycarbonate, Cordura nylon and leather.

Handles: Zytel®, Kraton®, aluminum and steel.

Features: Extremely strong blades, many featuring the company's trademark tanto point. Blade steels include Carbon V (a high-carbon, low-alloy steel), AUS stainless, 5150 or San Mai III, a three-layered, laminated construction. Many collaborations with custom knifemakers.

Retail price: $24.99 to $799.99

Voyager medium tanto point with a 3-inch AUS 8A stainless steel blade (offered in plain, serrated or 50/50 edges) with Zytel handle and stainless steel pocket clip. **$74.99**

Colonial
Knife Co. Inc.

287 Agnes at Magnolia St.
Providence, RI 02909-0327
800-556-7824
Fax: (401) 421-2047
www.colonialknife.com
E-mail: ckc1919@aol.com

Styles: Fixed-blade and folding knives for hunting, military and general use.

Sheaths: Leather or nylon.

Handles: Plastic, aluminum, stainless steel, ivory Delrin®, stag, resin butyrate and Kraton®.

Features: Some models feature locking blades, skeletonized handles, pocket clips and thumb studs for one-hand opening.

Retail price: $4.99 to $67.99

Drop- Point Hunter has a 4 1/4-inch high-carbon steel blade and "safety grip" handle. Includes leather sheath. **$24.99**

Bowie-Style Hunter has a 6-inch stainless steel blade and "safety grip" handle. Includes leather sheath. **$25.99**

Anvil Filet knife has a 5 3/4-inch stainless steel blade and "safety grip" handle. Includes leather sheath. **$23.99**

Coyote Series Lockback is 5 inches overall (closed) with a high-carbon steel blade and green synthetic handle. Also available in a 4-inch or 3-inch overall length. Includes leather sheath. **$28.99**

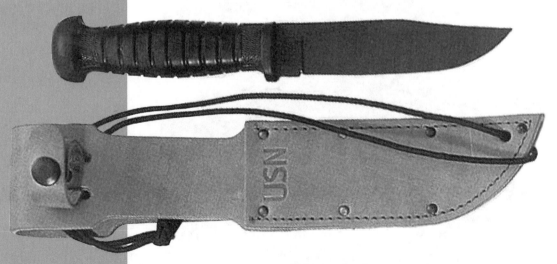

Mark I Navy Combat Utility Knife is made to the same specs as the one used in World War II. It has a 5 1/8-inch high-carbon steel blade with black anti-reflective finish and a black hard-resin butyrate handle. Includes leather sheath with lanyard hole and nylon cord. **$67.99**

Modified Drop Point Stiff K.I.S.S. has a 3 1/2-inch AUS 6M steel blade shaped for trout, bird and game skinning. Offered in straight or partially serrated edges. Includes Zytel® sheath and paracord. **$29.95**

Bear Claw has a 2-inch AUS 6M blade with a Zytel® handle and sheath. Offered in straight or serrated edge. **$39.95**

Columbia River Knife & Tool

9720 S.W. Hillman Ct.
Ste. 885
Wilsonville, OR 97070-7712
800-891-3100
Fax: (503) 682-9680
www.crkt.com
E-mail: info@crkt.com

Styles: Fixed-blade and folding knives for hunting, fishing, camping, tactical and general use.

Sheaths: Leather, Zytel® and polypropylene.

Handles: Carbon fiber, zinc alloy, Zytel®, stainless steel , titanium and G-10 fiberglass laminate.

Features: Most folders include thumb studs and pocket clips. Many collaborations with custom knife makers, including Ed Halligan (K.I.S.S. and P.E.C.K. designs), Michael Walker, Steve Ryan, Brian Tighe, Russ Kommer, Gary Paul Johnston, Al Polkowski and others.

Retail price: $21.99 to $175.00

M16 Carbon Fibre has a 2.6-inch ACUTO 440 stainless steel blade and carbon fiber handle, with an overall weight of 1.6 ounces. Offered in straight or partially serrated edge. M16 models also offered with aluminum and Zytel® handles, up to 3.9-inch blades of AUS 8 steel and Carson Flipper speed-openers. **$89.95 (shown)**

Columbia River Knife & Tool (cont.)

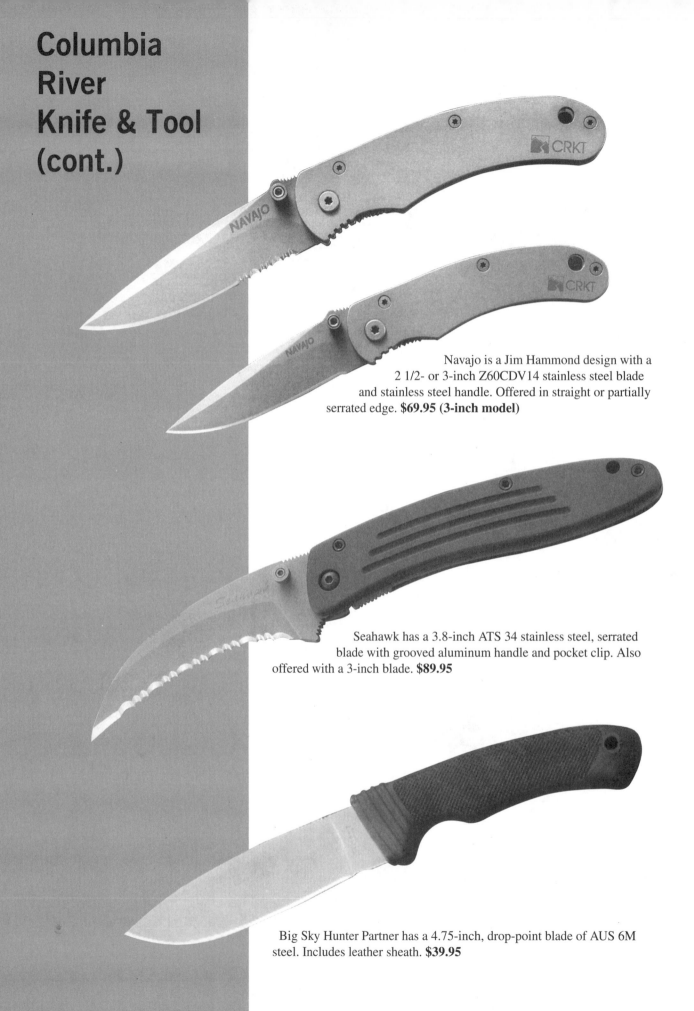

Navajo is a Jim Hammond design with a 2 1/2- or 3-inch Z60CDV14 stainless steel blade and stainless steel handle. Offered in straight or partially serrated edge. **$69.95 (3-inch model)**

Seahawk has a 3.8-inch ATS 34 stainless steel, serrated blade with grooved aluminum handle and pocket clip. Also offered with a 3-inch blade. **$89.95**

Big Sky Hunter Partner has a 4.75-inch, drop-point blade of AUS 6M steel. Includes leather sheath. **$39.95**

Point Guard
Damascus locking liner
has a 3 1/2-inch damascus
blade with a titanium handle.
Price unavailable.

Point Guard
locking liner has a 2
3/4-inch blade of ATS-34
stainless steel and a titanium
handle. **Price unavailable.**

Fancy Kasper Folding
locking liner has a 3 7/8-inch
blade of ATS-34 stainless steel and a
stag handle. **Price unavailable.**

Fancy Kasper Folding
Damascus locking liner has a 3
7/8-inch blade of damascus steel and an
ivory handle. **Price unavailable.**

Pat Crawford Knives

205 N. Center
West Memphis, AR 72301
501-735-4632

Styles: Semi-production
folding knives for
tactical and general use.

Sheaths: N/A

Handles: Stag, ivory,
titanium and other materials.

Features: Most models
have thumb studs for
one-hand opening; some
feature damascus steel blades.

Retail price: N/A

David Boye Knives

P.O. Box 1238
Dolan Springs, AZ 86441
(800) 853-1617
or (520) 767-4273
Fax: (520) 767-3030

Styles: Semi-production fixed-blade and folding knives for hunting and general use.

Sheaths: N/A

Handles: Ironwood, other hardwoods and synthetics.

Features: Exceptionally hard dendritic steel and dendritic cobalt blades.

Retail price: N/A

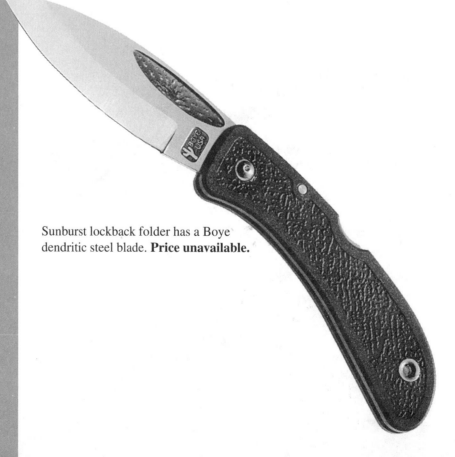

Drop point hunter has a 4-inch Boye dendritic cobalt blade and an ironwood handle. **Price unavailable.**

Sunburst lockback folder has a Boye dendritic steel blade. **Price unavailable.**

360-degree pivot Executive Knife has a 2.95-inch ATS-34 stainless steel blade with anodized blue aluminum handle. **$119.95**

California Legal Mini-Automatic; 1.9-inch stainless steel blade with green stained wood handle. **$79.95**

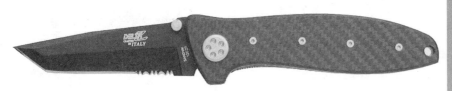

High Tech Liner Lock has a 3 1/2-inch tanto blade with serration and carbon fiber handle. **$219.95**

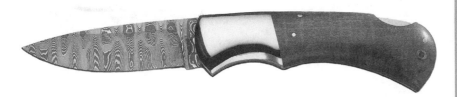

Drop Point Lock Back Folder; 3 1/2-inch super stainless Damascus blade with blue maple burl handle. **$289.95**

Fixed blade (with sheath) has a 5.25-inch 4116 stainless steel blade with African ox horn handle. **$169.95**

Liner Lock folder has a 3.25-inch 440A stainless steel blade with birch briar wood handle. **$109.95**

Delta Z Knives Inc.

P.O. Box 1112
Studio City, CA 91614
(818) 786-9488
Fax: (818) 787-8560
www.DeltaZ-Knives.com
E-mail: N/A

Styles: Wide range of folders and fixed-blade designs.

Sheaths: Leather.

Handles: Cocobolo, Micarta, maple burl, birch briar, olive briar, stag, African ox horn, cow horn, anodized aluminum, neoprene, bakelite and carbon fiber. Colors include blue, gold, silver, red, purple, green and black.

Features: Some feature damascus or stainless steel blades, back or liner locks, tanto points, pocket clips, blade studs for one-hand opening and 360-degree pivoting blades. Most models made in Italy.

Retail price: $52.95 to $359.95

Emerson Knives Inc.

P.O. Box 4180
Torrance, CA 90510-4180
(310) 212-7455
Fax: (310) 793-8730
www.emersonknives.com
E-mail: Eknives@aol.com

Styles: Fixed-blade and folding knives for tactical, hunting and general use.

Sheaths: Nylon and Kydex®.

Handles: G-10 epoxy/glass laminate, Kydron™, Kevlar®-reinforced polymer and skeletonized steel.

Features: Folders have thumb studs for one-hand opening; most offered with spear or tanto points and partially serrated edges; blades of 154 CM steel.

Retail price: $69.95 to $239.95

Commander has a 3 3/4-inch 154 CM steel blade with partially serrated edge and G-10 epoxy/glass laminate handle. Hook at top and back of blade is designed to quickly open knife by catching on pants pocket. **$219.95**

Police Utility has a 3 1/2-inch fixed blade of 154 CM steel blade with partially serrated edge and Kevlar®-reinforced polymer. Includes nylon sheath. **$179.95**

CQC-7 has a 3.3-inch 154 CM steel blade and black G-10 epoxy/glass laminate handle. Includes pocket clip. Offered with a tanto or spear point and satin or black finish. **$139.95**

Specwar has a 3 1/2-inch 154 CM steel blade and G-10 epoxy/glass laminate handle. Offered with a tanto or spear point and satin or black finish. **$199.95**

Raven has a 3 1/2-inch 154 CM steel blade and olive drab or black Kydron® handle. Offered in spear or tanto points. **$179.95**

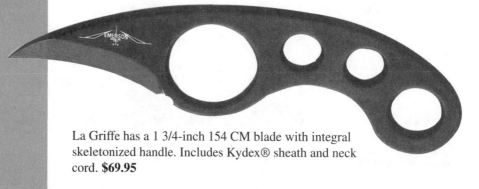

La Griffe has a 1 3/4-inch 154 CM blade with integral skeletonized handle. Includes Kydex® sheath and neck cord. **$69.95**

WM1 has a 2 3/4-inch VG10 blade and Thermorun handle. Neck Kydex or leather belt sheath available. **$79.95**

F1 Swedish Air Force survival knife has a 3.8-inch VG10 steel blade and Thermorun handle. **$99.95**

G1 Garm Fighter with 3 1/2-inch VG10 double-edged blade and Thermorun handle. **Price unavailable.**

H1 Hunting knife is a puukka design with 4-inch VG10 steel blade and Kraton handle. **Price unavailable.**

S1 Forest knife has a 5 1/8-inch VG10 blade and Thermorun handle. Kydex or leather belt sheath available. **$129.95**

A1 Survival knife with 6.3-inch VG10 blade and Kraton handle. **$178.95**

Fällkniven

P.O. Box 204
S-961 23 Boden
Sweden
(distributor: Blue Ridge Knives)
(540) 783-6143
(Blue Ridge Knives)
Fax: N/A
www.fallkkniven.com
E-mail: info@fallkniven.se
or (Blue Ridge Knives)
BRK@netva.com

Styles: Fixed-blade hunting and survival knives with some traditional Swedish designs.

Sheaths: Oxhide leather and Kydex.

Handles: Kraton, Thermorun, curly grained birch and sallow.

Features: Exceptionally strong blades of VG10 steel. Many models feature black Teflon coating on blade. Most feature two or three sheath choices.

Retail price: $79.95 to $178.95

Frost Cutlery Co.

P.O. Box 22636
Chattanooga, TN 37422
800-251-7768
or (423) 894-6079
Fax: (423) 894-9576
www.frostcutleryco.com
E-mail: N/A

Styles: Wide range of fixed -blade and folding knives with a multitude of handle materials.

Sheaths: N/A

Handles: Bone, mother of pearl, laminated wood, thermoplastic, rubber, stainless steel, synthetic scrimshaw, stag, imitation ivory and numerous colors of celluloid.

Features: Fantasy-style Bowie knives; novelty pocketknives featuring western heroes and Masonic symbols; keychain novelty knives; general-use pocketknives and tactical folders; all-stainless Flying Falcon folders. Most models feature 440 Solingen steel blades, nickel silver bolsters and brass liners.

Retail price: $3.00 to $239.95

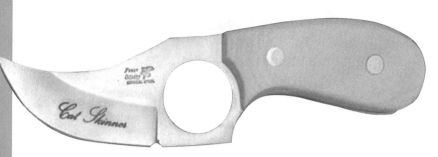

Cat Skinner is 6 inches overall and available with frostwood, smooth bone or wormgroove handle. **$22.95**

Marine Combat knife is 11 3/4 inches overall and includes sheath. **$16.95**

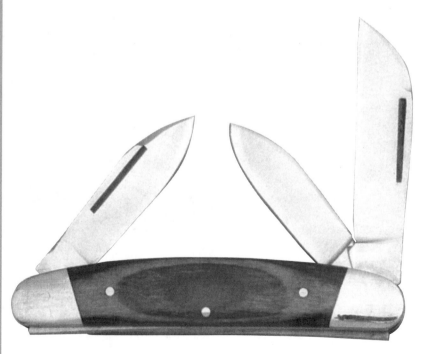

Tobacco Congress offers four blades in a 4 1/4-inch package. **$16.95**

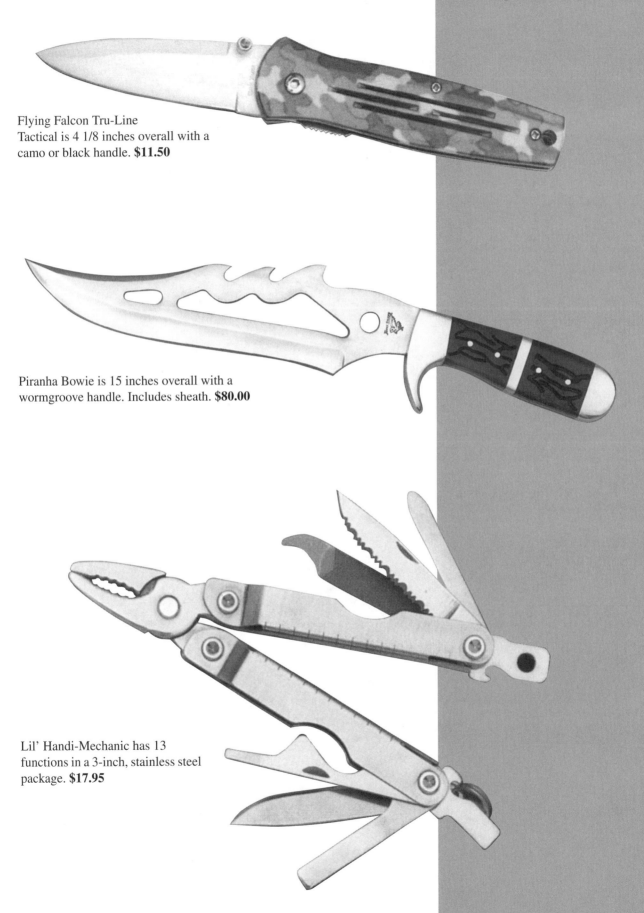

Flying Falcon Tru-Line Tactical is 4 1/8 inches overall with a camo or black handle. **$11.50**

Piranha Bowie is 15 inches overall with a wormgroove handle. Includes sheath. **$80.00**

Lil' Handi-Mechanic has 13 functions in a 3-inch, stainless steel package. **$17.95**

GATCO Sharpeners/ Timberline Knives

P.O. Box 600
Getzville, NY 14068-0600
800-548-7427
or (716) 877-2200
Fax: (716) 877-2591
www.timberlineknives.com
E-mail: gatco@buffnet.net

Styles: Fixed-blade and folding knives for hunting, camping, military and general use; Frog Tool multi-tool.

Sheaths: Nylon and Kydex®.

Handles: Fiberglass-reinforced nylon, aluminum, Kraton® and stainless steel.

Features: Folders have blade stud or hole for one-hand opening; some folders have pocket clips; NeeleyLock™ opens and closes by pushing the blade forward (no levers or buttons); Discovery™ lock is unlocked by sliding handle button.

Retail price: $23.99 to $400.00

Locking Liner is a Butch Vallotton design with a 3 1/2-inch AUS 8 bead-blasted blade and Zytel® handle with Kraton® inserts. Offered in partially serrated (shown) or straight edge. **$49.99**

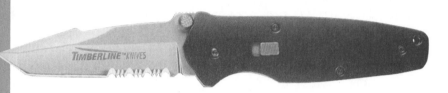

Discovery™ Lock has a 3.1-inch AUS 8 blade in plain or 40 percent serrated edge and aluminum handle. Also offered with nylon and Zytel® handles. **$99.99**

Warden Tactical is designed by Kelly Warden and offered with 2.9- or 3.9-inch blade of AUS 8 steel (combination or straight edge) and glass-filled nylon handle with pocket clip. **$59.99 (3.9-inch blade)**

Special Service Knife has a 3.4-inch AUS 8 partially serrated or straight-edge blade and stainless steel handle with pocket clip. **$120.00**

Aviator Pilot Survival Knife has a 3.4-inch 440 stainless steel blade with titanium nitride coating and a Kraton® sheath. **$220.00**

William Harsey-designed AirFrame has a 5-inch 154 CM steel blade with titanium handle and pocket clip. Offered in straight and serrated edges. **Price unavailable.**

Multi-Plier 800 Series Legend has a pliers with replaceable tungsten carbide wire-cutter inserts, jig saw coupler, Fiskars® scissors, file, bottle opener, regular and Phillips screwdrivers, Torx wrench with four Torx fasteners and knife blade. Aluminum handle with Gator TEX grips. Includes nylon sheath. **$136.00**

Gerber Legendary Blades — Fiskars

14200 SW 72nd Ave.
Portland, OR 97223
(503) 639-6161
Fax: (503) 684-7008
www.gerberblades.com
E-mail: N/A

Styles: Fixed-blade and folding knives and multi-tools for hunting, fishing, camping and general use.

Sheaths: Nylon, Concealex and plastic.

Handles: Santoprene® rubber/glass filled polypropylene, Kraton®, aluminum, G-10, carbon fiber, Zytel® and stainless steel.

Features: Multi-tools features include Torx wrench, saw coupler that takes standard jig saw blades, Fiskars® scissors, file, can opener, bottle opener, regular and Phillips screwdrivers, bit driver with bits, needlenose pliers with wire cutters, awl, standard and metric ruler, corkscrew, serrated and straight-edge knife blades. Some knife models have thumb studs or holes in the blade for one-hand opening.

Retail price: $20.00 to $240.00

Chameleon I has a stainless steel blade and ergonomic glass-filled nylon handle that is designed with a hole for the index finger. Overall length 3.4 inches closed. Also offered in 4.3- and 5.1-inch lengths. **$41.30**

Stud Gator has a 3 3/4-inch ATS-34 steel blade with straight or serrated edge and a stud on both sides of the blade for one-hand opening. Zytel® frame with Kraton® handle. Includes nylon sheath. Also offered as Gator Mate with 2 3/4-inch blade. **$57.60**

E-Z-Out has a 3 1/2-inch stainless steel blade with hole for one-hand opening and a Zytel®/Kraton® handle. Also offered with an ATS-34 steel blade and straight or partially serrated edges. **$32.00 to $60.00**

Expedition IB has a black-finish, 3 1/4-inch, high carbon steel blade with a Kraton® and glass-reinforced nylon handle. Includes plastic sheath. Also offered with a double-edge blade and stainless steel finish. **$68.00**

Fred Carter-designed Challenger Ti has a 4 1/2-inch ATS 34 stainless steel blade (plain or partially serrated with tanto or plain point) and titanium-coated aluminum handle. Includes nylon sheath and clip. **Price unavailable.**

Gigand
Company, Inc.

No. 4, Lane 130, Sec. 1
Kuang Fu Road
San Chung Taipei
Taiwan, R.O.C.
886-2-29952860
Fax: 886-2-29952860
www.gigand.com
E-mail: gigand@ms39.
hinet.net

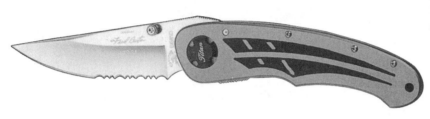

Fred Carter-designed Titan has a 4 1/2-inch ATS 34 stainless steel blade (straight or partially serrated edge) with titanium handle and blue or black inserts. **Price unavailable.**

Guardian neck knife has a 4 1/4-inch blade of AUS 8A stainless steel and an ABS plastic handle. Includes plastic sheath that holds knife with magnets. **Price unavailable.**

Mosquito neck knife has a 2-inch blade of AUS 8A stainless steel and ABS plastic handle. Includes plastic sheath that holds knife with magnets. **Price unavailable.**

Gigand Company, Inc. (cont.)

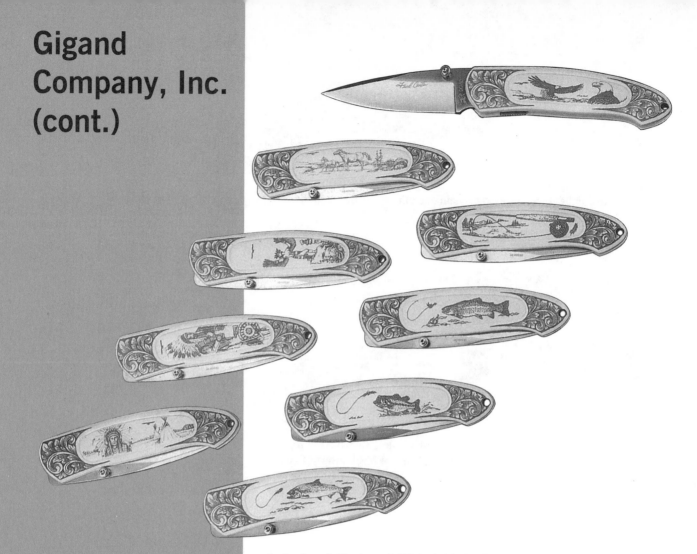

Scrimshaw folder has a 2 7/8-inch blade of 420 J2 stainless steel and ABS plastic handle with laser scrimshaw in nine fish, wildlife and Indian patterns. **Price unavailable.**

Spectrum LT is a Carter-designed model with a 3 1/8-inch ATS 34 blade and aluminum handle with carbon fiber overlay. Also offered with G10 overlay and solid aluminum handle in blue, gold, green, red, black or silver. **Price unavailable.**

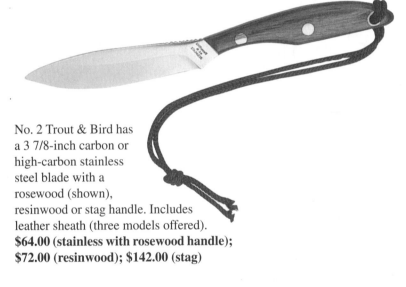

No. 1 Original Design has a 4-inch blade of carbon or high-carbon stainless steel and a rosewood (shown), water-resistant resinwood or stag handle. Includes oil-tanned leather sheath. Also offered with flap sheath and sheath with sharpening steel. **$69.00 (stainless with rosewood handle); $77.00 (resinwood); $147.00 (stag)**

No. 2 Trout & Bird has a 3 7/8-inch carbon or high-carbon stainless steel blade with a rosewood (shown), resinwood or stag handle. Includes leather sheath (three models offered). **$64.00 (stainless with rosewood handle); $72.00 (resinwood); $142.00 (stag)**

No. 4 Survival Knife has a 5 1/2-inch carbon or high-carbon stainless steel blade with a rosewood (shown), resinwood or stag handle. Includes leather sheath (three models offered). **$91.00 (stainless with rosewood handle); $99.00 (resinwood); $169.00 (stag)**

Grohmann Knives Ltd.

P.O. Box 40
116 Water St.
Pictou, Nova Scotia
Canada B0K 1H0
888-756-4837
or (902) 485-4224
Fax: (902) 485-5872
www.grohmannknives.com
E-mail: grohmann@
grohmannknives.com

Styles: Fixed-blade belt knives for hunting and fishing; folding pocketknives for hunting and general use.

Sheaths: Leather.

Handles: Rosewood, stag, laminated hardwood (resinwood) and Zytel®.

Features: Made in Canada. D.H. Russell and Grohmann belt knives with high-carbon stainless steel or carbon steel blades (in traditional Russell elliptical blade designs or Grohmann skinning blade designs).

Retail price: $37.00 to $197.00

Grohmann Knives Ltd. (cont.)

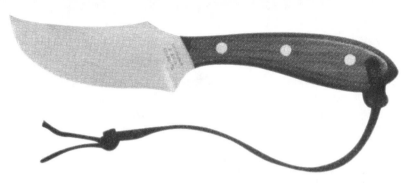

No. 103 Short Blade Skinner has a 3 1/2-inch carbon or high-carbon stainless steel blade with a rosewood (shown), resinwood or stag handle. Includes leather sheath (three models offered). **$88.00 (stainless with rosewood handle); $96.00 (resinwood); $166.00**

Featherlight Lockblade has a 3-inch high-carbon stainless steel blade and black Zytel® handle. **$37.00**

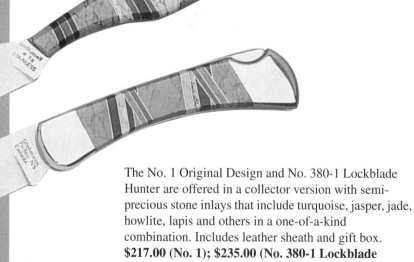

The No. 1 Original Design and No. 380-1 Lockblade Hunter are offered in a collector version with semi-precious stone inlays that include turquoise, jasper, jade, howlite, lapis and others in a one-of-a-kind combination. Includes leather sheath and gift box. **$217.00 (No. 1); $235.00 (No. 380-1 Lockblade Hunter)**

GT Knives Inc.

7734 Arsons Dr.
San Diego, CA 92126-4365
(858) 530-8766
Fax: (858) 530-8798
Web site: N/A
E-mail: N/A

Styles: Push-button and manual folding knives for sportsmen, law enforcement and the military.

Sheaths: N/A

Handles: Aircraft aluminum.

Features: ATS-34 stainless steel blades coated with titanium aluminum nitride. Most include pocket clip. Straight or serrated blades.

Retail price: $53.95 to $219.95

GT-302 is 4 7/8 inches closed, with an ATS-34 stainless steel blade with titanium aluminum nitride coating and an aircraft aluminum handle. Includes pocket clip. Also offered with a straight edge, and a model for law enforcement only. **$169.95**

GT-101 is 4 7/8 inches closed, with an ATS-34 stainless steel blade with titanium aluminum nitride coating and an aircraft aluminum handle. Includes pocket clip. Also offered with a partially serrated edge, and a model for law enforcement only. **$139.95**

Gutmann Cutlery Inc.

P.O. Box 2219
Bellingham, WA 98227
800-288-5379
or (360) 650-9141
Fax: (360) 676-1075
www.gutmanncutlery.com
E-mail: N/A

Styles: Wide range of folding and fixed-blade knives; multi-tools; compact pocket knives; Junglee folding and fixed hunting, military and fighting designs; axes; cleavers; cigar knives and kitchen knives.

Sheaths: Leather and ballistic nylon.

Handles: Kraton rubber, synthetic ivory, wood (some inlaid with turquoise or gemstones), aluminum, Zytel and stag.

Features: Variety of scrimshaw handles; Explora survival knife; Stubby designs; some models with pocket clips, skeletonized blades, one-hand openers and Walther logo; Smith & Wesson multi-tools.

Retail price: $11.95 to $345.00

Junglee® "Z" Knife™ has a 2 1/4-inch AUS-6 stainless steel blade with Zytel® handle fitted with rosewood inserts. Includes stainless steel pocket clip. Also offered in a Zytel®-only handle. **$24.95 (scrimshaw models with numerous wildlife scenes, $33.95)**

Junglee® Tri-Point™ has a partially serrated 3 1/2-inch AUS-10 stainless steel blade with a triangular hole for one-hand opening and a Zytel® handle. Also offered in a straight-edge or fully serrated blade. **$54.95**

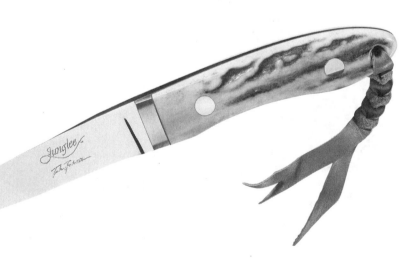

Junglee® Tak Fukuta Signature Series Hunter has a 4 1/8-inch AUS-8 stainless steel blade with brushed nickel bolsters and Sambar stag handle. Includes leather sheath and Fukuta's trademark braided lanyard. **$131.95**

Junglee® Tactical Gurkha has a slightly reverse-swept, 5-inch AUS-8 stainless steel blade in the spirit of traditional Gurkha knives, as well as a Kraton® rubber handle. Includes leather sheath. **$79.95**

Junglee® Baby Hattori™ has a 6 1/16-inch AUS-8 stainless steel blade and a handle that combines nickel silver guards, polished hardwood and Kraton® rubber. Includes leather sheath. **$199.95**

Walther® P99 Silhouette Folder has a 2 13/16-inch blade of 440C stainless steel with the outline of the famed Walther® P99 pistol cut into the blade. **$37.95**

Historic Edged Weaponry

1021 Saddlebrook Dr.
Dept. BT
Hendersonville, NC 28739
(828) 692-0323
Fax: (828) 692-0600
Web site: N/A
E-mail: N/A

Styles: Antique knives from around the world; importer of puukko and other knives from Norway, Sweden, Finland and Lapland.

Sheaths: Leather.

Handles: Reindeer antler, curly birch and great sallow.

Features: Traditional puukko and Viking designs, most with Swedish carbon or stainless steel blades.

Retail price: $25.00 to $1,700.00

This Jarvenpaa Co. Lapp Hunter has a 6-inch stainless steel blade and curly birch handle. Includes leather sheath. **$43.00**

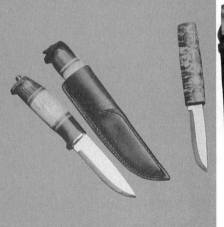

These Norwegian knives from the Helle Co. have triple-layered, laminated stainless steel blades and curly grained birch (knife on left has a rosewood, curly birch and leather-washer handle). From left are: Harding Hunter (**$67.00**); Viking Knife (**$43.00**); Laplander Hunter (**$67.00**); Mountaineer Knife (**$45.00**) and Super Fjording Camping Knife (**$39.00**). All include leather sheaths.

Schrade Buzz Saw Trapper has high carbon steel straight-edge and locking saw blades, pick and tweezers. Leather sheath included. **$47.95**

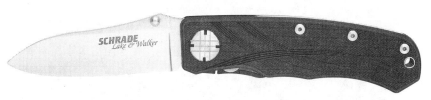

Schrade Lake & Walker folder designed by custom makers Ron Lake and Michael Walker has a one-hand-opening 2 7/8-inch blade with patented Tough Lock and Zylite (Kevlar/Zytel) handle, sliding safety and pocket clip. **$67.95**

Schrade Cliphanger Sportmate is 4 1/2 inches closed with a stainless steel blade, quick-release snap strap and a Zytel pocket clip permanently attached to the glass-reinforced nylon handle. Other Cliphangers are available with partially serrated blades and in 2 5/8-inch and 3 1/4-inch (closed) sizes. **$40.95**

Imperial Schrade Corp.

7 Schrade Court
P.O. Box 7000
Ellenville, NY 12428-0981
800-272-4723
or (845) 647-7600
Fax: (845) 210-8670
www.schradeknives.com
E-mail: info@
schradeknives.com

Styles: Schrade, Old Timer, Uncle Henry and Imperial brands of fixed-blade and folding knives for hunting, fishing, camping, survival and general use; Schrade and Tradesman multi-tools; numerous other specialty knives, including Schrade Cliphanger folders with quick-release straps.

Sheaths: Leather and ballistic nylon.

Handles: Stainless steel, oak, thermoplastic rubber, Delrin, Staglon, Zytel and Kevlar/Zytel.

Features: High carbon or Schrade+ stainless steel blades; brass linings with nickel silver or brass bolsters; multi-tools allow access to all blades when opened or closed; most models offer limited lifetime warranty; some models offer one year replacement guarantee against loss.

Retail price: $21.95 to $110.00

Imperial Schrade Corp. (cont.)

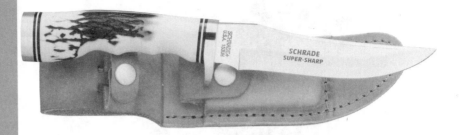

Schrade Uncle Henry Golden Spike is 9 1/4 inches overall with Schrade+ stainless steel blade, Staglon handle and leather sheath. **$65.95**

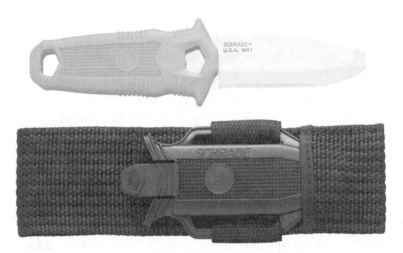

Schrade Water Rat is 7 3/8 inches overall with black or orange handle that locks into the Delrin sheath and is released with a push button. Sheath straps to an arm or leg, or can be clipped to a life vest. **$36.95**

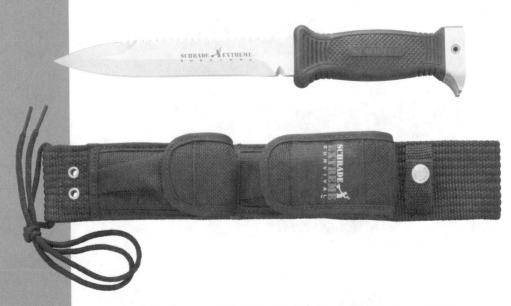

Schrade Extreme survival knife is 12 1/4 inches overall with saw/knife blade, hammer/claw pommel, file and ballistic nylon sheath. Similar Double Eagle model (not shown) is 11 3/8 inches overall with blackened blade and a molded sheath that holds a sharpening stone. **$110.00**

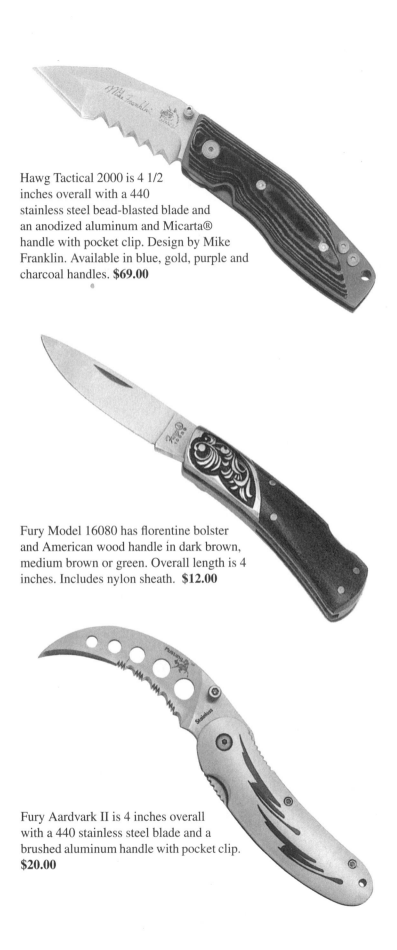

Hawg Tactical 2000 is 4 1/2 inches overall with a 440 stainless steel bead-blasted blade and an anodized aluminum and Micarta® handle with pocket clip. Design by Mike Franklin. Available in blue, gold, purple and charcoal handles. **$69.00**

Fury Model 16080 has florentine bolster and American wood handle in dark brown, medium brown or green. Overall length is 4 inches. Includes nylon sheath. **$12.00**

Fury Aardvark II is 4 inches overall with a 440 stainless steel blade and a brushed aluminum handle with pocket clip. **$20.00**

Joy Enterprises — Fury Cutlery

1104 53rd Court South
West Palm Beach, FL 33407
800-500-3879 or
(561) 863-3205
Fax: (561) 863-3277
www.joyenterprises.com or
www.furycutlery.com
E-mail:
mail@joyenterprises.com

Styles: Extensive variety of fixed-blade and folding knives for hunting, fishing, diving, camping, military and general use; novelty key-ring knives.

Sheaths: Leather and nylon.

Handles: Plastic, hardwoods, leather washers, rubber and stainless steel.

Features: Fury, Mustang, Hawg, Muela and Herbertz knife lines; models made in United States, Spain, Germany, Japan, Taiwan and China.

Retail price: 60 cents to $1,198.00

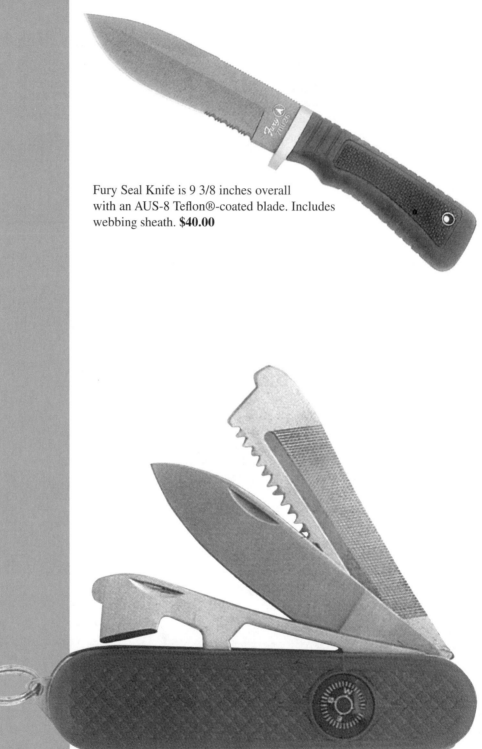

Fury Seal Knife is 9 3/8 inches overall with an AUS-8 Teflon®-coated blade. Includes webbing sheath. **$40.00**

Fury NATO-Type Knife has three blades, plus a compass in its olive-drab plastic handle. Overall length 4 inches. Includes nylon sheath. **$7.00**

The U.S.M.C. Fighting/Utility Knife is the same model used by the Marines in World War II. The 7-inch epoxy powder-coated blade is high-carbon steel. Available with straight edge or 2-inch serrated section and U.S.M.C. or U.S. Army leather sheath. **$59.79**

Next Generation Fighting/Utility Knife has a 7-inch Sandvik 12C27 high-carbon stainless steel blade with a bead-blasted finish and Kraton G® thermoplastic handle. Includes Kydex® or leather sheath. Also offered with straight edge. **$103.39 ($142.88 with Kydex® sheath).**

Black Tanto has an 8-inch, epoxy powder-coated blade with a 2-inch serrated section. Includes Kydex® sheath. **$76.37**

Warthog has a 5 3/8-inch, epoxy powder-coated blade with a straight, hollow-ground edge. Includes Kydex® sheath. **$76.37**

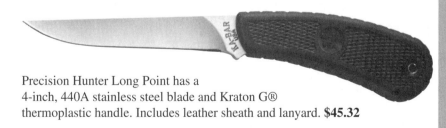

Precision Hunter Long Point has a 4-inch, 440A stainless steel blade and Kraton G® thermoplastic handle. Includes leather sheath and lanyard. **$45.32**

D2 Extreme Folder Drop Point has a 3-inch D2 tool steel blade with 1 1/4-inch serrated section and machined aluminum handle. Also available with clip, tanto or spear points. **$133.22**

KA-BAR
Knives Inc.

1125 East State St.
Olean, NY 14760
800-282-0130
Fax: (716) 373-6245
www.ka-bar.com
E-mail: info@ka-bar.com

Styles: Military-style fixed-blade knives (including the Marine Corps fighting knife design used in World War II), fixed-blade hunting knives and folding pocket and lockback knives.

Sheaths: Leather, Kydex and nylon.

Handles: Leather washers, Kraton thermoplastic, Staminawood, Delrin, stainless steel, ABS plastic, Zytel, glass-filled nylon and aluminum.

Features: High-carbon, 440 stainless steel, D2 tool steel or Sandvik 12C27 stainless steel blades; some models with black epoxy powder or bead-blasted blades; some with pocket clips and thumb studs.

Retail price: $4.21 to $206.55

Katz Knives Inc.

P.O. Box 730
Chandler, AZ 85244-0730
800-848-7084
or (480) 786-9334
Fax: (480) 786-9338
www.katzknives.com
E-mail: Katzkn@aol.com

Styles: Folding and fixed-blade knives in hunting, fishing, tactical and general-use designs.

Sheaths: Cordura nylon and leather.

Handles: Zytel, Kraton, ivory Micarta, cherrywood, Sambar stag and mother of pearl.

Features: XT80 or XT70 stainless steel blades; several models of military-style knives feature blades 5mm thick for extra strength; many folders feature pocket clips and one-hand opening.

Retail price: $20.55 to $299.99

Black Kat BK-900DP has an XT70 stainless steel, 3 3/4-inch drop-point blade with Katz One-Hand Opener thumb rest and Zytel® handle. Includes integral pocket clip. **$69.98**

Tanto K-1006WM has a 6 3/4-inch XT80 stainless steel blade and an ivory Micarta® handle. Includes Cordura® nylon sheath. Also offered with a Kraton® handle. **$294.98**

Wild Kat K-103CW has a 4 5/8-inch XT80 stainless steel blade and a cherrywood handle. Includes Cordura® nylon sheath. Also offered with sambar stag, ivory Micarta® and Kraton® handles. **$275.50**

Lion King K-302ST has a 6 1/8-inch XT80 stainless steel blade and sambar stag handle. Includes Cordura® nylon sheath. Also offered with cherrywood, ivory Micarta® and Kraton® handles. **$310.00**

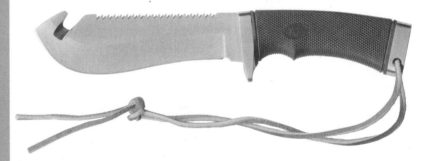

Hunter's Tool ™ Knife has a 5 1/2-inch XT80 stainless steel blade with a plain or partially serrated edge, a gut hook and bone saw. The handle is checkered Kraton®. Includes leather sheath and lanyard. **$215.00**

Cheetah K-900DP/CW has an XT80 stainless steel, 3 3/4-inch drop-point blade with cherrywood handle. Includes hip-hugger leather sheath. Also offered with a white Micarta® handle. **$190.00**

Ken Onion-designed Boa Model 1580 has a 3 3/8-inch blade of CPM-440V stainless steel coated with titanium-nitride and an aluminum handle. Features Speed-Safe assisted opening using index finger or thumb. Also offered in partially serrated blade. **$185.00**

Multi-Tool with Tool Adapter has six bits (screwdriver, Torx® and square-drive tips) that fit in the Tool Adapter and stow in the included nylon sheath. There is also a hacksaw blade, more screwdrivers, file, can opener, ruler and locking pliers with wire cutter. **$119.95**

Wade Officer has a 3 1/8-inch locking blade and a 2 1/8-inch serrated sheep-foot blade, both of 440A stainless steel, with a co-polymer handle available in black, blue, orange and yellow. **$49.95**

Kershaw Knives

25300 SW Parkway
Wilsonville, OR 97070
800-325-2891 or
(503) 682-1966
Fax: (503) 682-7168
www.kershawknives.com
E-mail: kershaw@
kershawknives.com

Styles: Fixed-blade and folding knives and multi-tools for hunting, fishing, camping and general use.

Sheaths: Nylon.

Handles: Polyamide, co-polymer, phenolic and brass, Kraton® rubber, metal alloy with ABS plastic inlay, steel with sandalwood inlay, aluminum with co-polymer inlay and stainless steel.

Features: 440V or 440A stainless steel blades; several folding models feature Ken Onion Speed-Safe assisted opening mechanism for fast one-hand opening; one fillet knife has adjustable blade length.

Retail price: $24.95 to $299.00

Kershaw Knives (cont.)

Deer Hunter has a 4-inch AUS 8A drop-point blade and co-polymer handle. Includes leather sheath. **$150.00**

Seven-Step Adjustable Fillet Knife has a unique blade design that allows the 420J2 blade to adjust from 5 1/2 to 9 inches. Includes ABS plastic sheath. **$24.95**

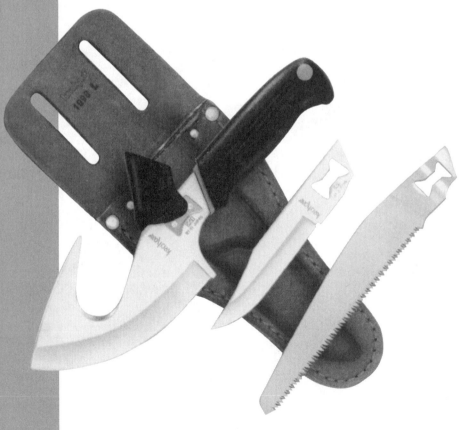

Alaskan Blade Trader has a 4 3/8-inch, AUS 6A skinning blade with gut hook, a 3 1/2-inch hunting blade of 420J2 steel and a 6-inch saw blade that share the same handle with a Quik-Lock mechanism. Includes leather sheath to hold everything. **$74.95**

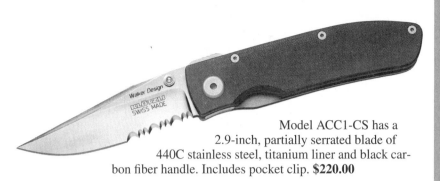

Model ACC1-CS has a 2.9-inch, partially serrated blade of 440C stainless steel, titanium liner and black carbon fiber handle. Includes pocket clip. **$220.00**

Klotzli

CH 3400
Burgdorf, Switzerland
800-922-6537 (Boker USA)
or 800-255-9034
(A.G. Russell)
Fax: N/A
www.klotzli.com
E-mail: info@klotzli.com

Styles: High-tech folding knives for tactical and general use.

Sheaths: N/A

Handles: Carbon fiber, G10 and titanium.

Features: Made in Switzerland.
Blades of 440C stainless steel. Collaborations with Michael Walker and Christian Wimpff.

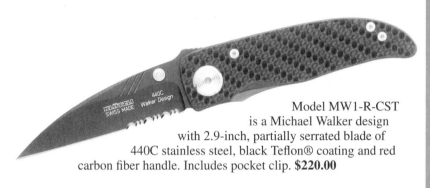

Model MW1-R-CST is a Michael Walker design with 2.9-inch, partially serrated blade of 440C stainless steel, black Teflon® coating and red carbon fiber handle. Includes pocket clip. **$220.00**

Retail price: $155.00 to $230.00

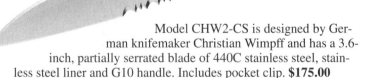

Model CHW2-CS is designed by German knifemaker Christian Wimpff and has a 3.6-inch, partially serrated blade of 440C stainless steel, stainless steel liner and G10 handle. Includes pocket clip. **$175.00**

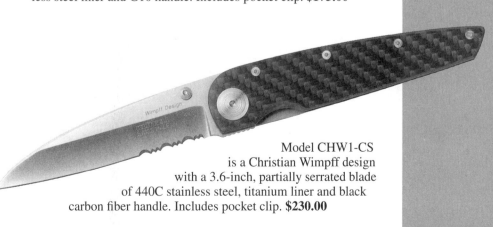

Model CHW1-CS is a Christian Wimpff design with a 3.6-inch, partially serrated blade of 440C stainless steel, titanium liner and black carbon fiber handle. Includes pocket clip. **$230.00**

Knives of Alaska

123 W. Main St.
Denison, TX 75021
800-572-0980 or
(903) 463-7112.
www.knivesofalaska.com
E-mail: info@
knivesofalaska.com

Styles: Folders, skinners, capers, fillet, cleavers, hatchets, unusual fixed-blade designs.

Sheaths: American leather.

Handles: Checkered rubberized, desert ironwood, Micarta, carbon fiber, titanium, mammoth ivory, stag.

Features: Two- and three-knife combination sets with single sheaths; round-pointed Muskrat and Alaska Brown Bear skinner/cleaver; outfitter-grade products field-tested in the Alaskan bush.

Retail price: $39.97 to $695.00

Alaskan Super Cub liner lock with 2 5/8-inch VG-10 steel blade and rubberized, carbon fiber or G-10 micarta handle. **$99.97 to $119.97**

Presentation Series liner lock with 2 1/2-inch VG-10 steel blade and mammoth ivory handle. **$595.00 (scrimshaw additional)**

Alaska Brown Bear skinner/cleaver with 6 1/2-inch D-2 steel blade and stag handle.**$169.97**

Handmade Series Wolverine clip point; 4 1/4-inch D-2 steel blade with stag handle. **$297.00**

Muskrat skinning/fleshing knife has a 2 1/4-inch D-2 steel blade with rubberized handle. **$44.97**

Grayling Fisherman and Hunter's Boning Knife; 6-inch AUS 8A stainless steel blade with rubberized, stag or desert ironwood handle. **$39.97 to $84.97**

Light Hunter mini-skinner/cleaver with 3 1/2-inch D-2 steel blade and rubberized, stag or desert ironwood handle. **$104.97 to $151.97**

Kopromed USA

P.O. Box 61485
Vancouver, WA 98666
888-735-8483 or
(360) 735-0570
Fax: (360) 735-0390
www.kopromed.com.pl/
E-mail: usako-pro@aol.com

Styles: Fixed blade and folding hunting and general-use knives.

Sheaths: Natural, brown or black leather.

Handles: Deer antler, African wood or rubber-plastic composite.

Features: Made in Poland. Stainless-steel alloy blades are hand-ground and polished. Designs electrochemically etched on blades.

**Retail price: $25.95 to $119.95
(also sold in sets)**

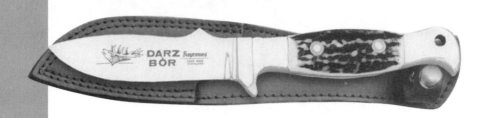

The Model 6 has a 3.9-inch stainless steel blade and stag handle. Includes leather sheath. **$79.95**

The Model 8 has a 3.9-inch stainless steel, drop-point blade with brass bolster and African hardwood handle. Includes leather sheath. **$69.95**

The Model 9 has a 3 3/4-inch stainless steel blade with a sure-grip rubber handle. Includes leather sheath. **$54.95**

The Model 14 has a 4.3-inch stainless steel blade with a top saw edge and African hardwood handle. Includes leather sheath. **$27.95**

The Model 17 has a 5.9-inch stainless steel blade with serrated top edge and stag handle. Includes leather sheath. **$109.95**

The Model 21 folding lockback has a 3 1/2-inch stainless steel blade and African hardwood handle. Includes leather sheath. **$99.95**

Crunch has a locking pliers, wire cutters and
stripper, wood/metal file, serrated knife, three screwdrivers, a hex-bit driver,
bottle opener and even a ruler. Includes leather or nylon sheath. **$98.00**

Flair has a needle-nose and regular pliers,
wire cutters, corkscrew with assist device, scissors, cocktail fork,
spreader knife, straight-edge/serrated knife, can/bottle opener, four
screwdrivers and a ruler. **$70.00**

Leatherman Tool Group Inc.

12106 NE Ainsworth Circle
Portland, OR 97220-9001
800-847-8665 or
(503) 253-7826
Fax: 800-367-1355 or
(503) 253-7830
www.leatherman.com
E-mail: N/A

Styles: A dozen models of
multi-tools, a category of knife
launched by founder Tim
Leatherman in 1983.
All include either a pliers
or scissors.

Sheaths: Nylon or leather.

Handles: Stainless steel or
painted stainless steel in red,
green or blue finishes
(Micra only).

Features: Blades include
needlenose or regular pliers,
wire cutters, scissors,
drop-point knife, clip-point
knife, diamond-coated file,
cross-cut file, flat screwdriver,
Phillips screwdriver,
bottle opener, ruler, hex-bit
driver, nail file, tweezers, awl,
cocktail fork, spreader knife
and corkscrew. Crunch
features locking pliers.
All models feature 100
percent stainless steel
construction. Some models
offered in black finish.

Retail price: $28.00 to $98.00

Leatherman Tool Group Inc. (cont.)

Wave features needle-nose and regular pliers, wire cutters and stripper, wood saw, serrated blade, scissors, file, five screwdrivers, a can/bottle opener and clip-point knife. **$100.00**

Sideclip has its namesake pocket clip, plus needle-nose and regular pliers, wire cutters, drop-point knife, four screwdrivers, can/bottle opener and a ruler. **$44.00**

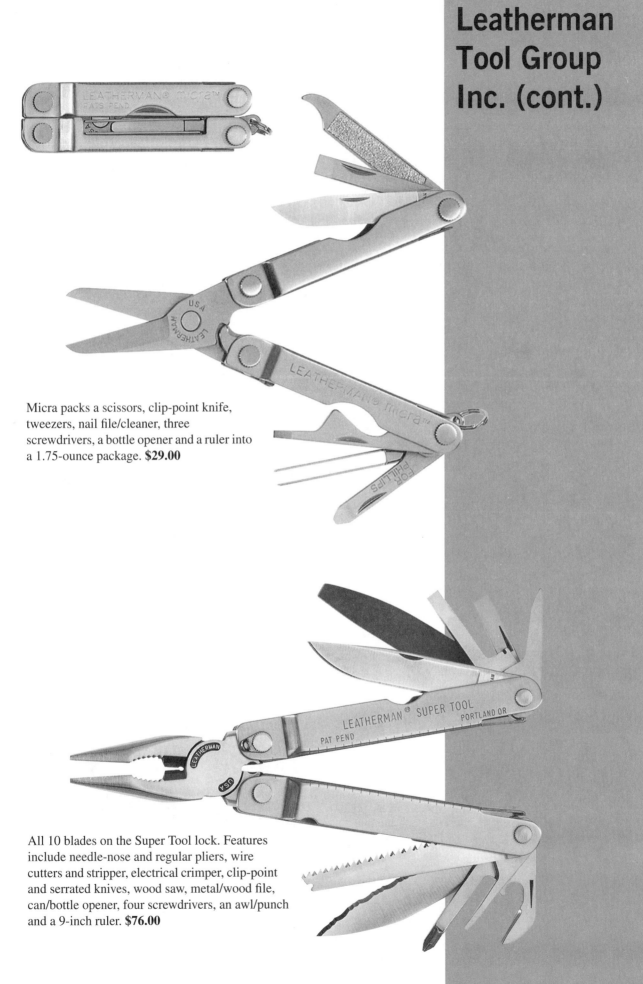

Micra packs a scissors, clip-point knife, tweezers, nail file/cleaner, three screwdrivers, a bottle opener and a ruler into a 1.75-ounce package. **$29.00**

All 10 blades on the Super Tool lock. Features include needle-nose and regular pliers, wire cutters and stripper, electrical crimper, clip-point and serrated knives, wood saw, metal/wood file, can/bottle opener, four screwdrivers, an awl/punch and a 9-inch ruler. **$76.00**

Marble Arms

420 Industrial Park
P.O. Box 111
Gladstone, MI 49837-0111
(906) 428-3710
Fax: (906) 428-3711
www.marblearms.com
E-mail: marble@up.net

Styles: Traditional fixed-blade knives for hunting, camping and general use.

Sheaths: Leather.

Handles: Stacked leather, curly maple, cocobolo Dymond®, India stag, black Micarta® and impala horn.

Features: 52-100 carbon steel blades offered in clip and drop points.

Retail price: $85.00 to $275.00

Trailcraft™ has a 3 1/2-inch blade of 52-100 carbon steel and a stacked leather handle. Includes leather sheath. **$85.00**

Trailcraft™ has a 3 1/2-inch blade of 52-100 carbon steel and a cocobolo Dymond® handle. Includes leather sheath. Also offered with curly maple, India stag, black Micarta® and impala horn handles. **$100.00**

Campcraft™ has a 4 1/2-inch blade of 52-100 carbon steel and a curly maple handle. Includes leather sheath. **$110.00**

Campcraft™ has a 4 1/2-inch blade of 52-100 carbon steel and an India stag handle. Includes leather sheath. Also offered with stacked leather, cocobolo Dymond®, black Micarta® and impala horn handles. **$135.00**

Sting Ray with speed-assisted 3 1/8-inch AUS8 blade and Fiberesin handle. **$64.95**

Rescue One with 3 1/2-inch AUS8 blade and Fiberesin handle. **$29.95**

The Paradox liner lock with 3 1/2-inch AUS8 blade, pliers and hex-bit screwdriver, with Fiberesin handle. **$75.00**

Tactical folder with 3 1/2-inch tanto-point ATS34 blade and G10 titanium handle. **$99.95**

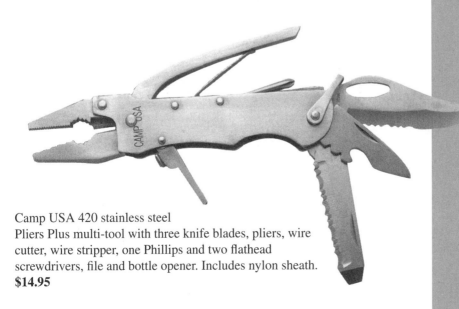

Camp USA 420 stainless steel
Pliers Plus multi-tool with three knife blades, pliers, wire cutter, wire stripper, one Phillips and two flathead screwdrivers, file and bottle opener. Includes nylon sheath. **$14.95**

Meyerco Manufacturing

4481 Exchange Service Dr.
Dallas, TX 75236
(214) 467-8949
Fax: (214) 467-9241
www.meyercousa.com
E-mail: N/A

Styles: Folding tactical, rescue and speed-assisted pocketknives; fixed-blade hunting and fishing designs; multi-function camping tools and machetes.

Sheaths: Nylon, Kydex or Fiberesin.

Handles: Fiberesin, G10 titanium, Kraton, rubberized and stainless steel.

Features: Variety of Blackie Collins designs, including speed-assisted Rascal, Big Rascal and Sting Ray, Speed Demon and Scamp; Camp USA knives, game shears and multi-tools.

Retail price: $5.25 to $110.00

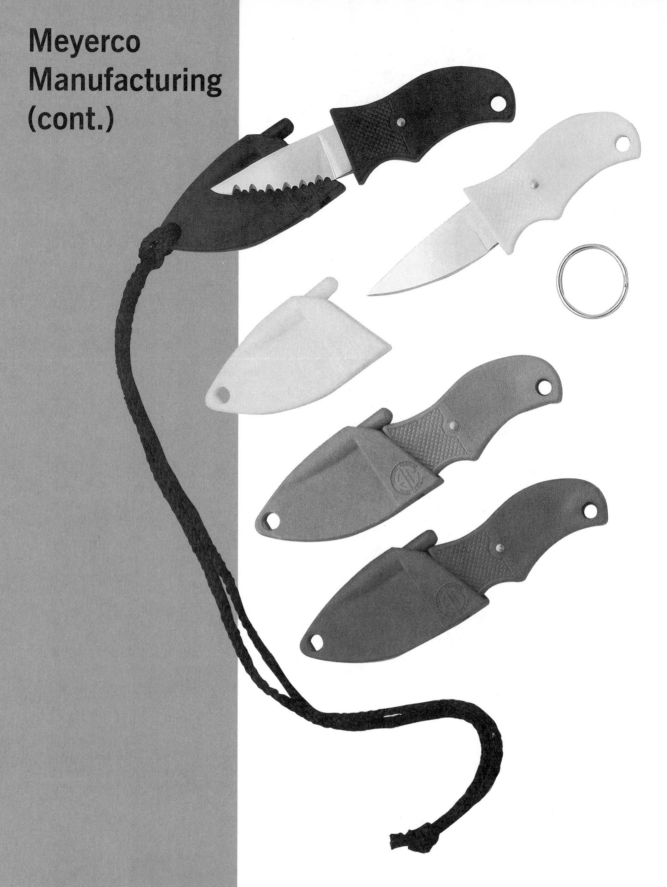

Buddy System with 2 1/8-inch AUS8 stainless steel blade and Fiberesin handle with spring-loaded sheath. **$19.95**

Mission Knives & Tools Inc.

13805 Alton Parkway
Suite D
Irvine, CA 92618
(949) 951-3879 or
(949) 951-0765
Fax: (949) 598-0258
www.missionknives.com
E-mail: info@
missionknives.com

Styles: Folding and fixed-blade survival, diving and battle knives.

Sheaths: Kydex.

Handles: Molded Hytrel/Kevlar, titanium, A2 steel.

Features: Variety of models made entirely of titanium for military and cold-weather applications, including mine defusing; one-piece A2 or titanium multi-purpose dive and utility knives with skeletonized handles.

Retail price: $98.00 to $389.00

MPK (Multi-Purpose Knife)
Standard has 7 1/8-inch titanium blade and Hytrel/Kevlar handle. Includes Kydex sheath. **$346.00 ($225.00 for A2 steel version)**

MPT (Multi-Purpose Tactical) has 6-inch titanium blade and Hytrel/Kevlar handle. Includes Kydex sheath. **$346.00**

MPS (Multi-Purpose Survival) has 5-inch titanium blade and integral, skeletonized handle. Includes Kydex sheath. **$346.00**

MPU (Multi-Purpose Utility) has a 3-inch titanium blade with integral, skeletonized handle. Includes Kydex® sheath. **$145.00 (stainless steel, $98.00)**

MPF (Multi-Purpose Folder) has a 4-inch titanium blade with drop or tanto point and partially serrated or straight edge; injection-molded handle. Includes titanium pocket clip. **$389.00 ($389.00 for A2 tool steel model)**

Myerchin Inc.

P.O. Box 911
Rialto, CA 92377
800-531-4890 or
(909) 875-3592
Fax: (909) 874-6058
www.myerchin.com
E-mail: N/A

Styles: Folding and fixed-blade hunting and offshore rigging knives.

Sheaths: Cordura nylon.

Handles: Sandalwood, white Micarta, black Micarta, Zytel.

Features: Blades of 440 high-carbon stainless steel; some models offered in a 70 percent serrated blade. Folders feature an oversized metal lanyard that unlocks the blade for one-hand closing. Many models feature a marlinspike for knot work or a gut hook for field dressing. Lightknife features built-in LED light.

Retail price: $65.95 to $113.95

A500 Safety/Dive knife is made from an 8-inch bar of steel with a sandblasted handle and 70 percent serrated blade. **$55.95**

B400 Alaska Guide has locking 440C stainless steel straight-edge and serrated blades. **$94.95**

B001 Offshore System includes 8 1/4-inch knife with black Micarta handle and 6.65-inch marlinspike in Cordura nylon sheath. Model used by U.S. Navy and U.S. Coast Guard. **$97.95**

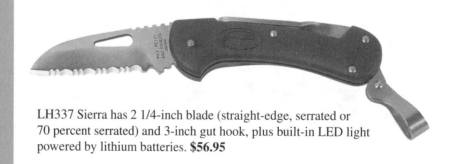

LH337 Sierra has 2 1/4-inch blade (straight-edge, serrated or 70 percent serrated) and 3-inch gut hook, plus built-in LED light powered by lithium batteries. **$56.95**

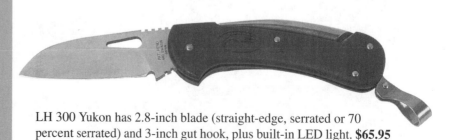

LH 300 Yukon has 2.8-inch blade (straight-edge, serrated or 70 percent serrated) and 3-inch gut hook, plus built-in LED light. **$65.95**

SP8 Machete has a 10-inch, 1095 carbon-steel blade with epoxy powder coating and a Kraton® polymer handle. Includes a combination leather/nylon sheath. **$61.80**

SP17 Army Quartermaster has a 6-inch, 1095 carbon-steel blade with epoxy powder coating and a Kraton® handle. Includes a leather/nylon sheath. **$57.00**

SP12 Tanto 6 has a 6-inch, 1095 carbon-steel blade with tanto point and a Kraton® handle. Includes a leather/nylon sheath. Design also offered with an 8- or 10-inch blade. **$44.00 (shown)**

SPC21 Navy Mark I has a 4 3/4-inch, brushed-finish 1095 carbon-steel blade and a Kraton® handle. Also offered with a black powder-coat finish. Includes leather/nylon sheath. **$35.72**

The Gambler Bagwell Bowie has a 9 3/8-inch blade of QS13 steel and a coffin-shaped wood handle. Includes leather sheath. **$175.00**

BC22 Heavy Duty chopper has a 22-inch 1095 steel blade with black oxide coating and polymer handle. **$24.00**

Ontario Knife Co.

26 Empire St.
Franklinville, NY 14737
800-222-5233 or
(716) 676-5527
Fax: 800-299-2618
www.ontarioknife.com
E-mail: salesOKC@aol.com

Styles: Fixed-blade and folding knives and machetes for hunting, camping, military and general use.

Sheaths: Leather, nylon, molded plastic and Kydex®.

Handles: Leather and fiber washers, molded plastic, Kraton® polymer and Gnvory®.

Features: Black powder-coated 1095 carbon-steel or 440A stainless steel blades; steel buttcaps.

Retail price: $19.14 to $275.00

Outdoor Edge Cutlery Corp.

6395 Gunpark Drive
Suite Q
Boulder, CO 80301
(303) 530-7667
Fax: (303) 530-7020
www.outdooredge.com
E-mail: outdooredge@
plinet.com

Styles: Fixed blade and folding hunting, skinning and general-purpose knives.

Sheaths: Leather and Delrin.

Handles: Delrin, aluminum, aluminum with Kraton inserts and Zytel.

Features: Wedge and Wedge II fixed-blade knives are held in Delrin sheaths that lock and unlock by pushing a button; can be clipped to a belt or worn around the neck on a cord. Skinning knives and saws feature T-shaped handles. Some folding knives feature pocket clips and partially serrated blades.

Retail price: $19.95 to $105.50

Impulse Model IM-10S (designed by Darrel Ralph) features a 3 3/4-inch skeletonized stainless steel blade with a serrated edge and bead blast finish; cast aluminum handle has Kraton inserts and pocket clip. Also offered in black Teflon-coated handle and straight edge. **$53.99**

Magna Model MZ-10 (designed by Kit Carson) has a 4-inch AUS-8A stainless steel blade and Zytel handle. Also offered in aluminum handle and 50 percent serrated edge. **$58.50**

Field-Spear has a 3 5/8-inch AUS-8A stainless steel blade and Zytel handle. Also offered in 2 7/8-inch blade and 50 percent serrated edge. **$59.50**

Whitetail Skinner has a 2 5/8-inch AUS-8A stainless steel blade with hook and T-shaped handle. Includes leather belt sheath. Also offered with 3-inch blade and partially serrated blade. **$48.50**

Outdoor Edge Cutlery Corp. (cont.)

Wedge has a 2 3/8-inch 6M stainless steel blade with a Delrin handle and a button that locks and unlocks the Delrin sheath. Can be clipped to a belt loop (with included swivel clip) or worn around the neck on a cord (included). Also offered as a 3-inch-blade Wedge II model. **$19.95**

Kodi-Pak includes a 2 1/2-inch-blade Kodi-Caper, 4 3/8-inch-blade Kodi-Skinner and 6-inch-blade Kodi-Saw, all in a leather belt sheath. Saw blade is replaceable. **$105.50**

Paragon Cutlery

P.O. Box 1008
Hendersonville, NC 28793
(828) 696-0777
Fax: (828) 697-5005
Web site: N/A
E-mail: N/A

Styles: Fixed-blade and folding knives for hunting, tactical and general use.

Sheaths: Leather.

Handles: Black Micarta® and cocobolo.

Features: Unique X-9 Para-Bow knife becomes the handle of a slingshot that shoots short arrows for survival situations. Collaborations by Tommy Lee, Larry Harley and George Herron.

Retail price: $45.00 to $250.00

X-9 Para-Bow™ is a lockback knife with a 4-inch surgical stainless steel blade and saw that doubles as the handle of a slingshot that can shoot small arrows. Compass is concealed in the fork assembly. **$250.00**

Larry Harley Battle Bowie has a 13 1/4-inch, non-reflective blade and a black Micarta® handle. Includes sheath. **$225.00**

Tommy Lee Boot Knife is 8 inches overall with cocobolo handle. **$160.00**

Larry Harley Humpback Skinner is 7 inches overall with a black Micarta® handle. **$125.00**

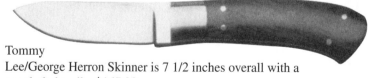

Tommy Lee/George Herron Skinner is 7 1/2 inches overall with a cocobolo handle. **$165.00**

George Herron Fixed Blade Classic Hunter is 8 inches overall with a cocobolo handle. **$180.00**

Model 11 Alaskan Skinner is offered in a 4-, 4 1/2- or 5-inch blade of tool steel or 440 stainless steel with a leather handle. Includes leather sheath. **$220.00 (4 1/2- and 5-inch blades)**

Model 18 Attack-Survival knife has a 5 1/2- or 7 1/2-inch tool steel or 440 stainless steel blade with a stainless steel, hollow handle and threaded brass cap. Includes leather sheath. **$275.00 (7 1/2-inch blade)**

Model 26 Pathfinder has a 4-inch drop-point blade of tool steel or 440 stainless steel with a stag handle. Includes leather sheath. **$215.00**

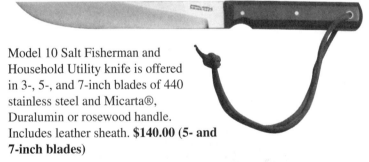

Model 10 Salt Fisherman and Household Utility knife is offered in 3-, 5-, and 7-inch blades of 440 stainless steel and Micarta®, Duralumin or rosewood handle. Includes leather sheath. **$140.00 (5- and 7-inch blades)**

Model 25 The Trapper has a 5- or 6-inch blade of tool steel or 440 stainless steel with a stag-and-leather handle. Includes leather sheath. **$280.00**

Model 12 Sportsman's Bowie is offered in a 6- or 9-inch blade of tool steel or 440 stainless steel with a leather handle, brass hilt and Duralumin butt cap. **$365.00 (9-inch blade)**

Randall
Made Knives

P.O. Box 1988
Orlando, FL 32802-1988
(407) 855-8075
Fax: (407) 855-9054
www.randallknives.com
E-mail: N/A

Styles: Handmade fixed-blade knives for hunting, fishing, diving, military and general use.

Sheaths: Leather.

Handles: Stag; black, white or maroon Micarta®; walnut; maple; rosewood and leather.

Features: Tool or 440 stainless steel blades; brass, nickel silver or duralumin butt cap; choice of handle shape, hilt shape, compass embedded in handle and other options.

Retail price: $135.00 to $435.00 (standard models)

Remington Arms Co.

870 Remington Dr.
Madison, NC 27025
800-243-9700
Fax: (336) 548-7801
www.remington.com
E-mail: info@remington.com

Styles: Fixed-blade and folding knives for hunting, fishing, camping and general use.

Sheaths: Leather, nylon or plastic.

Handles: Stag, G-10 composite, Delrin®, mother of pearl, stainless steel, laminated wood and Kevlar®-impregnated nylon.

Features: ATS 34 tool or 440A stainless steel blades; some blades have oval cuts for one-hand opening; some models feature multiple blades, including screwdriver, can opener, saw, pin punch, gut hook and 12/20 ga. choke tool.

Retail price: $9.58 to $143.92

This fixed-blade hunting knife has a 4-inch, tool-steel blade and a rosewood handle. Includes leather sheath. **Price unavailable.**

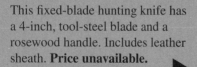

Bandit™ has a stainless steel clip-point blade and a black Delrin® handle; 3 inches overall. Other models include barlow-style with clip and pen blades, peanut with clip blade, trapper with clip blade and four- or six-blade camp with can opener, screwdriver, punch, spear blade and more. **Price unavailable.**

Delrin®-handle folding knife has a spear-point blade with hole for one-hand opening and a pen blade; 8 3/4-inches overall. Other models include a three-blade stockman; three-blade whittler; Upland with clip blade, 12/20 gauge choke tool and screwdriver, and gut hook; Waterfowl with clip blade, choke tool/screwdriver, pin punch and serrated bone blade; and Camp with four blades. **Price unavailable.**

Remington Arms Co. (cont.)

Rattlesnake™ One-Hander lockback has black-finish drop-point and saw blades with a camouflage nylon handle. Also offered with a serrated edge drop-point, drop-point and saw with gut hook, saw only or serrated clip blade and black nylon handle. **Price unavailable.**

Titanium Tactical One-Hander has a titanium-coated, spear-point blade with back saw and a G10 handle; overall length 5 1/8 inches. Also offered with a mini-spear blade. **Price unavailable.**

2001 Mariner Bullet™ Knife is a toothpick-style angler's knife design with 3 1/2-inch lockback blade and tortoise-shell celluloid handle. **Price unavailable.**

Richartz USA

1825 Walnut Hill Lane
Suite 120
Irving, TX 75038
800-859-2029
Fax: (972) 331-2566
www.richartz.com
E-mail: info@richartz.com

Styles: German-made, multi-blade folding knives for hunting, camping and general use.

Sheaths: N/A

Handles: Stainless steel with rubber nubs, sterling silver and rubber with stainless steel inlay.

Features: Box knives feature hollow handle with four mini-screwdrivers. Picnic knives separate into a knife and fork (with other blades included). Other blades include scissors, nail file, cuticle pusher, bottle opener, can opener, corkscrew, saw, pliers with wire cutter, Phillips and regular screwdrivers, awl and knife blade.

Retail price: $35.00 to $162.00

Blackwood maxi 9 has a blackwood handle and stainless steel blades. Thirteen other Blackwood models offered. **$90.00**

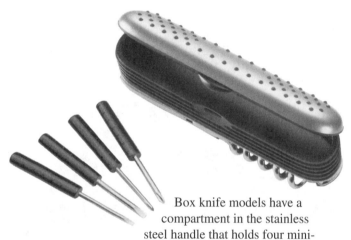

Box knife models have a compartment in the stainless steel handle that holds four mini-screwdrivers. Thirteen models offered, including one with Picnic knife features. **$34.00 to $66.00**

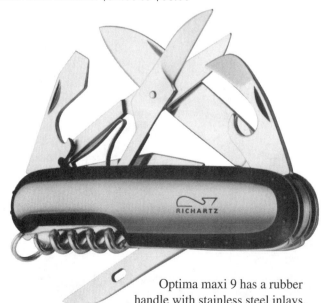

Optima maxi 9 has a rubber handle with stainless steel inlays, includes scissors, bottle opener, can opener, screwdriver, awl, corkscrew and knife blade. Thirteen other Optima models offered. **$85.00**

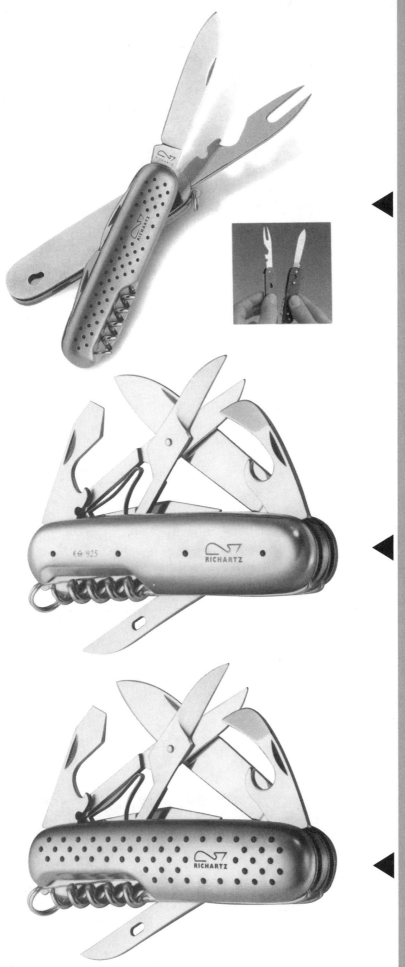

Richartz USA (cont.)

Picnic knife separates into a knife and fork, with additional blades in the knife handle (various blade options). Stainless steel construction; handle has rubber nubs. **$33.00 to $70.00**

Sterling maxi 7 has a sterling silver handle and stainless steel blades. Two other models offered. **$162.00**

Structure maxi 9 has a stainless steel handle with rubber nubs for better grip, includes scissors, bottle opener, can opener, screwdriver, awl, corkscrew and knife blade. Thirteen other Structure models offered. **$85.00**

Santa Fe Stoneworks

3790 Cerrillos Road
Santa Fe, NM 87505
800-257-7625 or
(505) 471-0036
Fax: (505) 471-0036
www.santafestoneworks.com
E-mail: knives@rt66.com

Styles: Camillus, Spyderco, Benchmade, Buck and other fixed-blade and folding knives enhanced with semi-precious stones, mother of pearl or inlaid woods.

Sheaths: N/A

Handles: Turquoise, malachite, azurite, lapis, chryscolla, apache gold, Picasso marble, mother of pearl and color-treated birch.

Features: Handle and bolster enhancements to factory knives.

Retail price: $41.00 to $330.00

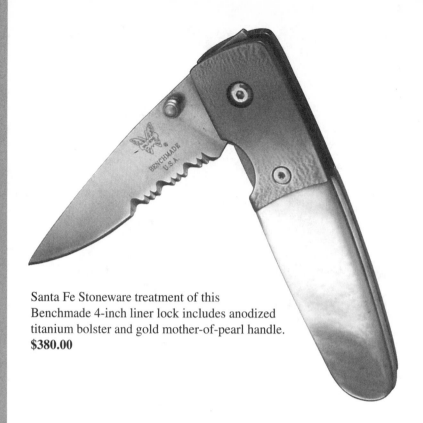

Santa Fe Stoneware treatment of this Benchmade 4-inch liner lock includes anodized titanium bolster and gold mother-of-pearl handle. **$380.00**

This two-blade Buck Pony has colored birch inlays. **$74.00**

This three-blade Buck Cadet features cross-pattern colored birch inlays. **$80.00**

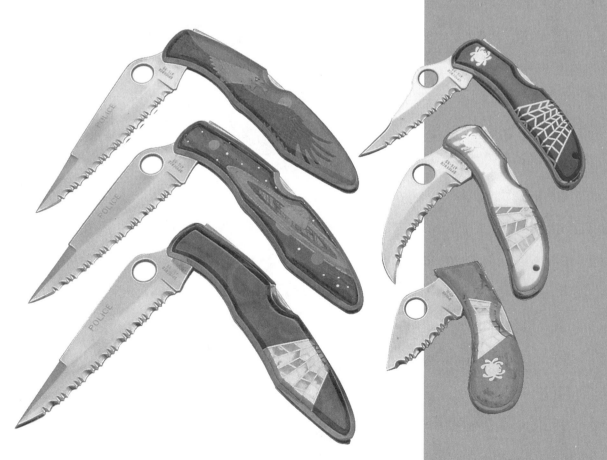

These Spyderco models have enhancements that include turquoise, jet, mother-of-pearl and colored birch handle inlays. **$180.00 to $260.00**

Sarco
Cutlery LLC

115 Fairground Road
Florence, AL 35630
(256) 766-8099
Fax: (256) 766-7246
www.sarcoproducts.com
E-mail: sarco@hiwaay.net

Styles: Fixed-blade camping knife.

Sheaths: N/A

Handles: N/A

Features: N/A

Retail price: N/A

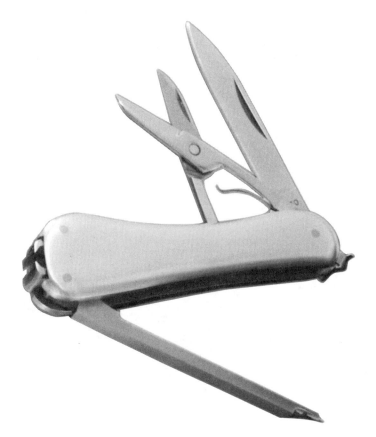

Tri Edge™ includes a file, clippers, manicure tip, scissors, and pen blade, with black Micarta® or Duraluminum handle. **$59.95**

Mini Pentagon has a 3 1/2-inch, powder-coated blade of 440A stainless steel and a Zytel® glass-reinforced handle. Includes black leather sheath with mounting clip. **54.95**

SOG Specialty Knives Inc.

6521 212th St. SW
Lynnwood, WA 98036
(425) 771-6230
Fax: (425) 771-7689
www.sogknives.com
E-mail: info@sogknives.com

Styles: Fixed-blade and folding knives and multi-tools for hunting, camping, tactical and general use.

Sheaths: Nylon, leather and Kydex®.

Handles: Zytel® glass-reinforced, Kraton®, lleather washers, Micarta® washers and stainless steel.

Features: Multi-tools feature pliers/wire cutters with an interlocking gear design that uses compound leverage for more gripping and cutting power. Titanium nitride finish on some multi-tools provides scratch- and corrosion-resistance. Many knife models feature semi-serrated edges, pocket clips and holes or thumb studs on the blades for one-hand opening.

Retail price: $24.95 to $274.95

PowerLock has stainless steel construction, folding handle covers for comfort and a pliers/wire cutter with a gear design that provides compound leverage. Four screwdrivers, scissors, wood saw, can/bottle opener, 1/4-inch drive, rulers and partially serrated blade included. **$79.95**

Recon Bowie has a 7-inch, gun-blued SK-5 carbon steel blade and a leather washer handle. Includes leather sheath and lanyard. **$225.00**

SOG Specialty Knives Inc. (cont.)

Seal Pup, a miniature version of the official SOG Navy SEAL knife, has a 4 3/4-inch, powder-coated blade of 440A stainless steel and a Zytel® glass-reinforced handle. Includes Kydex® sheath. **$74.95**

Tomcat has a 3 3/4-inch blade of 440A stainless steel and a Kraton® handle. Includes dual-mounting nylon pouch. **$129.95**

SwitchPlier is a push-button automatic pliers, plus a can opener, bottle opener, three screwdrivers, three-sided file, 1/4-inch socket drive and partially serrated blade. Aluminum handle. **$74.95**

Snap-It has a 3-inch AUS-8 stainless steel, serrated blade and fiberglass-reinforced nylon handle with Kraton® inserts. Snap shackle clips to belt loop, backpack or vest. **$56.95**

Dyad has a 3 3/8-inch straight-edge and a 3 3/4-inch serrated-edge blade, both of ATS-55 stainless steel . The handle is black Micarta. Includes black stainless steel pocket clip. **$152.95**

Spyderco Inc.

P.O. Box 800
Golden, CO 80402-0800
800-525-7770 or
(303) 279-8383
Fax: (303) 278-2229
www.spyderco.com
E-mail: custsvc@
spyderco.com

Styles: Primarily folding knives for law enforcement, hunting, fishing and general use. One style of fixed-blade hunting knife and SpydeRench multi-tool.

Sheaths: Concealex polymer.

Handles: Stainless steel, aluminum, fiberglass-reinforced nylon, G-10, G-10 with mother-of-pearl insets, Micarta®, Sermollan polymer, Kraton® insets and titanium.

Features: Most models feature Spyderco's trademark hole in the blade for one-handed opening, fully or partially serrated blade and pocket clip. Numerous collaborations with custom knifemakers, including Bob Lum, Frank Centofante, Bill Moran, Bram Frank, Tim Zowada, James A. Keating, Howard Viele, Tim Wegner, Bob Terzuola and others.

Retail price: $26.95 to $204.95

Spyderco Inc. (cont.)

Howard Viele has a 3 3/8-inch serrated blade of VG-10 steel with Viele's signature symbol: the Japanese God of War. The handle is black Micarta. Also offered with plain edge. **$146.95**

Bill Moran Featherweights have 3 7/8-inch blades of VG-10 stainless steel with an upswept or drop-point style. Handle is fiberglass-reinforced nylon with Kraton® inserts. Includes Kydex® sheath. **$89.95.**

SpydeRench combines a one-hand-opening knife with a 2 1/2-inch 440C stainless steel blade and a combination slip-joint pliers/adjustable wrench in one 4 5/8-inch package. Also includes a long bit with regular and Phillips screwdrivers, plus four bits that tuck inside. **$109.95**

Bram Frank Gunting has a 2 7/8-inch CPM-440V stainless steel blade that can be levered open by pushing it against an object, and is a defensive weapon with the blade closed. Handle is G-10. Dull-edged training model also offered. **$149.95**

Victorinox® SwissTool™ (shown) is made of stainless steel and has 24 tools, including five screwdriver blades, can opener, bottle opener, metal file, metal saw, ruler, pliers, wire cutter, wire stripper, electrical crimper, straight-edge blade and serrated blade. **$75.00** SwissTool Plus includes the Swiss Tool, plus wrench and six drive bits. **$95.00** SwissTool CS includes the SwissTool with detachable corkscrew. **$84.00**

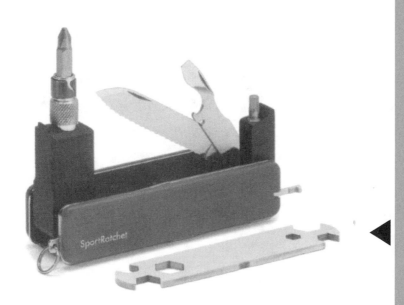

Swiss Army Brands Inc.

One Research Drive
P.O. Box 874
Shelton, CT 06484-0874
800-243-4045
Fax: 800-243-4006
www.swissarmy.com
E-mail: N/A

Styles: Folding multi-blade designs and multi-tools for hunting, fishing, camping, hiking, golfing and general use. One of the original brands (Victorinox) of Swiss Army knives.

Sheaths: Leather or nylon.

Handles: Stainless steel, sterling silver, solid plastic or translucent plastic.

Features: Wide variety of blades and tools (some removable), including straight-edge and serrated blades, saw blade, can opener, straight-edge screwdriver, Phillips screwdriver, file, scissors, ruler, hex socket with drive bits, pliers, wire cutter, awl, corkscrew, tweezers, toothpick, flashlight, hook, ball-point pen, hook disgorger, magnifying glass, sewing eye and digital altimeter.

Retail price: $10.00 to $175.00

SportRatchet has traditional red plastic handle and 19 features, including a locking ratchet drive, bit storage case with two Phillips and two hex bit tips, 1/4-, 3/8- and 7/16-inch wrenches; 8mm, 10mm and 12mm wrenches; bottle opener; toothpick; tweezers; and large serrated blade. Includes nylon pouch. **$51.00**

Swiss Army Brands Inc. (cont.)

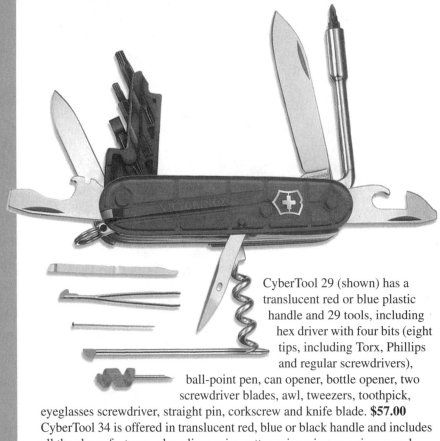

CyberTool 29 (shown) has a translucent red or blue plastic handle and 29 tools, including hex driver with four bits (eight tips, including Torx, Phillips and regular screwdrivers), ball-point pen, can opener, bottle opener, two screwdriver blades, awl, tweezers, toothpick, eyeglasses screwdriver, straight pin, corkscrew and knife blade. **$57.00** CyberTool 34 is offered in translucent red, blue or black handle and includes all the above features, plus pliers, wire cutter, wire crimper, scissors and hook. **$75.00** CyberTool 41 is offered in translucent red or blue handle and includes all these features, plus wood saw, metal saw, metal file, nail cleaner, chisel/scraper and 2.5mm screwdriver. **$90.00**

SwissChamp® XLT has a red translucent handle and 50 features, including a bit wrench, bit case with 10 bit points, pliers, magnifying lens, hook disgorger, ruler, wood saw, metal saw, metal file, wood chisel, ball-point pen, awl, straight pin, scissors and two knife blades. **$175.00**

Midnite MiniChamp® II is available with a translucent red or blue handle and includes 16 features, including scissors, bottle opener, magnetic Phillips screwdriver, scraper, ruler, cuticle pusher, nail cleaner, retractable ball-point pen, flashlight and two blades. **$38.00**

Altimeter (shown) has a translucent red handle and 17 features, including scissors, bottle opener, can opener, awl, hook, corkscrewer, mini-screwdriver, two knife blades, digital altimeter and digital thermometer. **$97.00** Altimeter Plus has the same features, plus a wood saw and fine screwdriver. **$102.00**

Taylor Cutlery

1736 N. Eastman Road
P.O. Box 1638
Kingsport, TN 37662-1638
800-251-0254 or
(423) 247-2406
Fax: (423) 247-5371
www.taylorcutlery.com
E-mail: taylor@preferred.com

Styles: Fixed-blade and folding knives for tactical, rescue, hunting and general use.

Sheaths: Nylon and leather.

Handles: Stag, aluminum with rubber inserts, aluminum with turquoise inlays, Zytel® with aluminum inserts, Zytel®, skeletonized steel, fiberglass, G-10.

Features: Smith & Wesson and Cuttin' Horse brands. Many models feature decorative scrimshaw or printed-scene inserts in handle; most have thumb studs or blade holes for one-hand opening.

Retail price: $11.60 to $92.24

Cuttin' Horse Smith & Wesson/John Deere Tractor Ride knife has a straight-edge and a serrated-edge blade, both with holes for one-hand opening. Also offered with four other John Deere-licensed paintings on the handle. **$32.00**

S.W.A.T. Scrimshaw Model SW23101 has a 3 3/8-inch 440 stainless steel blade with aluminum handle and black and white (shown) or black and silver bear inserts. Also offered with wolf, eagle, deer or trout scenes. **$49.20**

Smith & Wesson Tactical
Folder Model SW1250CF has a 4 3/4-inch 440 stainless steel blade with carbon fiber handle. Offered in drop or tanto point and straight or partially serrated edge, as well as aluminum or G-10 handles. **$84.36**

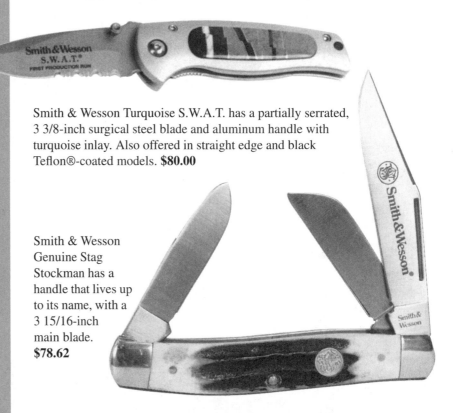

Smith & Wesson Turquoise S.W.A.T. has a partially serrated, 3 3/8-inch surgical steel blade and aluminum handle with turquoise inlay. Also offered in straight edge and black Teflon®-coated models. **$80.00**

Smith & Wesson Genuine Stag Stockman has a handle that lives up to its name, with a 3 15/16-inch main blade. **$78.62**

Cuttin' Horse Smith & Wesson 1999-2000 Duck Stamp knife has a 4-inch stainless steel blade with thumb stud and a handle inlaid with the 1999-2000 Federal duck stamp. Previous duck stamp designs also offered. **$32.00**

TiNives

1725 Smith Road
Fortson, GA 31808
888-537-9991
Fax: 706-322-2452
www.tinives.com
E-mail: N/A

Styles: High-tech folding knives for tactical, law enforcement and general use.

Sheaths: N/A

Handles: Machined aluminum.

Features: Ball-bearing mechanism for smooth opening. Aluminum handles available in a wide variety of colors and milled to create a texture for improved grip.

Retail price: $249.00 to $1,200.00

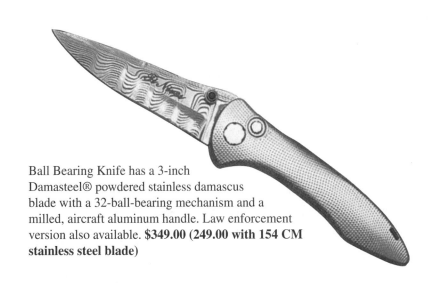

Stars and Stripes Forever Speedroller has a 4 1/4-inch blade of ATS-34 stainless steel and a milled aluminum handle. Law enforcement version also available. **$299.00**

Ball Bearing Knife has a 3-inch Damasteel® powdered stainless damascus blade with a 32-ball-bearing mechanism and a milled, aircraft aluminum handle. Law enforcement version also available. **$349.00 (249.00 with 154 CM stainless steel blade)**

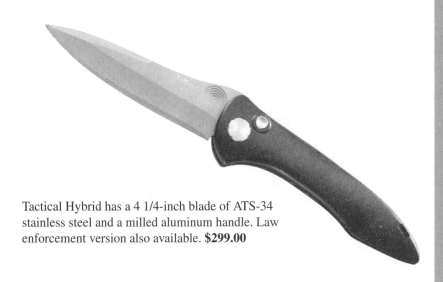

Tactical Hybrid has a 4 1/4-inch blade of ATS-34 stainless steel and a milled aluminum handle. Law enforcement version also available. **$299.00**

Utica Cutlery Co.

820 Noyes St.
Utica, NY 13503-1527
800-888-4223
Fax: (315) 733-6602
Web site: N/A
E-mail: Sales@kutmaster.com

Styles: Wide range of folding and fixed-blade designs, multi-tools and steak knives.

Sheaths: Nylon and leather.

Handles: Stainless steel, thermoplastic, Delrin Buckstag, hardwood, redwood, teakwood, brass, Uticryl.

Features: KutMaster and Mountain Quest brands; specialty multi-tools for archers, pruning shears/folding saw combo, folders with laser-engraved, scrimshaw or full-color wildlife scenes in clear handles; sculptured metal handles with die-struck wildlife scenes.

Retail price: $6.25 to $75.25

Mountain Quest Laser Series lockback with 3 1/2-inch blade and laser-engraved handles (offered in turkey, deer, mallard and Lab designs). **$15.95**

MiniMaster Archery Tool is 100 percent stainless steel with five modified Allen wrenches, broadhead tip assembly and removal wrenches, ruler, bottle opener, clip blade, screwdriver and locking "L" device. Nylon sheath includes loop for mini-flashlight. **$46.50** (Advantage Camo finish)

Gary Hawk Series lockback with 2 1/4-inch blade and brass sculptured handle (offered with deer, mallard, fishing and pointing dog scenes). **$31.99**

Teakwood Master Lockback with 2 1/4-inch stainless steel blade and laser-engraved teakwood handles (offered with eagle, deer, bass, mallard and trout designs). **$9.50**

Uticryl Whitetail Deer Model with 2 1/4-inch stainless steel blade and clear Uticryl handle (offered with deer, ring-necked pheasant, mallard, bass, eagle, turkey, wolf and grizzly bear designs). **$31.99**

Mountain Quest 25-function heavy duty folding multi-tool with locking hex-head driver and 12 bits (includes nylon pouch with storage for bits). **$22.99**

Wenger
North America

15 Corporate Drive
Orangeburg, NY 10962
800-431-2996 or
(914) 365-3500
Fax: (914) 425-4700
www.WengerNA.com
E-mail: N/A

Styles: One of the official makers of folding multi-blade Swiss Army Knives. Currently offers 81 models.

Sheaths: Nylon or leather pouch (some models).

Handles: Plastic (red, green, black), aluminum, stainless steel and titanium.

Features: Wide variety of stainless steel blades and tools (some removable) including straight edge and serrated blades, saw, ruler, fish hook disgorger, scissors, awl, can opener, flashlight, laser pointer, magnifier, fish hook file, nail file, compass, Allen wrenches, hex wrench, divot tool, cigar cutter and pliers.

Retail price: $15.00 to $125.00

MiniGrip™ features a flat-nose or needle-nose pliers, a removable bit holder with six screwdriver bits, bit adaptor tool, wood saw, metal saw and file, can opener, awl, wire stripper, locking screwdriver and knife blade. **$90.00**

Tool Chest Plus™ has 18 implements and 33 functions, including a double-cut wood saw, adjustable pliers with wire crimper and cutter, fish scaler/hook disgorger, mineral-crystal magnifier and even a compass, along with the usual knife blade. **$95.00**

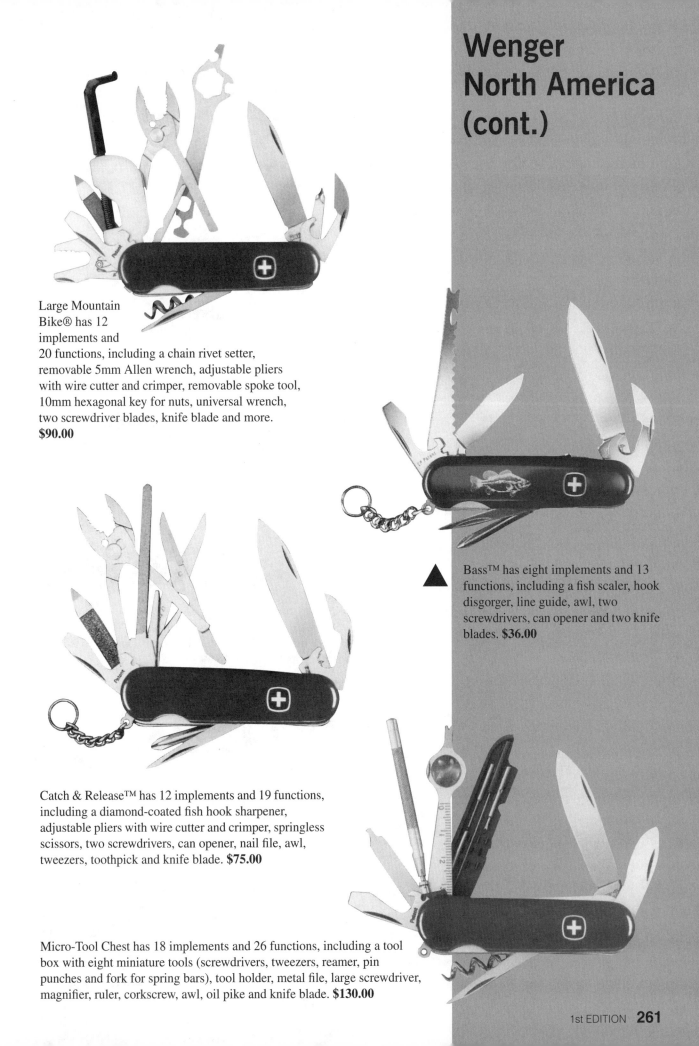

Wenger
North America
(cont.)

Large Mountain
Bike® has 12
implements and
20 functions, including a chain rivet setter,
removable 5mm Allen wrench, adjustable pliers
with wire cutter and crimper, removable spoke tool,
10mm hexagonal key for nuts, universal wrench,
two screwdriver blades, knife blade and more.
$90.00

Bass™ has eight implements and 13
functions, including a fish scaler, hook
disgorger, line guide, awl, two
screwdrivers, can opener and two knife
blades. **$36.00**

Catch & Release™ has 12 implements and 19 functions,
including a diamond-coated fish hook sharpener,
adjustable pliers with wire cutter and crimper, springless
scissors, two screwdrivers, can opener, nail file, awl,
tweezers, toothpick and knife blade. **$75.00**

Micro-Tool Chest has 18 implements and 26 functions, including a tool
box with eight miniature tools (screwdrivers, tweezers, reamer, pin
punches and fork for spring bars), tool holder, metal file, large screwdriver,
magnifier, ruler, corkscrew, awl, oil pike and knife blade. **$130.00**

William Henry Fine Knives

2125 Delaware Ave.
Suite C
Santa Cruz, CA 95060
(831) 454-9409
Fax: (831) 454-9309
www.williamhenryknives.com
E-mail: matt@
williamhenryknives.com

Styles: Semi-custom folding knives for hunting and general use; some limited editions.

Sheaths: Leather ClipCase.

Handles: nickel silver and jigged bone, mother of pearl, carbon fiber, ivory Micarta®, oak burl and others.

Features: Blades of ATS-34 or VG-10 stainless steel; stainless steel or titanium liners and components.

Retail price: $120.00 to $550.00

Pearl Series Kestrel Folder liner lock has a 2 1/8-inch ATS-34 stainless steel blade, three-piece titanium frame and nickel silver/mother-of-pearl handle. Hidden thong attachment in the handle's spine. **$270.00**

Amber Series Lancet Folder liner lock has a 2 5/8-inch ATS-34 stainless steel blade, three-piece titanium frame and nickel silver/jigged bone handle. Hidden thong attachment in the handle's spine. **$295.00**

Carbon Fiber Series Lancet Folder liner lock has a 2 5/8-inch ATS-34 stainless steel blade, titanium liner and pocket clip, and carbon fiber handle. Overall weight is 1 ounce. **$190.00**

Amber Series Spearpoint Folder liner lock has a 3 1/4-inch ATS-34 stainless steel blade, three-piece titanium frame and nickel silver/jigged bone handle. Hidden thong attachment in handle. **$270.00**

Carbon Fiber Series Spearpoint Folder liner lock has a 3 1/4-inch ATS-34 stainless steel blade, titanium liner and pocket clip, and carbon fiber handle. Weighs 1.6 ounces. **$220.00**

Pearl Series Spearpoint Folder liner lock has a 3 1/4-inch ATS-34 stainless steel blade, three-piece titanium frame and nickel silver/mother-of-pearl handle. Same hidden thong attachment as Kestrel. **$350.00**

Model Y299BK-SKT has a stainless steel blade wtih leaf-shaped cutouts and a metal alloy handle. 3 7/8 inches closed. **Price unavailable.**

Model YC9812 has a stainless steel blade with initation ivory handle and scrimshaw duck scene. **Price unavailable.**

Wuu Jau Co. Inc.

2600 S. Kelly Ave.
Edmond, OK 73013
800-722-5760
or (405) 359-5031
Fax: 877-256-4337
or (405) 340-5965
www.WuuJau.com
Email: N/A

Styles: Wide variety of imported fixed-blade and folding knives for hunting, fishing, camping, and general use.

Sheaths: Nylon or leather.

Handles: Cast metal, plastic, synthetic ivory, stainless steel and hardwood.

Features: Many models have thumb studs or holes in blades for one-hand opening. Variety of wildlife scenes scrimshawed on handles of some models.

Retail price: N/A

Zwilling J.A. Henckels Inc.

171 Saw Mill River Road
Hawthorne, NY 10532-1529
(914) 747-0300
Fax: (914) 747-1850
j-a-henckels.com
E-mail: N/A

Styles: Folding multi-blade utility knives for hunting, fishing, camping and general use.

Sheaths: Leather.

Handles: Plastic and stainless steel.

Features: Stainless steel blades and liners.

Retail price: $12.00 to $50.00

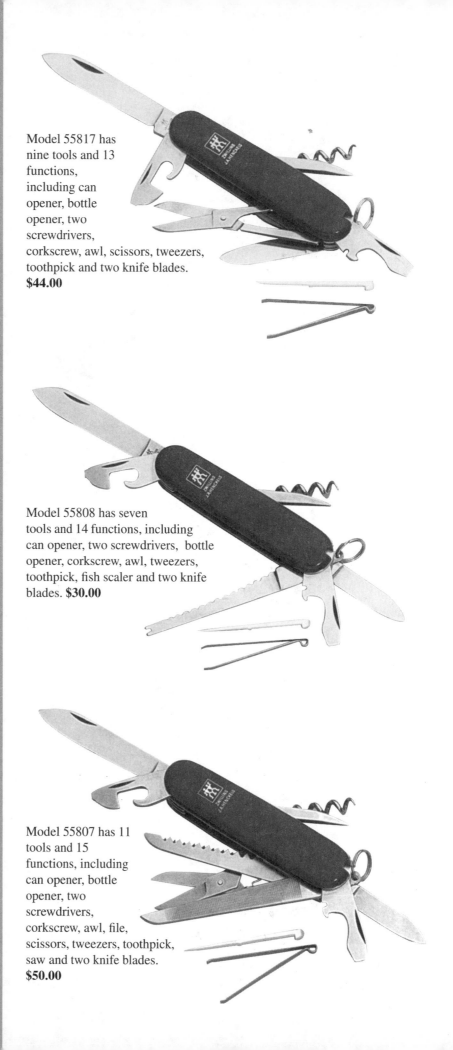

Model 55817 has nine tools and 13 functions, including can opener, bottle opener, two screwdrivers, corkscrew, awl, scissors, tweezers, toothpick and two knife blades. **$44.00**

Model 55808 has seven tools and 14 functions, including can opener, two screwdrivers, bottle opener, corkscrew, awl, tweezers, toothpick, fish scaler and two knife blades. **$30.00**

Model 55807 has 11 tools and 15 functions, including can opener, bottle opener, two screwdrivers, corkscrew, awl, file, scissors, tweezers, toothpick, saw and two knife blades. **$50.00**

MISCELLANEOUS COMPANIES

Beck's Cutlery & Specialties

SHP CENTER No. 109
McGregor Village
107 Edinburgh South Dr.
Cary, NC 27511
(919) 460-0203
Fax: (919) 460-7772

Burnt Chimney Cutlery Co.

P.O. Box 188
Forest City, NC 28043
800-447-4342
or (704) 245-4321
Fax: (704) 245-5121
Features: Burnt Chimney
pocketknives from Solingen, Germany.

Coast Cutlery Co.

2045 SE Ankeny St.
Portland, OR 97214

800-426-5858
or (503) 234-4545
Fax: (503) 234-4422
www.coastcutlery.com

Styles: Variety of fixed-blade and folding knives
and multi-tools for hunting, camping and
general use.
Sheaths: Leather and nylon.
Handles: Hardwoods, stag, mother of pearl,
plastic and steel.
Features: Exclusive distributor for Puma
knives.

Retail price: $35.00 to $190.00

Kellam Knives Co.

902 S. Dixie Hwy.
Lantana, FL 33462-4653
800-793-3481/(561) 588-3185
Fax: (561) 588-3186
www.kellamknives.com
E-mail: kellamknives@msn.com

Styles: Semi-production handmade knives from
Finland.

Lakota (Brunton USA)

620 E. Monroe
Riverton, WY 82501-4997
(307) 856-6559
Fax: (307) 856-1840
Features: AUS 8-A high-carbon stainless steel
blades.

Masters of Defense Knife Co.

1941 Camp Branch Road
Waynesville, NC 28786
(828) 452-4158
Fax: (828) 452-4158
www.mastersofdefense.com

Styles: Fixed-blade and folding knives for
tactical and general use.
Sheaths: Nylon or Kydex®.
Handles: Hardened 6061-T6 aluminum.
Features: Plain or serrated edge; satin
polished, matte bead blasted, satin gloss black
titanium carbo nitride or matte black titanium
carbo nitride finish; plunge lock mechanism;
some models have pocket clips; one model
has auxiliary cutter in handle.

Normark Corp.

10395 Yellow Circle Dr.
Minnetonka, MN 55343
800-874-4451
Fax: (612) 933-0046

Styles: Hunting knives, game shears and skinning ax.

Queen Cutlery Co.

P.O. Box 500
Franklinville, NY 14737
800-222-5233
Fax: 800-299-2618
www.cutlery.com
E-mail: salesOKC@aol.com

Quikut

P.O. Box 29
Airport Industrial Park
Walnut Ridge, AR 72476
(870) 886-6774
Fax: (870) 886-9162

Round Eye Knife & Tool

P.O. Box 818
Sagel, ID 83860
(208) 265-8858
Fax: (208) 263-0848
www.roundeye.com
E-mail: roundeye@nidlink.com

Styles: Folding and fixed-blade knives for hunting and general use.

Sheaths: Kydex®.
Handles: G-10 or carbon steel.
Features: Rolling Lock ™ with slide-bar operation is considered one of the strongest locking mechanisms for a folding knife. All R.E.K.A.T. folders feature this lock.

Retail price: $54.95 to $224.95

knifemaking supplies

The firms listed here specialize in furnishing knifemaking supplies in small amounts. Professional knifemakers have their own sources for much of what they use, but often patronize some of these firms. All the companies listed below have catalogs of their products, some available for a charge. For information about obtaining one, send a self-addressed and stamped envelope to the company. Firms are listed here by their request. New firms may be included by sending a catalog or the like to our editorial offices. We cannot guarantee any company's performance.

AFRICAN IMPORT CO.
ALAN ZANOTTI
20 BRAUNECKER RD.
PLYMOUTH, MA 02360

ALASKAN ANTLERCRAFT & IVORY
ROLAND AND KATHY QUIMBY
BOX 3175-RB
CASA GRANDE, AZ 85222

AMERICAN SIEPMANN CORP.
65 PIXLEY INDUSTRIAL PARKWAY
ROCHESTER, NY 14624

ART JEWEL ENTERPRISES, LTD.
460 RANDY RD.
CAROL STREAM, IL 60188

ATLANTA CUTLERY CORP.
2143 GEES MILL RD.
BOX 839XE
CONYERS, GA 30207

BATAVIA ENGINEERING
P.O. BOX 53
MAGALIESBURG, 2805
SOUTH AFRICA

BILL'S CUSTOM CASES
P.O. BOX 2
DUNSMUIR, CA 96025

BLADEMASTER GRINDERS
P.O. BOX 812
CROWLEY, TX 76036

BLADES "N" STUFF
1019 E. PALMER AVE.
GLENDALE, CA 91205

BOONE TRADING CO., INC.
BOX BB
BRINNON, WA 98320

BORGER, WOLF
BENZSTRASSE 8
76676 GRABEN-NEUDORF
GERMANY

BOYE KNIVES
P.O. BOX 1238
DOLAN SPRINGS, AZ 86441

BRIAR KNIVES
DARREL RALPH
7032 E. LIVINGSTON AVE.
RENOLDSBURG, OH 43068

BRONK'S KNIFEWORKS
C. LYLE BRUNCKHORST
23716 BOTHELL-EVERETT HWY.
COUNTRY VILLAGE, SUITE B
BOTHELL, WA 98021

CHRISTOPHER MFG., E.
P.O. BOX 685
UNION CITY, TN 38281

CUSTOM FURNACES
P.O. BOX 353
RANDVAAL, 1873
SOUTH AFRICA

CUSTOM KNIFEMAKER'S SUPPLY
BOB SCHRIMSHER
P.O. BOX 308
EMORY, TX 75440

CUSTOM KRAFT
14919 NEBRASKA AVE.
TAMPA, FL 33613

CUTLERY SPECIALTIES
DENNIS BLAINE
22 MORRIS LN.
GREAT NECK, NY 11024-1707

DAMASCUS-USA
149 DEANS FARM RD.
TYNER, NC 27980-9718

DAN'S WHETSTONE CO., INC.
130 TIMBS PLACE
HOT SPRINGS, AR 71913

DIAMOND MACHINING TECHNOLOGY, INC.
85 HAYES MEMORIAL DR.
MARLBOROUGH, MA 01752

DIXIE GUN WORKS, INC.
P.O. BOX 130
UNION CITY, TN 38281

EKLUND
P.O. BOX 483
NOME, AK 99762-0483

EZE-LAP DIAMOND PRODUCTS
3572 ARROWHEAD DR.
CARSON CITY, NV 89706

FIELDS, RICK B.
26401 SANDWICH PL.
MT. PLYMOUTH, FL 32776

FLITZ INTERNATIONAL, LTD.
821 MOHR AVE.
WATERFORD, WI 53185

FORTUNE PRODUCTS, INC.
HC 04, BOX 303
HWY. 1431 E. (SMITHWICK)
MARBLE FALLS, TX
78654

GILMER WOOD CO.
2211 NW ST. HELENS RD.
PORTLAND, OR 97210

GOLDEN AGE ARMS CO.
115 E. HIGH ST.
P.O. BOX 366
ASHLEY, OH 43003

GRS CORP.
DON GLASER
P.O. BOX 1153
900 OVERLANDER ST.
EMPORIA, KS 66801

HALPERN TITANIUM
LESLIE HALPERN
14 MAXWELL ROAD
MONSON, MA 01057

HARMON, JOE T.
8014 FISHER DRIVE
JONESBORO, GA 30236

HAWKINS CUSTOM KNIVES & SUPPLIES
110 BUCKEYE RD.
FAYETTEVILLE, GA 30214

HAYDU, THOMAS G.
2507 BIMINI LANE
FT. LAUDERDALE, FL 33312

HILTARY INDUSTRIES
7117 THIRD AVE.
SCOTTSDALE, AZ 85251

HOUSE OF TOOLS LTD.
#136, 8228 MACLEOD TR. S.E.
CALGARY, AB CANADA
T2H 2B8

HOV KNIVES & SUPPLIES
BOX 8005
S-700 08 OREBRO
SWEDEN

INDIAN JEWELERS SUPPLY CO.
P.O. BOX 1774
GALLUP, NM 87305-1774

INTERAMCO INC.
5210 EXCHANGE DR.
FLINT, MI 48507

JANTZ SUPPLY
P.O. BOX 584-GD
DAVIS, OK 73030-0584

JOHNSON, R.B.
I.B.S. INT'L. FOLDER SUPPLIES
BOX 11
CLEARWATER, MN 55320

JOHNSON WOOD PRODUCTS
34968 CRYSTAL RD.
STRAWBERRY POINT, IA 52076

K&G FINISHING SUPPLIES
P.O. BOX 980
LAKESIDE, AZ 85929

KNIFE & CUTLERY PRODUCTS, INC.
4122 N. TROOST AVE.
KANSAS CITY, MO 64116

KNIFE AND GUN FINISHING SUPPLIES
P.O. BOX 458
LAKESIDE, AZ 85929

KNIVES, ETC.
2522 N. MERIDIAN
OKLAHOMA CITY, OK 73107

KOVAL KNIVES, INC.
5819 ZARLEY ST.
NEW ALBANY, OH 43054

KWIK-SHARP
350 N. WHEELER ST.
FT. GIBSON, OK 74434

LINDER-SOLINGEN KNIFE PARTS
4401 SENTRY DR., SUITE K
TUCKER, GA 30084

LITTLE GIANT POWER HAMMER
420 4TH CORSO
NEBRASKA CITY, NE 68410

LIVESEY, NEWT
202 RAINES RD.
SILOAM SPRINGS, AR 72761

LOGISTICAL SOLUTION
P.O. BOX 211961
AUGUSTA, GA 30917

LOHMAN CO., FRED
3405 N.E. BROADWAY
PORTLAND, OR 97232

MARKING METHODS, INC.
LAURA JIMENEZ
301 S. RAYMOND AVE.
ALHAMBRA, CA 91803-1531

MASECRAFT SUPPLY CO.
170 RESEARCH PKWY #3
P.O. BOX 423
MERIDEN, CT 06450

MEIER STEEL
DARYL MEIER
75 FORGE RD.
CARBONDALE, IL 62901

MOTHER OF PEARL CO.
D.A. CULPEPPER
P.O. BOX 445, 401 OLD GA RD.
FRANKLIN, NC 28734

NICHOLAS EQUIPMENT CO.
730 E. WASHINGTON ST.
SANDUSKY, OH 44870

NORTHWEST KNIFE SUPPLY
525-L S.W. CALAPOOIA AVE.
SUTHERLIN, OR 97479

OREGON ABRASIVE & MFG. CO.
11303 NE 207TH AVE.
BRUSH PRAIRIE, WA 98606

OZARK KNIFE
3165 S. CAMPBELL
SPRINGFIELD, MO 65807

PAPAI, ABE
5013 N. 800 E.
NEW CARLISLE, IN 46552

PARAGON INDUSTRIES, INC.
2011 SOUTH TOWN EAST BLVD.
MESQUITE, TX 75149-1122

POPLIN, JAMES/POP KNIVES & SUPPLIES
103 OAK ST.
WASHINGTON, GA 30673

PUGH, JIM
P.O. BOX 711
AZLE, TX 76098

RADOS, JERRY
P.O. BOX 531
7523E 5000 N. RD.
RANT PARK, IL 60940

REACTIVE METALS STUDIO, INC.
P.O. BOX 890
CLARKDALE, AZ 86324

REAL WOOD
36 FOURTH ST.
DRACUT, MA 01826

REPRODUCTION BLADES
17485 SW PHEASANT LN.
BEAVERTON, OR 97006

RIVERSIDE KNIFE & FORGE SUPPLY
205 W. STILLWELL
DEQUEEN, AR 71832

ROCKY MOUNTAIN KNIVES
GEORGE L. CONKLIN
P.O. BOX 902, 615
FRANKLIN
FT. BENTON, MT 59442

RUMMELL, HANK
10 PARADISE LANE
WARWICK, NY 10990

SANDPAPER, INC. OF ILLINOIS
270 EISENHOWER LN. N.
UNIT 5B
LOMBARD, IL 60148

SCHELL, CLYDE M.
4735 N.E. ELLIOTT CIRCLE
CORVALLIS, OR 97330

SCHEP'S FORGE
BOX 83
CHAPMAN, NE 68827

**SHEFFIELD KNIFEMAKERS
SUPPLY, INC.**
P.O. BOX 741107
ORANGE CITY, FL 32774-1107

SHINING WAVE METALS
P.O. BOX 563
SNOHOMISH, WA 98290-0563

SMITH ABRASIVES, INC.
1700 SLEEPY VALLEY RD.
HOT SPRINGS, AR 71901

SMITH WHETSTONE, INC.
1700 SLEEPY VALLEY RD.
HOT SPRINGS, AR 71901

SMOLEN FORGE, INC.
NICK SMOLEN
RT. 2, BOX 191A
WESTBY, WA 54667

STOVER, JEFF
P.O. BOX 43
TORRANCE, CA 90507

STRANDE, POUL
SOSTER SVENSTRUP BYVEJ 16
DASTRUP 4130 VIBY SJ
DENMARK

TEXAS KNIFEMAKERS SUPPLY
10649 HADDINGTON, SUITE 180
HOUSTON, TX 77043

TRU-GRIT, INC.
760 E. FRANCIS ST. #N
ONTARIO, CA 91761

WASHITA MOUNTAIN
WHETSTONE CO.
P.O. BOX 378
LAKE HAMILTON, AR 71951

WILD WOODS
JIM FRAY
P.O. BOX 104
MONCLOVA, OH 43542

WILSON, R.W.
113 KENT WAY
WEIRTON, WV 26062

WOOD CARVERS SUPPLY, INC.
P.O. BOX 7500-K
ENGLEWOOD, FL 34295-7500

WYVERN INDUSTRIES
P.O. BOX 1564
SHADY COVE, OR 97539-1564

ZOWADA CUSTOM KNIVES
TIM ZOWADA
4509 E. BEAR RIVER RD.
BOYNE FALLS, MI 49713

knife services

custom grinders

Dozier, Bob, Dozier Knives & Grinders, PO Box 1941, Springdale, AR, 72765, 888-823-0023, 501-756-9139

High, Tom, Rocky Mountain Scrimshaw & Arts, 5474 S. 112.8 Rd., Alamosa, CO, 81101

Ingle, Ralph W., 112 Manchester Ct., Centerville, GA, 31028

Lamprey, Mike, Rose Cottage, Peters Marland, Torrington, Devon EX38 8QH, ENGLAND, 01805 601331

McLuin, Tom, 36 Fourth St., Dracut, MA, 01826, 978-957-4899, tmcluin@mediaone.net, www.people.ne.mediaone.net/tmcluin

Peele, Bryan, The Elk Rack, 215 Ferry St. P.O. Box 1363, Thompson, Falls, MT, 59873, Wilson, R.W., P.O. Box 2012, Weirton, WV, 26062

custom handle artisans

Bill's Custom Cases, P.O. Box 2, Dunsmuir, CA, 96025, 530-235-0177, 530-235-4959, billscustomcases@mindspring.com, Knife cases (cordura & leather)

Cooper, Jim, 2148 Cook Pl., Ramona, CA, 92065-3214, 760-789-1097, 760-788-7992, jamcooper@aol.com,

Eccentric Endeavors, Michel Santos and Peggy Quinn, P.O. Box 97, Douglas Flat, CA, 95229

Grussenmeyer, Paul G., 101 S. White Horse Pike, Lindenwold, NJ 08021-2304, 856-435-1500, 856-435-3786, pgrussentne@home.com

High, Tom, Rocky Mountain Scrimshaw & Arts, 5474 S. 112.8 Rd. Alamosa, CO, 81101

Holden, Larry, PO Box 2017, Ridgecrest, CA, 93556-2017, 760-375-7955, lardog44@yahoo.com

Holland, Dennis K., 4908-17th Pl., Lubbock, TX, 79416

Imboden II, Howard L., hi II Originals, 620 Deauville Dr., Dayton, OH, 45429

Ingle, Ralph W., 112 Manchester Ct., Centerville, GA, 31028

Kelley, Gary, 17485 SW Pheasant Lane, Aloha, OR, 97006, 503-848-9313, Custom buckle knives

Kelso, Jim, 577 Collar Hill Rd, Worcester, VT, 05682, 802-229-4254, 802-223-0595

Krogman, Pam, 838 Merlarkkey St., Winnemucca, NV, 89445

Lee,Ray, 209 Jefferson Dr., Lynchburg, VA, 24502

Lott Greco, Sherry, 100 Mattie Jones Rd., Greensburg, KY, 42743, 270-932-3335, 270-932-2225

Marlatt, David, 67622 Oldham Rd., Cambridge, OH, 43725, 740-432-7549

Mead, Dennis, 2250 E. Mercury St., Inverness, FL, 34453- 0514

Miller, Robert, 216 Seminole Ave., Ormond Beach, FL, 32176

Myers, Ron, 6202 Marglenn Ave., Baltimore, MD, 21206, 410-866-6914

Sayen, Murad, P.O. Box 127, Bryant Pond, ME, 04219

Schlott, Harald, Zingster Str. 26, 13051 Berlin, GERMANY, 03 01 929 33 46, 03 01 929 33 46, www.harald-schlott@t-online.de

Schönert, Elke, 18 Lansdowne Pl., Central, Port Elizabeth, SOUTH AFRICA

Smith, D. Noel, PO Box 702, Port Orchard, WA, 98366, knife2@kktv.com

Smith, Glenn, PO Box 54, Roscoe, MT, 59071

Snell, Barry A.,4801 96th St. N., St. Petersburg, FL, 33708- 3740

Vallotton, A., 621 Fawn Ridge Dr., Oakland, OR, 97462

Williams, Gary, (GARBO), 221 Autumn Way, Elizabethtown, KY, 42701

Willson, Harlan M., P.O. Box 2113, Lompoc, CA, 93438, hwillson@gte.net

display cases and boxes

Bill's Custom Cases, P.O. Box 2, Dunsmuir, CA, 96025, 530-235-0177, 530-235-4959, billscustomcases@mindspring.com, Knife cases (cordura & leather)

Brooker, Dennis, Rt. 1, Box 12A, Derby, IA, 50068

Clements', Custom, Leathercraft, Chas, 1741 Dallas St., Aurora, CO, 80010-2018, 303-364-0403, gryphons@home.com

Congdon, David, 1063 Whitchurch Ct., Wheaton, IL, 60187

Gimbert, Nelson, P.O. Box 787, Clemmons, NC, 27012

Haydu, Thomas, G., Tomway Products, 750 E Sahara Ave, Las Vegas, NV, 89104, 888 4 Tomway, 702-366-0626, tom@tomway.com, tomway.com

Mesa Case, Arne, Mason, 125 Wimer St., Ashland, OR, 97520, 541-482-2260, 541-482-7785

Miller, Michael K., M&M Kustom Krafts, 28510 Santiam Highway, Sweet Home, OR, 97386

Retichek, Joseph L., W9377 Co. TK. D, Beaver Dam, WI, 53916

Robbins, Wayne, 11520 Inverway, Belvidere, IL, 61008

S&D Enterprises, 20 East Seventh St., Manchester, OH, 45144, 937-549-2602, (937)-549-2602 or 2603, sales@s-denterprises.com, www.s-denterprises.com

Schlott, Harald, Zingster Str. 26, 13051 Berlin, GERMANY, 03 01 929 33 46, 03 01 929 33 46, www.harald-schlott@t-online.de

Schönert, Elke, 18 Lansdowne Pl., Central, Port Elizabeth, SOUTH AFRICA

engravers

Adlam, Tim, 1705 Witzel Ave., Oshkosh, WI, 54902, 920-235-4589, 920-235-4589

Alfano, Sam, 36180 Henry Gaines Rd., Pearl River, LA, 70452, 504-863-5120, sam@masterengraver.com, www.masterengraver.com

Allard, Gary, 2395 Battlefield Rd., Fishers Hill, VA, 22626

Allred, Scott, 2403 Lansing Blvd., Wichita Falls, TX

Alpen, Ralph, 7 Bentley Rd., West Grove, PA, 1939

Aoun, Charles, Galeb Knives, 69 Nahant St, Wakefield, MA, 01880, 781-224-3353, 781-224-3353

Baron, Technology Inc., David, David Baron, 62 Spring Hill Rd., Trumbull, CT, 06611, 203-452-0515, btinc@connix.com, "Polishing, plating, inlays, artwork"

Bates, Billy, 2302 Winthrop Dr. SW, Decatur, AL, 35603

Beaver, Judy, 48835 N. 25 Ave., Phoenix, AZ, 85027

Becker, Franz, Am Kreuzberg 2, 84533 Marktl/Inn, GERMANY

Bettenhausen, Merle L., 17358 Ottawa, Tinley Park, IL, 60477

Blair, Jim, P.O. Box 64, 59 Mesa Verde, Glenrock, WY, 82637, 307463-8115

Bleile, C. Roger, 5040 Ralph Ave., Cincinnati, OH, 45238

Bonshire, Benita, 1121 Burlington, Muncie, IN, 47302

Boster, A.D., 3744 Pleasant Hill Dr., Gainesville, GA, 30504

Bratcher, Dan, 311 Belle Aire Pl., Carthage, MO, 64836

Brooker, Dennis B., Rt. 1 Box 12A, Derby, IA, 50068

Churchill, Winston, G., RFD Box 29B, Proctorsville, VT, 05153

Collins, David, Rt. 2 Box 425, Monroe, VA, 24574

Collins, Michael, Rt. 3075, Batesville Rd., Woodstock, GA, 30188

Cupp, Alana, P.O. Box 207, Annabella, UT, 84711

Dashwood, Jim, 255 Barkham Rd., Wokingham, Berkshire RG11 4BY, ENGLAND

Davidson, Jere, 104 Fox Creek Dr, Goode, VA, 24556, 540-586-5150, JereDavidson@centralva.net

Dean, Bruce, 13 Tressider Ave., Haberfield, N.S.W. 2045, AUSTRALIA

DeLorge, Ed, 6734 W Main St, Houma, LA, 70360, 504-223-0206

Dickson, John W., P.O. Box 49914, Sarasota, FL, 34230

Dolbare, Elizabeth, P.O. Box 222, Sunburst, MT, 59482

Downing, Jim, P.O. Box 4224, Springfield, MO, 65808, 417-865-5953, www.thegunengraver.com

Drain, Mark, SE 3211 Kamilche Pt. Rd., Shelton, WA, 98584

Duarte, Carlos, 108 Church St., Rossville, CA, 95678

Dubben, Michael, 414 S. Fares Ave., Evansville, IN, 47714

Dubber, Michael, W., 8205 Heather Pl, Evansville, IN, 47710-4919, 812-476-0651, mwdub@aol.com

Eklund, Maihkel, Föne 1111, S-82041 Färila, SWEDEN, +46 6512 4192, maihkel.eklund@swipnet.se, http://euroedge. net/maihkeleklund/hems.shtml

Engel, Terry, (Flowers), P.O. Box 96, Midland, OR, 97634

Eyster, Ken, 6441 Bishop Rd., Centerburg, OH, 43011

Flannery, Engraving Co., Jeff, 11034 Riddles Run Rd., Union, KY, 41091, 606-384-3127, 606-384-2222, engraving@fuse.net, http://home.fuse.net/engraving/

Foster, Enterprises, Norvell, Foster, P.O. Box 200343, San Antonio, TX, 78220

Fountain Products, 492 Prospect Ave., West, Springfield, MA, 01089

French, James, Ronald, 1745 Caddo Dr., Irving, TX, 75060-5837

George, Tim and Christy, 3608 Plymouth Pl., Lynchburg, VA, 24503

Gipe, Sandi, Rt. 2, Box 1090A, Kendrick, ID, 83537

Glimm, Jerome C., 19 S. Maryland, Conrad, MT, 59425

Gournet, Geoffroy, 820 Paxinosa Ave., Easton, PA, 18042, 610-559-0710

Hands, Barry Lee, 26192 E. Shore Rte., Bigfork, MT, 59911

Harrington, Fred A., Winter: 3725 Citrus, St. James City, FL, 33956, 941-283-0721

Harrington, Fred A., Summer: 2107 W. Frances Rd, Mt. Morris, MI, 48458-8215, 810-686-3008

Henderson, Fred D., 569 Santa Barbara Dr., Forest Park, GA, 30297, 770-968-4866

Hendricks, Frank, HC03, Box 434, Dripping, Springs, TX, 78620

Holder, Pat, 7148 W. Country Gables Dr., Peoria, AZ, 85381

Hudson, Tommy, PO Box 1457, Yuba City, CA, 95992, 530-841-2966, 530-741-1670

Ingle, Ralph W., 112 Manchester Ct., Centerville, GA, 31028

Jiantonio, Robert, P.O. Box 986, Venice, FL, 34284

Johns, Bill, 6 Ptarmigan Drive, Cody, WY, 82414, 82414, 307-587-5090, Custom silver & gold handle inlays.

Kelly, Lance, 1723 Willow Oak Dr., Edgewater, FL, 32132

Kelso, Jim, RD 1, Box 5300, Worcester, VT, 05682

Koevenig, Eugene and Eve, Rabbit Gulch, Box 55, Hill City, SD, 57745-0055

Kostelnik, Joe and Patty, RD #4, Box 323, Greensburg, PA, 15601

Kudlas, John M., HC 66 Box 22680, Barnes, WI, 54873, 715-795-2031, jkudlas@ww.bright.net

Lee, Ray, 209 Jefferson Dr., Lynchburg, VA, 24502

Limings Jr., Harry, 959 County Rd. 170, Marengo, OH, 43334- 9625

Lindsay, Steve, 3714 West Cedar Hills Drive, Kearney, NE, 68847

Lyttle, Brian, Box 5697, High River AB CANADA, T1V 1M7

Lytton, Simon M., 19 Pinewood Gardens, Hemel Hempstead, Herts. HP1 1TN, ENGLAND, 01 442 25542

McCombs, Leo, 1862 White Cemetery Rd., Patriot, OH, 45658

McDonald, Dennis, 8359 Brady St., Peosta, IA, 52068

McFadden, John, PO Box 462, Coeur d'Alene, ID, 83816, 208-762-3090

McKenzie, Lynton, 6940 N. Alvernon Way, Tucson, AZ, 85718

Meyer, Chris, 39 Bergen Ave., Wantage, NJ, 07461, 973-875-6299

Morgan, Tandie, P.O. Box 693, 30700 Hwy. 97, Nucla, CO, 81424

Morton, David A., 1110 W. 21st St., Lorain, OH, 44052

Moschetti, Mitch, 1435 S. Elizabeth, Denver, CO, 80210

Nelida, Toniutti, via G. Pasconi 29/c, Maniago 33085 (PN), ITALY

Norton, Jeff, 2009 65th St., Lubbock, TX, 79412

Nott, Ron, Box 281, Summerdale, PA, 17093

Parsons, Michael, R., McKee Knives, 1600 S. 11th St., Terre Haute, IN, 47802-1722, 812-234-1679

Patterson, W.H., P.O. Drawer DK, College Station, TX, 77841

Perdue, David L., Rt. 1 Box 657, Gladys, VA, 24554

Peri, Valerio, Via Meucci 12, Gardone V.T. 25063, ITALY

Pilkington Jr., Scott, P.O. Box 97, Monteagle, TN, 37356

Poag, James, RR1, Box 212A, Grayville, IL, 62844

Potts, Wayne, 912 Poplar St., Denver, CO, 80220

Rabeno, Martin, Spook Hollow Trading Co., 92 Spook Hole Rd., Ellenville, NY, 12428

Raftis, Andrew, 2743 N. Sheffield, Chicago, IL, 60614

Roberts, J.J., 7808 Lake Dr., Manassas, VA, 22111, 703-330-0448, james.roberts@angelfire.com, www.angelfire.com/va2/engraver

Robidoux, Roland J., DMR Fine Engraving, 25 N. Federal Hwy., Studio 5, Dania, FL, 33004

Robyn, Jon, Ground Floor, 30 E. 81st St., New York, NY, 10028

Rosser, Bob, Hand Engraving, 1824 29th Ave. South, Suite 214, Birmingham, AL, 35209

Rudolph, Gil, 386 Mariposa Dr., Ventura, CA, 93001, 805-643-4005, 805-643-6416, gtraks@west.net

Rundell, Joe, 6198 W. Frances Rd., Clio, MI, 48420

Schickl, L., Ottingweg 497, A-5580 Tamsweg, AUSTRIA, 0043 6474 8583

Schlott, Harald, Zingster Str. 26, 13051 Berlin, GERMANY, 03 01 929 33 46, 03 01 929 33 46, www.harald-schlott@t-online.de

Schönert, Elke, 18 Lansdowne Pl., Central, Port Elizabeth, SOUTH AFRICA

Shaw, Bruce, P.O. Box 545, Pacific Grove, CA, 93950, 831-646-1937, 831-644-0941

Shostle, Ben, 1121 Burlington, Muncie, IN, 47302

Sinclair, W.P., 3, The Pippins, Warminster, Wiltshire BA12 8TH, ENGLAND

Smith, Jerry, 7029 East Holmes Rd., Memphis, TN, 38125

Smith, Ron, 5869 Straley, Ft. Worth, TX, 76114

Smith, Peggy, 676 Glades Rd., #3, Gatlinburg, TN, 37738

Smitty's Engraving, 800 N. Anderson Rd., Choctaw, OK, 73020

Snell, Barry A.,4801 96th St. N., St. Petersburg, FL, 33708- 3740

Spode, Peter, Tresaith Newland, Malvern, Worcestershire WR13 5AY, ENGLAND

Steduto, Giovanni, Gardone, V.T., ITALY

Swartley, Robert D., 2800 Pine St., Napa, CA, 94558

Takeuchi, Shigetoshi, 21-14-1-Chome kamimuneoka, Shiki shi, 353 Saitama, JAPAN

Valade, Robert B., 931 3rd Ave., Seaside, OR, 97138, 503-738-7672

Waldrop, Mark, 14562 SE 1st Ave. Rd., Summerfield, FL, 34491, 352-347-9034

Wallace, Terry, 385 San Marino, Vallejo, CA, 94589

Warenski, Julie, 590 East 500 N., Richfield, UT, 84701

Warren, Kenneth, W., P.O. Box 2842, Wenatchee, WA, 98807-2842, 509-663-6123, 509-663-6123

Whitehead, James D., 204 Cappucino Way, Sacramento, CA, 95838

Whitmore, Jerry, 1740 Churchill Dr., Oakland, OR, 97462

Williams, Gary, 221 Autumn Way, Elizabeth, KY, 42701

Winn, Travis A., 558 E. 3065 S., Salt Lake City, UT, 84106

Wood, Mel, P.O. Box 1255, Sierra Vista, AZ, 85636, melnan@dakotacom.net

Zietz, Dennis, 5906 40th Ave., Kenosha, WI, 53144

Baron Technology Inc., David Baron, 62 Spring Hill Rd., Trumbull, CT, 06611

Fountain Products, 492 Prospect Ave., West, Springfield, MA, 01089

Hayes, Dolores, P.O. Box 41405, Los Angeles, CA, 90041

Holland, Dennis, 4908 17th Pl., Lubbock, TX, 79416

Kelso, Jim, RD1, Box 5300, Worcester, VT, 05682

Larstein, Francine, David Boye Knives Gallery, 111-B Marine View, Davenport, CA, 95017, 831-426-6046, 831-426-6048, francine@boyeknivesgallery.com, www.boyeknivesgallery.com

Lefaucheux, Jean-Victor, Saint-Denis-Le-Ferment, 27140 Gisors, FRANCE

Leibowitz, Leonard, 1025 Murrayhill Ave., Pittsburgh, PA, 15217

MacBain, Kenneth, C., 30 Briarwood Ave., Norwood, NJ, 07648

Myers, Ron, 6202 Marglenn Ave., Baltimore, MD, 21206

Sayen, Murad, P.O. Box 127, Bryant Pond, ME, 04219

Smith, Glen, 1307 Custer Ave., Billings, MT, 59102

Vallotton, A., Northwest Knife Supply, 621 Fawn Ridge Dr., Oakland, OR, 97462

heat-treaters

Aoun, Charles, Galeb Knives, 69 Nahant St, Wakefield, MA, 01880, 781-224-3353, 781-224-3353

Bay State Metal Treating Co., 6 Jefferson Ave., Woburn, MA, 01801

Bodycote, Thermal, Processing, Tom, Tom Sidney, 710 Burns St., Cincinnati, OH, 45204, www.bodycote-na.com

Bos Heat, Treating, Paul, Shop: 1900 Weld Blvd., El Cajon, CA, 92020, 619-562-2370 / 619-445-4740 eves., paulbos@buckknives.com

El Monte Steel, 355 SE End Ave., Pomona, CA, 91766

Levine, Bernard, P.O. Box 2404, Eugene, OR, 97402, 541-484-0294, brlevine @ix.netcom.com, www.knife-expert.com/, Expert witness

Hauni Richmond Inc., 2800 Charles City Rd., Richmond, VA, 23231

Holt, B.R., 1238 Birchwood Drive, Sunnyvale, CA, 94089

Ingle, Ralph W., 112 Manchester Ct., Centerville, GA, 31028

O&W Heat Treat Inc., One Bidwell Rd., South Windsor, CT, 06074, 860-528-9239, 860-291-9939, owhti@aol.com

Texas Heat Treating Inc., 303 Texas Ave., Round Rock, TX, 78664

Texas Knifemakers Supply, 10649 Haddington, Suite 180, Houston, TX, 77043

The Tinker Shop, 1120 Helen, Deer Park, TX, 77536

Valley Metal Treating Inc., 355 S. East End Ave., Pomona, CA, 91766

Wilson, R.W., P.O. Box 2012, Weirton, WV, 26062

knife appraisers

Baker, Don and Kay, 5950 Foxfire Dr., Zanesville, OH, 43701

Levine, Bernard, P.O. Box 2404, Eugene, OR, 97402, 541-484-0294, brlevine@ix.netcom.com, www.knife-expert.com/, Expert witness

Russell, A.G., 1705 Hwy. 71 North, Springdale, AR, 72764

Vallini, Massimo, Via Dello Scalo 2/3, 40131 Bologna, ITALY

leatherworkers

Alfano, Sam, 36180 Henery Gaines Rd., Pearl River, LA, 70452

Baker, Don and Kay, 5950 Foxfire Dr., Zanesville, OH, 43701

Cheramie, Grant, 4260 West Main, Rt. 3, Box 940, Cut Off, LA, 70345

Clements', Custom, Leathercraft, Chas, 1741 Dallas St., Aurora, CO, 80010-2018, gryphons@home.com

Congdon, David, 1063 Whitchurch Ct., Wheaton, IL, 60187

Cooper, Harold, 136 Winding Way, Frankfort, KY, 40601

Cooper, Jim, 2148 Cook Pl., Ramona, CA, 92065-3214

Cow Catcher Leatherworks, 3006 Industrial Dr., Raleigh, NC, 27609, 919-833-8262, cowcatcher1@msn.com

Cubic, George, GC Custom Leather Co., 10561 E. Deerfield Pl., Tucson, AZ, 85749, 520-760-5988, gcubic@aol.com

Dawkins, Dudley, 221 N. Broadmoor, Topeka, KS, 66606-1254

Evans, Scott V, Edge Works Mfg, 1171 Halltown Rd, Jacksonville, NC, 28546, 910-455-9834, 910-346-5660, edgeworks@coastalnet.com, www.tacticalholsters.com

Fannin, David A., 2050 Idle Hour Center #191, Lexington, KY, 40502

Foley, Barney, 3M Reler Lane, Somerset, NJ, 08873

Genske, Jay, 2621/2 Elm St., Fond du Lac, WI, 54935

Gimbert, Nelson, P.O. Box 787, Clemmons, NC, 27012

Harris, Tom, 519 S. 1st St., Mount Vernon, WA, 98273

Hawk, Ken, Rt. 1, Box 770, Ceres, VA, 24318-9630

Hendryx Design, Scott, 5997 Smokey Way, Boise, ID, 83714, 208-377-8044, 208-377-2601, Kydex knife sheath maker

Homyk, David N., 8047 Carriage Ln., Wichita Falls, TX, 76306

K&J Leatherworks, P.O. Box 609, Watford, ON, N0M, 2S0, CANADA

Kravitt, Chris, HC 31 Box 6484, Rt 200, Ellsworth, ME, 04605-9805, 207-584-3000, sheathmkr@aol.com, www.treestumpleather.com, Reference: Tree Stump Leather

Larson, Richard, 549 E. Hawkeye, Turlock, CA, 95380

Lay, Robert J, Lay's Custom Knives, Box 122, Falkland, BC, V0J 3A0, CANADA V0E, 1W0, 250-379-2265

Layton, Jim, 2710 Gilbert Avenue, Portsmouth, OH, 45662

Lee, Randy, P.O. Box 1873, St. Johns, AZ, 85936, 520-337-2594, 520-337-5002, www.carizona.com/knives, Custom knifemaker

Marlatt, David, 67622 Oldham Rd., Cambridge, OH, 43725, 740-432-7549

Mason, Arne, 125 Wimer St., Ashland, OR, 97520, 541-482-2260, www.arnemason.com

McGowan, Liz, 12629 Howard Lodge Dr., Sykesville, MD, 21784, 410-489-4323

Metheny, H.A., "Whitey", 7750 Waterford Dr., Spotsylvania, VA, 22553

directory

Miller, Michael K., 28510 Santiam Highway, Sweet Home, OR, 97386

Mobley, Martha, 240 Alapaha River Road, Chula, GA, 31733

Morrissey, Martin, 4578 Stephens Rd., Blairsville, GA, 30512

Niedenthal, John, Andre, Beadwork & Buckskin, Studio 3955 NW 103 Dr., Coral Springs, FL, 33065-1551, 954-345-0447, a_niedenthal@hotmail.com, Native American beaded knife sheaths

Patterson, W.H., P.O. Drawer DK, College Station, TX, 77841

Poag, James H., RR #1 Box 212A, Grayville, IL, 62844

Red's Custom, Leather, Ed Todd, 9 Woodlawn Rd., Putnam Valley, NY, 10579

Riney, Norm, 6212 S. Marion Way, Littleton, CO, 71801

Rowe, Kenny, dba Rowe's Leather, 1406 W. Ave. C, Hope, AR, 71801, 870-777-8216, 870-777-2974, knifeart.com, rowesleather@yahoo.com

Ruiz Industries Inc., 1513 Gardena Ave., Glendale, CA, 53213-3717

Schrap, Robert G., 7024 W. Wells St., Wauwatosa, WI, 53213, 414-771-6472, 262-784-2996, rschrap@aol.com

Spragg, Wayne E., P.O. Box 508, Ashton, ID, 26241

Strahin, Robert, 401 Center Ave., Elkins, WV,

Stuart, V. Pat, Rt. 1, Box 447-S, Greenville, VA, 24440

Stumpf, John R., 523 S. Liberty St., Blairsville, PA, 15717

Tierney, Mike, 447 Rivercrest Dr., Woodstock ON CANADA, N4S 5W5

Turner, Kevin, 17 Hunt Ave., Montrose, NY, 10548

Velasquez, Gil, 7120 Madera Dr., Goleta, CA, 93117

Walker, John, 17 Laver Circle, Little Rock, AR, 72209, 501-455-0239

Watson, Bill, #1 Presidio, Wimberly, TX, 78676

Wegner, Tim, 8818-158th St. E., Puyallup, WA, 98373

Whinnery, Walt, 1947 Meadow Creek Dr., Louisville, KY, 40218

Williams, Sherman, A., 1709 Wallace St., Simi Valley, CA, 93065

photographers

Adlam, Tim, 1705 Witzel Ave., Oshkosh, WI, 54902, 920-235-4589, 920-234-4589

Alfano, Sam, 36180 Henery Gaines Rd., Pearl River, LA, 70452

Allen, John, Studio One, 3823 Pleasant Valley Blvd., Rockford, IL, 61114

Berisford, Bob, 505 West Adams St., Jacksonville, FL, 32202

Bilal, Mustafa, Turk's Head Productions, 908 NW 50th St., Seattle, WA, 98107-3634, 206-782-4164, 206-783-5677, turksheadp@aol.com, www.turkshead.com, "Graphic design, marketing & advertising"

Bittner, Rodman, 3444 North Apache Circle, Chandler, AZ, 85224

Bloomer, Peter L., Horizons West, 427 S. San Francisco, St., Flagstaff, AZ, 86001

Bogaerts, Jan, Regenweg 14, 5757 Pl., Liessel, HOLLAND

Box, Photography, Doug, 1804 W Main St, Brenham, TX, 77833-3420

Brown, Tom, 6048 Grants Ferry Rd., Brandon, MS, 39042- 8136

Buffaloe, Edwin, 104 W. Applegate, Austin, TX, 78753

Butman, Steve, P.O. Box 5106, Abilene, TX, 79608

Calidonna, Greg, 205 Helmwood Dr., Elizabethtown, KY, 42701

Campbell, Jim, 7935 Ranch Rd., Port Richey, FL, 34668

Catalano, John D., 56 Kingston Ave., Hicksville, NY, 11801

Chastain, Christopher, B&W Labs, 1462 E. Michigan St., Orlando, FL, 32806

Clark, John W., 604 Cherry St., Des Moines, IA, 50309

Clark, Ryerson, P.O. Box 1193, Dartmouth NS CANADA, B2Y 4B8

Cotton, William A., 749 S. Lemay Ave. A3-211, Fort Collins, CO, 80524

Courtice, Bill, P.O. Box 1776, Duarte, CA, 91010-4776

Crosby, Doug, RFD 1, Box 1111, Stockton Springs, ME, 04981

Danko, Michael, 3030 Jane Street, Pittsburgh, PA, 15203

Davis, Marshall, B., P.O. Box 3048, Austin, TX, 78764

Dikeman, Lawrence, 2169 Arbor Ave., Muskegon, MI, 49441

Durant, Ross, 316 E. 1st Ave., Vancouver BC CANADA, V5T 1A9

Earley, Don, 1241 Ft. Bragg Rd., Fayetteville, NC, 28305

Ehrlich, Linn M., 2643 N. Clybourn Ave., Chicago, IL, 60614

Ellison, Troy, P.O. Box 94393, Lubbock, TX, 79493, tellison@hiplains.net

Etzler, John, 11200 N. Island Rd., Grafton, OH, 44044

Fahrner, Dave, 1623 Arnold St., Pittsburgh, PA, 15205

Faul, Jan W., 903 Girard St. NE, Rr. Washington, DC, 20017

Fedorak, Allan, 28 W. Nicola St., Amloops BC CANADA, V2C 1J6

Fisher, Jay, 104 S. Main St., P.O. Box 267, Magdlena, NM, 87825, 509-854-2118, 505-854-2118, www.jayfisher.com

Fisher, Jay, P.O. Box 267, Magdalena, NM, 87825

Fitzgerald, Dan, P.O. Box 198, Beverly Hills, CA, 90213

Forster, Jenny, 1112 N. McAree, Waukegan, IL, 60085

Fox, Daniel, Lumina Studios, 6773 Industrial Parkway, Cleveland, OH, 44070, 440-734-2118, 440-734-3542, lumina@en.com

Gardner, Chuck, 116 Quincy Ave., Oak Ridge, TN, 37830

Gawryla, Don, 1105 Greenlawn Dr., Pittsburgh, PA, 15220

Godby, Ronald E., 204 Seven Hollys Dr., Yorktown, VA, 23692

Goffe Photographic, Associates, 3108 Monte Vista Blvd., NE, Albuquerque, NM, 87106

Graham, James, 7434 E Northwest Hwy, Dallas, TX, 75231, 214-341-5138, 214-341-5216, jags2dos@onramp.net

Graley, Gary W., RR2 Box 556, Gillett, PA, 16925

Griggs, Dennis, 118 Pleasant Pt Rd., Topsham, ME, 04086, 207-725-5689

Hanusin, John, 3306 Commercial, Northbrook, IL, 60062

Hardy, Scott, 639 Myrtle Ave., Placerville, CA, 95667

Hodge, Tom, 7175 S US Hwy 1 Lot 36, Titusville, FL, 32780-8172

Hoffman, Terrill, 7839 Old North Ct, Charlotte, NC, 28270, 704-364-0249

Holter, Wayne V., 125 Lakin Ave., Boonsboro, MD, 21713, 301-416-2855, mackwayne@hotmail.com

Jiantonio, Robert, P.O. Box 986, Venice, FL, 34284

Kelley, Gary, 17485 SW Pheasant Lane, Aloha, OR, 97006, 503-848-9313, Custom buckle knives

Kerns, Bob, 18723 Birdseye Dr., Germantown, MD, 20874

LaFleur, Gordon, 111 Hirst, Box 1209, Parksville BC CANADA, V0R 270

Landis, George E., 16 Prospect Hill Rd., Cromwell, CT, 06416

Lautman, Andy, 4906 41st N.W., Washington, DC, 20016

Lear, Dale, 6450 Cora Mill Rd, Gallipolis, OH, 45631, 740-245-5499, dalelear@yahoo.com, www.learz.com, Web page designer

LeBlanc, Paul, No. 3 Meadowbrook Cir., Melissa, TX, 75454

Lenz Photography, 939 S. 48th St., Suite 206, Tempe, AZ, 85281

Lester, Dean, 2801 Junipero Ave Suite 212, Long Beach, CA, 90806-2140

Leviton, David A., A Studio on the Move, P.O. Box 2871, Silverdale, WA, 98383, 360-697-3452

Long, Gary W., 3556 Miller's Crossroad Rd., Hillsboro, TN, 37342

Long, Jerry, 402 E. Gladden Dr., Farmington, NM, 87401

Lum, Billy, 16307 Evening Star Ct., Crosby, TX, 77532

McCollum, Tom, P.O. Box 933, Lilburn, GA, 30226

Moake, Jim, 18 Council Ave., Aurora, IL, 60504

Moya Inc., 4212 S. Dixie Hwy., West Palm Beach, FL, 33405

Mumford Photography, Phil, 2368 E Floyd Pl., Englewood, CO, 80110, 303-788-0384, 303-788-0384, Fotophil5@aol.com

Newton, Thomas, D., 136 1/2 W. 2nd St., Reno, NV, 89501

Norman's Studio, 322 S. 2nd St., Vivian, LA, 71082

Owens, William T., Box 99, Williamsburg, WV, 24991

Palmer Studio, 2008 Airport Blvd., Mobile, AL, 36606

Parker, T.C., 1720 Pacific, Las Vegas, NV, 89104

Parsons, 15 South Mission, Suite 3, Wenatchee, WA, 98801

Parsons, Michael R, 1600 S 11th St, Terry Haute, IN, 47802-1722, 812-234-1679

Patterson, W.H., P.O. Drawer DK, College Station, TX, 77841

Payne, Robert G., P.O. Box 141471, Austin, TX, 78714

Peterson Photography, Kent, 230 Polk St., Eugene, OR, 97402, kdp@pond.net, www.pond.net/kdp

Pigott, John, 231 Heidelberg Drive, Loveland, OH, 45140, 513-683-4875

Point Seven Inc., Eric, Eric R. Eggly, 810 Seneca St., Toledo, OH, 43608, 877-787-3836

Rasmussen, Eric L., 1121 Eliason, Brigham City, UT, 84302

Reinders, Rick, 1707 Spring Place, Racine, WI, 53404

Rhoades, Cynthia J., Box 195, Clearmont, WY, 82835

Rice, Tim, 310 Wisconsin Ave., Whitefish, MT, 59937

Richardson, Kerry, 2520 Mimosa St., Santa Rosa, CA, 95405, 707-575-1875, kerry@sonic.net, www.sonic.net/~kerry

Robertson, Kathy, Impress by Design, PO Box 211961, Augusta, GA, 30917, 706-650-0982, 706-860-1623, rccedge@csranet.com, Advertising/ graphic designer

Ross, Bill, 28364 S. Western Ave. Suite 464, Rancho Palos, Verdes, CA, 90275

Rubicam, Stephen, 14 Atlantic Ave., Boothbay, Harbor, ME, 04538-1202

Ruby, Tom, Holiday Inn University, 11200 E. Goodman Rd., Olive Branch, MS, 38654

Rush, John D., 2313 Maysel, Bloomington, IL, 61701

Schreiber, Roger, 429 Boren Ave. N., Seattle, WA, 98109, 206-622-3525

Semmer, Charles, 7885 Cyd Dr., Denver, CO, 80221

Silver Images Photography, 21 E. Aspen Ave., Flagstaff, AZ, 86001

Sims Photography, Bob, 3040 Andora Dr SW, Marietta, GA, 30064-2458

Slobodian, Scott, 4101 River Ridge Dr., P.O. Box 1498, San Andreas, CA, 95249, 209-286-1980, 209-286-1982, www.slobodianswords.com

Smith, Randall, 1720 Oneco Ave., Winter Park, FL, 32789

Stenzel Photography, P.O. Box 1504, Bozeman, MT, 59771

Storm Photo, 334 Wall St., Kingston, NY, 12401

Surles, Mark, P.O. Box 147, Falcon, NC, 28342

Tardiolo, 9381 Wagon Wheel, Yuma, AZ, 85365

Third Eye Photos, 140 E. Sixth Ave., Helena, MT, 59601

Thurber, David, P.O. Box 1006, Visalia, CA, 93279

Tighe, Brian, RR 1, Ridgeville ON CANADA, L0S 1M0, 905-892-2734, www.tigheknives.com, Knifemaker

Towell, Steven L., 3720 N.W. 32nd Ave., Camas, WA, 98607

Troutman, Harry, 107 Oxford Dr., Lititz, PA, 17543

Valley Photo, 2100 Arizona Ave., Yuma, AZ, 85364

Vara, Lauren, 4412 Waples Rd., Granbury, TX, 76049

Verhoeven, Jon, 106 San Jose Dr., Springdale, AR, 72764-2538

Verno Studio, Jay, 3030 Jane Street, Pittsburgh, PA, 15203

Wells, Carlene L., 1060 S. Main Sp. 52, Colville, WA, 99114

Weyer International, 2740 Nebraska Ave., Toledo, OH, 43607, 800-448-8424, 419-534-2697, law-weyer.international@msn.com, Books

Wise, Harriet, 242 Dill Ave., Frederick, MD, 21701

Worley, Holly, 6360 W David Dr., Littleton, CO, 80128-5708

scrimshanders

Adlam, Tim, 1705 Witzel Ave., Oshkosh, WI, 54902, 920-235-4589, 920-234-4589

Anderson, Terry Jack, 10076 Birnamwoods Way, Riverton, UT, 84065-9073

Arnold, Joe, 47 Patience Cres., London ON, CANADA, N6E 2K7

Bailey, Mary W., 3213 Jonesboro Dr., Nashville, TN, 37214

Baker, Duane, 2145 Alum Creek Dr., Cambridge Park Apt. #10, Columbus, OH, 43207

Barndt, Kristen A., RR3, Box 72, Kunkletown, PA, 18058

Barrows, Miles, 524 Parsons Ave., Chillicothe, OH, 45601

Beauchamp, Gaetan, 125 de la Riviere, Stoneham, PQ, G0A 4P0, CANADA, 418-848-1914, 418-848-6859, gaetanbeauchamp@uldectron.ca, www.pages.infinit.net/couteau/, "Custom grinder, custom handle artisan

Beaver, Judy, 48835 N. 25 Ave., Phoenix, AZ, 85027

Bellet, Connie, PO Box 151, Palermo, ME, 04354, 207-993-2327, pwhitehawk@juno.com or @palermo.org

Bonshire, Benita, 1121 Burlington Dr., Muncie, IN, 47302

Boone Trading Co. Inc., PO Box 669, Brinnon, WA, 98320, 360-796-4330, 360-796-4511

Bowles, Rick, 556 Pheasant Run, Virginia Beach, VA, 23452-8017

Brady, Sandra, P.O. Box 104, Monclova, OH, 43542, 419-866-0435, 419-867-0656

Bryan, Bob, 1120 Oak Hill Rd., Carthage, MO, 64836

Byrne, Mary Gregg, 1018 15th St., Bellingham, WA, 98225-6604

Cable, Jerry, 332 Main St., Mt. Pleasant, PA, 15666

Caudill, Lyle, 7626 Lyons Rd., Georgetown, OH, 45121

Collins, Michael, Rt. 3075, Batesville Rd., Woodstock, GA, 30188

Conover, Juanita Rae, P.O. Box 70442, Eugene, OR, 97401, 541-747-1726 or 543-4851

Courtnage, Elaine, Box 473, Big Sandy, MT, 59520

Cover Jr., Raymond, A., Rt. 1, Box 194, Mineral Point, MO, 63660

Cox, J. Andy, 116 Robin Hood Lane, Gaffney, SC, 29340

Davenport, Susan, 36842 Center Ave., Dade City, FL, 33525

DeYoung, Brian, 1448 Glen Haven Dr., Ft Collins, CO, 80526-2408

Dietrich, Roni, Wild Horse Studio, 1257 Cottage Dr., Harrisburg, PA, 17112, 717-469-0587, ronimd@aol.com

DiMarzo, Richard, 2357 Center Place, Birmingham, AL, 35205

Dolbare, Elizabeth, P.O. Box 222, Sunburst, MT, 59482

Drain, Mark, SE 3211 Kamilche Pt. Rd., Shelton, WA, 98584

Eklund, Maihkel, Föne 1111, S-82041 Färila, SWEDEN, +46 6512 4192, maihkel.eklund@swipnet.se, http://euroedge.net/maihkeleklund

Eldridge, Allan, 1424 Kansas Lane, Gallatin, TN, 37066

Evans, Rick M., 2717 Arrowhead Dr., Abilene, TX, 79606

Fisk, Dale, Box 252, Council, ID, 83612

Foster Enterprises, Norvell Foster, P.O. Box 200343, San Antonio, TX, 78220

Fountain Products, 492 Prospect Ave., West Springfield, MA, 01089

Garbe, Sandra, 1246 W. Webb, DeWitt, MI, 48820

Gill, Scott, 925 N. Armstrong St., Kokomo, IN, 46901

Halligan, Ed, 14 Meadow Way, Sharpsburg, GA, 30277, ehkiss@bellsouth.net

Hands, Barry Lee, 26192 East Shore Route, Bigfork, MT, 59911

Hargraves Sr., Charles, RR 3 Bancroft, Ontario CANADA, K0L 1C0

Harless, Star, c/o Arrow Forge, P.O. Box 845, Stoneville, NC, 27048-0845

Harrington, Fred A., Summer: 2107 W Frances Rd, Mt Morris MI 48458 8215 Winter: 3725 Citrus, St. James City, FL, 33956, Winter 941-283-0721,Summer 810-686-3008

Henderson, Fred D., 569 Santa Barbara Dr., Forest Park, GA, 30297, 770-968-4866

Henry, Michael K., Rte. 2, Box 161-J, Robbinsville, NC, 28771

Hielscher, Vickie, PO Box 992, 6550 Otoe Rd, Alliance, NE, 69301, 308-762-4318, hielscher@premaonline.com

High, Tom, 5474 S. 112.8 Rd., Alamosa, CO, 81101

Himmelheber, David R., 11289 40th St. N., Royal Palm Beach, FL, 33411

Holland, Dennis K., 4908-17th Place, Lubbock, TX, 79416

Hoover, Harvey, 5750 Pearl Dr., Paradise, CA, 95969-4829

Houser, Jesse, P.O. Box 993, Biscoe, NC, 27209

Imboden II, Howard L., 620 Deauville Dr., Dayton, OH, 45429, 937-439-1536, Guards by the "Last Wax Technic"

Johnson, Corinne, W3565 Lockington, Mindora, WI, 54644

Johnston, Kathy, W. 1134 Providence, Spokane, WA, 99205

Karst, Linda K., 402 Hwy. 27 E., Ingram, TX, 78025-3315, 830-896-4678,

Kelso, Jim, 577 Collar Hill Rd, Worcester, VT, 05682

Kirk, Susan B., 1340 Freeland Rd., Merrill, MI, 48637

Koevenig, Eugene and Eve, Koevenig's Engraving Service Rabbit Gulch, Box 55, Hill City, SD, 57745-0055

Kostelnik, Joe and Patty, RD #4, Box 323, Greensburg, PA, 15601

Kudlas, John M., HC 66 Box 22680, Barnes, WI, 54873, 715-795-2031, jkudlas@win.bright.net

Land, John W., P.O. Box 917, Wadesboro, NC, 28170

Lee, Ray, 209 Jefferson Dr., Lynchburg, VA, 24502

Lemen, Pam, 3434 N. Iroquois Ave., Tucson, AZ, 85705

Letschnig, Franz,RR1, Martintown ON, CANADA

Martin, Diane, 28220 N. Lake Dr., Waterford, WI, 53185

McDonald, René Cosimini-, 14730 61 Court N., Loxahatchee, FL, 33470

McGowan, Frank, 12629 Howard Lodge Dr., Sykesville, MD, 21784

McGrath, Gayle, 12641 Panasoffkee, N Ft Myers, FL, 33903

McLaran, Lou, 603 Powers St., Waco, TX, 76705

McWilliams, Carole, P.O. Box 693, Bayfield, CO, 81122

Mead, Faustina L., 2550 E. Mercury St., Inverness, FL, 34453-0514, 352-344-4751, scrimsha@citrus.infi.net, scrimshaw-by-faustina.com, Etcher (acid)

Minnick, Joyce, 144 N. 7th St., Middletown, IN, 47356

Mitchell, James, 1026 7th Ave., Columbus, GA, 31901

Moore, James B., 1707 N. Gillis, Stockton, TX, 79735

Ochonicky, Michelle "Mike", 31 High Trail, Eureka, MO, 63025, www.bestofmissourihands.com

Ochs, Belle, 124 Emerald Lane, Largo, FL, 33771, 727-530-3826, chuckandbelle @juno.com, www.oxforge.com

Pachi, Mirella, Via Pometta 1, 17046 Sassello (SV), ITALY, 019 720086, WWW.PACHI-KNIVES.COM

Pankova-Clark, Inna, P.O. Box 597, Andrews, NC, 28901

Parish, Vaughn, 103 Cross St., Monaca, PA, 15061

Peck, Larry H., 4021 Overhill Rd., Hannibal, MO, 63401

Peterson, Lou, 514 S. Jackson St., Gardner, IL, 60424

Poag, James H., RR #1 Box 212A, Grayville, IL, 62844

Polk, Trena, 4625 Webber Creek Rd., Van Buren, AR, 72956

Purvis, Hilton, P.O. Box 371, Noordhoek, 7985, REP. OF SOUTH AFRICA

Ramsey, Richard, 8525 Trout Farm Rd, Neosho, MO, 64850

Rece, Charles V., 2499 Pebble Creek Ct., Lincolntown, NC, 28092-6115

Riffe, Glen, 4430 See Saw Cir., Colorado Springs, CO, 80917, skrimmer@hotmail.com

Ristinen, Lori, 14256 Cty Hwy 45, Menahga, MN, 56464, 218-538-6608, grist@wcta.net, www.digitmaster.com/mnpro/lori/index-html

Roberts, J.J., 7808 Lake Dr., Manassas, VA, 22111

Robidoux, Roland J., DMR Fine Engraving, 25 N. Federal Hwy., Studio 5, Dania, FL, 33004

Rodkey, Sheryl, 18336 Ozark Dr., Hudson, FL, 34667

Rundell, Joe, 6198 W. Frances Rd., Clio, MI, 48420

Saggio, Joe, 1450 Broadview Ave. #12, Columbus, OH, 43212, jvsag@webtv.net

Sahlin, Viveca, Lövhagsgatan 39, S-724 71 Västerås, SWEDEN, + 46 21 358778, viveca@scrimart.u.se, www.scrimart.u.se

Satre, Robert, 518 3rd Ave. NW, Weyburn SK CANADA, S4H 1R1

Schlott, Harald, Zingster Str. 26, 13051 Berlin, GERMANY, 03 01 929 33 46, 03 01 929 33 46, www.harald-schlott@t-online.de

Schönert, Elke, 18 Lansdowne Pl., Central, Port Elizabeth, SOUTH AFRICA

Schulenburg, E.W., 25 North Hill St., Carrollton, GA, 30117

Schwallie, Patricia, 4614 Old Spartanburg Rd. Apt. 47, Taylors, SC, 29687

Selent, Chuck, P.O. Box 1207, Bonners Ferry, ID, 83805

Semich, Alice, 10037 Roanoke Dr., Murfreesboro, TN, 37129

Sherwood, George, 46 N. River Dr., Roseburg, OR, 97470

Shostle, Ben, 1121 Burlington, Muncie, IN, 47302

Sinclair, W.P., 3, The Pippins, Warminster, Wiltshire BA12 8TH, ENGLAND

Smith, D. Noel, PO Box 702, Port Orchard, WA, 98366, knife2@kktv.com

Smith, Jerry, 8770 Hunters Run, Olive Branch, TN, 38654, 662-890-5533, jsmith2098@aol.com

Smith, Peggy, 676 Glades Rd., #3, Gatlinburg, TN, 37738

Smith, Ron, 5869 Straley, Ft. Worth, TX, 76114

Snell, Barry A.,4801 96th St. N., St. Petersburg, FL, 33708- 3740

Stahl, John, Images In Ivory, 2049 Windsor Rd., Baldwin, NY, 11510, 516-223-5007

Steigerwalt, Jim, RD#3 Sunbury, PA, 17801

Stuart, Stephen, 15815 Acorn Circle, Tavares, FL, 32778, 352-343-8423, 352-343-8916, scrim@cde.com

Talley, Mary, Austin, 2499 Countrywood Parkway, Cordova, TN, 38018

Thompson, Larry D., 23040 Ave. 197, Strathmore, CA, 93267

Tong, Jill, P.O. Box 572, Tombstone, AZ, 85638

Toniutti, Nelida, Via G. Pascoli, 33085 Maniago-PN, ITALY

Tucker, Steve, 3518 W. Linwood, Turlock, CA, 95380

Tyser, Ross, 1015 Hardee Court, Spartanburg, SC, 29303

Velasquez, Gil, Art of Scrimshaw, 7120 Madera Dr., Goleta, CA, 93117

Walker, Karen, PO Box 3272, Alpine, WY, 83128-0272, gwknives@silverstar.com

Warren, Al, 1423 Santa Fe Circle, Roseville, CA, 95678, warrenives@juno.com

Williams, Gary, (Garbo), 221 Autumn Way, Elizabethtown, KY, 42701

Winn, Travis A., 558 E. 3065 S., Salt Lake City, UT, 84106

Young, Mary, 4826 Storeyland Dr., Alton, IL, 62002

Zima, Russell, 7291 Ruth Way, Denver, CO, 80221

directory

carvers

Marlatt, David, 67622 Oldham Rd., Cambridge, OH,
43725, 740-432-7549

DiMarzo, Richard, 2357 Center Place, Birmingham, AL,
35205

writers

Kelley, Gary, 17485 SW Pheasant Lane, Aloha, OR,
97006, 503-848-9313, Custom buckle knives

etchers

Baron Technology Inc., David Baron, 62 Spring Hill Rd.,
Trumbull, CT, 06611

Kostelnik, Joe and Patty, RD #4, Box 323, Greensburg,
PA, 15601

Schlott, Harald, Zingster Str. 26, 13051 Berlin,
GERMANY, 03 01 929 33 46, 03 01 929 33 46,
www.harald-schlott@t-online.de

Schönert, Elke, 18 Lansdowne Pl., Central, Port
Elizabeth, SOUTH AFRICA

Snell, Barry A.,4801 96th St. N., St. Petersburg, FL,
33708- 3740

hand-forged fancy knives

Patterson, W.H., P.O. Drawer DK, College Station, TX,
77841

knife videos

Congdon, David, 1063 Whitchurch Ct., Wheaton, IL,
60187

Gimbert, Nelson, P.O. Box 787, Clemmons, NC, 27012

antique knife dealers

Congdon, David, 1063 Whitchurch Ct., Wheaton, IL,
60187

Gimbert, Nelson, P.O. Box 787, Clemmons, NC, 27012

mail order sales

AMERICAN TARGET KNIVES
1030 BROWNWOOD NW
GRAND RAPIDS, MI 49504

ARIZONA CUSTOM KNIVES
JAY AND KAREN SADOW
8617 E. CLYDESDALE
SCOTTSDALE, AZ 85258

ARTHUR, GARY B.
RT. 7 BOX 215
FOREST, VA 24551

ATLANTA CUTLERY CORP.
2143 GEES MILL RD., BOX 839XZ
CONYERS, GA 30207

ATLANTIC BLADESMITHS/PETER
STEBBINS
32 BRADFORD ST.
CONCORD, MA 01742

BALLARD CUTLERY
1495 BRUMMEL AVE.
ELK GROVE VILLAGE, IL 60007

BARRETT-SMYTHE, LTD.
30E 81ST GRD FLOOR
NEW YORK, NY 10028

BECK'S CUTLERY SPECIALTIES
748F EAST CHATHAM ST.
CARY, NC 27511

BELL SR., R.T. "BOB"
P.O. BOX 690147
ORLANDO, FL 32869

BLAIRS BLADES & ACCESSORIES
531 MAIN ST., SUITE 651
EL SEGUNDO, CA 90245

BLUE RIDGE KNIVES
RT. 6, BOX 185
MARION, VA 24354-9351

BOONE TRADING CO., INC.
P.O. BOX BB
BRINNON, WA 98320

CARMEL CUTLERY
DOLORES & 6TH; P.O. BOX 1346
CARMEL, CA 93921

CLASSIC CUTLERY
39 ROOSEVELT AVE.
HUDSON, NH 03051-2828

COHEN & NEAL CUSTOM KNIVES
P.O. BOX 831
COCKEYSVILLE, MD 21030

CORRADO CUTLERY
OTTO POMPER
26 N. CLARK ST.
CHICAGO, IL 60602

CREATIVE SALES & MFG.
BOX 550
WHITEFISH, MT 59937

CUTLERY SHOPPE
P.O. BOX 610
MERIDIAN, ID 83680-0610

DENTON, J.W.
102 N. MAIN ST., BOX 429
HIAWASSEE, GA 30546

EDGE CO. KNIVES
P.O. BOX 826
BRATTLEBORO, VT 05302

FAZALARE, ROY
P.O. BOX 1335
AGOURA HILLS, CA 91376

FROST CUTLERY CO.
P.O. BOX 22636
CHATTANOOGA, TN 37422

GENUINE ISSUE, INC.
949 MIDDLE COUNTRY RD.
SELDEN, NY 11784

GODWIN, INC., G. GEDNEY
2139 WELSH VALLEY RD.
VALLEY FORGE, PA 19481

HAWTHORN GALLERIES, INC.
P.O. BOX 6071
BRANSON, MO 65616

HERITAGE ANTIQUE KNIVES
BRUCE VOYLES
P.O. BOX 22171
CHATTANOOGA, TN 37422

HOUSE OF TOOLS LTD.
#136, 8228 MACLEOD TR. SE
CALGARY, ALBERTA, CANADA
T2H 2B8

HUNTER SERVICES
FRED HUNTER
P.O. BOX 14241
PARKVILLE, MD 64152

IRONSTONE DISTINCTIVE BLADEWARE
16350 S. GOLDEN RD.
GOLDEN, CO 80401

JENCO SALES, INC.
P.O. BOX 1000
MANCHACA, TX 78652

KELLEM KNIVES CO.
3422 OLD CAPITOL TRAIL, STE. 831
WILMINGTON, DE 19808

KNIFE-AHOLICS UNANIMOUS
P.O. BOX 831
COCKEYSVILLE, MD 21030

KNIFEART.COM
13301 POMPANO DR
LITTLE ROCK AR 72211
ADDED 12/00

KNIFE & CUTLERY PRODUCTS, INC.
P.O. BOX 12480
NORTH KANSAS CITY, MO 64116

KNIFE IMPORTERS, INC.
P.O. BOX 1000
MANCHACA, TX 78652

KNIFEMASTERS CUSTOM KNIVES/J&S
FEDER
P.O. BOX 2419
WESTPORT, CT 06880

KNIVES PLUS
2467 I 40 WEST
AMARILLO TX 79109

KRIS CUTLERY
P.O. BOX 133 KN
PINOLE, CA 94564

LDC CUSTOM KNIVES
P.O. BOX 211961
AUGUSTA, GA 30917

LES COUTEAUX CHOISSIS DE ROBERTS
RON ROBERTS
P.O. BOX 273
MIFFLIN, PA 17058

LONDON, RICK
P.O. BOX 21303
OAKLAND, CA 94620

LONE STAR WHOLESALE
PO BOX 587
AMARILLO TX 79105

MATTHEWS CUTLERY
4401 SENTRY DR., SUITE K
TUCKER, GA 30084

MORTY THE KNIFE MAN, INC.
4 MANORHAVEN BLVD.
PORT WASHINGTON, NY 11050

MUSEUM REPLICAS LTD.
2143 GEES MILL RD., BOX 840XZ
CONYERS, GA 30207

NASHOBA VALLEY KNIFEWORKS
373 LANGEN RD., BOX 35
LANCASTER, MA 01523

NORDIC KNIVES
1634CZ COPENHAGEN DR.
SOLVANG, CA 93463

PARKER'S KNIFE COLLECTOR SERVICE
6715 HERITAGE BUSINESS COURT
CHATTANOOGA, TN 37422

PEN AND THE SWORD LTD., THE
1833 E. 12TH ST.
BROOKLYN, NY 11229

PLAZA CUTLERY, INC.
3333 S. BRISTOL ST., SOUTH COAST PLAZA
COSTA MESA, CA 92626

RAMSHEAD ARMOURY, INC.
P.O. BOX 85
MARYVILLE, IL 62062-0085

ROBERTSON'S CUSTOM CUTLERY
P.O. BOX 211961
AUGUSTA, GA 30917

ROBINSON, ROBERT W.
1569 N. FINLEY PT.
POLSON, MT 59860

RUSSELL CO., A.G.
1705 HIGHWAY 71 NORTH
SPRINGDALE, AR 72764

SHAW, GARY
24 CENTRAL AVE.
RIDGEFIELD PARK, NJ 07660

SMOKY MOUNTAIN KNIFE WORKS
P.O. BOX 4430
SEVIERVILLE, TN 37864

STIDHAM'S KNIVES
P.O. BOX 570
ROSELAND, FL 32957-0570

STODDARD'S, INC.
COPLEY PLACE
100 HUNTINGTON AVE.
BOSTON, MA 02116

STONEWORKS
P.O. BOX 211961
AUGUSTA, GA 30917

organizations & publications

organizations

AMERICAN BLADESMITH SOCIETY
c/o Joseph G., Cordova, P.O. Box, 977, Peralta, NM 87042

AMERICAN KNIFE THROWERS ALLIANCE
c/o Bobby, Branton, 4976, Seewee Rd., Awendaw, SC 29429

ART KNIFE COLLECTOR'S ASSOCIATION
c/o Mitch Weiss, Pres., 2211 Lee, Road, Suite, 104, Winter Park, FL, 32789

AUSTRALIAN KNIFEMAKERS GUILD INC.
P.O. Box 659, Belgrave, 3160, Victoria, AUSTRALIA

CALIFORNIA KNIFEMAKERS GUILD
c/o Barry Evan, Posner, Mbrshp, Chairman, 5222, Beeman Ave., N. Hollywood, CA, 91607

CANADIAN KNIFEMAKERS GUILD
c/o John, Freeman, Sec./Treas., 160, Concession, St., Cambridge, Ont., CANADA, N1R 2H7

JAPANESE SWORD
SOCIETY OF THE U.S., P.O. Box 712, Breckenridge, TX 76424

KNIFE COLLECTORS CLUB INC, THE
1705 N, Thompson St., Springdale, AR 72764, (501) 751-7341, (800) 255-9034, (501) 751-4520, club@k-c.com. The oldest and largest association of knife collectors. Issues limited edition knives, both handmade and highest quality production, in very limited numbers. The very earliest was the CM-1, Kentucky Rifle.

KNIFEMAKERS GUILD
c/o Billy Mace Imel, Sec./Treas., 1616 Bundy Ave., New Castle, IN, 47362

KNIFEMAKERS GUILD OF SOUTHERN AFRICA, THE
c/o Bertie, Rietveld, Chairman, P.O. Box 53, Magaliesburg, SOUTH AFRICA

MIDWEST KNIFEMAKERS ASSOCIATION
c/o Corbin Newcomb, Pres., 628 Woodland Ave., Moberly, MO 65270

MINIATURE KNIFEMAKERS' SOCIETY
c/o Gary F. Bradburn, Sec., 1714 Park Pl., Wichita, KS 67203

MONTANA KNIFEMAKERS' ASSOCIATION, THE
14440 Harpers Bridge Rd, Missoula, MT 59808, (406) 543-0845, Annual book of custom knife makers' works and directory of knife making supplies; $19.99

NEO-TRIBAL METALSMITHS
P.O. Box 44095, Tucson, AZ 85773-4095

NORTH CAROLINA CUSTOM KNIFEMAKERS GUILD
c/o Tommy McNabb, Pres., 4015 Brownsboro Rd., Winston-Salem, NC 27106

PROFESSIONAL KNIFEMAKERS ASSOCIATION
2905 N. Montana Ave., Ste. 30027, Helena, MT 59601

TRIBAL NOW!
Neo-Tribal Metalsmiths, P.O. Box 44095, Tucson, AZ 85733-4095

UK BLADE
United Kingdom Blade Associations, P.O. Box 1, Brampton CA67GD, ENGLAND

UNITED KINGDOM BLADE ASSOCIATION (UKBA)
P.O. Box 1, Brampton, CA67GD, ENGLAND

WEYER INTERNATIONAL BOOK DIVISION
2740 Nebraska Ave., Toledo, OH 43607-3245

publications

BLADE MAGAZINE
Krause Publications, 700 E. State St., Iola, WI 54990/800-272-5233
Editor: Steve Shackleford. Monthly. Official magazine of the Knifemakers Guild. $3.25 on newsstand; $19.95 per year. Also publishes *Blade Trade*, a cutlery trade magazine; *Dream Teams; Tek-Knives; Knives of Europe* and knife books.

CUTTING EDGE, THE
1705 N, Thompson St, Springdale, AR 72764-1294, (501) 751-7341, (800) 255-9034, (501) 751-4520, buyer@cuttingedge.com, After-market, knives since 1968. We offer about 1,000 individual knives each month. Subscription by first class mail, in U.S. $20 per year, Canada or Mexico by air mail, $25 per year. All overseas by air mail, $40 per year. The oldest and the most experienced in the business of buying and selling knives. We buy collections of any size, take knives on consignment or we will trade. Every month there are eight pages in color featuring the work of top makers.

KRAUSE PUBLICATIONS, INC.
700 E. State St., Iola, WI 54990/715-445-2214; FAX: 715-445-4087
In addition to *Sporting Knives* and the *Knives* annual, Krause and its DBI Books division publish many knife books, including *American Premium Guide to Knives and Razors* by Jim Sargent; *IBCA Price Guide to Antique Knives* by J. Bruce Voyles; *Levine's Guide to Knives and Their Values* by Bernard Levine; *The Wonder of Knifemaking* by Wayne Goddard; *How To Make Knives* by Richard W. Barney and Robert W. Loveless; *The Tactical Folding Knife* by Bob Terzuola; *How to Make Folding Knives* by Ron Lake, Frank Centofante and Wayne Clay; *Complete Book of Pocketknife Repair* by Ben Kelly Jr.; *Knife Talk* by Ed Fowler; *Collins Machetes and Bowies 1845-1965* by Daniel E. Henry; and *Collecting Indian Knives* by Lar Hothem.

KNIFE WORLD

P.O. Box 3395, Knoxville, TN 37927/800-828-7751
Editor: Mark Zalesky. Monthly. Tabloid size on newsprint. Covers custom knives, knifemakers, collecting, old factory knives, etc. General coverage for the knife enthusiast. Subscription $15 year.

KNIVES ILLUSTRATED

265 S. Anita Dr., Ste. 120, Orange, CA 92868/714-939-9991
Editor; Bud Lang. $3.50 on newsstands; $14.95 for six issues. Plenty of four-color, all on cutlery; concentrates on handmade knives.

NATIONAL KNIFE MAGAZINE

P.O. Box 21070, Chattanooga, TN 37424/423-899-9456
For members of the National Knife Collectors Association. Emphasis on pocketknife collecting, of course, together with association show news. Membership $25 year; $28 for new members.

RESOURCE GUIDE AND NEWSLETTER / AUTOMATIC KNIVES

2269 Chestnut St., Suite 212, San Francisco, CA 94123/415-731-0210
Editor: Sheldon Levy. In its eighth year as a quarterly. Deep coverage of automatic folders. $30 year by mail.

TACTICAL KNIVES

Harris Publications, 1115 Broadway, New York, NY 10010/212-807-7100; FAX: 212-627-4678

Editor: Steve Dick. Aimed at emergency-service knife designs and users. Price $4.95; $14.95 for six issues. On newsstands.

TRIBAL NOW!

Neo-Tribal Metalsmiths, P.O. Box 44095, Tucson, AZ 85733-4095
Editor: Bill Randall. (See Neo-Tribal Metalsmith under Organizations.) Price: $10 per year for four issues with two- to four- page supplements sent out on a regular basis.

TWO KNIFE GUYS PUBLISHING

Ken Warner/J Bruce Voyles, PO Box 24477, Chattanooga TN 37422, (423) 894-6640

UK BLADE

United Kingdom Blade Associations, P.O. Box 1, Brampton CA67GD England
On a base of UK knifemakers, the UKBA, seeks to sweep the knife fancy of Britain all into one tent. Membership dues: Ordinary £16 year; husband and wife (one magazine) £20 year; trade £30 year. And they have no phone yet.

WEYER INTERNATIONAL BOOK DIVISION

2740 Nebraska Ave., Toledo, OH 43607, 419-534-2020, 419-534-2697
Publishers of the *Knives: Points of Interest* series. Sells knife-related books at attractive prices; has other knife-publishing projects in work.

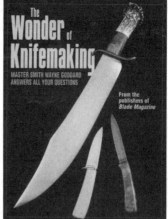

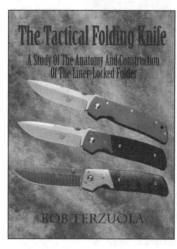

BOOKS FOR HUNTERS

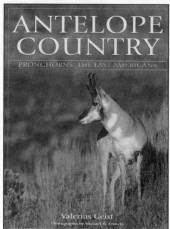

Antelope Country
Pronghorns: The Last Americans
by Valerius Geist, Photography by Michael H. Francis
Professor Valerius Geist shares his fascinating insights into pronghorn antelope, the last surviving larger mammal of an era when the Great Plains was teeming with more species of wildlife than the African plains. Learn how the fleet, beautiful pronghorn was nearly wiped off the plains along with its bigger brother, the American bison, in the late 1800s, and then returned to abundance through myriad conservation efforts. The book is illustrated with striking photography by Michael Francis.
Hardcover • 8-1/4 x 10-7/8 • 176 pages • 150 color photos
Item# ALPCY • $39.95

Big Bucks the Benoit Way
Secrets from America's First Family of Whitetail Hunting
by Bryce Towsley
Finally, the long-awaited second book on the tried-and-true hunting strategies of the legendary Benoit family. Although tracking and woodsmanship are emphasized, hunters of all ages, no matter where they hunt, will gain the knowledge needed to bag trophy bucks.
Hardcover • 8-1/2 x 11
208 pages
150 b&w photos
16-page color section
Item# HBB • $24.95

Elk
Strategies for the Hunter
by Durwood Hollis
If you want to bag a trophy elk, author Durwood Hollis provides a detailed map to success. He'll guide you through the complicated process of applying for a license and hiring a guide and show you exactly what you need to succeed at elk camp. If you're serious about the most majestic animal in North America, this book is for you.
Softcover • 8-1/2 x 11
208 pages
125 b&w photos
Item# ELK • $19.95

Rub-Line Secrets
by Greg Miller, Edited by Patrick Durkin
In Rub-Line Secrets, Greg Miller takes deer hunters to the graduate level in teaching them proven tactics for finding, analyzing and hunting a big buck's rub-line. No one has enjoyed more rub-line success than Miller. His straight-forward approach to hunting rub-lines is based on more than 30 years of intense hunting and scouting. The book is illustrated with photos and diagrams that help Miller explain his proven rub-line tactics.
Softcover • 6 x 9 • 208 pages
100 b&w photos
Item# HURU • $19.95

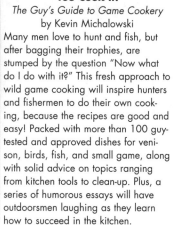

You Cook It!
The Guy's Guide to Game Cookery
by Kevin Michalowski
Many men love to hunt and fish, but after bagging their trophies, are stumped by the question "Now what do I do with it?" This fresh approach to wild game cooking will inspire hunters and fishermen to do their own cooking, because the recipes are good and easy! Packed with more than 100 guy-tested and approved dishes for venison, birds, fish, and small game, along with solid advice on topics ranging from kitchen tools to clean-up. Plus, a series of humorous essays will have outdoorsmen laughing as they learn how to succeed in the kitchen.
Spiral • 6 x 9 • 208 pages • 30 illustrations
Item# YCI • $14.95

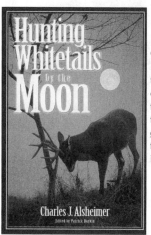

Hunting Whitetails by the Moon
by Charles J. Alsheimer, Edited by Patrick Durkin
Charles J. Alsheimer, *Deer & Deer Hunting* magazine's Northern field editor, explains how deer hunters can use autumn moon cycles to predict peak times in the North and South to hunt rutting white-tailed bucks. He details the ground-breaking research conducted that unlocked the mysteries of the moon's influence on deer activity and behavior.
Softcover • 6 x 9 • 256 pages
100 b&w photos
Item# LUNAR • $19.95

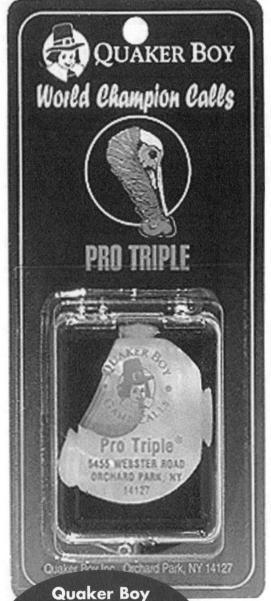

FREE CALL

SPORTING KNIVES READER INTEREST SURVEY

1. **Check all that apply:** In which of the following knife-using activities are you currently active?

   - ☐ Model making
   - ☐ Whittling
   - ☐ Woodworking
   - ☐ Construction
   - ☐ Boating
   - ☐ Hunting
   - ☐ Fishing
   - ☐ Camping/Hiking
   - ☐ Military service
   - ☐ Law enforcement
   - ☐ None of these
   - ☐ Other:_____

2. **Check all that apply:** What are your reading interests?

   - ☐ Vintage Models
   - ☐ History of manufacturers
   - ☐ History of knife design
   - ☐ Collecting *new* sporting knives
   - ☐ Collecting *old* sporting knives
   - ☐ Making sporting knives
   - ☐ Customized sporting knives
   - ☐ Personal protection knives
   - ☐ Knife Accessories
   - ☐ U.S. sporting knives
   - ☐ European sporting knives
   - ☐ World-wide sporting knives
   - ☐ None of these
   - ☐ Other:_____

3. **Check all that apply:** Which of the following <u>publications</u> do you read regularly, that is, at least three out of every four issues?

   - ☐ American Handgunner
   - ☐ Blade
   - ☐ Guns & Ammo
   - ☐ Guns Magazine
   - ☐ Knife World
   - ☐ Knives Illustrated
   - ☐ Shooting Times
   - ☐ Shotgun News
   - ☐ Tactical Knives
   - ☐ Other:_____

4. **Check all that apply:** Which of the following gun/knife <u>books</u> do you purchase regularly?

   - ☐ Gun Digest
   - ☐ Guns Illustrated
   - ☐ Handguns
   - ☐ Knives
   - ☐ Shooter's Bible
   - ☐ Other:_____

5. **Check all that apply:** Which of the following did you read in this year's edition of SPORTING KNIVES?

   - ☐ **Feature Articles**

   Field Editors New Product/S.H.O.T. Show Reports:
   - ☐ Sporting Folders
   - ☐ Sporting Fixed Blades
   - ☐ Tactical Folders
   - ☐ Pocketknives
   - ☐ Swords & Fantasy
   - ☐ Neck & Boot Knives
   - ☐ Multi-Tools
   - ☐ Factory-Custom Collaborations
   - ☐ Accessories
   - ☐ Industry Website Directory

   - ☐ **Knife Marketplace**   ☐ **Catalog of Sporting Cutlery**

   Reference Section:
   - ☐ Directory of Sporting Cutlers
   - ☐ Collectors Associations
   - ☐ Library of Sporting Cutlery & Edged Weapons
   - ☐ Periodical Publications

   ADDITIONAL COMMENTS? _____
   _____
   _____

   Thank you for filling out the Sporting Knives Reader Interest Survey. Please return your completed survey no later than June 1, 2002. This offer expires on June 1, 2002.

YOU RECEIVE <u>TWO</u> <u>FREE</u> ISSUES OF BLADE MAGAZINE FOR TAKING THE TIME TO COMPLETE OUR SURVEY!**

☐ Please send me my gift — 2 issues of BLADE magazine (a retail value of $9.90). BLADE is the world's #1 knife publication. It is the largest and most comprehensive knife magazine available today.

Name: ☐☐☐☐☐☐☐☐☐☐☐☐☐☐☐☐☐☐☐☐☐☐☐☐☐☐☐☐

Address: ☐☐☐☐☐☐☐☐☐☐☐☐☐☐☐☐☐☐☐☐☐☐☐☐☐☐☐

City: ☐☐☐☐☐☐☐☐☐☐☐☐☐☐☐☐☐☐☐☐☐☐☐☐☐☐☐

State: ☐☐   Zip Code: ☐☐☐☐☐   Phone: ☐☐☐—☐☐☐—☐☐☐☐

** <u>PLEASE NOTE</u>: You must complete all of the survey questions and return this by June 1, 2002 to qualify to receive your free gift (2 issues of BLADE).

ABA4JX

Tape Here   Tape Here

BUSINESS REPLY MAIL
FIRST-CLASS MAIL PERMIT NO. 12 IOLA, WI

POSTAGE WILL BE PAID BY ADDRESSEE

KRAUSE PUBLICATIONS
MARKETING RESEARCH DEPT
700 E STATE ST
IOLA WI   54945-9989

NO POSTAGE
NECESSARY IF
MAILED IN
THE UNITED
STATES